3D STUDIO
MAX FUNDAMENTALS

Michael Todd Peterson
Contributions by Larry Minton
Cover Art Designed by Frank Delise

**New
Riders**

New Riders Publishing, Indianapolis, Indiana

3D Studio MAX Fundamentals

By Michael Todd Peterson

Published by:
New Riders Publishing
201 West 103rd Street
Indianapolis, IN 46290 USA

Printed in the United States of America 1 2 3 4 5 6 7 8 9 0

Library of Congress Cataloging-in-Publication Data

```
Peterson, Todd, 1969-
    3D studio MAX fundamentals / Todd Peterson.
        p.   cm.
    Includes index.
    ISBN 1-56205-625-5
    1. Computer animation.  2. 3D studio.  3. Computer
    ➥graphics.
I. Title
TR897.7.P47  1996                        96-19479
006.6--dc20                              CIP
```

Warning and Disclaimer

Publisher	Don Fowley
Publishing Manager	David Dwyer
Marketing Manager	Mary Foote
Managing Editor	Carla Hall

Product Director
Alicia Buckley
Development Editor
John Kane
Project Editor
Laura Frey
Copy Editors
Gail Burlakoff
Chuck Hutchinson
Tad Ringo
Technical Editors
Larry Minton
Kevin Ochs
Associate Marketing Manager
Tamara Apple
Acquisitions Coordinator
Stacey Beheler
Publisher's Assistant
Karen Opal
Cover Designer
Karen Ruggles
Cover Production
Aren Howell
Book Designer
Anne Jones
Production Manager
Kelly Dobbs
Production Team Supervisor
Laurie Casey
Graphics Image Specialists
Stephen Adams, Daniel Harris, Clint Lahnen, Ryan Oldfather, Casey Price, Laura Robbins, Jeff Yesh
Production Analysts
Jason Hand
Bobbi Satterfield
Production Team
Dan Caparo, Terrie Deemer, Tricia Flodder, Aleata Howard, Christine Tyner, Karen Walsh
Indexer
Tim Griffin

About the Author

Michael Todd Peterson is currently an instructor at Pellissippi State Community College, an ATC. He previously taught at the University of Tennessee College of Architecture. Todd also owns MTP graphics, a rendering and animation firm that specializes in architecural visualization and multimedia. In addition to this book, Mr. Peterson has authored or co-authored *Inside AutoCAD for DOS, 3D Studio for Beginners*, and *Autocad in 3D*.

Acknowledgments

Todd would like to thank John Kane and Laura Frey at New Riders for all their help and patience during the creation of this book. Todd would also like to extend thanks to Larry Minton and Kevin Ocks for making sure the excercises and text are technically correct.

Contents at a Glance

Table of Contents

Introduction

3D Studio MAX (referred to simply as MAX) is a breakthrough modeling, rendering, and animation software developed by Autodesk for the Windows NT 3.51 or later operating system. With MAX comes a new level of productivity, capability, and customizability. Some of the new features of MAX include the following:

▲ New updated user interface to provide greater flexibility and power.

▲ New operating system (Windows NT) that provides a greater level of power and expandability than the old DOS platform.

▲ New modeling commands and editing commands.

▲ The Stack. The Stack is a list of modifiers applied to a piece of geometry. You can go back and change any applied modifier at any time. This gives you parametric modeling capabilities.

▲ New multithreaded renderer to take advantage of multiprocessing.

▲ New Material Editor and material types. The new interface and types provide you with just about all the material types you could ever need.

▲ New Track View dialog box to control and edit animation sequences with ease.

▲ New plug-in architect called Core Component Plug-In technology. Plug-ins can now take over any part of the rendering pipeline, including modeling, rendering, video display, and so on.

▲ HEIDI shaded display technology. Now you can work in a real-time shaded environment that can take advantage of hardware acceleration from special video cards based on the GLint chip.

3D Studio MAX Fundamentals is your guide to these features of 3D Studio MAX, and much more. Within this book, you'll explore this new version of the 3D Studio program through concise explanation and dozens of hands-on examples. And to help you work your way through MAX's new interface, *3D Studio MAX Fundamentals* features hundreds of screen captures that depict the various elements of the MAX interface.

Who Should Read This Book

3D Studio MAX Fundamentals is intended for anyone who is using 3D Studio MAX, beginning to use 3D Studio MAX, or considering switching to 3D Studio MAX.

Although it is geared toward the beginning user, even more advanced users will find the information in *3D Studio MAX Fundamentals* useful. This book focuses on the basics of creating, rendering, and animating geometry in 3D Studio MAX. Each topic is thoroughly covered through both explanation and exercise. Any previous experience with 3D Studio MAX is beneficial, but not really necessary.

For people who have never used 3D Studio MAX, it is beneficial, but not necessary to have some experience in one of the following areas:

▲ AutoCAD (or any CAD program, for that matter)

▲ 3D drawing

▲ 3D Studio for DOS, or any rendering and animation program

▲ Art or freehand drawing

Even if you do not have experience with one of these items, you can still learn and use 3D Studio MAX by following along with the examples in this book. It just might take you a little longer than someone who does have experience in these areas.

How This Book Is Organized

3D Studio MAX Fundamentals is intended to give you an overview of the MAX system and how you can best use it. To help provide a clear understanding of working with MAX, this book is divided into the following parts:

▲ **Part I: Introducing MAX.** This is the place to go if you've not yet installed MAX, or if you are brand-new to the workings of MAX. The chapters within Part One will help you understand the relationship between MAX and the Windows NT operating system, familiarize you with the MAX interface, and get you up and running with a quick introductory exercise.

▲ **Part II: Geometry Fundamentals.** Part II begins the in-depth exploration of MAX's new features by demonstrating how to create objects within MAX. As you work your way through the many hands-on exercises within this part of the book, you'll discover the power that MAX brings to object creation and lofting.

▲ **Part III: Geometry Modification Fundamentals.** Here, you'll go beyond the basics of creating objects to editing and modifying them to suit your needs. You'll learn about the various selection controls used in MAX, enhance your modeling skills by editing 2D shapes and 3D loft objects, and examine what may be the most-used aspect of the new MAX interface: the command rollouts.

▲ **Part IV: Composition and Rendering Fundamentals.** Moving beyond objects, Part IV demonstrates how you can use MAX's tools to create entire scenes. First, you'll learn how to use lighting, cameras, and materials to compose scenes in MAX. The middle chapters expose you to more advanced materials, and Chapter 15 demonstrates the ins and outs of rendering, culminating in an in-depth composition and rendering exercise. The final chapter explores the use of environmental effects to add realism to your scenes.

▲ **Part V: Animation Fundamentals.** In Part V, you will see the power MAX brings to animation. You'll first learn about animation basics, such as keyframing, and how time works in computer animation. MAX's new Track View tool is explained in its own chapter and featured in the "Motion Controllers" chapter. You will work through demonstrations of character animation and inverse kinematics, and then finish the part with a look at rendering animations, including discussion on network rendering.

▲ **Part VI: Special Effects Fundamentals.** For those of you who just can't resist going beyond the fundamentals, Part VI shows off MAX tools you will use to enhance your animations. You'll learn about the video post, which will enable you to add effects to each frame immediately after the frame is rendered. Chapter 23 introduces you to MAX's space warps and particle systems, with which you can add all sorts of special effects to your animations. The last chapter in the book highlights all that you've learned about MAX in an in-depth exercise.

▲ **Part VII: Appendices.** The two appendices in *3D Studio MAX Fundamentals* provide valuable reference information. Appendix A explains the file extensions you'll work with in MAX, and Appendix B shows the numerous cursors that help indicate the working state of MAX.

This organization also enables you to move from one part to another when you feel you are comfortable with the material in that part.

Notes, Tips, and Warnings

3D Studio MAX Fundamentals includes special sidebars, which are set apart from the normal text by icons. This book includes three distinct types of sidebars: Notes, Tips, and Warnings. These passages have been given special treatment so that you can instantly recognize their significance and easily find them for future reference.

Note

A *Note* includes extra information you should find useful. A Note might describe special situations that can arise when you use MAX under certain circumstances, and might tell you what steps to take when such situations arise. Furthermore, Notes will alert you to when topics are covered in different sections in the book.

Tip

A *Tip* provides quick instructions for getting the most from your MAX setup. A Tip might show you how to speed up a procedure, or how to perform one of many time-saving and system-enhancing features.

Warning

A *Warning* tells you when a procedure can be dangerous—that is, when you run the risk of serious problem or error, even losing data or crashing your system. Warnings generally tell you how to avoid such problems, or describe the steps you can take to remedy them.

3D Studio MAX brings a new level of power and flexibility to you, the computer animator. Through the use of the Core Component technology, the power and flexibility of 3D Studio MAX is only going to increase in the future. By learning the fundamentals of MAX, you can quickly and easily make the transition to this new platform and begin to take advantage of all the new features and capabilities that are now at your fingertips!

New Riders Publishing

The staff of New Riders Publishing is committed to bringing you the very best in computer reference material. Each New Riders book is the result of months of work by authors and staff who research and refine the information contained within its covers.

As part of this commitment to you, the NRP reader, New Riders invites your input. Please let us know if you enjoy this book, if you have trouble with the information and examples presented, or if you have a suggestion for the next edition.

Please note, though: New Riders staff cannot serve as a technical resource for 3D Studio MAX or for questions about software- or hardware-related problems. Please refer to the documentation that accompanies 3D Studio MAX or to the applications' Help systems.

If you have a question or comment about any New Riders book, there are several ways to contact New Riders Publishing. We will respond to as many readers as we can. Your name, address, or phone number will never become part of a mailing list or be used for any purpose other than to help us continue to bring you the best books possible. You can write us at the following address:

New Riders Publishing
Attn: Publisher
201 W. 103rd Street
Indianapolis, IN 46290

If you prefer, you can fax New Riders Publishing at (317) 581-4670.

You can also send electronic mail to New Riders at the following Internet address:

abuckley@newriders.mcp.com

NRP is an imprint of Macmillan Computer Publishing. To obtain a catalog or information, or to purchase any Macmillan Computer Publishing book, call (800) 428-5331.

Thank you for selecting *3D Studio MAX Fundamentals*!

PART I

INTRODUCING MAX

CHAPTER 1

MAX and Windows NT

One of the most important changes in 3D Studio MAX is the move to the Windows NT operating system. This fact alone brings a whole new level of power and flexibility that 3D Studio for DOS never had. Windows NT provides many operating system-level features such as built-in networking, multi-processor support, multi-threading, multi-tasking, and so on that DOS could not provide.

This chapter focuses on some of the features of Windows NT and how they relate to MAX. By the end of this chapter, you should have a good understanding of how to install and run MAX under NT, what the hardware requirements are, and how MAX takes advantage of NT's new features. To this end, this chapter focuses on the following topics:

- ▲ Installing MAX
- ▲ Hardware requirements for MAX and NT
- ▲ Networking MAX under NT
- ▲ Windows NT advantages

If you already have MAX installed and running and are comfortable configuring and running NT, you can skip to the next chapter to begin learning how to use the MAX interface. If you are not sure about your skill level with NT, you should probably go ahead and read this chapter to make sure you know everything you will need to know.

Note

MAX is designed for Windows NT version 3.51; this is stated specifically in the Documentation. NT 4.0 is due out sometime late in the summer of 1996, and will become the standard MAX platform in the future. For this reason, all the screen shots of MAX are taken on a Beta (test) version of NT 4.0. Although it is unlikely, some of the interface dialog boxes might look slightly different in the final version of NT 4.0. If you are using NT 3.51, the dialog boxes should be very similar to those under NT 4.0, and you should not have any problems with the figures.

Installing MAX

Installing 3D Studio MAX is a fairly quick and easy process. MAX ships on a CD-ROM and a single floppy. You will need between 30 and 100 MB of free disk space on the drive where you install MAX, depending upon the options that you choose to install. For example, MAX ships with many sample scenes, bitmaps for use in materials, and sample images. You do not necessarily need to install these options to have a functional MAX system, but they will help you learn and use MAX. To install MAX, simply follow the following steps:

1. Load the MAX CD-ROM into your CD drive and the floppy into your floppy drive. Make sure the floppy disk is *not* write-protected.

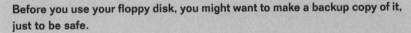

Note

Before you use your floppy disk, you might want to make a backup copy of it, just to be safe.

It is always a good idea to make backup copies of your software before installation. This helps to alleviate problems if the disk gets damaged or corrupted at any point in the future. You always will have a clean copy to fall back on.

2. Double Click on the My Computer Icon on your desktop. This displays all the drives on your system.

3. Double click on the CD-ROM drive icon. This displays the contents of the CD.

4. You will see an icon titled Setup. Double click on this icon to start the setup process. Figure 1.1 shows you the initial setup screen after starting the setup process.

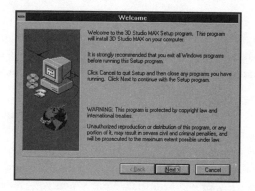

Figure 1.1

*The Welcome screen
indicating that you are
getting ready to install
3D Studio MAX 1.0.*

5. Choose the Next button. This displays the Setup Type dialog box, where you can choose which parts of MAX you want to install and where.

6. You can choose from three installation options: Typical, Compact, and Custom. Typical installs MAX with the most common components. Compact installs the minimal software necessary to run MAX. Custom enables you to pick and choose the parts you want to install. Select the installation type you want to use.

7. At the bottom of the Setup Type dialog box, you can select the directory and drive where you will install MAX. The default will be *X*:\3DSMAX, where *X* is the drive in which your NT system is installed. If you want to change this, choose Browse and select the correct drive and directory.

8. If you chose Custom, you are then prompted to select the installation options (see fig. 1.2). Otherwise, the installation process will begin. When it is finished, you will have a new folder (program group under NT 3.51) with the 3D Studio MAX icon in it.

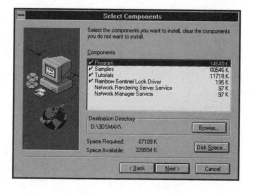

Figure 1.2

*The Select Components
dialog box where you
can select which parts of
MAX you are going to
install.*

9. If you choose Custom, you can install the network rendering services at this point. Before you can install the network rendering services, however, you must have TCP/IP correctly installed and running. If it is not, exit the installation now and install

TCP/IP. (Check your NT documentation for how to do this.) If you choose to install the network rendering services at this point, read the following steps; otherwise, skip to the end of the steps. (Remember, you can install the network rendering services at a later point. See Chapter 21, "Rendering Animations," for more information on how to do this.)

10. There are two network rendering services: Manager and Server. Manager is used to control the network rendering. Server is used to launch MAX on each slave machine and notify the Manager when the slave is working on a frame. Generally, Manager is installed on only one machine in the network. You will need to know the IP address of the machine Manager is, or will be, installed on. When you choose to continue installing MAX, you will be prompted for the IP address of the Manager. (See Chapter 21, "Rendering Animations," for more information on network rendering.)

To make sure everything is installed and correctly registered in the registry, you should reboot NT at this point by choosing Start, Shutdown. Then, select Restart the computer from the Shut Down Windows dialog box and choose Yes. When NT comes back up, log on as usual. To start MAX, simply double-click on the icon that the installation routine created.

The first time you launch MAX after you have installed it, you must configure MAX. Because MAX takes advantage of advanced display technologies such as HEIDI, you need to configure the display first. A small dialog box appears, as shown in figure 1.3. Here, you select the driver for the type of display that you are running in your system. After you have configured the display, you will not have to reconfigure it unless you reinstall MAX. Each configuration option is listed below and is briefly described:

▲ **Software Z Buffer (SZB).** This is the most commonly used display driver because it requires no special hardware. SZB enables MAX to perform all the 3D video calculations in software, instead of using specialized hardware.

▲ **GLint-Based Card.** This option enables you to use one of the many GLint-based accelerator cards that are available today. These cards are available from ELSA, Omnicomp, Fujitsu, and others. A GLint card must be installed and running properly under NT before you configure MAX to run with this option—otherwise, MAX will crash.

▲ **Other.** This option enables you to use third party drivers written by other software or hardware manufacturers. For example, MAX uses a HEIDI display driver, not OpenGL. At the time of this writing, an OpenGL driver was not available for MAX. But, at some point in the future, one will be available. When it is, you will have to install the driver. Then, it will appear under the Other option of this dialog box.

Figure 1.3

The 3D Studio MAX Driver Setup dialog box where you select the video driver that MAX uses.

When you select the video driver and choose OK, MAX will successfully load, as shown in figure 1.4.

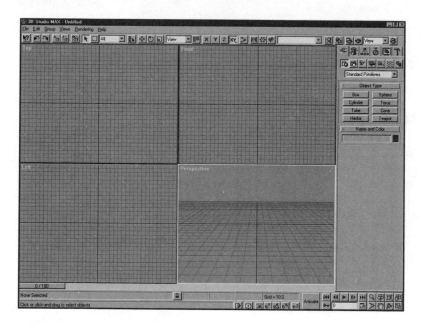

Figure 1.4

How the 3D Studio MAX Interface appears after you load MAX for the first time.

Now that MAX is up and running, there are a couple of other configuration issues to be aware of, such as MAX preferences and Bitmap material paths. These issues will be discussed in later chapters as they are needed. For example, bitmap paths are used to define the location of any bitmap that MAX might use for a material; this is covered in Chapter 13, "Mapped Materials." As you work with MAX and progress through this book, you will configure and customize MAX to the settings that you want.

Hardware Requirements for MAX

One of the downsides to running MAX under Windows NT is the increased hardware requirements necessary for running MAX. Some of these requirements might come as a shock to the average DOS user, but they are more than worth the price when you see the power and flexibility that MAX brings you. This section discusses four areas of hardware requirements:

▲ Processor

▲ Memory and swap file space

▲ Video cards

▲ Other hardware

Processor

The processor is the brains of your computer, and defines how fast your system can do calculations. The minimum processor for running MAX under Windows NT is a 486-66. MAX will run on a slower processor such as a 486-33 or even a 386-33, but you will be very disappointed with the performance of MAX.

The preferred processor for running MAX is a Pentium 90 or faster. If you can afford it, you should purchase a Pentium-Pro processor, the fastest processor available on an Intel platform as of this book's initial printing. The following table lists Intel processors that provide good performance for MAX, and their respective speeds:

Intel Processors and Speeds

Processor	Speeds
Pentium	90, 100, 120, 133, 150, 166, 200
Pentium Pro	150, 166, 180, and 200

Of course, by the time you read this, there probably will be faster processors available.

For MAX, you should buy the absolute fastest processor you can afford. MAX needs to perform many complex calculations, not only for the shaded viewports, but for rendering as well. Some features, such as a volumetric light, can really slow down the rendering process. The faster the processor you get, the easier MAX will be to use and the less time it will take you to get your work done. If you can afford it, a Pentium Pro 200 provides exceptional performance that is close to that of an SGI (Silicon Graphics) workstation.

Memory and Swap File Space

Memory—specifically, the amount of RAM in your system—is a huge consideration for MAX. As you work with MAX, you will begin to use up the RAM in your system as your file grows. If the file get large enough, MAX can run out of physical RAM. When this happens, MAX begins to use hard disk space (through the NT swap file) as virtual RAM. The problem is, MAX can access physical RAM over 200 times faster than it can the hard disk. When MAX begins to swap (sometimes swapping is called *paging*) to disk, the performance of MAX drops dramatically. The only solutions are to purchase more RAM or live with the slower performance when dealing with larger files.

The memory requirements for MAX are rather stringent. Windows NT itself takes between 12–16 MB of RAM. Add to that another 8–10 MB for MAX to load, and you are already at 24–26 MB. The minimum requirements for running MAX on an NT system are 32 MB of RAM with a 100 MB swap file. Kinetix recommends at least 64–128 MB of RAM and a 200–300 MB swap file. This is, of course, dependent upon the complexity of the scene you are working on.

Fortunately, NT provides features that DOS could not. NT enables MAX to access up to 2 GB of RAM, whereas under DOS, 3D Studio could only physically address 64 MB. NT also provides a flat memory model, so you do not have to worry about the old DOS 640 KB barrier. There are no longer any memory managers, TSRs, high memory, or anything else of that nature.

If you do run out of physical RAM, MAX will resort to using NT's swap file as virtual RAM and begin swapping to disk. MAX performance will drop noticeably when this happens, but sometimes you simply cannot avoid it. By using proper modeling, material management, and lighting, you can help to reduce the chances of swapping, but there will always be a case where you will be swapping, no matter what you do.

When you installed NT, you were asked to specify a drive and size of a swap file. NT then created a file called PAGEFILE.SYS on that drive. This is the NT swap file. For running large complex operations under MAX, especially when using large particle systems, you will probably need a large swap file—around 200–300 MB—unless you have enough RAM to compensate for it. You should make sure that you have enough disk space to compensate for this. Fortunately, NT provides another neat feature: The swap file can be split across different drives. By splitting the swap file across drives, you can utilize the additional free space on a second drive, instead of being limited to the amount of space on the first drive. Unless you need the space, though, you probably should not split your swap file.

Tip

When running Windows NT, the type of hard drive you are using can make a significant different in the performance of your system. SCSI drives, especially new Ultra SCSI drives, have much higher performance ratings than IDE drives. When you begin to swap to disk, you will want the fastest possible hard drive to help alleviate performance problems caused by the swapping.

NT loves to use SCSI drives and works best with them because NT is a 32-bit operating system. If at all possible, you should be using the fastest SCSI drives you can afford. These can include Fast and Fast-Wide SCSI-2 or Ultra and Ultra Wide SCSI. Having 4 or 9 GB of disk space is not unreasonable in today's world. Not to mention the fact that you can chain seven or more drives together, depending upon your controller. IDE simply is too limiting for serious animation work under NT because you are limited to either two or four devices (hard drives or CD-ROMs) and they do not perform as well as SCSI drives.

The following steps briefly show you how to configure the NT swap file:

1. Choose Start, Settings, Control Panel to start the NT control panel (see fig. 1.5).

Figure 1.5

You can set NT system options in the NT control panel.

2. Double click on the System control panel applet icon. This displays the System dialog box (see fig. 1.6).

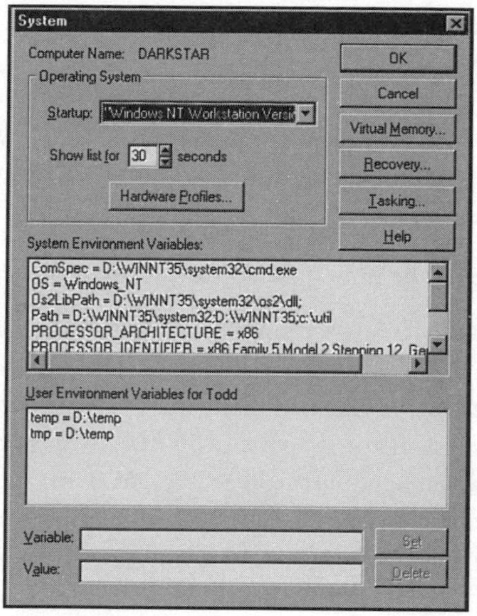

Figure 1.6

The NT System dialog box.

3. Choose the Virtual Memory button. This displays the Virtual Memory dialog box (see fig. 1.7).

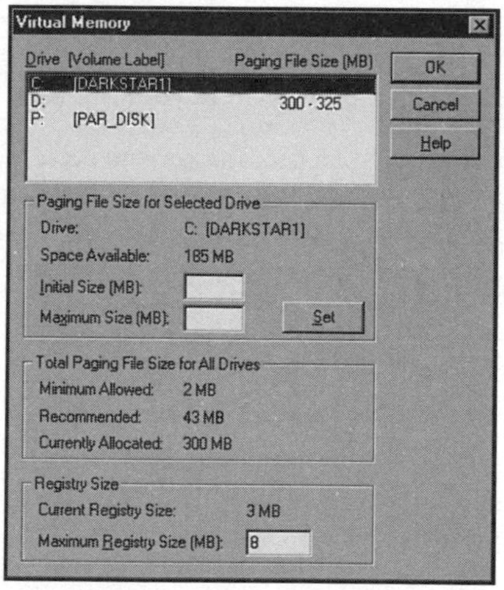

Figure 1.7

The Virtual Memory dialog box.

4. A list of the drives on your system appears in the window at the top of the dialog box. The swap file size, if any, for the drive is listed to the right. To change a swap file size, click on the drive letter. Then, under the Paging File Size for Selected Drive section of the dialog box, enter an initial and a maximum size for the swap file. For a 200 MB swap file, for example, you might enter 200 as the initial and 225 as the maximum.

5. Choose the Set button to set the values you entered.

6. Choose OK to return to the System control panel applet.

7. Choose OK again to return to the control panel. If you made any changes to the swap file, you are prompted to reboot the system at this point. If so, choose Restart Computer in the dialog box and NT will reboot.

When NT comes back up, it will be running with the new swap file settings.

If you ever get an Out of Virtual Memory warning when you are running MAX, you have run out of swap file space. If this happens, save your work in MAX and exit, repeat the preceding steps and increase your swap file size, then restart NT and MAX and try again. Generally, you should try increasing the swap file in 50 MB increments. If you did not increase the size of the swap file enough, you might get the same error again. Alternatively, you can try to localize the problem in your scene and try various methods of creating the section of the scene that is giving you problems, without using so much memory.

Video Cards

MAX can make great use of advanced video cards. Basically, any video card that works with NT and has NT drivers will work with MAX. This includes ISA, VLB, and PCI video cards. MAX is intended to be run using 24-bit color, or 16.7 million colors on the screen at the same time. This gives you the greatest realism in your previews.

You should purchase or upgrade your video card so that you can run 24-bit color at at least 800×600 resolution. Running MAX at a resolution smaller than 800×600 makes the interface cluttered and difficult to use. The most common resolutions for running MAX will be 1024×768 or 1280×1024. As a matter of fact, the MAX interface was designed for 1024×768 resolution and looks very cluttered at 800×600. The higher the resolution you run, the more working space you will have, not only for viewports, but also command rollouts. You might notice this as you work through the exercises in this book. Table 1.1 lists video resolutions, their color depths, and the amount of RAM necessary on the video card to achieve these resolutions and color depths.

Table 1.1

Video Card Resolutions and Video Memory Requirements

Resolution	Color Depth (In Bits)	Memory Needed
800×600	8	1 MB
800×600	16	1 MB
800×600	24	2 MB

Resolution	Color Depth (In Bits)	Memory Needed
1024×768	8	1 MB
1024×768	16	2 MB
1024×768	24	4 MB
1280×1024	8	2 MB
1280×1024	16	4 MB
1280×1024	24	8 MB
1600×1200	24	8 MB

As you can see, a 4 MB video card is almost necessary to get the full use of color in MAX. But, if you do not have a 4 MB card, make sure you have at least a 2 MB video card because you can still run 16 bit color at 1024×768, which is still very good.

If you can, you should also try to get at least a PCI-based video card because they provide the best performance. VESA local bus (VLB) and ISA cards do not provide the very high video performance that is necessary for the MAX display to run efficiently. This is especially true when you are using shaded viewports in MAX. You can run MAX on ISA or VLB cards, but the performance will not be as good as with a PCI card. The better the performance in your video card, the better MAX will perform for you. The following list shows you some popular video cards that can be used with MAX:

Matrox Millenium

ATI Graphics Pro Turbo

Diamond Stealth 64 Vram

Number 9 128 Imagine

Remember, if you can get your card to work with NT, you can run MAX on it. Consult your video card manufacturer if you are not sure about your card's compatibility with NT.

Other Hardware

There are several other pieces of hardware that can be used with MAX to increase your productivity. These include, but are not limited to, the following:

▲ Perception Board

▲ GLint Chip Video Card

▲ Accom WSX Video Recorder

The Perception board is a popular nonlinear video recording device designed to work under Windows NT. The Perception board is composed of a video output device linked to a SCSI-2 hard-drive controller. Animations and still frames can be stored to a dedicated hard drive and then recorded to videotape in real time. The Perception card supports composite, SVHS, and Betacam SP outputs. After the Perception board and drivers are installed, it appears simply as another drive under your system. All you have to do is send your Targa files directly from the renderer to the Perception drive. Then, use the Perception's playback utility to record the animation to tape. The Perception also works great with non-linear video editors such as Adobe Premiere and Speed Razor Pro.

If you are doing animations and recording them to videotape, owning a Perception board is a great idea. This is because a Perception board is fairly inexpensive, easy to use, and is great for making rough drafts of animations and recording animations out to tape. The Perception board can handle as high as D1 quality and up to one or more hours of digital video, depending upon how many hard drives you have hooked up to the board.

GLint chip-based video cards are high-end video acceleration cards used to speed up the display of graphics programs such as MAX that support high-end 3D graphics APIs such as OpenGL and HEIDI. 3D3D Kinetix recommends—if you can afford it—to run MAX with a GLint card or other accelerator card for optimal performance. In fact, installing a GLint chip card in your system will give you almost Unix workstation-level video display performance for a fraction of the cost of purchasing a high-end Unix workstation.

Note

> MAX uses a technology called HEIDI developed by Autodesk. HEIDI provides you with the capability to view your MAX scenes in any of a variety of modes, including wireframe and shaded views, with a high level of performance. HEIDI runs in software, but can also be accelerated by any of a variety of accelerator cards, such as GLint or OpenGL cards, provided by a number of manufacturers.

All GLint chip boards are PCI-based and have 4 MB, 8 MB, or more RAM, depending upon their configuration. A GLint chip video card can be implemented in a system in either of two ways. The first type is a single-slot solution where the GLint board has on board SuperVGA acceleration and can handle both 2D and 3D acceleration on the same board. The Elsa GLoria card is an example of a single-slot solution. The other, more popular, kind of solution is the two-slot solution where you have a VGA video card with a pass through to the GLint card. Two-slot solutions are more popular because they are much cheaper to implement than single-slot solutions. When your system boots, it uses the VGA card for 2D acceleration until NT is loaded. When NT is loaded, the GLint card takes over. Depending upon the configuration of the GLint card, you can generally pick one up for around $1,500–$3,000. Video boards in this price range provide video performance around 300,000–500,000 shaded polygons per second. If you like working in the shaded view in MAX, you should definitely consider getting a GLint chip board. See the section "Video Acceleration" for more information on how this works.

Note

3DLabs, the makers of the GLint chip, have recently introduced an accelerator chip called a Delta chip that can be used to increase the performance of the GLint chip. This chip takes over from your main system processor many of the floating point calculations necessary for 3D acceleration. This results in between 1.2 and 3 times the performance, depending upon the type of scene being accelerated and which 3D API is being used. HEIDI can make some use of this new chip, but not as much as OpenGL will. Many of the GLint card manufacturers already are shipping cards with the Delta processor on it.

Additionally, the Delta card can support up to two GLint processors. In the future, you will probably see multiprocessing video cards. Either way, a GLint card with a Delta chip will provide you with better performance than a GLint card alone.

The last piece of extra hardware worth mentioning is the Accom WSX digital video recorder. This rather expensive piece of hardware is used to hold 30 or 60 seconds of uncompressed D1 digital video for recording directly to a Betacam SP deck. The hardware is directly supported by MAX and NT. If you need this high a level of quality for 30 or 60 seconds, you should look into getting an Accom WSX recorder. Otherwise, stick with a Perception board.

The hardware requirements for MAX running under NT are rather large, but after you have the hardware to run MAX effectively, you will find yourself pleased with the performance of the system and what you can do with it.

Networking MAX under NT

One of the most powerful advantages of MAX running under NT is that of built-in networking for network rendering. Like 3D Studio for DOS, MAX has built-in network rendering. 3D Studio for DOS could make use of any network OS or protocol as long as 3D Studio for DOS could access a shared network drive. Unlike the DOS version, however, MAX uses TCP/IP (Transmission Control Protocol/Internet Protocol) to do its network rendering. TCP/IP is used because it is a fairly common network protocol and can be used on networks that combine Unix, Macintosh, and PC machines.

With TCP/IP, you can perform both network rendering and network rendering management across the Internet. Even though you can do this, you probably will not want to, because the network rendering probably will be slow simply due to the amount of traffic on the Internet. Whether you are running the network rendering locally or across the Internet, setting up and running a MAX rendering network is covered in Chapter 21, "Rendering Animations." This section takes a look at installing and running the TCP/IP software under NT.

Installing TCP/IP

When you installed NT, you had the option of installing a network. If you chose to install the network, you were given options as to what software to install. If you installed TCP/IP at that time, it should be up and running, If not, you can do the following steps to install TCP/IP and get it up and running:

1. Choose Start, Settings, Control Panel to access the control panel settings.

2. Double click on the Network icon in the Control Panel. Figure 1.8 shows you the resulting dialog box.

Figure 1.8

You can install, configure, or remove network protocols and adapters in the Network dialog box.

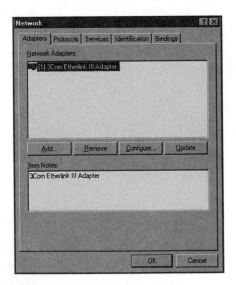

3. If you have a network adapter installed and running on the network, it appears on the list. If you have an adapter in your system, but no network is running, choose Add and follow the instructions for adding a network card.

4. To add the TCP/IP software, Click on the Protocols tab to see the Protocols section of the dialog box (see fig. 1.9).

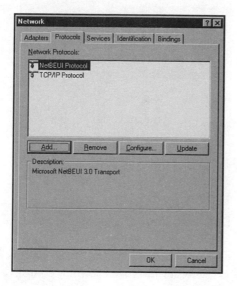

Figure 1.9

The Network Protocols dialog box.

5. If you have TCP/IP installed, it appears on this list. You might have more than one protocol installed and running. If TCP/IP is not installed, choose the Add button to display the Select Network Protocol dialog box (see fig. 1.10).

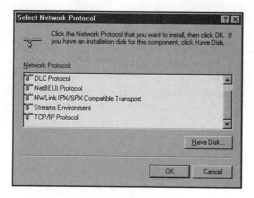

Figure 1.10

The Select Network Protocol dialog box.

6. Click on TCP/IP Protocol and choose OK.

7. At this point, you are asked to insert your NT CD-ROM into the drive, or a specific disk if you are using 3.5" disks for NT. NT then copies over the appropriate files. When it is finished, you are prompted to configure TCP/IP (see fig. 1.11).

Figure 1.11

*The TCP/IP
Configuration
dialog box.*

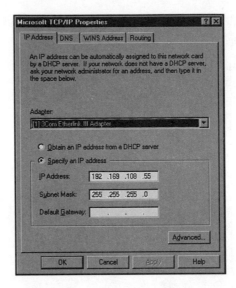

8. An IP address is composed of four numbers from 0 to 255. An example of an IP address is 192.169.108.55. Internet addresses are broken down by domains and ranges. The last number represents the individual machines in your network domain. (Consult your NT documentation for a full explanation of IP addresses and how they work.) You should number your machines sequentially using the last number of the series to make it easier to keep up with your machines. Enter your IP address in the provided fields. Alternatively, if you are on a large network, get an IP address from your network administrator.

9. Enter a subnet mask of 255.255.255.0 unless otherwise told by your network administrator.

10. Click on the WINS Address tab. This displays the WINS address dialog box as shown in figure 1.12.

11. Make sure all options are disabled here, unless directed by your network administrator.

12. Choose OK to return to the Network dialog box.

13. Choose Close to return to the Control Panel. At this point, you will be asked to reboot the machine. Choose Yes and reboot.

Now you have your networking installed and running. If you encounter any difficulty in getting the network up and running, consult your NT documentation.

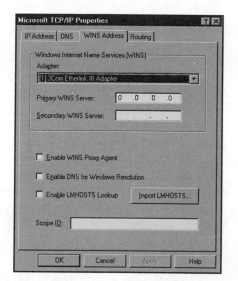

Figure 1.12

The WINS Address dialog box.

Note

In later chapters of the book, it is assumed that you have your network configured correctly and properly running.

Windows NT Advantages

Before moving on to the user interface in Chapter 2, you should be aware of some advantages that NT brings to you. These advantages include, but are not limited to, the following:

▲ The Windows 95 Shell

▲ Preemptive multitasking

▲ Multithreading and multiprocessing

▲ Crash protection

▲ Alternative processor architectures

The Windows 95 Shell

3D Studio MAX was designed to specifically take advantage of the new Windows 95 Shell that ships with Windows NT 4.0. The NT shell provides you with a more advanced interface to NT that is much easier to learn, use, and be more productive with. For example, the new shell provides you with quick access to commands, files, network connections, and system configuration options. MAX takes advantage of this environment by supporting the new Windows 95 dialog boxes, which support long filenames up to 256 characters in length. See your NT documentation for more information on using the 95 shell. Figure 1.13 shows you the Windows 95 shell running under NT 4.0.

Preemptive Multitasking

One of NT's biggest advantages is preemptive multitasking. Multitasking is the capability to run more than one program at the same time. So, while you are rendering an animation on an NT workstation, you can switch over and do some word processing with MAX rendering in the background. Unfortunately, you cannot run two sessions of MAX at the same time.

Note

> There are two types of multitasking in Windows systems: Windows 3.11 uses cooperative multitasking, whereas NT and Windows 95 use preemptive multitasking. Under cooperative multitasking, several programs that are running at the same time are trying to access the processor. But, a program with a higher priority can take over the processor and not relinquish control until it is done with its task. This causes 3.11 to appear to hang or run very sluggishly. Preemptive multitasking, on the other hand, assigns a different level of priority to each running application. Then, based on their priority, each application is given a certain amount of time to access the processor. The amount of time is defined by the OS, not the application. Hence, NT and Windows 95 systems using preemptive multitasking run multiple programs much more smoothly than cooperative multitasking systems.

A better example of multitasking for a MAX user might be the capability to switch between MAX and Adobe Photoshop when doing some serious image editing. This alone can save you hours of time versus 3D Studio for DOS where you have to load Windows or reboot to run Adobe Photoshop.

If you are going to do multitasking, you should have enough RAM to support all programs that are running. If you do not, all programs that are running will slow down considerably.

Multi-Threading and Multi-Processing

Another big advantage of NT that MAX was specifically designed to use is multi-threading. Under NT, each task is considered a thread. This thread is monitored by the system and executed in order of the thread's priority. A single-threaded application has only one thread and hence, can only perform a single task at a time. A multi-threaded application can spawn new threads as needed to run at the same time.

Multi-threading works great with multi-processing. Whereas most PCs contain only one microprocessor, multiprocessing machines have more than one microprocessor. As each thread in a multiprocessor NT machine needs to be run, it is sent to the next available processor. This has the effect of almost doubling the performance of multi-threaded applications. To demonstrate, the following table shows you a typical rendering time for a large complex scene on four different types of computers.

Machine Type	Rendering Time
Pentium 133	53 Min
Dual Pentium 133	32 Min
Pentium Pro 200	25 Min
Dual Pentium Pro 200	12 Min

As indicated in the previous table, a dual processor machine provides you with almost double the performance, for about $1,000–$2,000 more in price. Typically, in MAX, you will see between 1.6 and 1.9 times better performance when rendering on a dual processor machine versus a single processor machine. In the future, you can expect to see quad and six processor machines that will show similar scalability when running multi-threaded applications such as MAX.

Crash Protection

Another nice advantage of NT is crash protection. To put it simply, NT protects running applications from one another. For example, if you had Photoshop and MAX running at the same time and Photoshop crashes, MAX will not. Under Windows 3.11, the crash of Photoshop would bring down all other running applications. So, you have some measure of safety when MAX is running long processes in the background.

Video Acceleration

As mentioned earlier, MAX takes advantage of video acceleration through HEIDI. NT has built-in support for OpenGL, a similar 3D API that provides much higher video performance than software acceleration alone. With support for HEIDI built into MAX, all you have to do to get a video accelerator to work is install the card, then install the appropriate driver. Once the driver is installed, simply select the appropriate MAX driver when you run MAX for the first time after installation and you are off and running.

Alternative Processor Architectures

The last big advantage of NT does not affect MAX as of the first release of MAX. NT can run on a variety of processor architectures including Intel (x86), PowerPC, Digital Alpha, and MIPS. MAX has not been ported to these other architectures, but it may at some point in the future.

The standout of the alternative architectures is the Digital Alpha processor. NT running on an Alpha looks the same as NT running on an Intel processor, except that it is exceptionally faster. The current Alpha speed champ is the 21164 Alpha, running at 333 MHz, which is more than six times faster than a Pentium 90. As with other machines, you also can purchase multi-processing Alpha machines. If and when MAX is ported over to the Alpha processor, speed freaks will have access to the fastest microprocessor on the planet! This will bring an entirely new level of performance to desktop animation.

Note

At this point, you might be thinking that you need to learn more about NT. Resources that can help you learn more about Windows NT include the following:

▲ *Windows NT for Graphics Professionals* from New Riders Publishing
▲ *Inside Windows NT Workstation* from New Riders Publishing
▲ *Inside Windows NT Server* from New Riders Publishing
▲ The Windows NT documentation
▲ Windows NT courses from a local college or business

To put it simply, the more you know about NT, the less likely you are to have problems installing and running MAX or any other NT software.

Summary

3D Studio MAX was designed for Windows NT for a reason. This chapter showed you why and how you can take advantage of NT's features. You should learn as much as you can about NT because it probably will be the operating system of the future for desktop animation.

Before doing anything with MAX, you should learn a little about its interface so you know how to access commands and perform basic tasks. Chapter 2 focuses on how to use MAX's new user interface.

CHAPTER 2

The MAX User Interface

One of the largest and most powerful differences between 3D Studio MAX and 3D Studio for DOS is the new user interface. This updated interface provides you with much greater control over MAX's features and commands; it also provides you with a single integrated environment within which you can work.

This chapter focuses on the new user interface and how to use it. In particular, this chapter covers the following topics:

▲ The MAX interface layout

▲ Changing the way your work is displayed

▲ Ways to access commands

▲ Customizing the user interface

The MAX Interface Layout

The layout of the MAX interface is quite different from 3D Studio for DOS. The DOS version has five different modules, each dedicated to a specific task in 3D Studio. MAX has one interface that handles all tasks. Figure 2.1 shows a typical MAX interface with the important areas of the interface labeled.

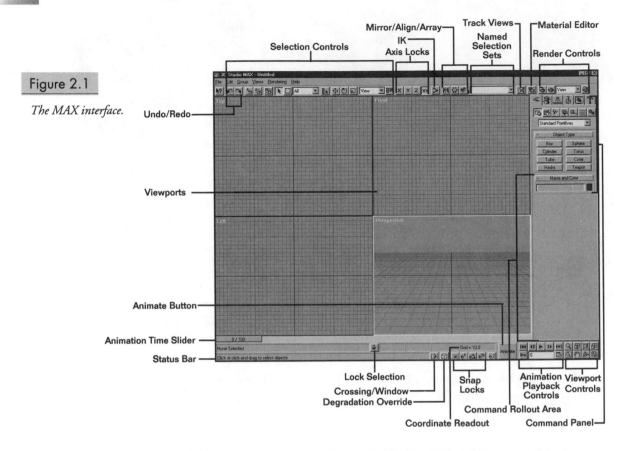

Figure 2.1

The MAX interface.

Each of the interface components is described in the following list:

▲ **Pulldowns**. These pull-down menus provide you with access to many of MAX's commands, including File, Edit, Group, View, Rendering, and Help menus.

▲ **Undo/Redo**. Max enables you to have unlimited undo and redo. These two buttons provide one method of accessing these commands. On the Undo button, the arrow points to the left, and on the Redo button, the arrow points to the right.

▲ **Selection Controls**. Many of the commands in MAX require the use of a selection set. This group of buttons enables you to select and manipulate objects in a variety of ways. See Chapter 7, "Selection Controls," for more information on some of these buttons.

▲ **Axis Constraints**. Axis constraints restrict the transformations of objects in MAX to a single direction or plane. See Chapters 8–10 for more information on using Axis locks with modifiers and transforms.

▲ **IK**. This button enables the use of Inverse Kinematics for Character animation. See Chapter 20, "Linking and IK," for more information on IK.

▲ **Mirror/Align/Array**. This group of buttons enables you to use the basic Mirror, Align, and Array commands in MAX.

▲ **Named Selection Sets**. Because selection sets are so important to MAX's modifiers and transforms, MAX enables you to save selection sets under unique names. This drop-down list provides you with quick access to the named selection sets.

▲ **Material Editor**. This button provides you with access to the Material Editor dialog box, so you can create and assign materials to objects.

▲ **Track View**. This button provides you with access to the Track View dialog box. You use Track View to control any and all animated parameters in your scene.

▲ **Render Controls**. This set of buttons provides you with access to MAX's rendering options and dialog boxes.

▲ **Command Panel**. The command panel is the heart of the MAX system. Through the command panel, you can find most of the commands. The command panel is broken down into six different tabs: Create, Modify, Hierarchy, Motion, Display, and Utility. Through each tab, you can reach commands of these types.

▲ **Command Rollout Area**. In the command rollout area, the parameters for a specific command appear when the command is selected from the command panel. They are called rollouts because many of the command areas are longer than the screen. Each of the rollouts can be collapsed or expanded to view the commands and parameters associated with them. See the section titled "Accessing Commands" later in this chapter for more information on using the command rollouts.

▲ **Viewport Controls**. These buttons provide you with all the necessary controls to manipulate and change any of your currently configured viewports.

▲ **Animation Playback Controls**. These buttons enable you to control the interactive animation playback system in MAX.

▲ **Animate Button**. This button controls the creation of animation keys. When this button is active, it turns red, and the active viewport will have a red outline. While this button is active, any time you transform or modify an object, an animation key is created.

Tip

> If you manually add the following 2 lines to the 3DSMAX.INI file, which is located in your 3DSMAX root directory, the time slider background also turns red when the Animate button is on.
>
> ```
> [RedSliderWhenAnimating]
> Enabled=1
> ```

▲ **Snap Locks**. In MAX, a variety of different types of snaps can help you draw accurately. These buttons provide you with the capability to enable and disable the different snap locks at will.

▲ **Adaptive Degradation Override**. When MAX is playing back an animation, it tries to play back the animation as fast as it can with the best shading method. When the speed drops below a certain point, MAX uses a less complex shading method to increase the speed. This override button disables the degradation of the shading method in the active viewport.

▲ **Crossing Selection**. This button controls how windowed selection sets are created. When the button is active, any objects completely or partially in the selection window are selected. When the button is inactive, only objects completely in the selection window are selected. See Chapter 7, "Selection Controls," for more information on how to use selection sets.

▲ **Lock Selection**. After you create a selection set, you can lock the selection set. This button activates the lock. When a selection set is locked, you cannot add more objects to the set or remove objects from the set.

▲ **Status Window**. The status window shows you messages about what is going on in MAX. If you are not sure what is going on, you can always check the status window to find out.

▲ **Coordinate Readout**. The coordinate readout area is helpful for telling where the cursor is in 3D space. This readout gives you the x, y, and z readouts of the cursor position, as well as percentage readouts for operations such as scale.

▲ **Animation Time Slider**. The animation time slider sets the current frame of the animation. If you grab the slider using your mouse and drag it, you are "scrubbing" the slider. When you scrub, you can interactively view the animation.

▲ **Viewports**. The viewports enable you to view the geometry, materials, lights, cameras, and scenes that you create in MAX. These viewports are fully configurable.

▲ **Command Help**. When you choose this button, you can click on any command or spinner in MAX and the help for that command will appear. This works everywhere except the menu bar.

The MAX interface features many options and capabilities. After you get used to using it, you will find that it is a joy to work with, and it is much easier to use than the old DOS interface that 3D Studio used to have.

Viewport Configurations

Each of the viewports in MAX is highly configurable to match your needs. Each viewport is capable of supporting the following MAX features:

▲ Displaying all geometry, lights, cameras, and so on

▲ Displaying geometry in wireframe or shaded views

▲ Displaying the working grid

▲ Displaying textures on surfaces

You can turn on each of the preceding options in several different ways. The first way is to choose Views, Viewport Configuration to access the dialog box shown in figure 2.2.

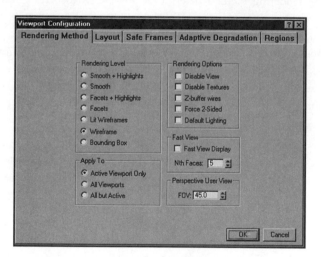

Figure 2.2

The Viewport Configuration dialog box.

The second method of accessing viewport configuration controls is by placing your mouse pointer over the title of the viewport. Then, simply right-click to access the menu (see fig. 2.3).

The Viewport Configuration menu contains shortcuts to some of the option settings in the Viewport Configuration dialog box. You can also access the same dialog box by choosing Configure at the bottom of this menu.

Figure 2.3

*The Viewport
Configuration menu.*

Using the Viewport Configurations

The configuration of your viewports has a direct impact on the performance of MAX. The following three tabs in the Viewport Configuration dialog box are worth examining:

▲ Rendering Method

▲ Layout

▲ Adaptive Degradation

You can also access some of these options by right-clicking on the name of a viewport to access the Viewport Configuration menu.

Rendering Method

The rendering method determines how MAX displays geometry on the screen. Thanks to the new HEIDI rendering engine, you have the option of choosing either wireframe or shaded displays. In either case, you can also choose different levels of display quality. The higher the quality, the slower the MAX display becomes. Some of the options that you can enable for the viewports can also speed up the display, but the same options also take up more of your system's memory.

Note

> HEIDI is a specialized 3D interactive rendering API that is based partly upon the HOOPS technology developed by Autodesk. HEIDI enables you to have shaded interactive viewports. HEIDI also enables you to make use of hardware accelerators such as Glint cards and other such devices. Basically, HEIDI provides high end 3D display acceleration in both hardware and software.

The Rendering Methods table of the Viewport Configuration dialog box contains five sections, as shown in figure 2.2. Each of the sections is described in the following list:

▲ **Rendering Level**. These options enable you to select the method that MAX uses to render the viewport. The default is Wireframe.

▲ **Rendering Options**. You can use these options in a viewport to enhance the functionality and quality of the viewport. Sometimes the enhanced functionality occurs by sacrificing free RAM, speed, or both.

▲ **Apply To**. This section enables you to choose where you are going to apply the rendering method settings. The default is the active viewport.

▲ **Fast View**. This option increases the speed of the display. It works by not displaying some of the faces in the scene. You can set the Nth Faces spinner to determine which faces to display in the viewport. For example, a setting of 5 will not display every fifth face in the objects in the viewport.

▲ **Perspective User View**. A new default perspective view is now available in MAX instead of the old user view. This option enables you to configure the *field of view* (FOV) for the perspective view. You can adjust the spinner field to increase or decrease the FOV. This option is only available when a perspective view is active.

In the Rendering Level section of the dialog box, many options are available for the display of rendered objects. Figures 2.4 through 2.10 show the results of using each type of rendering level.

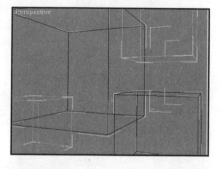

Figure 2.4

Bounding box.

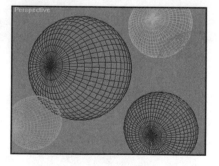

Figure 2.5

Wireframe.

Figure 2.6

Lit wireframe.

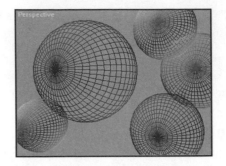

Figure 2.7

Facets.

Figure 2.8

Facets + Highlights.

Figure 2.9

Smooth.

Figure 2.10

Smooth + Highlights.

Tip

A shaded viewport redraws slower than a wireframe. The higher the rendering level, the longer it takes to redraw the screen. You can compensate for the longer redraw times by purchasing a hardware accelerator such as a GLint chip card, as mentioned in Chapter 1, "MAX and Windows NT."

You can help to control the speed and quality of the viewport display by adjusting the Rendering Options in the Rendering Method tab of the Viewport Configuration dialog box. Each option is described in the following list:

▲ **Disable View**. This option disables the current viewport. You can turn on this option to increase the redraw speed of the viewports by removing one of the viewports that MAX needs to redraw. MAX will only redraw the disabled viewport, if it is the active viewport.

▲ **Disable Textures**. This option disables your ability to view textures in the scene. Viewing textures on objects can slow down the display enormously. By enabling this option, you disable the texture display and increase the redraw speed.

▲ **Z-buffer wires**. This option forces MAX to Z-buffer all wireframe displays. A Z-buffer sorts the wireframe objects by depth in the viewport and displays the wireframe objects in their appropriate order. Figures 2.11 and 2.12 show the difference between a Z-buffered wire display and a non-Z-buffered display. A Z-buffered display takes up more memory and is a little slower than a standard wireframe display.

Figure 2.11

Z-buffered wireframe viewport.

Figure 2.12

Non-Z-buffered wireframe viewport.

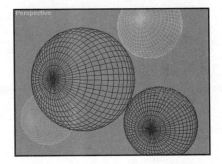

▲ **Force 2-Sided**. Each surface in MAX has a front side and a back side. The front side is defined by a *surface normal*, which is a vector that is perpendicular to the surface. When the normal faces away from the view, the surface is invisible. Force 2-sided makes the surface visible, regardless of the location of the normal. Using this option tends to slow down the screen display.

▲ **Default Lighting**. This option tells MAX to use the default lighting in the viewport, instead of any lighting that you have defined. The default lighting is two lights, one to the upper-left corner of the scene and one to the lower-right corner of the scene.

When you set these options, you can pick where you are going to apply the options in the Apply To section of the Rendering Method tab of the Viewport Configuration dialog box.

After you set the options you want, you can either move to a different tab in the dialog box, or you can choose OK to return to MAX and implement the changes you have just made. You should strive to set the options for MAX viewports to best match a combination of performance and features for which you are looking.

Layout

When you're working in three dimensions, as you do in MAX, the control and layout of the viewports on the screen become very important. For example, if you have a layout of Top, Left, Right, and a perspective view, you can see the geometry from almost every side. But many times you might want other layouts.

With MAX, like 3D Studio for DOS, you can control the layout of the viewports. The Layout tab of the Viewport Configuration dialog box enables you to configure the MAX viewports in a wide variety of methods (see fig. 2.13).

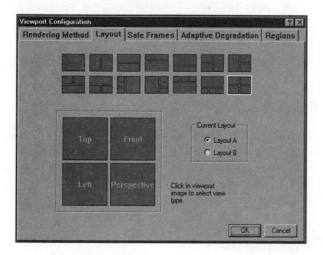

Figure 2.13

The Layout tab of the Viewport Configuration dialog box.

At the top of the dialog box, you see a set of predefined viewport configurations. These configurations define the size and locations of viewports, but not the contents of the viewports. You define the contents of the viewports individually. In the lower-left corner, a larger view of the selected configuration appears, listing the current viewport contents. To change the contents of a viewport, simply click on the viewport. A drop-down list appears in which you can select the view you want (see fig. 2.14).

The last thing to note here is the Current Layout section of the Layout tab in this dialog box. In many cases, you might want to work with more than one viewport layout. MAX enables you to use up to two predefined layouts. You can switch between layouts by choosing A or B from this list, pressing the | (vertical bar) key on your keyboard when you are working in MAX (see the "Customization" section later in this chapter for more information on keyboard shortcuts), or choosing Swap Layouts from the Viewport Configuration pull-down menu, which you can access by right-clicking on any viewport name. (See "The Right Mouse Button" section later in this chapter for more information on this pull-down menu.)

Figure 2.14

*Viewport Contents
pop-up menu.*

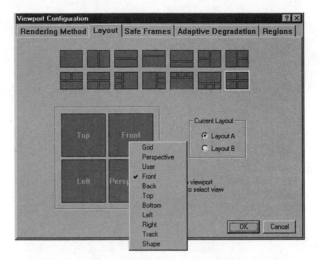

Tip

Because of the importance of Track View to animation in MAX, you might want to keep a second layout of viewports with one of the viewports configured to show Track View. This is especially true when you're using certain plug-ins, such as Biped, that make extensive use of Track View.

Adaptive Degradation

One of the largest enhancements in MAX is the capability to work in a shaded mode. By working in a shaded mode, you can easily tell where objects are in 3D space, and you can tell the relationships between different objects. Shaded views also make the previews of animations more useful. Unfortunately, previewing an animation in shaded mode takes up a lot of processing power and requires a fast video card.

To help compensate for the need for a faster video card, MAX uses adaptive degradation. When it's playing back a shaded animation, MAX uses the current shading mode, unless the speed of the playback drops below a certain point. Then MAX reduces, or *degrades*, the shading mode to the next shading mode that is selected for use by the adaptive degradation. Because the newer mode is less costly in terms of processing power, the playback speed increases. In the Adaptive Degradation tab of the Viewport Configuration dialog box, you control these functions in MAX (see fig. 2.15).

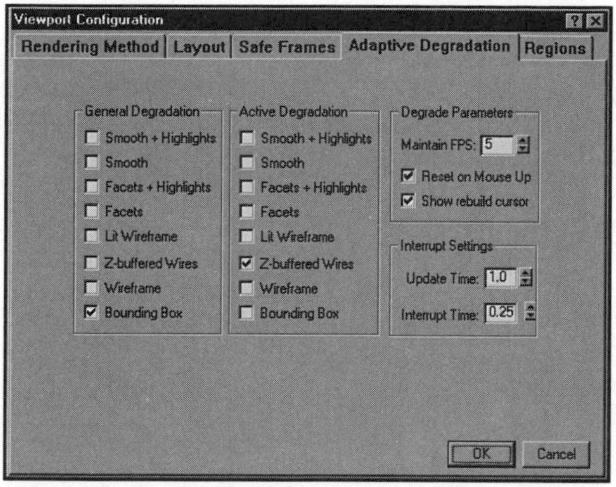

Figure 2.15

*The Adaptive
Degradation tab.*

Two types of viewport degradation exist in MAX: general and active. The general degradation affects all viewports, including inactive viewports. The active degradation affects only the active viewport. Simply select the rendering levels through which you want the degradation to step down. You can select as many levels as you like. For example, if you choose Facets in the Active Degradation section, when MAX plays back an animation and cannot keep the specified frame rate, it drops back to a faceted shading mode and continues to play back the animation.

In the upper-right corner of the Adaptive Degradation tab of this dialog box, you can specify the degrade parameters. In this section, you can tell MAX what frame rate to maintain before degrading the rendering method. The default is five frames per second, or FPS. If MAX cannot maintain this speed in animation playback, it uses the next lower level of degradation to try to keep the specified FPS. The Reset on Mouse Up check box tells MAX to reset the viewports rendering level back to its normal level when the playback of the animation is done. The Show rebuild cursor check box activates a special cursor to let you know that MAX is rebuilding the viewport after you stop the animation. The rebuild cursor is an arrow with a small, dark gray rectangle underneath it.

Under the interrupt settings, you can control how often MAX updates or redraws the screen. You have two options here: Update Time and Interrupt Time. Update Time sets the interval between updates during viewport rendering. At each interval, a new section of the rendering is drawn on screen. If set to 0, nothing is drawn until the rendering is complete. Interrupt Time sets the interval between times when the program checks for a mouse-down event during viewport rendering. Small values free the mouse more quickly, so you can use the mouse elsewhere without waiting for it to "wake up."

Tip

Do not disable the Show rebuild cursor option because it is one of the clues to tell you what **MAX** is doing. In large, complex shaded scenes, rebuilding the viewport can take anywhere from a few seconds to 30 or 40 seconds. Without the cursor indicating what is going on, you might think that **MAX** is frozen because you cannot do anything else.

Of course, if you want, you can also override the adaptive degradation by choosing the Override button located at the bottom of the MAX screen (refer to figure 2.1). Alternatively, you can press the O key to set the override as well. When the override is on, adaptive degradation is disabled, and the viewport uses the current rendering method, no matter how slow the playback is.

By using the various tabs of the Viewport Configuration dialog box, you can control the rendering method, layout, and degradation properties of MAX. But you cannot change how you are viewing the contents of the viewports themselves.

Controlling the View in MAX

MAX provides you with a wide variety of button controls and keyboard shortcuts to control the view of a MAX viewport. These controls include functions such as zooming, panning, rotating, and so on.

The Viewport Control Buttons

To control the viewport contents, you use the viewport control buttons located in the lower right corner of the MAX screen. Each button enables you to control various aspects of the active viewport. In MAX, the configuration of the view control buttons changes with each type of viewport. For example, a perspective view has one set of viewport control buttons, whereas any planar view such as Top or Left has another set. (Camera and Spotlight view controls are covered in Chapter 11, "Composition Basics: Lights and Cameras.")

Additionally, if the button has a small triangle in the lower-right corner, the button has an associated flyout. You can access the flyout by clicking and holding the left mouse button. Figure 2.16 shows a button and its flyout. Whichever button you choose from the flyout becomes the button that appears on top.

Zoom Extents All button

Zoom Extents All flyout

Figure 2.16

The Zoom Extents All button and flyout.

Figure 2.17 shows the most common command buttons. Each button is described in the following list:

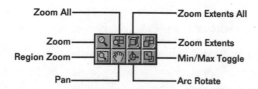

Zoom All — Zoom Extents All

Zoom — Zoom Extents

Region Zoom — Min/Max Toggle

Pan — Arc Rotate

Figure 2.17

The Viewport control panel.

Zoom. The Zoom command enables you to zoom in and out of viewports, including the perspective view. When you choose this button, an icon that looks like a magnifying glass appears. Simply click in the viewport you want to zoom. As you hold down the mouse button, move the pointer toward the top to zoom in and toward the bottom to zoom out. The zoom control stays active until you choose another command.

Zoom All. The Zoom All command works just like the Zoom command, except that the Zoom All command affects all viewports at the same time. Like Zoom, Zoom All is active until you choose another command.

Zoom Extents. The Zoom Extents command zooms in or out of the active viewport until the extents of all geometry show in the viewport. This button also has a flyout with a second version of the Zoom Extents command; it is called Zoom Extents Selected (see fig. 2.18). The selected version zooms to the extents of any selected object instead of all objects in the scene.

Figure 2.18

The Zoom Extents flyout.

Zoom Extents All. The Zoom Extents All command works just like the Zoom Extents command, except it affects all viewports in MAX at the same time. Also, like Zoom Extents, it has a flyout with a Zoom Extents All Selected button (see fig. 2.16).

Field of Vision (FOV). The FOV button affects only Perspective viewports. In Planar viewports, this button is replaced with the Region Zoom button (see the next description). The FOV button essentially works the same as the Zoom command, except that it adjusts the field of vision, or the cone, of the perspective view and does not move the view physically closer to the geometry.

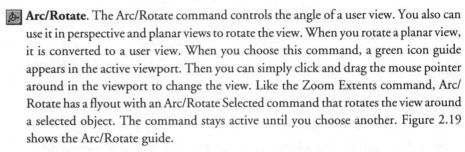

Region Zoom. The Region Zoom commands enable you to zoom in on a specific area of a viewport by specifying opposite corners of a window surrounding the area you want to view. Simply click and drag to create the window. This command stays active until you choose another command. If you switch to a perspective view, the command changes to the FOV command, and FOV is then active.

Pan. The Pan command enables you to move around in a viewport without changing the zoom level. When you choose the Pan command, simply click in the viewport in which you want to pan. Then, click and hold the mouse button as you move it around. Wherever you move the mouse pointer, the view moves as well.

Figure 2.19

The Arc/Rotate guide.

Arc/Rotate. The Arc/Rotate command controls the angle of a user view. You also can use it in perspective and planar views to rotate the view. When you rotate a planar view, it is converted to a user view. When you choose this command, a green icon guide appears in the active viewport. Then you can simply click and drag the mouse pointer around in the viewport to change the view. Like the Zoom Extents command, Arc/Rotate has a flyout with an Arc/Rotate Selected command that rotates the view around a selected object. The command stays active until you choose another. Figure 2.19 shows the Arc/Rotate guide.

Min/Max Toggle. The Min/Max Toggle changes a viewport into a full-screen viewport or vice versa. Simply click in the viewport you want to maximize, and click on the Toggle button. The viewport then takes up all the viewport area. If you choose the Min/Max Toggle again, the viewport is returned to its original size and position.

You use each of the viewport control commands extensively during the exercises in this book. Through the completion of the exercises, you will learn how and when to use these commands, in the context of working with MAX. For now, you just need to know the location of the commands and which commands do what.

Accessing Commands

One of the most important aspects of using a new user interface, of course, is how you access commands. MAX provides you with a variety of methods for accessing commands that are both intuitive and unique. You can basically access commands using the following ways:

▲ Pull-down menus

▲ The toolbar

▲ The command panel

▲ The right mouse button

By using one of these methods, you can access all the commands that are available in 3D Studio MAX.

Pull-Down Menus

The pull-down menus are located at the top of the MAX screen. Each pull-down menu is dedicated to a specific set of tasks under MAX. As in any other Windows application, if a command is grayed out or dimmed on a menu, it is not available at that time. In MAX, many commands require the selection of an object before they become available. Also, any keyboard shortcuts for the commands on the menus are listed to the right of each command on the menu. Each menu is described in the following list:

▲ **File**. The File menu enables you to open, save, import, and export a variety of files. Through the File menu, you can also access the MAX preferences and path configurations for MAX (see fig. 2.20).

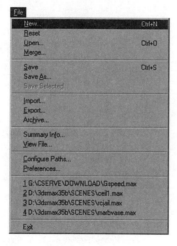

Figure 2.20

The File menu.

▲ **Edit**. The Edit menu enables you to access a variety of important MAX commands (see fig. 2.21). These commands include selection commands, undo and redo, TrackView, Material Editor, and a variety of other commands.

▲ **Group**. The Group menu enables you to create, edit, and destroy named groups of objects (see fig. 2.22). See Chapter 7, "Selection Controls," on selection sets for more information on groups.

▲ **Views**. The Views menu enables you to control all aspects of viewing objects in MAX, including viewport configurations, unit settings, drawing aids settings, and an undo for viewport commands only (see fig. 2.23).

Figure 2.21

Figure 2.21

The Edit menu.

Figure 2.22

The Group menu.

Figure 2.23

The Views menu.

▲ **Rendering**. The Rendering menu enables you to access rendering commands, the video post, and environment settings (see fig. 2.24).

Figure 2.24

The Rendering menu.

▲ **Help**. The Help menu provides you with access to the online Help system for MAX. You can also obtain version information about MAX and all the plug-ins in the system through this menu (see fig. 2.25).

Figure 2.25

The Help menu.

Many of the commands that are available on the menus are also available through a variety of other methods discussed later in this chapter. You may choose whichever methods you like.

The Toolbar

The toolbar is located directly below the pull-down menus; it provides access to some of the most common commands in MAX (see fig. 2.26). As with many buttons on the MAX screen, if you hold the mouse pointer over a button, a tooltip appears, telling you what the command is. If you forget what a button is, use the tooltips to find out what the button is.

Figure 2.26

The MAX toolbar.

Two forms of the MAX toolbar are available: a long toolbar (standard) and a short toolbar. The short toolbar is intended for use on systems that use an 800×600 video resolution or less, such as a laptop or notebook computer.

To access the short toolbar, follow these steps:

1. Choose File, Preferences.

2. Under the General tab of the Preferences dialog box, choose Short Toolbar in the Layout section.

3. Choose OK. The short toolbar then appears as shown in figure 2.27.

Figure 2.27

The Short MAX toolbar.

The short toolbar is the same as the long toolbar, with the exception of a few missing commands. You can find the missing commands, such as TrackView and Material Editor, under the Edit menu. Commands on both toolbars are discussed as they are needed.

The Command Panel

The most important new feature of the MAX interface is the command panel, as shown in figure 2.28. The command panel provides you with access to all the drawing and editing commands in MAX.

Each command panel is made up of three areas. At the top of the panel is a set of buttons that you can use to access different types of commands. For example, Create enables you to create a variety of objects. Each object type is listed as a button.

Below the buttons is a drop-down list for subcommand types. For example, under Create, you can choose the Geometry button. The five types of geometry that you can create appear in this drop-down list.

Below the drop-down list is the command rollout area. Here, the actual commands and parameters appear. Not all command panels have the buttons and drop-down lists, but all of them have the command rollout area.

The command panel is broken down into six different tabs, each representing a different set of commands for you to use. When a tab is visible, all of its commands are displayed.

Figure 2.28

The command panel.

Command Panel Details

Each command panel has an intricate set of details. For the purpose of this example, the Create command panel is described as an example of how to use the typical command panel. You use other command panels in a similar fashion.

The Create command panel (refer to figure 2.28) enables you to create a variety of objects in MAX. The Create panel contains seven buttons below the tabs. Each button represents a different type of object that you can create. Each is described in the following list:

▲ **Geometry**. The Geometry button enables you to access commands that include the creation of 3D geometry such as boxes, spheres, cones, and so on. You have access to five subcategories of geometry. (See later in this section for descriptions of the subcategories.)

▲ **Shapes**. This button enables you to access 2D shape commands. You can create a 2D shape and loft the shape into a 3D object along a path.

▲ **Lights**. This button enables you to create lights to illuminate your 3D scene.

▲ **Cameras**. This button enables you to create a camera through which you can view your 3D scene.

▲ **Helpers**. This button enables you to create helper objects to accomplish certain tasks in MAX.

▲ **Space Warps**. This button enables you to create *space warps*, which are animated special effects such as wind and gravity.

▲ **Systems**. This button enables you to create systems such as bones and ring arrays.

Below the buttons in the command panel is a drop-down list. For each type of object you can create in MAX, you may be able to create subtypes. For example, under Geometry, you can create five different subtypes of objects. Each geometry subobject is described in the following list:

▲ **Standard Primitives**. These objects are boxes, cones, and so on.

▲ **Patch Grids**. These Bézier surfaces are easily manipulated into 3D organic objects.

▲ **Compound Objects**. These objects are created by combining two or more existing objects.

▲ **Particle Systems**. These objects produce complex effects such as sprays and snows. Rain is also an example of a particle system.

▲ **Loft Object**. These 2D objects are lofted along a 3D path to form a 3D object.

The rest of the command panels are described in the following list:

▲ **Modify**. The Modify command panel enables you to access and change the parameters of any selected existing object (see fig. 2.29). You can also apply any of a variety of modifiers to your geometry, such as bend, twist, and so on. In this command panel, you can also access the Modifier stack.

▲ **Hierarchy**. The Hierarchy command panel enables you to create geometry hierarchies for IK linking and animation (see fig. 2.30).

▲ **Motion**. The Motion command panel enables you to assign parametric or trajectory motion controllers to an object or convert the path of an object to or from a spline (see fig. 2.31).

▲ **Display**. The Display command panel enables you to control the display of any objects in MAX, including hiding, unhiding, and display optimizations (see fig. 2.32).

Figure 2.29

The Modify command panel.

Figure 2.30

The Hierarchy command panel.

▲ **Utility**. The Utility command panel provides access to several small utility programs (see fig. 2.33).

The specifics of each command panel and the command usage are covered in the appropriate chapters throughout the book.

Figure 2.31

The Motion command panel.

Figure 2.32

The Display command panel.

Figure 2.33

The Utility command panel.

Working with Command Panel Rollouts

When you actually select a command in MAX, the button turns green to indicate it is active, and the parameters for the command appear in the rollout area. Depending on the command, a few or many command options appear. Consider, for example, the box command. You use it to create a box in MAX. You access the command by choosing the Create command panel and then clicking on the Box button. When you do, the box button turns green to indicate it is active, and the command rollout appears (see fig. 2.34).

Each set of parameters is subdivided by a horizontal button. This button has either a – or + and a title. For example, the Keyboard entry button has a +. It indicates that if you click on the button, the keyboard entry parameters will rollout, as shown in figure 2.35. When the rollout expands, the + turns into a –, and the commands are now available. The exact opposite occurs when you click on a – bar. The commands are hidden until you expand the rollout again.

If you expand the keyboard rollout area, you may notice that the rollouts extend below the bottom edge of the command rollout area. (If you are running at 1280×1024 or higher resolution, this may or may not be true.) You can dynamically move the rollout if necessary. If you place the cursor over the rollout area but not over a command, a hand appears. Simply click and drag up and down, and you can move the rollout area so that you can access the sections that are now hidden.

Figure 2.34

The Box Command rollout area.

Figure 2.35

The Keyboard Entry rollout expanded.

In the keyboard rollout area, you see parameters such as length, width, and height. Next to each is a text entry field and a spinner. If you click in the white area, you can type in a new value for the field. Alternatively, you can click on the up or down arrow on the spinner and drag the mouse vertically. Moving the mouse toward the top of the screen increases the value; moving the mouse toward the bottom of the screen decreases the value.

 Tip

> Many commands in MAX make use of the spinner fields, so make sure that you are comfortable adjusting them.

The command panels and rollouts are very important in MAX. As you learn commands, you will get more and more practice with them. Make sure that you are familiar with what each command panel does and how to access commands on each panel.

The Right Mouse Button

Many of the commands and features of MAX are also accessible by using the right mouse button. This feature takes awhile for some users to get used to, especially if you are coming from an environment in which you never used the right mouse button.

You can use the right mouse button, for example, to work with the viewport configurations. If you right-click on the name of any viewport, a menu appears where you click (see fig. 2.36). This menu provides you with a subset of the viewport configuration tools that are quickly and easily accessible. Right-clicking on the viewport name is much easier than choosing Views, Viewport Configuration to access the same features.

The right mouse button can also be used to cancel an operation in MAX, or a right click on a spinner sets the value of the corresponding field to the smallest value allowed for that field. Additional uses of the right mouse button are introduced in the appropriate chapters.

Figure 2.36

The Right-Click viewport menu.

Customization

Another nice feature of MAX is the ability to customize the interface to some degree. You can customize the following items:

▲ Modify command panel

▲ Keyboard shortcuts

▲ MAX preferences

▲ Map paths

Customizing the Modify Command Panel

The Modify command panel, by default, shows 10 buttons with 10 different commands. But, in actuality, it has 21 modify commands. If you have any plug-ins, the command panel may have even more commands. You can access the additional commands by choosing the More button at the top of the Modify command panel. The More button is not available unless an object has been created and selected. Choosing this button displays a dialog box that enables you to access the commands (see fig 2.37), but you may want to configure some of the commands as buttons.

Figure 2.37

The Modifiers dialog box.

The following steps show you how to customize the Modify command panel:

1. Choose the Configuration button. (To the right of the More button is the Sets button. To the right of the Sets button is the Configuration button.) A dialog box appears, as shown in figure 2.38.

Figure 2.38

*The Configure Button
Sets dialog box.*

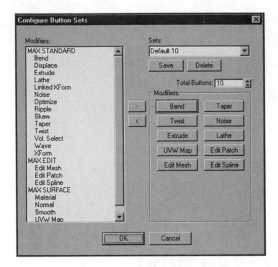

2. Using the spinner, increase the Total Buttons field to 12. Two new blank buttons appear, as shown in figure 2.39.

Figure 2.39

*The newly configured
buttons.*

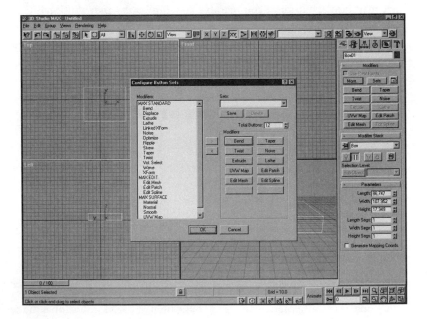

3. Click on one of the new buttons. Then double-click on the Optimize command in the list of Modifiers on the left. The button now reflects the new command.

4. Click on the other blank button. Then double-click on Displace in the Modifiers list. The button now reflects the new command.

5. In the Sets field at the top of the dialog box, type **set1**. Then choose Save. Now you have a second set of buttons that you can access through the Sets button in the Modify command panel.

6. Choose OK. The Modify command panel is updated.

Modifying the command panel is a rather easy process. After you practice with MAX for a while, you will have a good idea of which buttons you want to display on the Modify panel. The panel can have a maximum of 16 buttons.

MAX Preferences

Many of the customization settings for MAX are located in the Preference Settings dialog box, as shown in figure 2.40. You can access this dialog box by choosing File, Preferences. Like other dialog boxes in MAX, the Preference Settings dialog box is tabbed into different sections. You look at three preferences in this chapter:

▲ General

▲ Files

▲ Keyboard

Other Preference Settings tabs are covered during the course of the book.

General

You use the General tab of the Preferences Settings dialog box to change overall settings for MAX (see figure 2.40). This tab is divided into six different sections. Each is described in the following list:

▲ **Preview Options**. If you create a preview animation file, MAX automatically begins to play the animation after the preview is generated when this setting is checked.

▲ **Layout**. As mentioned previously, you can turn on the option for the short toolbar here. Also, you can reposition the command panel on the left side of the screen instead of the right, if that position makes you more comfortable.

▲ **Virtual Framebuffer**. This setting is a performance optimization button. If you are running MAX in 256 colors, you should turn on this option. It optimizes the frame buffer to work with 8-bit or 256-color screens.

▲ **Spinner Precision**. This field set the decimal precision for all spinner fields that make use of decimal places.

▲ **System Unit Scale**. This section sets the overall system unit scale. Unless you have a very good reason to change these settings, don't. You can always change the units for your scene, independent of this setting.

▲ **Interaction**. These options help to define how you interact with MAX. First is the spinner snap. If you want to have it jump from number to number, click the Use Spinner Snap option. You can set the number intervals in the Spinner Snap box. You can also set the number of undo levels and the amount of time in milliseconds before the tooltips appear.

Figure 2.40

The general preferences.

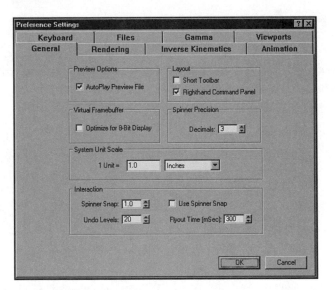

Tip

Setting the number of undo levels directly affects the amount of memory used by MAX. The more undo levels you have, the more memory MAX uses. If you have plenty of memory (greater than 32 MB), you should probably set this value to a higher number.

Files

If you click on the Files tab of the Preference Settings dialog box, you can access the file preferences (see fig. 2.41). These preferences directly affect how MAX saves files.

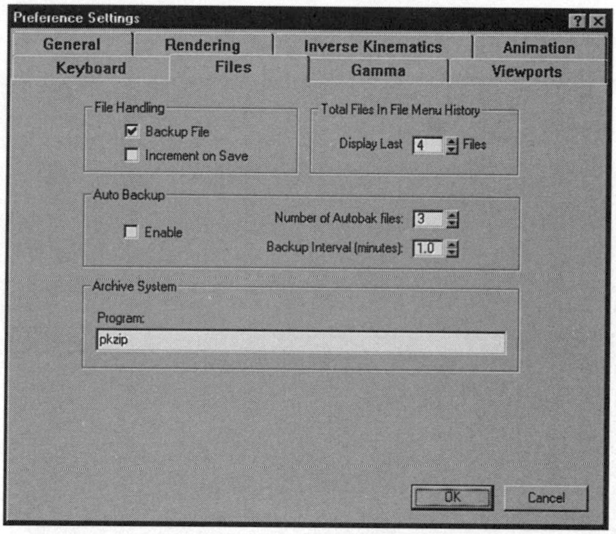

Figure 2.41

The Files tab.

This tab contains four options. Each is described in the following list:

▲ **File Handling**. These two options control how you save files. The first option is to save a backup. You should always leave this option enabled. The second option is to increment on save. It is handy to help you keep multiple versions of the scene on which you are working. Every time you save, the file name automatically increases by one.

▲ **Total Files in File Menu History**. The File menu keeps a history of the files you opened most recently. This spinner keeps track of how many files appear on the menu. The maximum is nine files.

▲ **Auto Backup**. You should take advantage of this powerful feature. If you enable this option, MAX automatically saves your file at set intervals. You can set the number of automatically backed up files it keeps on the hard drive, as well as the time interval between backups. Generally speaking, a time between 10 and 60 minutes is good.

▲ **Archive System**. MAX has a built-in system to archive files. The only option here is to enter the command for the compression program. The default is PKZIP. For this feature to work, PKZIP must be in your NT system path so that MAX can locate it and use it.

Several good file preferences are available here, including file handling and automatic backups. Make sure that you set them to the settings you want.

Keyboard

One of the more powerful features of MAX is the ability to tie a command to a keyboard shortcut. If you click on the Keyboard tab in the Preference Settings dialog box, you can set the keyboard shortcuts for MAX (see fig. 2.42).

Figure 2.42

The Keyboard tab.

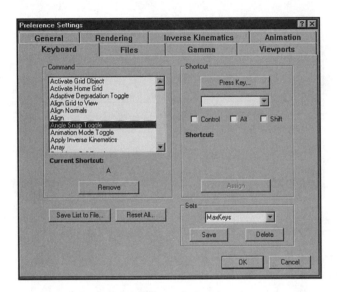

In the Command section of the tab, you see a list of all the commands in MAX that can have a keyboard shortcut assigned to them. If you click on a command, the keyboard shortcut, if any, appears below the list. Click on Angle Snap Toggle, for example, to see its keyboard shortcut.

Warning

Because you can save your own set of keyboard shortcuts, make sure that you do not overwrite the default MAX keyboard shortcuts. They are saved as a set named MAXKeys. The MAXKeys are saved internally. If you overwrite them, you can only restore the original configuration by reinstalling MAX.

The following steps show you how to set a keyboard shortcut and save your own shortcut:

1. From the Command list of the Keyboard tab, select the command to which you want to assign the keyboard shortcut.

2. In the Shortcut section, click either Control, Alt, or Shift if you want to use one of these modifiers. Otherwise, click on the Press key button.

3. Press any key.

4. Choose the Assign button, and that key is assigned as the keyboard shortcut. If you choose a modifier, you have to hold down the modifier and press the key to use the shortcut.

5. Click in the Sets drop-down list; then type a new name for your set.

6. Choose the Save button.

7. Choose OK, and the keyboard shortcuts are put into effect.

With a little practice and some thought, you should be able to set up enough keyboard shortcuts to substantially increase your productivity.

Many other preferences are worth a look. They are covered in later chapters when necessary.

Configuring Map Paths

The last interface issue for this chapter is map paths. A *map path* is the location of a bitmap image that you are using in a material or as a background in MAX. To configure map paths, choose File, Configure Paths. The Configure Paths dialog box appears, as shown in figure 2.43.

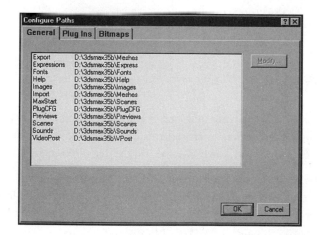

Figure 2.43

The Configure Paths dialog box.

Click on the Bitmaps tab to access the box for bitmaps, as shown in figure 2.44.

Figure 2.44

The Bitmaps tab.

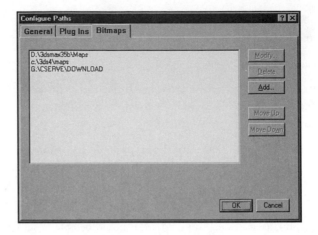

To add a new path, simply choose the Add button. A standard Windows NT file dialog box then appears, as shown in figure 2.45. Navigate to the directory you want, and choose the Use Path button. The path then appears in the list. Choose OK to save the list. The list is saved in the 3DSMAX.INI file in your 3DSMAX directory.

Figure 2.45

The Choose New Bitmap Path dialog box.

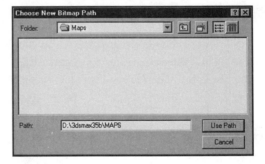

Summary

Many issues are related to the new user interface in 3D MAX Studio. It may take a couple of hours before you start to feel comfortable using the new interface. But, after you get used to it, you will see just how powerful and flexible it really is.

To help you get used to the interface and how it works, the next chapter provides an introductory exercise in which you create a small animation. This exercise should give you a rough overview of some of the features of MAX, as well as give you an idea of how easy MAX is to use. So, get yourself ready to experience MAX.

A Quick Overview

Before diving into the guts of MAX, you need a quick overview of the features and capabilities of MAX. This chapter introduces you to the features of MAX through a quick exercise. You might not understand all the commands and their results as you progress through the exercise, but you will get a great overview of how powerful MAX is and how much fun it is to use.

This exercise shows you how to do the following:

▲ Create geometry

▲ Modify the geometry

▲ Create lights and cameras

▲ Assign materials to the geometry

▲ Create a few special effects

▲ Animate the geometry

▲ Render the animation

Before you start this exercise, make sure that you have 3D Studio MAX installed and running on Windows NT. This exercise makes use of several memory intensive features of MAX. You need to have at least 32 MB of RAM to do this exercise and the other exercises in this book. You should also create a virtual memory swap file of around 200 MB in size. Refer to Chapter 1, "MAX and Windows NT," if you do not have MAX up and running yet or you need to configure your swap file.

Producing Your First Animation in MAX

This exercise, which runs through the entire chapter, demonstrates the creation of an animation in MAX. A rendered frame of the model you will create is shown in figure 3.1.

Figure 3.1

After creating the model described in this chapter, you can render any frame of the animated model to the screen or to disk.

When you are finished, you will have a complete animation. If you want, you can see the final animation by playing back the MAXFINT.AVI file, which is provided on the accompanying CD. You can use the Windows NT Media Player to play back the animation.

Now it is time to get started learning how to use MAX.

Creating the Stage for the Scene

In the following steps, you will create and adjust geometry for the scene using MAX's geometric object tools. These steps introduce the basic techniques for creating geometric objects and adjusting their creation parameters.

1. Load 3D Studio MAX.

2. In the command panel, click on the Create command panel tab to open the Create command panel. (By default, it should be showing already.)

3. Choose the Box button in the command panel Object Type rollout. The Box button turns green to show that it is active.

4. Activate the Top viewport by right-clicking in the viewport. Click at approximately –100,–100, and drag at a 45-degree angle to 100,100. (Watch the coordinate readout at the bottom of the screen. Don't worry about trying to hit –100,–100 exactly. You just need to be somewhat close.) Release the mouse button. Now move the mouse cursor toward the bottom of the screen until you see some thickness in the box; the actual thickness does not matter. Click again. The box should appear as shown in figure 3.2.

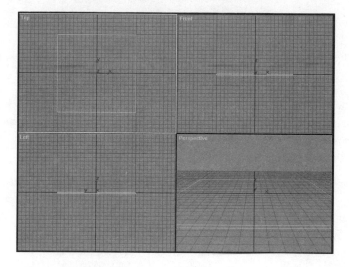

Figure 3.2

As you create an object, the object is shown in the MAX viewports.

5. In the Create command panel rollout area, change both the length and width to 200 by using the spinners or by clicking in the box and typing **200**. In the Height field, enter a height of **0**. Figure 3.3 shows the command panel with these changes. (Note that as you make the changes, the display interactively updates.)

6. In the Name and Color rollout in the command panel, click in the name box and change the object name from Box01 to **Ground**.

Figure 3.3

The creation parameters for an object can be modified after the object is created.

7. Double-click on the color swatch to the right of the object name. The Object Color dialog box appears (see fig. 3.4). By default, MAX randomly picks colors for the objects. You can choose any color you like and then choose OK. This new color then appears as the object's wireframe color, and as the object's color in the shaded display until you assign a material to the object in a step later in this chapter.

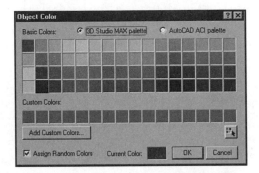

8. In the Perspective viewport, right-click on the title of the viewport. In the menu that appears, choose Smooth + Highlight to change the shading mode. For the rest of this exercise, this viewport is always a shaded view.

9. With the Box command still active, right-click in the Top viewport to make it active, click at –70,–20, and drag to 70,20. Release the mouse button, and then drag the mouse cursor vertically to assign a height. Drag the mouse cursor until you have a height of 30 (watch the Height field in the command panel), and then click. Notice that the shaded display is updated interactively as you create the box.

10. In the Parameters rollout in the command panel, set the Length to 40, the Width to 140, and the Height to 30. This way, you get exact measurements. Figure 3.5 shows the Perspective view with the second box.

Figure 3.5

You can configure MAX to perform real-time shading of the objects displayed in any viewport.

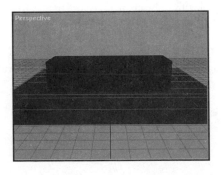

11. Go to the Name and Color rollout in the command panel. For the object name, enter **Base**, and choose another color if you want. (Note that choosing a different color is optional.)

12. Choose File, Save to save the file. In the Save dialog box, name the file **MAXCH3.MAX,** and choose the Save button. This way, you save the file to the Scenes directory of your MAX installation.

At this point, you have created two basic objects: two boxes. Notice that the creation process is simple, and accuracy does not matter. You can easily create an object, and then go back and add precise measurements to the object. In later chapters, you learn how to draw more precisely.

Figure 3.6

The Shape-Creation commands are shown when the Shapes button in the Create command panel is selected.

Creating Lofted Objects and 3D Text for the Scene

Now, you are ready to create three more complex objects. The first two objects are "lofted." They are drawn as 2D shapes and lofted along a 3D path to create a 3D shape. If you have used 3D Studio for DOS, you are undoubtedly used to using the 2D Shaper and 3D Lofter to accomplish this task. The third object is extruded text.

1. In the Create command panel, choose the Shapes button to display the shape-creation commands, as shown in figure 3.6.

2. Choose the Star button to create a star shape.

3. Click at 40,0 and drag out to 60,0 in the Top viewport to specify the outer radius. When you release the mouse button, move the mouse cursor back toward the center of the star, and click to set an inner radius.

4. In the Parameters rollout, set Radius 1 to **20**, Radius 2 to **5**, and the number of points to **8**. Figure 3.7 shows the resulting star in the Top viewport.

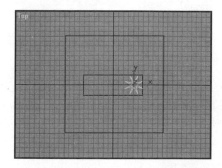

Figure 3.7

The star is placed over the right side of the box.

5. Choose the Line button in the Create command panel.

6. Click at 0,–120, and then click at 30,–120 to draw a 30-unit long horizontal line. Right-click to exit the Line command. You will use this line as the loft path. Do not drag the mouse cursor between points because doing so will curve the line. If you do, simply right-click to cancel, and then press Delete to delete the line. Figure 3.8 shows the Top viewport.

Figure 3.8

The Top viewport showing the shape and the path that will be used to create the loft object.

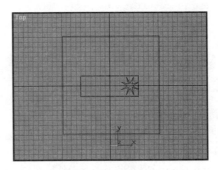

7. Choose the Geometry button in the command panel to display the geometry-creation tools.

8. Choose Loft Object from the drop-down list. Figure 3.9 shows the command panel at this point.

9. Choose the Loft button to display a new rollout so that you can create the loft object.

10. In the Creation Method rollout, choose Get Path. The Get Path button turns green at this point. When you place the cursor over the top of the line, a different cursor appears telling you that you can select this object as the path. Then click on the line in the Top viewport.

Figure 3.9

The Loft command is accessed by selecting the Create command panel tab and choosing Loft Object from the pull-down list.

11. Choose Get Shape. Then click on the star in the Top viewport. The lofted shape appears in the shaded viewport, as shown in figure 3.10.

12. Click on the Skin Parameters rollout header to display the Skin Parameters rollout (see fig. 3.11).

13. Click on the Skin check box under Display. Checking this box causes the lofted object to appear in all nonshaded viewports as well. When you enable this option, you can see the complexity of the object.

14. Choose the Select Object button from the main toolbar. Then click on the original star shape in the Top viewport, and press Delete to delete the object.

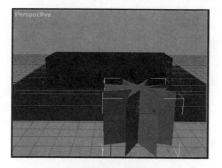

Figure 3.10

The lofted star shape as seen in the shaded Perspective viewport.

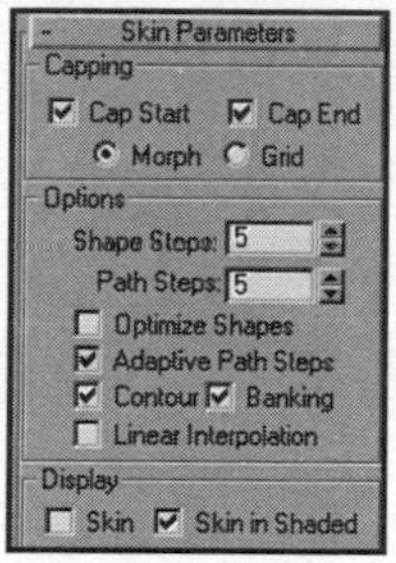

Figure 3.11

The Skin Parameters rollout enables you to set various options for skinning the loft object.

15. Click on the lofted object to select it again.

16. In the Top viewport, place the cursor over the lofted object and right-click. The Object Transform menu then appears, as shown in figure 3.12. Choose Move, and a new four-arrow cursor appears when you are over the object.

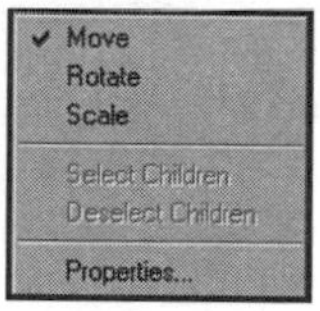

Figure 3.12

The Object Transform menu allows you to specify which type of transform to apply to the object.

17. In the Top viewport, while the four-arrow cursor is showing, click and drag the lofted object. Place it directly over where the original star shape was.

18. Right-click in the Front viewport to activate it. Place the cursor over the lofted object, and click and drag. Drag the object vertically so it is sitting on top of the base object (see fig. 3.13).

Figure 3.13

The lofted star is moved to its correct position on top of the box.

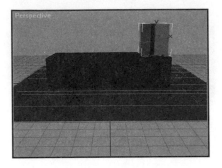

19. Now, you can make a copy of the object. Right-click in the Top viewport to make it active. Hold down the Shift key, click on the loft object, and then drag it to the opposite end of the base object. The Clone Options dialog box appears, as shown in figure 3.14. Make sure that Copy is selected, and choose OK.

Figure 3.14

The Clone Options dialog box enables you to create one or more copies of an object.

20. Choose the Shapes button on the Create command panel to display the shape-creation tools. Then choose Text.

21. In the Text area of the Parameters rollout, enter the first nine characters of your name in place of MAX Text.

22. In the Parameters rollout, set the size to 15, and click on the I button for italics. By default, the font should be Arial, so you use this font throughout the exercise. If Arial is not chosen in the Font drop-down list, click on the arrow to display the list, and choose Arial. Figure 3.15 shows the Text rollout with these settings.

23. Click anywhere in the Front viewport below the existing objects. The text shape appears, as shown in figure 3.16.

24. Click on the Modify command panel tab to display the Modify commands. Choose the Extrude button.

25. In the Parameters rollout in the command panel, set the Amount to 5 to add thickness to the text.

26. Right-click on the text object to access the Object Transform menu. Choose Move.

27. Click on the text object and drag it so it is positioned between the two lofted star objects (see fig. 3.17).

28. Choose File, Save to save the file to your hard drive.

Creating a Light and Camera

At this point, you have created all the basic geometry necessary for this exercise. Now, you can create a light to light the model and a camera through which you can view the model. Then you will be ready to apply materials, render, and animate the scene.

1. Choose the Create command panel tab to access the Create commands.

2. Choose the Lights button on the command panel so you can create a light.

3. Choose the Target Spot button. This button enables you to create a spotlight with both a light and a target.

4. Right-click in the Top viewport to make it active, click at –130,130, and drag to 0,0 and release the mouse button. The light is then created on the ground.

Figure 3.15

The Text rollout enables you to specify the font, attributes, size, and text to be placed in the scene.

Figure 3.16

When you click in a viewport, the text shape is created, centered around that point.

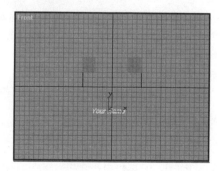

Figure 3.17

*The Perspective view
of the text object
positioned between the
lofted star objects.*

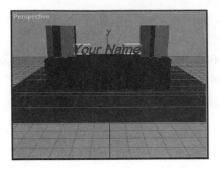

5. Right-click in the Left viewport to activate it and right-click on the light icon (it looks like a small yellow cone at the top of the blue cone) to access the Object Transform menu. Choose Move.

6. Click and drag the light vertically 260 units. Click on the Zoom Extents All button to magnify the views in all viewports so all the objects in the scene are shown. Figure 3.18 shows the scene with the light in the correct position.

Figure 3.18

*To illuminate a scene,
create and place lights
to shine on your objects.*

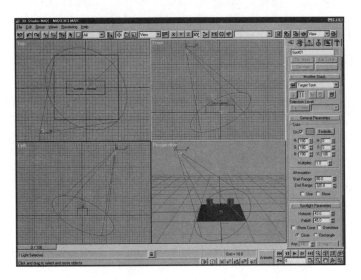

7. Choose the Modify command panel tab while the light is still highlighted. The light parameters appear. Scroll the command panel up until you find the Shadow Parameters rollout. Click on Casts Shadows so this light casts shadows for added realism.

8. Click on the Create command panel tab again. Then click on the Cameras button to access the Camera commands.

9. Choose the Target camera type. This option enables you to create a camera similar to the light.

10. Right-click in the Top viewport to activate it, click at 100,–100, and drag to 0,0 to create the camera on the ground.

11. Right-click in the Front viewport to activate it. Right-click to access the Object Transform menu, and choose Move.

12. Move the camera vertically 60 units.

13. Click on the camera target icon to select it. (It is probably fairly close to the spotlight target icon, so make sure you choose the correct one. You will know you have the right icon because the cone of the camera remains visible. If you select the light target, the cone of the light will be displayed.) Move the target of the light vertically 30 units.

14. Right-click in the Perspective viewport to activate it. Press C on your keyboard. The viewport is now the camera viewport (see fig. 3.19).

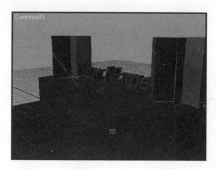

Figure 3.19

You can view your scene through a camera by setting a viewport as a camera view.

15. Because this camera view is a little too close, click and highlight the camera icon in the Top viewport.

16. Choose the Modify command panel tab. The camera parameters then appear.

17. Click on the 35mm button in the Stock Lenses section of the command panel to set the lens length of the camera to 35mm. The view updates and is now correct (see fig. 3.20).

18. Choose File, Save to save the file.

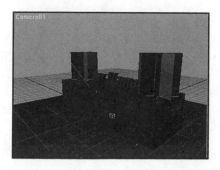

Figure 3.20

MAX provides many camera options, including a range of stock lens sizes.

Assigning Materials and Rendering the Model

Now, you have created all but one piece of geometry for the model. The last piece of geometry is a particle system effect. At this point, you can assign some materials to the model and test render it.

1. Start with the ground object. Choose the Select Object button from the main toolbar, and click on the ground object in any viewport. The object turns white when highlighted.

2. Click on the Material Editor button on the main toolbar. A Material Editor dialog box appears in which you can assign the material to the object (see fig. 3.21).

Figure 3.21

The Material Editor is where materials are defined and assigned to objects.

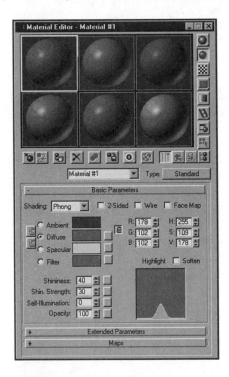

3. The sphere in the upper-left corner of the Material Editor should have a white box around it. This box indicates that it is the current material. Click on the color swatch next to the Diffuse option in the Basic Parameters rollout in the dialog box. A color selector then appears, as shown in figure 3.22.

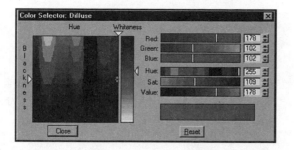

Figure 3.22

The Color Selector dialog box provides many different ways of adjusting the color to achieve the exact color you want.

4. On the left side of the color selector is a rainbow of colors. Click on a shade of blue that you like. If you want, you can use the whiteness slider next to the rainbow of colors to increase or decrease the intensity of the color.

5. When you are happy with the color, click on the color swatch next to Ambient in the Material Editor. Set this color to a darker blue in the Color Selector dialog box.

Tip

> **To copy the diffuse color to the ambient color, click on the diffuse color swatch, drag it over the ambient color swatch, and release the mouse button. In the dialog box that appears, choose the Copy button.**

6. In the Shading drop-down list, select Metal as the shading type. This option gives the material the illusion of a blue polished metal.

7. Set the Shininess spinner to 75, and the Shininess Strength spinner to 90. This will give the metal nice highlights.

8. Choose the Assign Material to Selection button in the upper portion of the Material Editor (third icon from left under sample spheres). This option assigns the material to the selected object. When you choose this option, the ground turns blue in the shaded viewport to reflect the new material assigned to it. Figure 3.23 shows the Material Editor and viewports at this point.

9. Click on the base object, repeat steps 2 to 8, and assign a new material to the object. Before you repeat the steps, however, click on the upper-middle sample sphere in the Material Editor to highlight it. If you don't select this object, you will change the material you just created. Make the base a green material. For the base material color, use a Phong shading instead of Metal shading.

10. Repeat the preceding steps for the lofted stars and the text in the scene. Create and assign materials with colors you like. Use Phong shading instead of Metal shading. Make sure that you use a different material window for each different material you are assigning to an object. Figure 3.24 shows one possible rendering of the scene.

Figure 3.23

*The Material Editor
settings for the ground
object and a shaded
Perspective view of
the scene.*

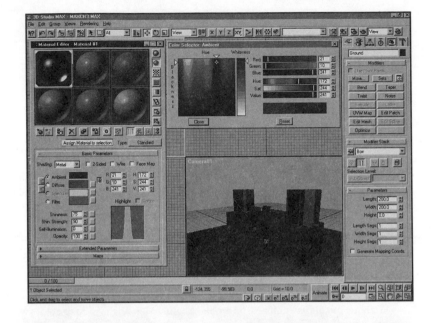

Figure 3.24

*A sample rendering of
the scene with materials
assigned to the objects.*

11. Click in the Camera viewport to make sure that it is the current active viewport.
Choose the Render Scene button from the main toolbar. The Render Scene dialog
box appears, as shown in figure 3.25.

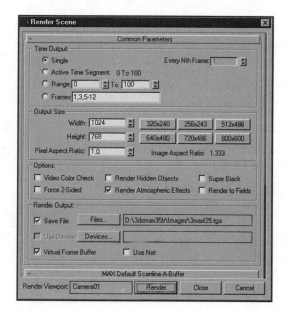

12. Choose the Render button. The scene is rendered to the screen and should look similar to figure 3.24.

13. After you finish the rendering, choose File, Save to save the file.

Animating the Scene

Now that you have rendered your first scene, you're ready to do a little animation. First, you animate a text rotate and a change of materials. Then you animate the lofted objects to make them twist.

1. Close the Render Scene dialog box and the Material Editor if they are still open from the preceding steps.

2. To start animating the text, click on the text object in the Top viewport to highlight it.

3. Click on the Animate button. The Animate button turns red and a red outline appears around the Top viewport to indicate that you are about to create some animation.

4. Click on the animation time slider at the bottom of the screen, and drag it to the right until it reads 50/100. This number indicates that the current frame of the animation is 50.

5. Right-click on the text object in the Top viewport to access the Object Transform menu. Choose Rotate. Press A on your keyboard to turn on the angle snap. Using angle snap makes it easier for you to rotate the text.

6. Click and drag the cursor toward the bottom of the screen. As you do, the text rotates. Rotate the text 180 degrees; then release the mouse button.

7. Drag the animation time slider to frame 100. Rotate the text again another 180 degrees. This way, you create a full 360 degrees of animation. (Note that if you want to, you can simply go to frame 100 and rotate the text a full 360 degrees.)

8. Click on the Animate button to turn it off.

9. For a quick preview of the animation, click in the Camera viewport to make it active.

10. Click on the Degradation override button at the bottom of the screen. Clicking this button keeps the animation playing back in shaded mode.

11. Click on the Play Animation button in the lower-right corner of the screen. The animation then plays back in the Camera viewport. If you have a slow machine, such as a Pentium 90, the animation may appear jumpy (unless you are using an accelerator card—then it should be rather smooth). If the animation looks bad, you can overcome this problem by following the next step. If the animation is playing back fine, skip the next step.

12. Stop the animation by clicking on the Stop button. Then right-click on the Stop button to display the Time Configuration dialog box (see fig. 3.26). In the Playback section of the dialog box, turn off Real Time. Choose OK, and play back the animation again. This time, it should be slower but smoother.

Figure 3.26

The Time Configuration dialog box provides access to the settings for animation creation and playback.

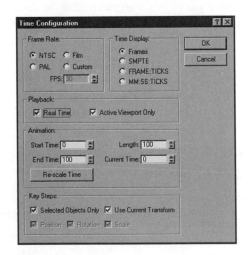

13. Click on the Stop button to stop the playback of the animation.

14. To animate the material of the text, click on the text object to highlight it in any viewport.

15. Choose the Material Editor button from the main toolbar.

16. In the Material Editor, click on the material window that you have assigned to the text object. Then click on the Animate button at the bottom of the MAX screen to turn on animation.

17. Drag the animation time slider to frame 50.

18. Change the material color to a shade of blue.

19. Drag the animation time slider to 100, and change the material color to a shade of red. Turn off the Animate button and close Material Editor.

20. Play back the animation. As the text rotates, it should change materials.

21. Stop the animation by clicking on the Stop button, and set the animation time slider back to 0.

22. To animate the lofted objects, first click on one of the lofted star objects to highlight it. Then click on the Modify command panel tab.

23. At the bottom of the command panel is a rollout called Deformations. Click on this rollout to expand it (see fig. 3.27).

Figure 3.27

The Loft Deformations rollout provides a set of dialogs for creating complex objects using loft deformation curves.

24. Click on the Scale button in the rollout. A deformation grid then appears on-screen. (see fig. 3.28). This grid enables you to deform the lofted object by scaling it along the loft path.

25. In the Scale Deformation dialog box, click on the black box on the right end of the red line. At the bottom of the dialog box is a readout. Drag the right end of the line down until the readout reads 50. This way, you can scale the top of the loft object down 50 percent from its original size.

26. Close the Scale Deformation dialog box.

Figure 3.28

*The Scale Deformation
dialog box enables you
to scale the cross-section
of the lofted object
along the loft path.*

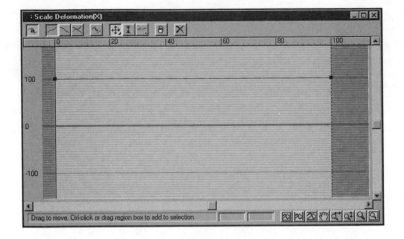

27. Set the frame slider to 50. Turn on the Animate button at the bottom of the MAX screen, and choose the Twist button in the Deformation section of the rollout. The Twist Deformation dialog box appears (see fig. 3.29).

Figure 3.29

*The Twist Deformation
dialog box enables you
to rotate the cross-
section of the lofted
object along the loft
path.*

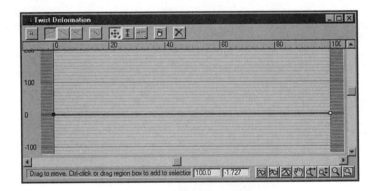

28. In the dialog box, drag the right end of the red line to 150 and release it. This way, you can add a 150 percent twist to the object, as shown in figure 3.30.

Figure 3.30

*The object that is
created when a scale
and twist deformation
is applied to the loft
object.*

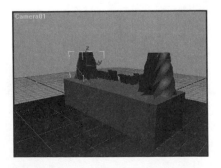

29. Drag the animation time slider to 100.

30. Drag the right end of the twist deformation line back to 0.

31. Close the Twist Deformation dialog box, and turn off the Animate button.

32. Repeat steps 23 to 31 with the other loft object selected. But, instead of moving the twist to 150 and then back to 0, move the twist to −150 in frame 50 and back to 0 in frame 100. This way, you can make the two loft objects twist opposite of each other.

34. Choose File, Save to save the file.

35. Click in the Camera viewport to make sure that it is active. Choose the playback button to see how the animation looks right now. It should look pretty good here but not quite complete.

Adding a Special Effect

At this point all of the scene geometry is created and animated. To complete the scene, you add a gold-like spray of sparks behind the text.

1. To create a special effect, first choose the Create command panel tab.

2. Choose the Geometry button. Then choose Particle systems from the drop-down list. A list of particle systems that you can create appears (see fig. 3.31).

3. Choose the Spray button to create a spray particle system.

4. Click at −15,20 and drag to 15,40 in the Top viewport to create the emitter for the spray.

5. Set the speed in the Parameters rollout to −10. This speed causes the spray to shoot up into the air. At this point, because the spray is an animated effect, you cannot see it. Drag the animation time slider to 50. There, you should see some of the effect, as shown in figure 3.32.

6. In the Parameters rollout, set the drop size to 4, the Viewport count to 1000, and the Render count to 2000. Set the variation to 2. As you adjust these settings, you can see their effect. Only the render count does not affect the screen. This render count affects how many particles appear when the animation is rendered.

Figure 3.31

The Particles Systems rollout enables you to select the type of particle system to be generated.

Figure 3.32

The particles generated by the spray particle system can be seen in the MAX viewports.

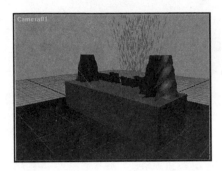

7. Now, you have a fairly random spray. To see what is missing, however, play back the animation. The spray goes up, but it never comes back down. So, you need to add a little gravity.

8. First, choose the Create command panel tab. Then choose the Space Warps button on the Create command panel.

9. Choose Gravity.

10. Click at 100,0 and drag to 115,0 in the Top viewport to create a little square that represents the gravity effect.

11. Right-click in the Front viewport to activate it. Then right-click on the gravity space warp to access the Object Transform menu, and choose Move.

12. Move the space warp so it is positioned above the particle spray.

13. In the Top viewport, move the space warp so it is directly above the particle spray, as shown in figure 3.33.

14. The space warp is in place, but it does not affect anything yet. First, you must bind the space warp to the particle spray. Choose the Bind to Space Warp button from the main toolbar.

15. In the Front viewport, click on the particle spray to highlight it. When you move the cursor over the highlighted spray, you see the Space Warp Bind cursor.

16. Click and drag up to the gravity space warp until you see the same bind cursor over the space warp. Then release the mouse button. The warp and the spray are highlighted briefly to indicate the binding. Then you see the effect of the gravity.

17. Click on the Select Object button on the main toolbar, and choose the gravity space warp in the scene. Then choose the Modify command panel tab.

18. In the Parameters rollout, set the strength of the space warp to 0.75 instead of 1 to reduce the gravity effect.

19. Choose File, Save.

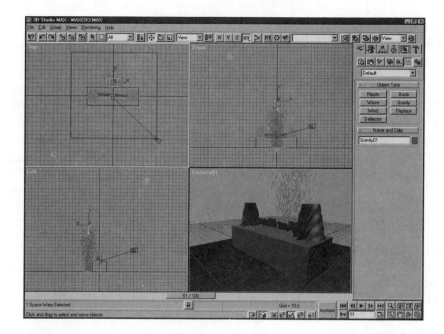

20. Now click on the particle spray to highlight it. Then choose the Material Editor button.

21. Click on the lower-right sphere in the Material Editor. Set the color to a bright yellow with a Metal shading limit. Set Shininess to 60 and Shininess Strength to 100. Set Self-illumination to 50.

22. Click on the Assign Material to Selection button. The particle spray now looks like a gold spray.

23. Close the Material Editor, and choose File, Save again.

RENDERING THE ANIMATION

At this point the scene is complete. In the following steps, the animation is rendered to an AVI file.

1. To render the scene, first click in the Camera viewport to make it active.

2. Choose the Render Scene button from the main toolbar. The Render Scene dialog box then appears.

3. In the Time Output section of the dialog box, choose Active Time Segment. In the Output Size section, click on the 320×240 button to set the resolution because this size is a good test resolution.

4. In the Render Output section of the dialog box, click on the Files button. In the resulting File dialog box, enter the filename as **MAXCH3.AVI**. Choose OK to return to the Render Scene dialog box.

5. Choose Render at the bottom of the dialog box. The animation is generated. Depending on the speed of your machine, rendering may take anywhere from 10 minutes to 2 or 3 hours. When you are done, an AVI file is created in the Images directory of the 3D Studio MAX directory. (If you do not want to render, you can use the AVI file that has been provided on the CD under the name MAXFINT.AVI. Use the Media Player of Windows NT to view it.)

6. After the file is done rendering, choose File, Save and then choose File, Exit to exit the program.

Now, you have completed your first model in 3D Studio MAX. Impressed yet? You should be. This type of animation would not be very easy to create in 3D Studio for DOS or many other animation packages. If you are familiar with other animation packages, imagine trying to create the particle spray and the twisting loft objects. This typically is not an easy task. With the capabilities MAX provides for object creation and modification, your scenes are limited only by your imagination.

Summary

This chapter has shown you the basics of using 3D Studio MAX in the hopes of sparking your interest to a high level. By this time, you may be dreaming of many things you want to do or think you can do in MAX. So, without further ado, you can set off on your voyage into the world of MAX.

The next section of the book covers geometry fundamentals. In this section, you find chapters on creating the different types of geometry in MAX. If you feel comfortable creating geometry in MAX and want to move on to other topics, feel free to skip the Geometry fundamentals section. But, because MAX offers many new features, you are highly encouraged to go through the fundamentals so that you have the best possible foundation before you begin working with this powerful modeling, rendering, and animation package.

In Chapter 4, you learn about creating basic 3D shapes such as boxes and cones. Most scenes you create will be at least partially based on these basic 3D shapes. These shapes can be thought of as the basic building blocks upon which the rest of the model is built.

PART II

GEOMETRY FUNDAMENTALS

3D Objects

One of the first things to look at in MAX is how to create basic objects. Even though basic objects may seem simple to you, they have many parameters that you can adjust and manipulate to change how the basic objects look.

3D Studio MAX actually has five categories of basic objects:

▲ Standard primitives

▲ Patch grids

▲ Compound objects

▲ Particle systems

▲ Loft objects

Each of these five categories corresponds to the items on the drop-down list on the Create command panel. One category, Loft objects, is a basic object itself and deserves coverage in its own chapter; see Chapter 5, "Creating Lofted Objects." Particle systems are more like a special effect and have special uses; therefore, they are covered in Chapter 23, "Special Effects Fundamentals." Another type of object, a Morph Compound Object, also is not covered in this chapter; because it is an animation topic, it is covered in Chapter 17, "Basic Animation."

This chapter covers the basics of creating standard primitives and patch grids in MAX and all the parameters associated with creating each type of object.

Object Naming and Color Conventions

Every object in MAX should have a unique name. You can name all the objects in your scene the same, but you will have problems later when you try to select them using Select by Name. As a general rule, make all object names unique. Object names can use just about any character and can have spaces in them. Object names are also case sensitive. So, names such as *Box* and *box* are different. You should strive to name each object with a name that you can recognize for that object.

If, for example, you create a box that you are going to use as a wall, you might call it SouthWall if it is the wall on the south side of the building. Use names that are associated with what the object is in the scene. That way, you can quickly recognize them.

Each object in MAX also has a color assigned to it. By default, MAX randomly picks the color of objects as you create them. You then have the option of changing the color of the object if you want. These colors show on-screen until you assign a material to the object. Then the object appears the color of the material. Because MAX supports full 24-bit color (16.7 million colors), you can use any color in the spectrum on your object.

When you create objects, the top command rollout in the Create command panel is the Object Type rollout, followed by the name and color rollout, as shown in figure 4.1. The Name and Color rollout has a name field and a color swatch. You can change the name by clicking in the field and entering a new name.

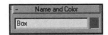

Figure 4.1

The Name and Color rollout where you can change the name and color of objects that you create.

You change the color by clicking on the color swatch beside the name field to access the Object Color dialog box (see fig. 4.2).

In the lower left corner of the Object Color dialog box is the Assign Random Colors check box. Unless you have a good reason to change it, you should probably leave this option turned on so each object in the scene will have a different color. You can turn off random color selections and choose a specific color if you want a group of objects that you create to be the same color. To change the color of an object, simply click on the color you want to use in the display area. The current color is indicated with a black outline.

This dialog box contains two special capabilities. The first is the ability to add your own custom colors. The second is the ability to pick an existing object and use its color.

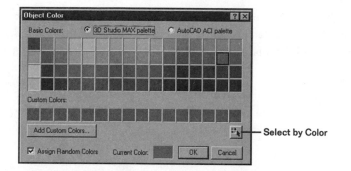

Figure 4.2

The Object Color dialog box where you can select any of a number of colors for an object that you create to use.

To create your own custom object colors, click on the Add Custom Colors button in the Object Color dialog box. The Color Selector dialog box then appears, as shown in figure 4.3.

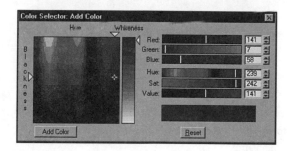

Figure 4.3

The Color Selector: Add Color dialog box where you can select a color from the entire color spectrum by HSV or RGB color methods.

This dialog box is the same dialog box you use to pick any color in MAX. On the left side is the Hue box where you can choose the basic color of the object. In the middle is the Whiteness slider to control the intensity of the color. On the right are the RGB (which stands for Red, Green, and Blue) and HSV (which is Hue, Saturation , and Value) color sliders.

You can easily use the Hue box and Whiteness and Blackness slider to choose just about any color you could possibly want. You use the RGB and HLS sliders for precise control over a specific color. Adjusting the RGB values directly affects the HSV or Hue, Whiteness, and Blackness settings, and vice versa.

Red, Green, and Blue are considered color channels. By combining different levels of each of these colors, you can create any color you want. Each channel has up to 255 (8-bit) shades of that color. By combining all 3 channels, you get 24-bit color, or 16.7 million colors (255×255×255).

HLS is a slightly different color scale. You pick the overall color by using the Hue channel. Then, using Luminance and Value, you can have a fine control over the Hue color. Luminance controls how bright the color is. The Value controls how deep and rich the color is.

To use the Color Selector dialog box, simply choose a color using any of the sliders or pick areas. Then choose the Add Color button. Your new color then appears in the select color swatch in the Custom Colors section of the Object Color dialog box, as shown in figure 4.4.

Figure 4.4

The Object Color dialog box with a custom color.

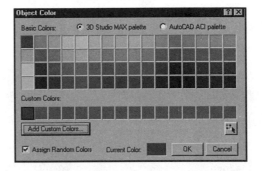

The other method for choosing colors is to use the Select by Color button in the Object Color dialog box. It is on the right side, above the OK and Cancel buttons. When you choose this button, the Select Objects dialog box appears (see fig. 4.5). You can choose any object from this list, and its color is assigned as the current color. Click on the object in the list, and choose Select. After you have finished creating the color, close the Color Selector dialog box and you are returned to the Object Color dialog box. The color is then highlighted as the current color.

Figure 4.5

The Select Objects dialog box.

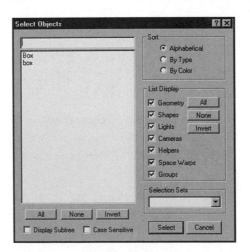

Note

> The Select Objects dialog box is used heavily in many operations in MAX. Please refer to Chapter 7, "Selection Controls," for more information on this dialog box and how to use it.

When you choose OK in the Object Color dialog box, you return to the name and color rollout, and the new color is applied to the object.

Standard Primitives

Standard primitives are objects such as boxes, cones, spheres, and so on. By combining standard primitives, you create more complex objects such as bridges, bicycles, and so on. But you have to start with the basic building blocks before you can create the skyscraper. 3D Studio MAX utilizes eight basic object types:

▲ Box

▲ Sphere

▲ Cylinder

▲ Torus

▲ Tube

▲ Cone

▲ Hedra

▲ Teapot

Each of these standard primitives appears on the Create command panel when the Geometry button is active (see fig. 4.6). Each standard primitive is discussed in the following sections.

Figure 4.6

You select the type of geometry you want to create in the Create Geometry command panel.

Box

A box is the simplest building block in MAX. A box is any two- or three-dimensional rectangular shape. When you choose the Box command from the Create command panel, the box-creation parameters are displayed, as shown in figure 4.7.

Figure 4.7

Define the various parameters for a box in the Box-Creation Parameters.

The Box command has three rollout areas besides the Name and Color rollout. These rollouts are Creation Method, Keyboard Entry, and Parameters.

The creation method defines how you create the box. The default is the box method. In this method, you must specify two opposite corners by clicking in any viewport with your mouse and dragging to the opposite corner. Then you must specify the height. With the cube method, you create the box by choosing a center point and dragging out. The cube is created equally on all sides.

The Keyboard Entry rollout enables you to create the box by specifying the length, width, and height of the box, along with X, Y, and Z creation points when the Create button is clicked. The box is created on the XY plane (this is called the home grid and is discussed in Chapter 6, "Drawing with Precision") at the coordinates you specify. As with all spinner boxes, you can change the numbers in this rollout by clicking in the fields and typing in the new value or by clicking and dragging on the spinner.

The last section is the Parameters rollout. When you create a box by clicking and dragging on the screen, these parameters adjust according to your mouse clicks. You can then come back and adjust these parameters for more precise control after you have created the box.

Of special note here are the segment spinners. They define how complex the box is. If, for example, you create a box that is under the influence of a space warp such as explode or ripple, you will want a fairly complex box; otherwise, the space warp will not have much effect. Each segment that you add subdivides the surface into smaller faces. Figure 4.8 shows a box with one segment and a box with ten segments in each direction.

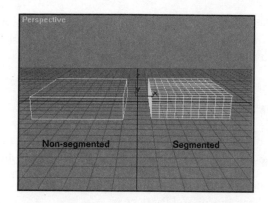

Figure 4.8

A box with one segment and a box with ten segments.

You also can have the system generate mapping coordinates for the box by checking the Generate Mapping Coordinates checkbox at the bottom of the Parameters rollout. This option applies standard box mapping to the box for use with mapped materials. (See Chapter 13, "Mapped Materials.")

The following exercise shows you how to create a box using a couple of methods:

METHOD 1: CREATING A BOX USING THE BOX METHOD

1. Choose the Box button in the Create command panel.

2. Click at −50,−50 and drag to 50,50.

3. Move the mouse cursor toward the top of the screen ten units. Watch the Height field in the Parameters rollout.

4. Adjust any parameters in the Parameters rollout for precise box creation.

METHOD 2: CREATING A BOX USING KEYBOARD ENTRY

1. Click on Keyboard Entry in the Create command panel to expand the rollout.

2. Enter **50** in the Length field, **50** in the Width field, and **10** in the Height field.

3. Enter **100** in the X field, **100** in the Y field, and **0** in the Z field.

4. Choose Create. The box appears at the specified coordinates with the correct dimensions.

5. Choose a name and a color for the box.

Figure 4.9

*The Sphere
Command rollout.*

Boxes are the most basic primitive and are heavily used. As you gain experience with modifiers and other effects, you will learn which box parameters to adjust to create certain effects.

Sphere

The sphere object has fewer parameters than the box and is easier to create. Figure 4.9 shows the Sphere command rollout in the Create command panel.

As with the box rollouts, three rollouts are worth mentioning here: Creation Method, Keyboard Entry, and Parameters.

> **Note**
>
> All the standard primitives contain the Creation Method, Keyboard Entry, and Parameters rollouts. For the rest of the standard primitives commands, only the parameters rollouts are covered.

The Creation Method rollout provides two methods for creating the sphere: Edge and Center. You will probably create more spheres using the Center method than the Edge method. In the Center method, you choose a center point and drag out to the radius of the sphere. In the Edge method, you choose one edge location and drag to create the opposite edge of the sphere.

The Keyboard Entry rollout enables you to create the sphere by specifying parameters and a location for the sphere before you create it (see fig. 4.10). All keyboard rollouts have a location in X, Y, and Z coordinates, along with the necessary object parameters to create the object.

Figure 4.10

*The Keyboard Entry
rollout for sphere.*

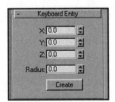

The Parameters rollout of the Create command panel enables you to control how you create the sphere. To create a sphere, you simply click and drag in any viewport when the Sphere command is active. Then you can come back and adjust both the radius of the sphere and the number of segments in this rollout. The higher the number of segments, the smoother the sphere is.

Below the Segments field is a Smooth checkbox. Enabling this option turns on smoothing for the renderer. Then, when the sphere is rendered, it always appears smooth instead of faceted.

You also can use the Hemisphere spinner in the Parameters rollout. This spinner enables you to create a hemisphere from the sphere. The spinner can have a value of 0 to 1. When the value is 0, the whole sphere appears. As you adjust the value toward 1, the sphere begins to disappear from the bottom up, until, at a value of 1, the sphere completely disappears.

You can use two methods for creating the hemisphere: Chop and Squash. Chop creates the hemisphere by chopping the sphere from the bottom to the top, reducing the number of segments in the hemisphere. The Squash option keeps the number of segments in the hemisphere consistent.

Below the Chop and Squash radio buttons are two other checkboxes. Base to Pivot controls where the sphere is created. When the Base to Pivot option is turned off, the sphere is created with the center point on the X,Y plane. When Base to Pivot is enabled, the sphere is created with the bottom edge of the sphere on the X,Y plane. You can easily see how this option works by turning Base to Pivot on and off when you create the sphere. The last option, Generate Mapping Coordinates, creates spherical coordinates for use with mapped materials.

Note

Any object that has a curve in it, such as a sphere or a cone, has a smoothing field. Because it is defined here, it is not mentioned in the description of other objects. The same applies to Generate Mapping Coordinates. All objects that you can create in MAX have the Generate Mapping Coordinates option, so it is not discussed further either.

The following exercise shows you how to create a sphere in two different ways:

METHOD 1: CREATING A SPHERE USING THE CENTER METHOD

1. Choose Sphere from the Create command panel.

2. Click at 0,0 and drag out to 20,0 in the Top viewport to create a sphere of radius 20.

3. Adjust the Segments field in the Parameters rollout to 20 to increase the complexity of the sphere.

4. Turn on the Base to Pivot checkbox.

5. Name the sphere and give it a color.

1. Choose Edge in the Creation Method rollout.

2. Click and drag from 0,0 to 40,0 in the top viewport. The sphere is then created.

3. Set the Hemisphere spinner to .5 in the Parameters rollout and then turn on the Squash option.

4. Choose Base to Pivot to turn on this option. When the squash is applied to the sphere, the sphere remains correctly oriented to the ground.

Cylinder

When you choose the Cylinder button in the Create command panel, the Cylinder rollout appears (see fig. 4.11). You create a cylinder by choosing a center point and then a radius. Then you specify a height by using the mouse.

In the Parameters rollout, you can adjust several cylinder-creation parameters to create different cylinders. The Radius and Height define the overall size of the cylinder. The Height Segments, Cap Segments, and Sides determine the complexity of the cylinder.

Another option in the command rollout is called Slice On. It appears in the Parameters rollout for the cylinder. The Slice On option enables you to create a sliced version of the object, much like a taking a slice out of a cake. When you turn on Slice On, you can adjust two fields: Slice From: and Slice To:. Both are degree spinners. When you adjust one, you define how much of a 360-degree circle you are slicing. Figure 4.12 shows a sliced cylinder versus a nonsliced cylinder.

Figure 4.11

The Cylinder rollout appears when you choose the Cylinder button.

Figure 4.12

A sliced cylinder versus a nonsliced cylinder.

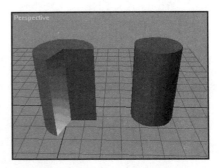

Note

> The Torus, Tube, Cone, and Cylinder commands all contain the Slice On option in the Parameters rollout. Because it is discussed here, it is not discussed for Torus, Tubes, or Cones.

The following exercise shows you how to create a cylinder and a sliced cylinder:

METHOD 1: CREATING A CYLINDER USING THE CENTER METHOD

1. Choose Cylinder from the Create command panel.

2. Click at –50,0 and drag to –30,0 in the Top viewport.

3. Move the mouse cursor vertically until the Height spinner in the Parameters rollout reads approximately 60.

METHOD 2: CREATING A CYLINDER USING THE EDGE METHOD

1. Choose Cylinder from the Create command panel.

2. Select the Edge creation method.

3. Click at 50,0 and drag to 30,0 in the Top viewport.

4. Move the mouse cursor vertically until the Height spinner in the Parameters rollout reads 30.

5. Turn on Slice On.

6. Set the Slice From value to 270.

7. Name the object and assign a color to it.

Torus

A torus is a donut-like cylinder. When you create a torus, you must specify both an inner and outer radius point as well as a center point. When you choose Torus from the Create command panel, the torus rollout appears (see fig. 4.13).

Figure 4.13

The Torus rollout, where you can specify parameters for creating a torus.

The Parameters rollout for the torus contains two Radius fields, one Rotation field, and one twist field. Using the Radius1 and Radius2 fields, you can adjust the inner and outer radius of the torus. The first radius you pick on-screen is assigned Radius1. This radius could be the inner or outer radius, depending on where you choose Radius2 and vice versa.

The Rotation field controls how much the cylinder is rotated. This field affects only the placement of generated mapping coordinates and does not generally affect the overall look of the torus. The Twist field, in contrast, dramatically affects the look of the torus. The twist is given in degrees, and this number affects how much twist the torus has. Imagine, for example, if you straighten the torus into a cylinder. Then you twist one end of the cylinder 360 degrees and place it back into the torus shape. This process is the same as placing a twist in the torus. Figure 4.14 shows a twisted torus.

The last new options to look at in this Parameters rollout are the smoothing options. Unlike the other rollouts you have seen to this point, the torus has two types of smoothing instead of one. The first type is All, and the second type is Sides. Sides applies smoothing to the sides of the torus, around the radius, but not along the length of the torus where the segments are. All applies smoothing to the sides and the length. Figure 4.15 shows the torus shown in figure 4.14 with just Sides smoothing turned on. The torus in figure 4.14 has All smoothing turned on.

Figure 4.14

A Torus with a 720-degree twist showing you some of the flexibility in the primitive commands.

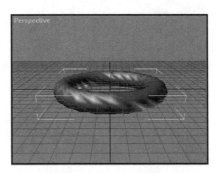

Figure 4.15

The Torus with Sides smoothing turned on.

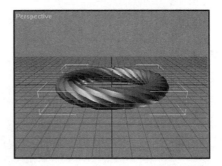

The following exercise shows you how to create a torus:

CREATING A TORUS

1. Choose Torus from the Create command panel.

2. Click and drag at 0,0 in the Top viewport.

3. Drag to 30,0 and release the mouse button to set the inner radius of the torus.

4. Click at 50,0 to set the outer radius of the torus. Depending on where you choose this second radius point, it could be the inner or outer radius of the torus. For this example, it is the outer radius.

5. The torus is created, and you can adjust other parameters such as the number of segments or sides and the smoothing.

Tube

A tube is a hollow cylinder, like a water pipe. You create the tube by choosing the inner and outer radius of the tube as well as its length. When you choose Tube from the Create command panel, the Tube rollout appears (see fig. 4.16).

In the Parameters rollout for the tube, you have the same parameters as a cylinder, except for the Radius1 and Radius2 parameters. As you do with a torus, you select a center point and then a radius point. The first radius point you choose is Radius1, and the second radius point you choose is Radius2. Depending on where you choose Radius1 and Radius2, they may be either the inner or outer radius of the tube.

All the other parameters are the same as a cylinder.

The following exercise shows you how to create a tube:

CREATING A TUBE

1. Choose Tube from the Create Command panel.

2. Click at 0,0 in the Top viewport and drag out to 30,0 to set Radius1.

3. Click at 40,0 to set Radius2.

Figure 4.16

The Tube rollout, where you can specify parameters for creating a tube.

4. Move the mouse cursor toward the top of the screen to set the height of the tube.

5. Adjust any other creation parameters you feel necessary.

Cone

A cone is a slanted cylinder with an upper and a lower radius. When the upper radius is 0, the cone has a point; otherwise, the cone slopes up to a flat top. When you choose Cone from the Create command panel, the Cone rollout appears (see fig. 4.17).

Creating a cone is just like creating a cylinder, except that you have one extra step. A cone has both Radius1 and Radius2 parameters. Radius1 is the radius of the base of the cone, and Radius2 is the radius of the top of the cone. The extra step is defining Radius2. Otherwise, the parameters are exactly the same as those of a cylinder.

Figure 4.17

The Cone rollout, where you can specify parameters for creating a cone.

Figure 4.18

The Hedra rollout, where you can specify parameters for creating hedra.

The following exercise shows you how to create a cone:

CREATING A CONE

1. Choose Cone from the Create command panel.

2. Click at 0,0 and drag out to 50,0, in the top viewport, to set Radius1, or the lower radius of the cone.

3. Move the mouse cursor toward the top of the screen, and click to set the height of the cone. Set the height to any value you want.

4. Move the mouse cursor left or right to set the upper radius, or Radius2. Click when you have a radius you want.

5. Set the rest of the creation parameters that you want in the Parameters rollout.

Hedra

A hedra is a group of geometric shapes such as a tetrahedron or an octahedron. These shapes are defined by a center and a radius. When you choose Hedra from the Create command panel, the Hedra rollout appears (see fig. 4.18).

The following are the five different types of hedras: Tetra, Cube/Octa, Dodec/Icos, Star1, and Star2. Figure 4.19 shows a basic example of each type.

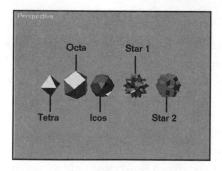

Figure 4.19

The different types of hedra.

Two sets of parameters affect how each hedra type looks: Family Parameters and Axis Scaling. A third set of parameters called Vertices affects how MAX builds the hedra but not how the hedra looks. You use the Vertices rollout to place the hedra vertices in different locations for different editing effects.

Figure 4.20

The Teapot rollout, where you can specify a center point and radius for creating a teapot.

The Family Parameters affect the overall look of the object. The P and Q fields control the size of the points in the hedra in the P and Q axes. Valid values are from 0 to 1.

The Axis Scaling parameters affect how large the hedra points are along the P, Q, and R axes. You can set these values to any numbers that you like.

The P, Q, and R axes change from hedra to hedra. The best way to understand these axes is to create one of each type of hedra and adjust the values of the P, Q, and R axes to see how the values affect the geometry.

The following exercise shows you how to create a hedra:

CREATING A HEDRA

1. Choose Hedra from the Create command panel.

2. In the Family section of the Parameters rollout, select the Hedra type that you want to create. For this exercise, choose Star1.

3. Click at 0,0 and drag out to 50,0 in the top viewport. The hedra is created.

4. Adjust the Family Parameters and Axis Scaling parameters to create the hedra you want.

Teapot

The last item on the Standard Primitive Create command panel is the teapot. The teapot is a standard computer graphics problem from the early days of rendering and animation. Developed and modeled at the University of Utah, the teapot represented a difficult object to model. Back in the early days of computer modeling, curved surfaces such as those shown in the teapot, were very difficult to model. Today, with Bézier spline and NURBS surfaces, these are rather simple tasks. MAX provides it as an example of how easy modeling is these days. If you have any scenes that need a teapot, you have a prebuilt teapot at your disposal. When you choose Teapot from the Create command panel, the Teapot rollout appears (see fig. 4.20).

You create the teapot by specifying a center point and a radius. The only other options are to enable or disable the various parts of the teapot, including body, handle, spout, and lid. You can find checkboxes for each of these items in the Parameters rollout. Simply check the box if you want that part of the teapot, or turn it off if you don't.

The following exercise shows you how to create a teapot:

CREATING A TEAPOT

1. Choose Teapot from the Create command panel.

2. Click at 0,0 and drag to 50,0 in the top viewport. The teapot is created.

3. Turn on or off any parts of the teapot in the Parameters rollout, or adjust the complexity as you need.

This section concludes the discussion of standard primitives that you can create in MAX. You can combine these simple primitives in many ways to create more complex objects. More times than not, you also have to edit these primitives to achieve the geometry you are looking for. Chapter 6, "Drawing with Precision," introduces you to the basics of editing geometry.

Patch Grids

Patch grids are Bézier surfaces that you can create in MAX. A Bézier surface is a flat surface of triangles or squares that you can adjust through the manipulation of control points. You can create patch grids by selecting the Patch Grids option from the Geometry type drop-down list in the Create command panel. The Patch Grid rollout appears, as shown in figure 4.21.

Figure 4.21

The Patch Grid rollout.

You use patch grids to create nonuniformly curved surfaces by adjusting the control points. When you adjust a control point, it affects an area of the patch grid instead of a single vertex or point. Figure 4.22 shows a patch grid and one that has been modified. In the adjusted patch grid in the figure, only one control point was moved to create the curved surface.

You can create two types of patch grids in MAX: quad patches and tri patches.

Figure 4.22

A flat Patch Grid versus an adjusted Patch Grid.

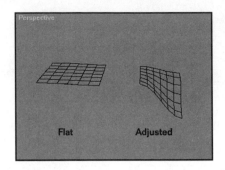

Quad Patch

A quad patch is formed from quads or squares. This type of patch is less complex and more uniform than a tri patch (discussed next). When you create a quad patch, you always create it as a flat surface that must be edited to create a curved surface. You create the patch by choosing two opposite corners of the patch. When you choose the Quad Patch button on the Patch Grid command panel, the Quad Patch rollout appears (see fig. 4.23).

The only parameters here influence the size and complexity of the grid. The Length and Width fields in the Parameters rollout define the overall size of the patch. The Length and Width Segments define how dense the patch is.

The following exercise shows you how to create a quad patch:

Figure 4.23

The Quad Patch rollout.

CREATING A QUAD PATCH BÉZIER SURFACE

1. Choose Quad Patch from the Create command panel.

2. Click at –50,–50 and then at 50,50 in the top viewport to create the patch.

3. Adjust the Length and Width Segments in the Parameters rollout as you like.

Tri Patch

A tri patch is the same as a quad patch except for two differences. First, you create a tri patch out of triangles instead of quads. Second, you cannot adjust the complexity of the tri patch. Otherwise, the two are the same. Refer to the preceding exercise on "Creating a Quad Patch" to create a tri patch. In step one, however, choose Tri Patch instead.

Compound Objects

A compound object combines two or more existing objects into one. The most common form of a compound object is a Boolean object. Boolean objects are based on Boolean mathematics, invented by Charles Boole several hundred years ago. Boolean objects enable you to combine two objects into one in three ways: Intersection, Union, and Subtraction. Figure 4.24 shows you the two original objects and the resulting objects after having one of the Boolean operations applied to them.

Generally, to create a Boolean object, the two objects you are going to combine must overlap in some way. If they do, the Boolean operations work best. To actually perform a Boolean operation, you must select one object first, (which will be called operand A) and then select the type of Boolean operation you want to perform. Then you select the second object (called operand B) to complete the Boolean operation. Each Boolean operation is described in the following list:

▲ **Union**. This operation combines the volumes of operand A and B into one large object.

▲ **Intersection**. This operation combines the volumes of operands A and B by creating an object that is the shared volume between A and B.

▲ **Subtraction**. This operation combines the volumes of A and B by subtracting one from the other. You are given the option of subtracting A from B or vice versa.

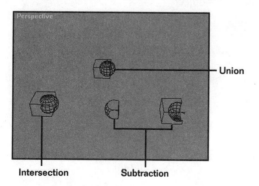

Intersection   Subtraction

Figure 4.24

The different Boolean operations performed on the same two objects.

You can access the Boolean commands by first selecting one of the two objects you want to combine. The selected object becomes Operand A. Then choose Compound Objects from the Create command panel. Two types of compound objects are available: Morphs and Booleans. When you choose the Boolean option, you get the rollout shown in figure 4.25.

The rollout is broken down into two separate rollouts: Pick Boolean and Parameters. Under Pick Boolean, you can select Operand B and determine whether a reference, copy, instance, or a moved version of the selected object is used in the Boolean operation.

Figure 4.25

The Boolean Object rollout where you can perform Boolean operations.

Under Parameters, you can determine the type of Boolean operation, how it is displayed, updated, and whether the finale Boolean object is optimized. Generally, you set the parameters for the Boolean operation before you select Operand B. When you do select Operand B, the Boolean is created the as soon as you select the object.

 Tip

> If you perform a complex Boolean operation and the final object appears to have faces missing or to be positioned incorrectly, disable the optimize result option.

The following exercise shows you how to create a Boolean object:

CREATING A BOOLEAN OBJECT

1. Create a box starting at 0,0 that is 100 units wide, 10 units long, and 50 units high.

2. Create a sphere that has a radius of 30 and is centered at 50,0. Set Base to Pivot on.

3. Choose Select objects.

4. Select the box.

5. Select compound objects from the drop-down list.

6. Select Boolean as the compound object type.

7. Set the operation type to Subtract (A-B).

8. Choose Pick Operand B.

9. Click on the sphere. The Boolean object is created.

Summary

MAX contains two types of basic 3D objects: Standard Primitives and Patch Surfaces. By creating and combining these objects, you can create a variety of simple scenes. Each object that you create in MAX must have a unique name, and it is automatically assigned a random color.

MAX also enables you to create other types of objects. The next chapter introduces you to creating lofted objects where a 2D shape is lofted along a 3D path to create a 3D object.

Creating Lofted Objects

One of the most powerful tools that MAX provides for creating complex geometry is the capability to loft a 2D or 3D shape along a predefined path into a 3D object. Using this method, you can create complex objects such as telephone handles, molding around the top of a room, or a bottle. The process is fairly simple:

1. Create one or more shapes and edit them into a form you want.

2. Create another shape to act as the loft path.

3. Attach the shape to the loft path to create the lofted object.

4. Edit the lofting parameters to create a variety of objects.

This chapter focuses on the first three steps of the process. (The fourth step, editing the lofted object, is covered in Chapter 10, "Modifying Objects at Different Levels," as is the use of the Edit Spline modifier to edit shapes.)

In particular, this chapter covers the following topics:

▲ Creating shapes

▲ Creating the loft object

Figure 5.1

*The shape-creation
commands are shown
when the Shapes button
in the Create command
panel is selected.*

Creating Shapes

A *shape* is defined as an object that consists of one or more splines. A *spline* consists of two or more vertices and the line that connects the vertices. A *segment* is the line connecting two vertices. Depending on the values assigned to the vertices, a segment can be either linear or curved. Examples of shapes include lines, arcs, circles, flat text, stars, and any of a number of other polygons. You create shapes in MAX by choosing the Shapes button on the Create command panel, which displays the shape-creation buttons shown in figure 5.1.

The 3D Studio MAX shape-creation system is a little unusual. By default, each spline you draw in MAX is a separate shape. This is important because you cannot combine splines of two different shapes into a single spline using an operation such as a Boolean. Rather, you must either create the two splines in the same shape, or attach the two shapes using the EditSpline Modifer described in Chapter 10, "Modifying Objects at Different Levels," to be able to combine the splines.

Immediately above the shape-creation buttons in the Object Type rollout is the Start New Shape button, which is on by default. If you make the button available by unchecking the check box next to the button, every spline you create will be the same shape. To start a new shape, click on the Start New Shape button. When a shape consists of more than one spline, you can apply modifiers and transforms to the splines as a set, or you can combine the splines in the shape to create a more complex spline. (For clarification, see Chapter 10, "Modifying Objects at Different Levels," which explores how to edit the shapes you create in this chapter.)

All splines created in MAX are *Bézier splines*, an easily edited form of a Bézier curve. Bézier splines are very easy to curve and manipulate. A Bézier spline passes through the vertices that define the spline, and the curvature of the spline between the vertices is controlled by tangent vectors at the vertices. A spline can be adjusted in MAX by either moving individual vertices or by adjusting the tangent vectors for the vertices.

Like 3D objects in MAX, each spline you create is automatically assigned a different color. Fortunately, different splines in the same shape have the same color. Following are the ten types of Bézier splines you can create in MAX:

▲ Line

▲ Donut

▲ NGon

▲ Rectangle

▲ Circle

▲ Ellipse

▲ Arc

▲ Star

▲ Helix

▲ Text

Line

A line is the most basic denominator of a shape. Most of the shapes you create use some form of line. In MAX, a line can be straight or curved, depending upon how it is created. To draw a line in MAX, you can draw from point to point and create a standard straight line. You can also draw from point to point, click on the second point, and drag the mouse to create a curve around the point you just placed.

Choosing the Line button in the command panel displays the Line rollout, as shown in figure 5.2. The two main rollouts to pay attention to in the Line command are Interpolation and Creation Method. Interpolation enables you to control the shape's complexity. Lofted shapes tend to become fairly complex very quickly. You can start to control their complexity by reducing the complexity at the beginning.

MAX subdivides spline curves into smaller straight lines that approximate the true curve. The three options under Interpolation control how this subdivision occurs. These options are Steps, Optimize, and Adaptive. The Steps option determines the number of interpolation points between adjacent vertices. For example, if you drew a spline using six as the Steps setting, there would be seven smaller lines between adjacent vertices. The step value is more important for curved lines than for straight lines. The more steps in the line, the smoother the curve. The Optimize button, which is on by default, tells MAX to optimize the spline by setting the number of steps for linear segments of the spline to 0. All curved segments use the number of steps specified by the Steps option. Clicking on the Adaptive button disables the Optimize

Figure 5.2

The Line rollout enables you to set the creation parameters and options for line shapes.

button and the Steps setting. Adaptive interpolation automatically tries to adapt new step settings for each segment to reduce the number of steps in the segment while maintaining its curve.

Note

> Because the interpolation options are common to all shapes, they are not discussed elsewhere in this chapter. For a reminder of what they do, refer to this section.

The creation methods are very important for specifying the curvature of the line as the vertices are created. The first of these options—Initial Type—determines the initial shape of the curve as it passes through the vertex. The default is an angular corner. Choose Smooth to create a smooth curved line based on the location of the next vertex in the line.

The second type of creation method—Drag Type—affects what happens when you drag the mouse around a vertex that you place. There are three options: Corner, Smooth, and Bézier. By default, the Bézier option is enabled. This means that when you click and drag the mouse around a line vertex, MAX creates a Bézier curve instead of an angular corner. You use the other options to create a smooth or angular corner, instead.

If you continue to draw line segments, you can create a closed spline by clicking on the start vertex. When a warning message appears, asking whether you want to create a closed spline, you answer yes or no by choosing the appropriate option with the mouse.

The following exercise shows you how to create a line in several different ways:

CREATING A LINE WITH ANGULAR CORNERS

1. Choose the Line button from the command panel.
2. Set both the Initial Type and the Drag Type to Corner.
3. Click at 0,0 in the top viewport. Then click at 30,30, and then at 50,30 to create a line.
4. Right-click to exit the Line command.

CREATING A LINE WITH BÉZIER CORNERS

1. Choose the Line button from the command panel.
2. Set the Initial Type to Corner and the Drag Type to Bézier.

3. Click at 0,0 in the top viewport.

4. Click and hold at 30,30. Drag the mouse vertically until you see a curve in the line, then let go.

5. Click at another point of your choice on the screen to place the end point of the line.

6. Right-click to exit the command.

Donut

A donut is a fairly simple 2D shape to create. You simply choose a center, then an inner and outer radius. To display the Donut rollout (see fig. 5.3), click on the Donut button in the command panel.

As with the 3D tube object, the Donut rollout provides two radius fields. You do not need to specify which field is the inner or outer radius; MAX will know from the measurements whether Radius 1 is the inner or outer radius. And also as with 3D tube creation, you have both center and edge creation methods.

The following exercise shows you how to create a 2D donut:

CREATING A DONUT

1. Choose the Donut button from the command panel.

2. Click at 0,0 in the top viewport, drag out to 30,0, and let go.

3. Click at 40,0 to set the outer radius.

4. In the Parameters rollup, use the spinner to increase the value for Radius 1 to 50.

5. In the Creation Method rollup, click on Edge.

6. Click at 50,0 in the top viewport, drag out to 100,0, and let go.

7. Click at 90,0 to set the inner radius.

Figure 5.3

The Donut rollout enables you to set the creation parameters and options for donut shapes.

NGon

An *NGon* is a polygon with *n* sides. (For example, an octagon is an NGon with eight sides.) You create the NGon by specifying the number of sides, then a center and radius for the polygon. When you choose the NGon button in the command panel, the NGon rollout appears (see fig. 5.4).

The Parameters rollout contains three creation parameters: Radius, Sides, and Circular. The Radius value defines how large the NGon is. The Sides value determines how many sides the NGon has. The Circular option determines whether the NGon is circular or flat-faced. (For example, an octagon is a flat-faced NGon.) The Circular option is used to create circles with a specific number of vertices for use in lofting and morphing animation sequences.

The following exercise shows you how to create an NGon:

CREATING AN NGON

1. Choose the NGon button in the command panel.

2. Set the number of sides to eight for an octagon.

3. Click at 0,0 in the top viewport, then drag to 100,0 and let go. The NGon appears.

4. In the Parameters rollup, click on Circular. The NGon becomes a circular object.

Rectangle

A *rectangle* is a simple four-sided figure created by choosing two opposite corners of the rectangle. When you choose the Rectangle button in the command panel, the Rectangle rollout appears (see fig. 5.5).

The following exercise shows you how to create a rectangle shape:

CREATING A RECTANGLE

1. Choose the Rectangle button in the command panel.

2. Click at 0,0 in the top viewport, then drag to 50,50. The rectangle shape is created.

3. While holding down the Control key, click at 50,50 in the top viewport, then drag in any direction. A square shape is created.

Figure 5.4

The NGon rollout enables you to set the creation parameters and options for NGon shapes.

Figure 5.5

The Rectangle rollout enables you to set the creation parameters and options for rectangle shapes.

Figure 5.6

The Circle rollout enables you to set the creation parameters and options for circle shapes.

Figure 5.7

The Ellipse rollout enables you to set the creation parameters and options for ellipse shapes.

Circle

A *circle* is a shape created by specifying a center and a radius. When you choose the Circle button in the command panel, the Circle rollout appears (see fig. 5.6). To create a circle, simply select the creation method, then drag between two points in the viewport.

Ellipse

An *ellipse* is created exactly like a rectangle but inscribed within the rectangle area. The length and width of the rectangle determine the size and shape of the ellipse. When you click on the Ellipse button in the command panel, the Ellipse rollout appears (see fig. 5.7). To create an ellipse, simply select the creation method, then drag between two points in the viewport.

Arc

An *arc* is a spline created by specifying two end points and either a center or radius point of the curve. Because an arc is simply a section of a circle, it has the same properties as a circle (such as a center point and a radius). If you click on the Arc button in the command panel, the Arc rollout appears (see fig. 5.8).

In the Creation Method rollout there are two ways to define an arc—End-End-Middle and Center-End-End. In the first method, you choose one end point, then the other. The location of the middle point determines the position and size of the arc. In the second method, you choose the center point of the arc first. Then the size and position of the arc are determined by the location of the end points.

In the Parameters rollout there are three creation parameters and one option: Radius, From, To, and Pie Slice. Radius is the overall radius of the arc. From is the start point of the arc on the radius of the arc (in degrees). To is the end point of the radius of the arc (in degrees). If you enable the Pie Slice option, the start and end points of the arc are connected to the center point of the radius, creating a closed shape that looks like part of a pie chart.

The following exercise shows you several ways to create an arc:

Figure 5.8

The Arc rollout enables you to set the creation parameters and options for arc shapes.

CREATING AN END-END-MIDDLE ARC

1. Click on the Arc button in the command panel.

2. Click at 0,0 in the top viewport to place the start point, then drag to 40,40 to place the end point.

3. Move the mouse around on the screen to make the arc change. Click when you find an arc you like. The arc is then created.

4. Click on Pie Slice to see its effect. You can also adjust any of the other parameters to see their effect.

CREATING A CENTER-END-END ARC

1. Click on the Arc button in the command panel.

2. Click at 0,0 in the top viewport to set the center point, then drag to 30,0 to set the start point of the arc.

3. Click at –40,50 to set the end point of the arc. The arc appears as you move the cursor.

Star

A *star* shape is defined by an outer and inner radius, and has *n* number of points on each radius. The star is formed by lines alternately connecting the points on the outer and inner radii. When you click on the Star button in the command panel, the Star rollout appears (see fig. 5.9).

In the Parameters rollout are four parameters you can set: Radius 1, Radius 2, Points, and Distortion. You do not need to specify which field is the inner or outer radius; MAX will know from the measurements whether Radius 1 is the inner or outer radius. Points determines how complex the star is by specifying the number of points on the inner and outer radii. The Distortion field has the effect of rotating the star points created at Radius 2, but not those at Radius 1, which makes the star look less uniform and perfect.

The following exercise shows you how to create a star:

CREATING A STAR

1. Choose the Star Button from the command panel.

2. Click at 0,0 in the top viewport, and drag out to 50,0.

3. Click at 100,0 to set the outer radius. The star appears.

4. Set the distortion to 20 to make the star look less perfect.

5. Increase the number of points to 8.

6. Reduce Radius 2 to 25.

Figure 5.9

The Star rollout enables you to set the creation parameters and options for star shapes.

Figure 5.10

The Helix rollout enables you to set the creation parameters and options for helix shapes.

Helix

A *helix* is defined by moving a point around a circle that is moving vertically through space. As such, MAX's helix is the only shape that is created as a 3D spline as opposed to a 2D spline. Click on the Helix button in the command panel to display the Helix rollout, as shown in figure 5.10.

You can define five parameters for a helix: Radius 1, Radius 2, Height, Turns, and Bias. Radius 1 is the radius of the helix at the bottom; Radius 2, the radius of the helix at the top. Height is the overall height of the helix. The value in the Turns field determines how many full circles the line forming the helix makes as it travels from bottom to top. Finally, Bias determines whether the helix circles are closer to the top or the bottom of the helix. Valid values for the Bias field are from –1 to 1. The default is 0, with the helix perfectly balanced. Setting the bias to 1 moves the helix radii closer to the top of the helix.

At the bottom of the Parameters rollout are two check boxes that specify whether the line forming the helix rotates clockwise (CW) or counterclockwise (CCW) from bottom to top.

The following exercise shows you how to create a helix:

CREATING A HELIX

1. Click on the Helix button in the command panel.

2. Click at 0,0 in the top viewport, drag to 100,0, and let go. This sets Radius 1 and the initial value for Radius 2.

3. Move the mouse toward the top of the screen to set the height. Set a height that looks reasonable to you, then click.

4. Move the mouse up or down to set the upper radius. Pick a radius you like, then click to create the helix.

5. Click in the Turns field, and enter 3.

6. Click in the Bias field and enter .5. To better understand the Bias field, adjust this number using the spinner until you get a sense of how the Bias parameter works.

Text

The last option of the shape-creation tools, and one of the more important 2D shapes, is that of text. Text is defined by a font and a height—all you have to do is place the location. Clicking on the Text button in the command panel displays the Text rollout, as shown in figure 5.11.

The Text command has three fields that you can control. The first is the font field. In the Parameters rollout, a drop-down list displays the fonts you can use to create text. A font determines the look of the text itself. MAX can use any TrueType font installed in NT or Type 1 PostScript fonts located in MAX's font directory. MAX cannot use other Post-Script fonts (because NT does not support PostScript) nor the FNT files that 3D Studio for DOS used. Fortunately, thousands of TrueType fonts are available.

After you select a font, you can set whether it is italic or underlined by clicking on the appropriate button under the Font drop-down list. If you want a bold font, you must select the bold version of the font in the Font drop-down list. After setting the Italic or Underline feature, you must set the height of the font in the Size field. This height is given in drawing units. Finally, in the white box, you type the text you want. You can simply use the mouse to highlight the default (MAX Text), and type your text. After you have set all the parameters, all you have to do is place the text by clicking anywhere in any viewport. The text will be centered around the point you choose.

The following exercise shows you how to create some text:

Figure 5.11

The Text rollout enables you to set the creation parameters and options for text shapes.

CREATING SOME TEXT

1. Choose the Text command from the command panel.

2. Choose Times New Roman from the Font drop-down list.

3. Click on the Italic button.

4. Set the height (Size) to 20.

5. In the Text field, type your name instead of MAX Text.

6. Click at 0,0 in the Top viewport to place the text.

Now you have seen all of MAX's shape-creation tools. You can edit these shapes by using the tools discussed in Chapter 10, "Modifying Objects at Different Levels." If you are interested, feel free to jump to that chapter and see what you can do. Otherwise, you can explore the tools when you get to that chapter.

Figure 5.12

The Loft command is accessed by selecting the Create command panel tab and choosing Loft Object from the pull-down list.

Figure 5.13

The Loft rollout, where you can select the loft shapes.

Creating the Loft Object

A loft object is a 3D object created by generating a surface across one or more shapes positioned along a path. The loft shapes can be thought of as the cross-sections of the loft object. The path controls the placement of the shapes in the loft object. To create a loft object, you need at least two shapes—one or more to act as the loft shapes and another to act as the loft path. If only one loft shape is used, MAX uses that shape at both ends of the path.

The only restrictions on loft shapes are that each shape contain the same number of splines, and that the splines in each shape have the same nesting order. For example, if you have two shapes, the first containing a donut and the second containing a circle, these two shapes could not be used as loft shapes for the same object because one contains two splines, and the other only one. The same is true if the second shape contained two circles side by side, because the first contains one spline nested within another, whereas the second does not contain a nested spline.

The only restriction on the path shape is that the shape must contain only one spline. For example, a donut cannot be a path shape because it contains two splines.

After you have created the two shapes, you must select one before you can access the Loft command. After selecting a shape, choose the geometry button on the Create command panel, then choose Loft Object from the drop-down category list to display the Loft command button (see fig. 5.12). Clicking on the Loft button in the command panel displays the Loft rollout, as shown in figure 5.13.

The Loft rollout enables you to select the loft shapes and path, and the various options for smoothing, mapping, and skinning the loft object. The Loft command panel contains four rollouts: Creation Method, Surface Parameters, Skin Parameters, and Path Parameters.

The shape you selected prior to entering the Loft command can be used as either the loft shape or as the loft path. Which one it is used as depends on whether you now choose the Get Shape or Get Path button in the Creation Method rollout. If the originally selected shape is to be used as the path shape, you would choose the Get Shape button and select the remaining shape as a loft shape. If the originally selected shape is to be used as a loft shape, you would choose the Get Path button and select the remaining shape as the loft path.

The shape selected before entering the Loft command is checked by MAX to verify that it is a valid loft path (that it contains only a single spline). If it is not, it can only be a loft shape, and only the Get Path button will be available in the Creation Method rollout.

The Creation Method rollout has three options to control what happens to a shape when you perform a Get Path or a Get Shape. If the Move option is selected, the shape is moved into the loft object and removed from the scene. If the Copy option is selected, an independent copy of the shape is used in the loft object. If the Instance option is selected, an instance of the shape is used in the loft object. The default option is Instance. An instance of the shape selected when entering the Loft command is always used in the loft object.

When you perform a Get Path or Get Shape on a shape, you will see the loft shape attach itself to the start of the loft path. At this point, the loft object has been created, even though you cannot really see it at this point.

Two rollouts in the Loft command panel are not expanded when you enter the Loft command. Click on the Surface Parameters and the Skin Parameters rollout headers to expand these rollouts. Figure 5.14 shows you these expanded rollouts.

The Surface Parameters rollout enables you to apply both smoothing and mapping to the loft object. Smoothing creates a nice smooth object. Length Smoothing smoothes the object along the loft path, whereas Width Smoothing smoothes the object around its loft shapes. Mapping enables you to apply mapped materials correctly to the object. (For more information, see Chapter 12, "Basic Materials.")

The Skin Parameters rollout enables you to control the capping, the options of the loft process, and how the loft object is displayed in the viewports. *Capping* places surfaces over the start and end of the loft object, creating a closed 3D object. The loft options control the complexity of the loft object. Brief descriptions of these options follow:

▲ **Shape steps**. Controls the number of steps or linear segments between each vertex in the loft shapes. The more steps, the smoother curved shapes appear.

▲ **Path Steps**. Controls the number of steps between each main division in the path. This helps to control the smoothness of loft object when using curved paths or loft deformations.

Figure 5.14

The Surface and Skin Parameters rollouts enable you to set various options for smoothing and mapping the surface and for skinning the loft object.

▲ **Optimize Shapes**. Optimizes the linear spline segments in loft shapes before they are lofted, thus reducing the complexity of the loft object.

▲ **Adaptive Steps**. Adds additional steps to the loft object between loft path vertices to create the best possible skin object. Steps are added where a shape lies on the path and where deformation curve control points lie.

▲ **Contour**. Forces the loft shape to stay perpendicular to the loft path. Otherwise, loft shapes remain parallel to each other.

▲ **Banking**. Forces the loft shape to rotate with the loft path. For example, a helix loft path should have banking turned on to create the correct type of loft object. Otherwise, the loft shape might not line up correctly to the path in all three dimensions.

▲ **Linear Interpolation**. Determines whether MAX interpolates the loft skin using a linear or smooth change between shapes. The default is to use smooth interpolation, which results in a smoother, less rigid object. A linear interpolation creates a surface using straight lines between shapes, making a much more rigid object.

In the Display box at the bottom of the Skin Parameters rollout are two buttons: Skin and Skin in Shaded. The default selection, Skin in Shaded, causes the skinned loft shape to appear in shaded viewports only. If you click on the Skin option, the skinned loft object will appear in wireframe viewports as well.

The last rollout—Path Parameters—enables you to place different loft shapes at different points along the loft path. For example, at the start of the loft path you could have a circle, at the center a star, and at the end a box. As described earlier, the only restrictions are that all loft shapes must contain the same number of splines, and that the splines have the same nesting level.

There are two Path Parameter options: Path and Snap. The Path option enables you to select either a Distance or Percentage along the path to place the next shape. You can use the Snap option to place shapes at set distances along the loft path. When you choose a new location for the next loft shape, a yellow cross appears on the loft path to indicate the location for the new shape. Then, simply choose Get Shape and select the next shape you want to use.

At the bottom of the Path Parameters rollout are three buttons. These buttons are used to determine which path level is active (the active level is marked by the yellow cross). The first button, Pick Level, enables you to click a shape on the path to set the active path level. The second button, Previous Shape, switches the active path level to the previous shape along the path. The third button, Next Shape, switches the active path level to the next shape along the path.

Warning

When you use multiple shapes, be sure to carefully line up the first vertex of the shapes. The first vertex is defined as the start point of the shape. When you select a shape, the first vertex appears as a white box on the shape. If you make sure that all the first vertices of the shapes are oriented in the same direction before you add the loft shape to the loft path, you should be okay. Otherwise, the loft object might seem to twist as it is lofted.

The following exercise shows you how to create a loft object:

CREATING A LOFT OBJECT

1. Create a star shape that has an inner radius of 5 and an outer radius of 10.

2. Create a helix with a Radius 1 of 100 and a Radius 2 of 5. Set Turns to 4. Set Height to 100 units.

3. Click on the Geometry button in the Create command panel, then choose Loft object from the drop-down list.

4. Click on the Loft button.

5. Choose Get Shape in the Loft Object rollout. The shape is attached to the helix path, as shown in figure 5.15.

6. Click on Skin Parameters to display the rollout. Turn Skin on. The loft object appears in the viewport.

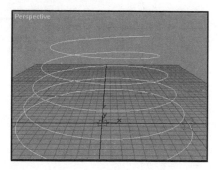

Figure 5.15

A perspective view of a star lofted on a helix path.

For further practice, try to create a loft object with multiple path shapes. Also create a loft object and adjust some of the parameters to see the effect.

Loft objects are a powerful method of creating geometry. They become even more powerful when you add loft deformations. For more information on this topic, see Chapter 8, "Object Editing, Transforms, and Modifiers."

Summary

Creating shapes and lofting them is a relatively easy process that can produce very powerful results in terms of unique and complex geometry. Remember the following key information about loft objects:

▲ Be careful when you create splines, because each spline you create can be a different shape. If you want to combine two splines into a single spline, make sure the Create New Shape button is off. Then you can change the shape, using the edit commands discussed in Chapters 8 and 10.

▲ Use the loft object skin parameters to control the display of the loft shape.

▲ You must select a shape, whether it is the path or loft shape, before you can create the loft object.

▲ If you are going to use multiple shapes on the same loft path, make sure that you line up the first vertices of each shape and that each shape contains both the same number of splines and the same spline nesting.

If you make sure you accomplish these key things you should be able to create a wide variety of lofted objects.

Now that you have an idea of how to create most of the basic geometry objects in MAX, it is time to learn how to create them accurately. The next chapter shows you how to create precise objects in MAX.

Drawing with Precision

When you work in MAX, you often will want to create geometry free of the restrictions of accuracy so that you can freely explore your creativity. At other times, however, you need to draw with accuracy and precision. MAX has many built-in tools to help you accomplish just this task.

This chapter focuses on how you can use MAX's precision drawing tools to draw with the commands you worked with in Chapters 4 and 5. In this chapter, you learn how to work with the following:

▲ Units of Measurement

▲ Grids

▲ Snaps

▲ Keyboard entry

▲ Grid objects

▲ Tape objects

One additional drawing aid is the keyboard transform type-in. This drawing aid will not be described in this chapter because it makes use of the Rotate, Move, and Scale commands. This aid is described in Chapter 7, "Selection Controls," and Chapter 8, "Object Editing, Transforms, and Modifiers."

Setting Units of Measurement

In MAX, you can set up specific units of measurement to match the type of work you do. An architect, for example, might use architectural units, whereas a civil engineer might stay with decimal units. You can set the units in MAX by choosing Units Setup from the Views pull-down menu. The Units Setup dialog box then appears, as shown in figure 6.1.

Figure 6.1

The units of measurement and how the units are displayed in MAX are specified in the Units Setup dialog box.

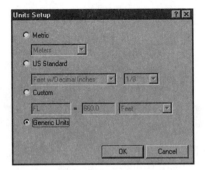

The default units setting in MAX is generic units. Generic units are decimal units, and are accurate up to three decimal places. You also can set up three other kinds of units in MAX: Metric, US Standard, and Custom.

Metric units are the European standard units. If you click on the radio button next to Metric in the Units Setup dialog box, you activate the metric units. Then, in the drop-down list, you can choose four kinds of metric units: millimeters, centimeters, meters, and kilometers. When you choose one of these settings, the coordinate readouts at the bottom of the screen reflect this change by adding the appropriate suffix to the coordinates. If you choose Metric Meters, for example, an "M" is appended to the end of the coordinate readouts to reflect the meter measurement.

US Standard units are the basic units used in the United States. Like Metric units, when you click on the radio button next to this option in the Units Setup dialog box, you activate the units. Then you can use the two drop-down lists to set the units. The first drop-down list enables you to choose the unit type, and the second drop-down list determines how accurate coordinates are measured. You can choose from six different US Standard unit settings. Each is described in the following list:

▲ **Fractional Inches**. Fractional Inches forces all coordinates to be read in inches with fractions. A coordinate, for example, might read 89 $\frac{1}{8}$". This is 89.125 inches, not 89.125 feet. Because it is a fractional unit, you can set how accurate the fractions are displayed. The default is $^1/_8$", which means no coordinate will display less than $^1/_8$ inch measures.

▲ **Decimal Inches.** Decimal Inches is like Fractional Inches, except that it uses decimal places after the inch measurement instead of fractions. Accuracy is always three decimal places.

▲ **Fractional Feet**. Fractional Feet works like Fractional Inches, except that units are measured in feet instead of inches. So, 89$^1/_8$' represents 89.125 feet, not 89 feet and $^1/_8$ inch.

▲ **Decimal Feet**. Decimal Feet is the same as Fractional Feet, except that fractions are expressed as decimals. Accuracy is always three decimal places.

▲ **Feet w/ Fractional Inches.** Feet w/ Fractional Inches is the most common US standard unit, especially for architectural work. Here, coordinates are read as feet and inches using fractions. The coordinate 89' $^1/_8$", for example, is 89 feet and $^1/_8$ inch.

▲ **Feet w/ Decimal Inches.** Feet w/ Decimal Inches is the same as Feet w/ Fractional Inches, but fractions are expressed as decimals up to three places of accuracy.

The last unit type that you can set in the Units Setup dialog box is a Custom unit. Here, you can make up your own unit settings. You could create, for example, a unit measure called 5mile where 1 unit equals 5 miles. All you have to do is enter the unit name, in this case 5mile, in the first field. Then, in the second field, enter 5 and select Miles from the drop-down list. Then all units are measured as 5mile units.

You should set your units to the type and readout that you are most familiar with. An architect, for example, may use US Standard Feet w/ Fractional Inches. When you use a unit setup such as this, make sure that you correctly enter coordinates using the unit format. The coordinate 89' 3" is correct, for example, whereas 89' 3 is not correct.

Note

If you have used AutoCAD before and used Architectural units, you know that 89'3 is a valid unit setting. In MAX, however, it is not. You must include both the feet and inch markers; otherwise, MAX does not accept the value.

Defining Grid Settings

The default grid seen in the MAX viewports is called the home grid, and is located on the major axis planes. A typical home grid is shown in figure 6.2. The grid in the Top viewport appears on the X,Y plane, for example, whereas the grid in the Front viewport appears on

Figure 6.2

The home grid is the plane upon which objects are created and is shown in each MAX viewport.

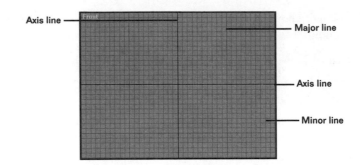

the X,Z plane. There are three different colors for the lines on the grid. The darkest two lines are the axes lines. These lines meet at the world origin, and reflect the world coordinate axes. The lighter lines are called the major lines, and the lightest lines are called the minor lines.

You can change the spacing of the major and minor lines by choosing Grid and Snap Settings from the Views pull-down menu. The Grid and Snap Settings dialog box then appears, as shown in figure 6.3.

Figure 6.3

The spacing of the lines in the home grid is set in the Home Grid tab of the Grid and Snap Settings dialog box.

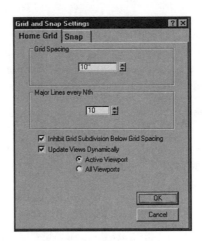

The default spacing of the home grid is 10 units. The units value depends on the unit settings. If you are using US Standard units with feet and fractional inches, for example, the home grid is 10" by default. In this case, a home grid spacing of 12" may be more appropriate as this will result in a grid line appearing every foot. After you set the grid spacing, you can determine the major lines spacing. The default major line spacing is 10 grid lines.

The last few settings for the home grid affect how the grid appears when you zoom in or out of the viewport. If the grid lines always maintained the same spacing, when you zoomed out in a viewport the grid would become very dense at a certain point. To prevent this, MAX automatically redraws the screen using a new subdivision when the grid density reaches a certain point. In the new subdivision, the major lines of your grid become minor lines, and your smaller minor lines disappear. This change does not affect the scale of the drawing, only how large the grid is. The Inhibit Grid Subdivision Below Grid Spacing check box affects how small the grid spacing will appear when you zoom in. When you choose the Inhibit check box, the grid does not subdivide below the grid spacing when you zoom in on a viewport.

The Update View Dynamically options affect which views are dynamically updated as you change the grid and major line spacing values. If Active Viewport is selected, only the grid spacing in that viewport will be updated. The other viewports will update when you close the dialog. If All Viewports is selected, the grid spacing in all viewports will be updated. If Update Views Dynamically is unchecked, none of the viewports will be updated until you close the dialog.

Configuring and Using Snaps

The most common helpful precision drawing aid in MAX is snaps. Snaps control where objects are placed when created or moved, the incremental values used when rotating and scaling objects, and the incremental values used when adjusting parameter fields using their spinner. For example, you can force MAX to snap to grid intersection points or vertices of other objects for more accurate drawing.

MAX provides four different types of snaps: Spatial, Angle, Percent, and Spinner. Before using snaps, you need to configure the snap settings.

Snap Settings

Most of the snap setting are found in one dialog box. To access the snap settings, choose Grid and Snap Settings from the Views pull-down menu, and click on the Snap tab of the Grid and Snap Settings dialog box (see fig. 6.4). The Spinner snap setting is not adjusted in this dialog, and is described separately in the next section.

The Snap tab of this dialog box has four sections: Snap Strength, Snap Priority, Snap Values, and Relative/Absolute. The Snap Strength setting determines how large an area on the screen spatial snaps will affect. (See the following section describing snap types for an explanation of Spatial snaps.) When you choose a point on the screen with a spatial snap active, MAX searches around that point the snap strength distance in pixels to find the nearest correct snap. If you have a vertex snap active, for example, and you click in the Top viewport to draw a new box, MAX looks for the nearest vertex that is within 8 pixels of where you clicked in the viewport, assuming that you are using the default Snap Strength of 8. The higher you set this value, the less accurate you have to be to select a snap correctly, but the more likely you are to choose the wrong snap item.

Figure 6.4

The settings for spatial, angle, and percent snaps are adjusted in the Snap Tab of the Grid and Snap Settings dialog box.

Note

Snap Strength is dependent on your screen resolution. A Snap Strength value of 8 pixels, for example, affects a larger area on an 800×600 screen than it does on a 1024×768 or a 1280×1024 screen. You may need to play with this value to reach a setting that you are comfortable with for your resolution.

The Snap Priority sets which geometry type it is most important to snap to when performing spatial snaps. You can set priority to four geometry types: Vertex Point, Edges, Grid Intersections, and Grid Lines. You can set four levels of priority or turn off snap for a geometry type. The default, for example, has a vertex point snap with the highest priority. Under this situation, if you click in a fairly dense viewport with grid lines, edges, intersections, and vertices all within the 8-pixel snap strength area, MAX chooses the vertex point first because it has highest priority. You can set the priorities as you like.

The Snap Values enable you to set how the Angle and Percent snaps work. Angle snap restricts rotations to certain angle increments. The default is 5 degrees. Percent snap restricts operations such as scale-to-percent increments. The default is 10 percent. (See the following section describing Snap Types for an explanation of Angle and Percent snaps.)

Finally, you can set whether snaps are relative or absolute. Most of the time, when you use a snap, you want to restrict yourself to working on the home grid intersections and grid lines. Sometimes, however, you may want to use the snap spacing but not adhere to the grid lines. To do so, you use a relative snap. If Absolute Snap is selected, you will always snap to the grid lines and intersections. By default, Relative Snap is enabled.

Snap Types

After you set the snap settings, choose OK to close the Grid and Snap Settings dialog box and put the changes into effect. After you set the snap options, you can enable or disable the various snap types using the snap buttons at the bottom of the screen. Figure 6.5 shows these buttons.

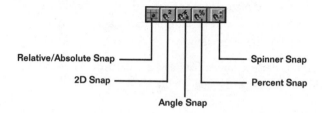

Relative/Absolute Snap

2D Snap

Angle Snap

Spinner Snap

Percent Snap

Figure 6.5

The Snap Toggle buttons are used to select Absolute or Relative snap, select the type of Spatial snap, and to turn on Individual snaps.

Spatial snaps snap to geometry based on the distance of the geometry types from the cursor, and the priorities set for the geometry types. One of the buttons, the Spatial Snap button, has a flyout to enable you to access the 2D, 2.5D, and 3D spatial snap control buttons. Figure 6.6 shows this flyout.

Figure 6.6

Click and hold on the Spatial Snap button to choose the type of Spatial snap you want to use.

If you right-click on any of these buttons, you can also quickly access the Grid and Snap Settings dialog box mentioned previously. Each of the buttons is described in the following list:

Relative/Absolute Snap. This button enables Relative or Absolute Snap. You can use Relative Snap only in an orthogonal viewport such as the Top or Front views. Relative Snap is automatically disabled in Perspective, Spotlight, and Camera views. When this button is enabled, the button changes to show the snap ball on a grid intersection point to represent Absolute Snap. Relative/Absolute Snap only affects the moving of objects while a spatial snap is active.

2D Snap. 2D Snap enables snaps only on the current grid plane. In the Top viewport, for example, this plane is the X,Y plane. If you are using a grid object as a work plane, 2D Snap works on this plane as well. (See "Using Helper Objects" later in this chapter for more information on grid objects.) You cannot snap to a vertex or edge unless the vertex or edge is on the current grid plane.

2.5D Snap. 2.5D Snap enables you to draw on the current grid plane but snap to vertices on objects above or below the grid plane. This process is similar to holding up a piece of transparency and tracing objects that are behind the transparency, and then having the lines appear on the plane of the transparency.

3D Snap. 3D Snap works in all three dimensions and enables accurate snapping to all vertices, grid lines, grid intersections, and edges.

Note

Only one of the 2D, 2.5D, or 3D spatial snaps can be active at a time. You cannot enable 2D and 3D snaps at the same time. Again, these options are located on the 2D Snap flyout.

Angle Snap. Angle Snap restricts the rotation of object-to-angle increments set in the Snap tab of the Grid and Snap Settings dialog box. Angle Snap works for any operation that involves rotation.

Percent Snap. Percent Snap restricts any operation that uses percentages to a certain increment. Again, you set this snap in the Grid and Snap Settings dialog box. Scale and nonuniform scale are examples of commands that use percents to work.

Spinner Snap. Spinner Snap restricts all spinners in MAX to certain increments. If you never need three decimal places of accuracy, for example, you could set the Spinner Snap setting to 1 and enable this option. Then all spinner snaps would never have a value smaller than 1. The Spinner Snap value is set by choosing File, Preferences. The Spinner Snap setting is in the Interaction section under the General tab.

You can use different snap types and settings at different times as you draw to accurately place and transform objects quickly. The following exercise shows you how to use some of these drawing aids to draw a few boxes:

USING A VARIETY OF SNAPS WHEN DRAWING

1. Choose Views, Units Settings. The Units Setup dialog box appears.

2. In the dialog box, set your units to US Standard, Feet w/ Fractional Inches, and set the increment to $1/2$.

3. Choose OK to close the dialog box.

4. Choose Views, Grid and Snap Settings. The Grid and Snap Settings dialog box appears.

5. On the Home Grid tab, set the home grid spacing to 12".

6. Click on the Snap tab of the dialog box.

7. Set the snap type to 3D by choosing the 3D radio button.

8. Choose OK to close the dialog box.

9. Click on the 3D Snap Toggle button at the bottom of the screen to enable 3D snaps.

10. Choose Box from the Create command panel.

11. Click at 0,0 in the Top viewport, drag to 10'0", 10'0", and let go.

12. Move the mouse cursor up until you have set a height of 2'0" and click the mouse.

13. Click on Zoom Extents All in the lower-right corner of the screen.

14. Click on Zoom All and Zoom Out in the Top viewport. All views adjust at the same time.

15. Choose Box in the Create command panel again. Click on the upper-right corner of the box in the Front viewport, and make a new box that is 2'0" cubed. Figure 6.7 shows the resulting box configurations.

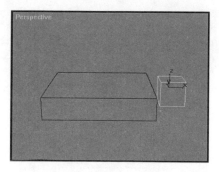

Figure 6.7

Using 3D Snap enables you to snap to the vertices or edges of objects in your scene.

The preceding exercise shows you how easy and powerful a 3D snap is to use. You should try setting different geometry type priorities to see the affect of these settings on the snap points. Also try using Angle Snap and Percentage Snap while rotating and scaling the boxes you previously created.

Using Keyboard Entry

As mentioned in Chapter 4, "3D Objects," each of the drawing creation commands in the Create command panel such as Box or Circle contains a Keyboard Entry rollout in the command panel. You can use this section to build objects quickly and precisely with exact measurements and locations. Figure 6.8 shows an example of the Tube Keyboard Entry rollout.

Keyboard entry is the most precise method of creating any type of geometry. It does not, however, lend itself to being very creative or very intuitive. It is useful, however, when you know the exact sizes and positions of the objects you are creating.

Using Helper Objects

The final drawing aids discussed in this chapter are "helper" objects. You create these objects to help you draw or animate other objects. Helper objects do not render in the final scene, but they do appear on the screen.

You can access the helper objects by choosing the Helpers button on the Create command panel. The helper commands then appear, as shown in figure 6.9.

In this command panel are four helper objects: Grid, Dummy, Tape, and Point. Two of these helper objects are worth looking at now: Grid and Tape. The other two are useful for animation and editing purposes.

Grid Objects

Grid objects are used to create new work planes on which you can draw objects in MAX. Say, for example, you want to create a series of objects on a plane that is rotated 45 degrees from the home grid in the X axis. You can create these objects in two ways. The hard way is to create the objects and then manually rotate and move them into position. The easy way is to create a Grid object, and move and rotate it into position. Then you can draw objects on the new Grid object. Grid objects are also useful for drawing objects on planes above and below the home grid plane.

Grid objects are similar to construction planes in 3D Studio Release 4. While construction planes were limited to being parallel to the orthographic views, Grid objects can be moved and rotated the same as any other object.

If you choose the Grid button in the Create command panel, the Grid object rollout appears (see fig. 6.10).

You create a Grid object much like you create a rectangle—by choosing two opposite corners. The size of the Grid object can be adjusted in the Length and Width fields in the Parameters rollout. The only other option you can set is the grid spacing on the Grid object. After creating the Grid object, you should set this spacing to match the spacing of the home grid for consistency in your drawing. The Grid object appears as shown in figure 6.11.

Figure 6.10

Grid objects enable you to create objects at any location and at any angle.

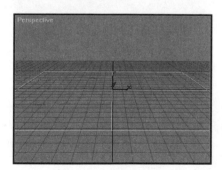

Figure 6.11

The Grid object acts as a replacement to the home grid and provides a visual indication of the plane upon which objects will be created.

You can now rotate and move this grid object into any three-dimensional position in space. (See Chapter 8, "Object Editing, Transforms, and Modifiers," on how to move and rotate objects.) Figure 6.12 shows the grid rotated in 3D space.

The Grid object can be moved and rotated into any position in 3D space.

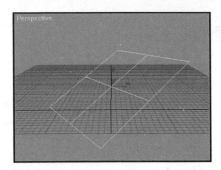

To work on the Grid object, you must first activate it. After it is activated, it acts like your home grid, and everything you create is drawn on the plane of the Grid object. You can activate the Grid object by choosing Views, Grids, Activate Grid Object. If you have multiple Grid objects in your scene, you must select the Grid object you want to activate before you choose Views, Grids, Activate Grid Object. Then the appropriate Grid object is used.

Now, if you draw a box, it will appear on the plane of the Grid object, regardless of the viewport you use. Figure 6.13 shows an example of a box drawn on an active Grid object.

Figure 6.13

When an object is created on an Active Grid object, it has the same orientation as the Grid object.

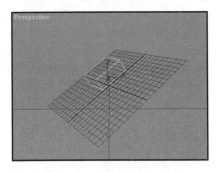

Working at an awkward angle, of course, can be disconcerting and difficult. So, you can use a special viewport, called a *grid view* to align one of the viewports to the active Grid object. Working in this view is the same as working in a Top viewport, except that your objects are drawn on the Grid object plane. You can activate the grid view by first activating the Grid object, and right-clicking on the title of the viewport that you want to change. Then choose Views, Grid. Figure 6.14 shows the viewport layout with a grid view.

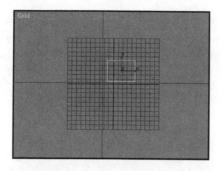

Figure 6.14

A viewport can be aligned to an active Grid object to provide an undistorted view of objects created on the Grid object.

The last thing you can do to a Grid object is align it to a viewport. For example, you might want to perform this task in a Camera viewport. Say you want to have some text, such as a title for the scene, move across the screen in front of your scene. To create this text, you need to use a view-aligned Grid object. Then you can create the text and animate it on the Grid object plane without worrying about trying to rotate and position the text so that it lines up with the camera viewport.

To align a Grid object, first you must make it the active Grid object. Then click on the title of the viewport to which you want to align the Grid object. Then choose Views, Grids, Align to View. The Grid object is then automatically aligned to the viewport, and you are ready to begin creating geometry.

After you are done using a Grid object and want to return to the home grid, choose Views, Grids, Activate Home Grid.

The following exercise shows you how to use a Grid object. In this exercise, you use Select and Move and Select and Rotate. Both of these commands are covered in Chapter 8, "Object Editing, Transforms, and Modifiers," so don't feel like you missed something when you use these commands here. This exercise also explores some more uses of snaps.

USING A GRID OBJECT

1. Choose the Helpers button in the Create command panel.

2. Choose Grid.

3. Click at 0,0 in the Top viewport, drag to 100,100, and let go. The Grid object then appears in the viewport.

4. Choose the Select and Rotate button from the main toolbar.

5. Click on the Angle Snap button at the bottom of the screen.

6. In the Front viewport, click on the Grid object and drag the mouse cursor vertically until you have rotated the object –45 degrees. Watch your coordinate readouts. Notice how the rotation snaps thanks to the angle snap.

7. Repeat the Rotate command in the Top viewport this time. You should end up with a Grid object similar to the one shown in figure 6.15.

Figure 6.15

Grid objects can be moved and rotated just like any other object.

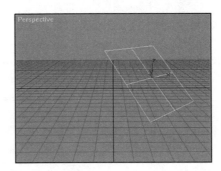

8. Choose Views, Grids, Activate Grid Object. The grid is now activated.

9. Choose the Geometry button on the Create command panel.

10. Choose Box.

11. Create a box in the Front viewport. Notice how it appears on the grid plane.

12. Right-click on the Top viewport name to activate it and display the viewport menu. Choose Views, Grid from the viewport menu. The Top viewport is now a grid view.

13. Repeat the Box command. Now, when you draw in the Grid viewport, like you are used to, the object still appears correctly aligned.

14. To return to your initial settings, right-click on the Grid viewport name, and choose Views, Top from the viewport menu. Choose Views, Grids, Activate Home Grid to turn the home grid back on.

Figure 6.16

The Tape object enables you to measure the distance between any two points, or provides a tape of a specified length.

Tape

The Tape helper object has one use. You use it to measure the distance from one point to another in a scene. If you click on the Tape button in the Create command panel, the Tape rollout appears (see fig. 6.16).

The only two options are Length and Specify Length. If you enable the Specify Length option, when you draw a Tape object, it will always have the same length. This capability is useful for placing objects a specific distance apart. You can also use the Tape object as a guide. If Specify Length is disabled, you simply click and drag a line. The Tape object appears, and the length of the Tape object appears grayed out in the Length box. Figure 6.17 shows a typical use of the Tape object.

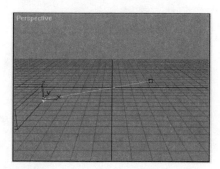

Figure 6.17

The Tape object can be used to measure the distance between objects in your scene.

Summary

MAX provides you with several tools to help you draw accurately. These tools include snaps, grid objects, tapes, and keyboard entry systems.

Now that you have an idea of how to draw accurately, you're ready to look at how to modify existing objects to create any type of geometry you want. Because of this capability, MAX is a very powerful modeling system. Before looking at some of the editing commands, however, you must understand selection sets because many of the editing commands make extensive use of selection sets. The next chapter focuses on how to create and use the variety of selection methods that MAX provides. Chapters 7 through 10 cover the fundamentals of geometry modification.

PART III

GEOMETRY MODIFICATION FUNDAMENTALS

Selection Controls

When applying a modifier or transform to an object in MAX, you generally must select the object before you can apply the modifier or transform. This also applies to operations such as applying materials, animation controllers, and editing animation in TrackView. All of these depend on the correct selection of objects. Hence, MAX provides many methods for selecting objects so that you can apply a variety of modifiers and transforms to the selection set. (For more information about transforms and modifiers, see Chapter 8, "Object Editing, Transforms, and Modifiers.")

This chapter shows you how to create the different selection sets that MAX can use, with particular focus on the following topics:

▲ Selection commands

▲ Named selection sets

▲ Locking selection sets

▲ Groups

Using Selection Commands

Selecting a single object in MAX is a relatively straightforward process. Selecting more than one object, or selecting an object and then applying a transform to the object is a little more complex, but still easy. MAX provides several powerful selection commands, including the following:

▲ Select Object

▲ Select by Name

▲ Select All

▲ Select None

▲ Select Invert

▲ Select by Color

The first two selection commands are available in the main toolbar (see fig. 7.1). The last five selection commands are available in the Edit menu (see fig. 7.2). (Select by Name is available both in the main toolbar and in the Edit menu.)

Four composite selection tools are also shown in the main toolbar—Select and Link, Select and Move, Select and Rotate, and Select and Scale. Each of these tools enables you to select one or more objects, and then immediately perform an action on the selected objects. Each of these composite selection tools uses the same selection techniques as Select Object. More information on these composite selection tools can be found in Chapter 8, "Object Editing, Transforms, and Modifiers."

 Warning

Be careful when you use composite selection tools that have built-in transforms. You can easily forget that you are using such a selection tool, select an object, and accidentally move or rotate it. The point is, make sure that you are aware of which type of selection tool you are using *before* you use it.

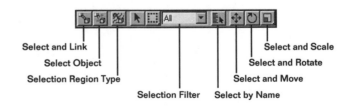

Figure 7.1

The selection tools that are most commonly used are contained on the main toolbar.

Select and Link
Select Object
Selection Region Type
Selection Filter
Select by Name
Select and Move
Select and Rotate
Select and Scale

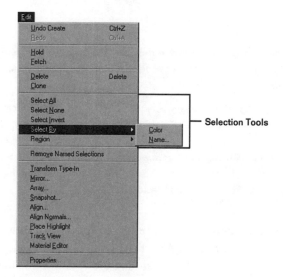

Figure 7.2

Additional selection tools are provided on the Edit menu.

Select Object

The Select Object command enables you to select one or more objects at a time for use in a transform or a modifier. When you select this command, the cursor changes to a cross whenever it is positioned over an object that you can select. When you select an object, it turns white to indicate that it has been selected. After an object has been selected, you can apply modifiers, transforms, or any other operation in MAX that requires a selection.

You can use the Select Object command not only to select a single object, but also to create a selection set. A *selection set* is a group of objects selected together so that the same modifier or transform can be applied to them.

You can create a selection set by using the Select Object command in several ways. The easiest way to create a larger selection set is to hold down Ctrl while selecting objects. When you do, a small black cross (+) appears next to the arrow to indicate that you are adding to the selection set. When you move the cursor over an object that can be added, the cursor changes from an arrow to a cross. If you then click on the object, the object is selected and added to the selection set. If, while holding down Ctrl, you click on an object that has already been selected, the object is deselected and removed from the selection set. All objects in the selection set are white.

Tip

> Because objects turn white when they are selected, you should try to avoid creating any white objects. (Knowing whether white objects are selected or were created white is difficult.)
>
> In only one circumstance will a selected object not appear white. When you apply either an Edit Mesh, Edit Patch, or Edit Spline modifier to a selection, you can select and modify portions of the geometry of the selected objects. The selected geometry turns red to indicate what geometry is selected. The rest of the selection set remains white. (See Chapter 10, "Modifying Objects at Different Levels," for more information on this subject.)

Clearly, having to click individually on multiple objects to add them to the selection set can be difficult and tedious. In MAX, the process is easier—you can create a larger selection set by simply drawing a border around the objects you want to select and select them all at once. This selection method is called *region selection.*

To use region selection, you simply choose the Select Object button, click in the viewport in an area in which no geometry exists, and then drag to create a window. Depending on the region inclusion type, all or some of the objects in the window will be selected. Again, you can use the Ctrl key modifier to add more objects using this method also.

There are two types of region inclusion types—crossing and window—and three region types you can use. The following sections discuss these region inclusion types and region types.

Crossing Inclusion Type

A region selection using the *crossing* inclusion type selects any objects inside the window or that *touch* the window. By default, MAX uses the crossing inclusion type. To control which inclusion type MAX uses, you toggle the Window/Crossing button at the bottom of the screen (see fig. 7.3). Alternatively, you can choose Edit, Region, Crossing to set the inclusion type.

Figure 7.3

The Window/Crossing button showing that crossing inclusion type is being used.

Window Inclusion Type

A region selection using the *window* inclusion type is similar to using the crossing inclusion type, except for one difference—only objects that exist *completely inside* the window boundary are selected. Anything that touches or is outside the window boundary will not be selected. To activate the window inclusion type, choose the Crossing/Window button at the bottom of the screen. When the button is depressed, the icon changes to signify a window inclusion type (see fig. 7.4). Alternatively, you can choose Edit, Region, Window to set the inclusion type.

Window/Crossing in Window Mode

Region Types

Region selection defaults to a rectangular region type, or selection shape, that is sometimes difficult to work with. Fortunately, however, MAX also provides two other region types you can work with—Circular and Fence. You can change the region type by clicking and holding on the Selection Region Type button next to the Select Object button on the main toolbar, which displays the Region Type flyout (see fig. 7.5).

A rectangular region type works like any other rectangle—you choose two opposite corners. A circular region type is defined by a center and a radius. A fence region type is defined, like a line, by clicking in the viewport to choose a start point, dragging out to the second point on the line, and then clicking to set successive points on the line. The fence is closed by clicking on the start point, or by double-clicking at the last point. Double-clicking causes a point to be set at the cursor location, and a line to be drawn from that point to the start point.

The region types, combined with region inclusion types, provide powerful methods for selecting objects. The following exercise shows you how to use these selection methods to select a variety of objects. Be sure to load the file CH7A.MAX from the CD-ROM for this exercise.

USING SELECT OBJECTS

1. Load CH7A.MAX from the CD-ROM. Figure 7.6 shows this file's initial screen. MAX can display viewports in several different ways. For this exercise, the active viewport is displayed in full-screen mode.

Figure 7.4

The Window/Crossing button showing that window inclusion type is being used.

Figure 7.5

The Region Type flyout enables you to change between rectangular, circular, and fence region types.

Figure 7.6

Figure 7.6

*The initial screen
shown when file
CH7A.MAX is loaded.*

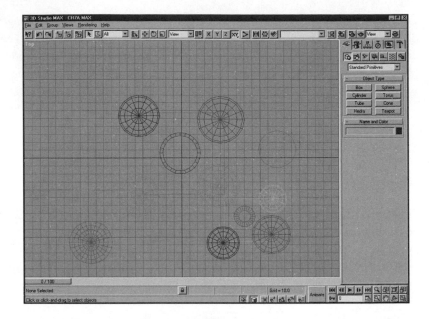

2. Choose Select Object from the main toolbar.

3. Click on the box in the lower right quadrant to select it.

4. Hold down Ctrl and click on the four spheres around the box, and the cylinder in the center of the box. As you click on the objects, they are added to the selection set and turn white. Figure 7.7 shows you the correct selection set.

Figure 7.7

*Objects selected while
holding down Ctrl are
added to the selection
set.*

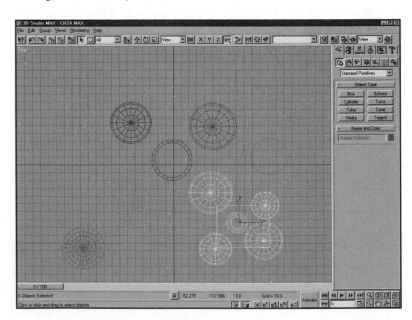

5. Choose Edit, Select None to deselect the objects.

6. Click on the Window/Crossing button at the bottom of the screen to set it to a window inclusion type.

7. Click in the lower right viewport and create a window that encompasses only the objects you selected before (see fig. 7.8).

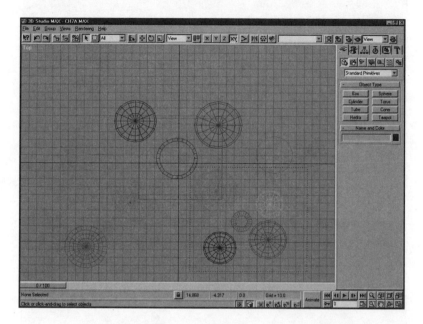

Figure 7.8

When performing region selects using the window inclusion type, only objects completely within the window are selected.

8. Choose Edit, Select None to deselect the objects.

9. Click and hold on the Selection Region Type button to display the Region Type flyout. Set the Region Type to Fence.

10. Draw an outline around the boxes, including the sphere that is common to both boxes, as shown in figure 7.9.

11. The objects are selected, as shown in figure 7.10.

12. Repeat steps 8 through 10, but use a crossing inclusion type this time to see the difference.

The exercise shows you how easy and powerful MAX's selection tools are. You should practice using these basic selection tools because they are very important to almost any MAX operation you will do from this point on. Use the file CH7A.MAX and try using the different selection methods described earlier to select various combinations of objects.

Figure 7.9

*The use of the Fence
Region Type enables
you to draw an
irregular shape as the
selection region.*

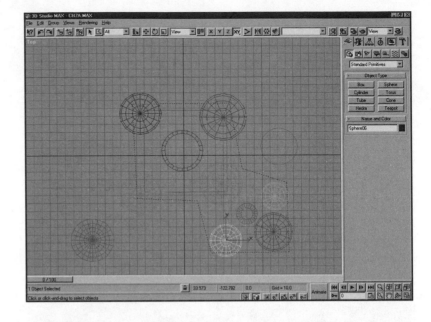

Figure 7.10

*The resulting selection
set when using a fence
region type and a
window inclusion type.*

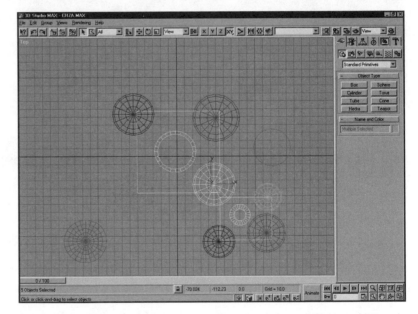

Warning

Be careful when you use region selection. In a front or right viewport, it will select not only the objects you want, but also all objects behind the object closest to you. If this is what you want to select, great. If not, then you need to use a different viewport to make the selection correctly. Remember, by holding down Ctrl, you can remove objects from the selection set, as well as add them.

Selection Filters

In addition to the window and crossing inclusion types, you also can apply selection filters to select only objects of a specified object type. MAX enables you to select objects based on one of the following object types: All, Geometry, Shapes, Lights, Cameras, Helpers, and Space Warps. You enable selection filtering by choosing the appropriate object type from the Selection Filter drop-down list located to the right of the region type button. MAX then allows you to select only objects of the specified object type.

For example, if you choose to filter your selection set for lights, when you perform a region select, only lights will be chosen. All other objects in the scene are ignored, regardless of whether they exist in the selection window. The default in MAX is All. Selection filters can be very helpful if you get tired of having lights and cameras chosen in your selection set when you only want to select geometry objects. In this case, you can simply set the selection filter to select only geometry objects.

Select by Name

Another powerful selection method is Select by Name. Each object that you create in MAX must have a name. If you are careful and name your objects so that they are easily recognizable, you can use Select by Name very quickly and easily. You can access this selection method by choosing the Select by Name button located to the right of the selection filters drop-down list, which displays the Select by Name dialog box shown in figure 7.11.

This dialog box is very heavily used in MAX. On the left is a list of all the currently viewable objects in the scene (hidden or frozen objects are not included in the list). Any objects that are selected are highlighted in blue. Options are visible on the right and across the bottom of the dialog box.

Figure 7.11

The Select Objects dialog box presents a sorted list of objects in the scene, and enables you to select objects singly or in groups.

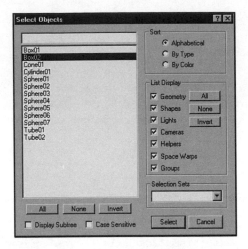

The dialog box is easy to use. Simply select the objects you want from the list and choose Select. The objects are selected. You can use the Ctrl key modifier again to select individual objects and add them to the list or remove them from the list. You can also use the Shift key modifier, as follows: Choose one object, hold down Shift, and choose another object. All objects on the list between the two you selected with the Shift key modifier are selected. Alternatively, you can click on an object and drag up or down the list, selecting all objects the mouse cursor touches. You can use this last method in combination with either the Ctrl or Shift key modifier.

Perhaps a more powerful method is to select objects by using a wildcard modifier. In the blank box at the top of the dialog box you can enter all or part of a name and select all objects with that name. Say, for example, that you have a group of objects, all of which have names that start with *Site* (Site Bench, Site Pole, and so on). Well, you can select all objects whose names start with *Site* by typing **Site*** in the blank box and pressing Enter. (The asterisk (*) wildcard means "everything.")

At the bottom of the dialog box, under the list, are three buttons to help you select objects in the list. All, as its name implies, selects all objects in the list. None deselects all objects. Invert chooses any objects that are not selected and deselects all objects that are selected.

The Display Subtree check box organizes your list of objects, based on the parent-child relationship. (See Chapter 20, "Linking and IK" for more on this.) Use the Case Sensitive check box when you want to differentiate between upper- and lowercase names. (For example, MAX sees no difference between *Site* and *site* unless Case Sensitive is turned on.)

In the upper right corner of the dialog box is a set of sort options that allows you to sort the list of objects and make it easier to find the objects you want. With a list of several hundred objects, sorting becomes very important. The default is to sort the objects alphabetically. You can also sort them by object type or color. The List Display options define what types of objects are displayed in the list. The List Display options affect the display of the list only, and not which objects are currently selected. To view each type of object, simply check or uncheck the appropriate option.

Finally, you can select objects based on their membership in a named selection set. (See "Using Named Selection Sets," later in this chapter.)

When you choose the Select button, any objects you highlighted on the list are selected, and all other objects are deselected. Say, for example, that you select a sphere and then, in the Select by Name dialog box, select a box (and only a box) on the list and choose Select. The box will be selected and the sphere will be deselected.

The following exercise shows you how to use the Select by Name dialog box:

USING SELECT BY NAME

1. Load the CH7A.MAX file from the CD-ROM. If you still have this file loaded from the previous exercise, you do not need to reload it.

2. Choose the Select by Name button on the main toolbar.

3. Click on Sphere01 and drag down until Sphere07 is highlighted.

4. Choose Select. All spheres in the scene are selected.

5. Choose the Select by Name button again.

6. Click on the None button at the bottom of the dialog box. All the previously highlighted object names are unhighlighted.

7. Hold down Ctrl and click on all objects whose name starts with Box or Tube.

8. Choose Select. All the spheres are deselected and the boxes and tubes are selected.

Edit Menu Selection Commands

Four other powerful selection methods are worth a brief mention here. These selection methods, located on the Edit menu, are Select All, Select None, Select Invert, and Select by Color. Select All selects all objects in the scene. Select None deselects all objects in the scene. Select Invert deselects any currently selected objects and selects all objects that were not previously selected. Select by Color, is accessed by choosing Edit, Select By, Color. When you do, a special cursor that looks like a small rainbow is displayed. When you select a single object with this cursor, all objects that have the same object color as that object are selected also.

All of the Edit menu selection commands except Select by Name honor the selection filter setting. If you set the selection filter to Lights and choose Edit, Select All, all the lights will be selected, but objects of other types will not be selected.

Using Named Selection Sets

When you have many objects in a scene in MAX, you will find yourself regularly selecting and unselecting certain sets of objects. To help speed up your work, MAX has named selection sets. A *named selection set* is a group of selected objects that are referred to by a name. This allows you to easily reselect the same set of objects by name.

You can easily create a named selection set by selecting all the objects you want in the set, clicking in the Named Selection Set field on the main toolbar (see fig. 7.12), and typing the name of the selection set. A single object may be a member of as many selection sets as you like. Objects are not restricted to use in only one named selection set.

Figure 7.12

The Named Selection Set field on the main toolbar allows you to define and retrieve named selection sets.

Now, when you use features such as the Select by Name box, you can select a group of objects based on their selection set name. In this case, a much quicker method is simply to choose the name from the drop-down list in the selection set name box. The objects in the selection set will be selected automatically.

Another application of named selection sets is to control the number of objects shown on the screen. The fewer the objects on-screen, the faster the screen redraws. By defining groups of objects that you will be working on together as named selection sets, you can easily hide objects that don't need to be displayed.

You may have as many different named selection sets as you want. Selection set names can be as long as the selection name window. Anything longer than that will be truncated to fit the window.

To remove any named selection, simply choose the named selection in the drop-down list and then, while the objects are highlighted, choose Edit, Remove Named Selections. This does not delete the objects, but simply destroys the named selection set.

The following exercise shows you how to create and use a named selection set:

USING NAMED SELECTION SETS

1. Load the CH7A.MAX file from the CD-ROM. If you still have this file loaded from the previous exercise, you do not need to reload it.

2. Choose Select by Name from the main toolbar.

3. Choose all objects in the list that are not spheres.

4. Choose Select. All objects except spheres are selected.

5. Click in the Named Selection box. Type **Non-Sphere** and press Enter. You have just created the named selection set.

6. Choose Edit, Select None to deselect all objects.

7. Click on the Named selection drop-down list and choose Non-Sphere. All nonsphere objects are again selected.

You should make a habit of using named selection sets in your work. They can save an enormous amount of time when you need to edit, manipulate, and transform groups of objects.

Locking Selections

When you are working with selection sets, especially large selection sets, you probably want to be able to lock the selection set so that you cannot accidentally add objects to or remove them from the selection set. For example, if you were to use the Select and Move selection command (see Chapter 8, "Object Editing, Transforms, and Modifiers"), you could easily click on the wrong object and deselect the object(s) you wanted to move. A locked selection set prevents this.

You can lock a selection set in two different ways. First, having created the selection set, lock it by pressing the spacebar. To unlock the selection set, press the spacebar again. Alternatively, you can click on the Lock Selection Set button at the bottom of the screen to lock or unlock the selection (see fig. 7.13).

Figure 7.13

Selection sets can be locked to prevent inadvertently deselecting the selection set.

Using Groups

Another powerful method for controlling sets of objects in MAX is something called Groups. A *group* is a collection of objects that have been grouped together and act as one object. When you select one object in the group, all are selected. The difference between this and a named selection set or some other method of combining objects is that you can open the group, move objects, and then close the group. It will act as one object again, but you were able to move individual elements.

All the group commands are located in the Group menu (see fig. 7.14). You must select one or more objects before any of the Group commands become available.

Following are brief descriptions of the seven commands on the Group pulldown menu:

▲ **Group**. Enables you to create a group from the selected objects and give the group a name. You must select one or more objects before creating the group. When you choose the Group command, the dialog box shown in figure 7.15 appears so that you can name the group. You can create as many groups as you like. Groups can even be *nested* (one group can contain other groups).

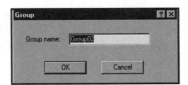

▲ **Open**. Enables you to manipulate individual objects in the group. When you open a group, a magenta boundary line appears, showing you the outer edges of the group. Each object in the group may now be manipulated individually.

▲ **Close**. Enables you to change an open group back to a closed group in which the objects act as a single object.

▲ **Ungroup**. If you select a group and choose this command, the group is destroyed and only the individual objects remain, unless there are nested groups in the larger group. Then, the larger group is reduced to the smaller groups.

▲ **Explode**. Like ungroup, this command destroys the grouping of objects. Explode removes all groups, even nested ones.

▲ **Detach**. When you have an object selected in an open group, you can detach it from the group by selecting this command.

▲ **Attach**. Enables you to attach the selected object(s) to any group. When you select this command, the cursor changes to a cross whenever it is positioned over a group.

Warning

> Because the group is selected when you select one object in the group, the group can be selected if you have a restricted selection filter set and at least one object in the group satisfies the selection filter. For example, if a group contains a box and a light, the selection filter is set to Lights, and you choose Edit, Select All, the group will be selected along with any other lights.

Grouping is a powerful method for handling sets of objects as a single entity. The following exercise shows you how to use groups:

USING GROUPS

1. Load the CH7A.MAX file from the CD-ROM. If you still have this file loaded from the previous exercise, you do not need to reload it.

2. Select four of the spheres in the scene.

3. Choose Group, Group and name the group **Spheres.**

4. Choose Edit, Select None.

5. Choose Select Object and click on one of the spheres in the group. All four spheres are highlighted.

6. Choose Group, Open to open the group.

7. Choose Select and Move.

8. Click and hold on one of the spheres, and move it to a new location by dragging the mouse. Let go to place the sphere.

9. Choose Group, Close. The group is again present, but with the new location of the moved sphere.

10. Choose Group, Open to open the group again.

11. Choose Select Objects.

12. Click on a sphere that is not a member of the group.

13. Choose Group, Attach.

14. Click on the group. The sphere is added to the group.

15. Choose Edit, Select None.

16. Click on the sphere that you just added to the group. All five spheres are highlighted.

Summary

MAX provides you with many tools that enable you to select individual or groups of objects for use in combination with other commands. The selection process is vital to the correct functioning of most commands in MAX. You must be able to select one or more objects in a variety of ways to be able to model and work efficiently in MAX.

Now that you know how to use selection sets, it is time to look at how to modify geometry. MAX provides many different ways to modify and transform geometry. The next chapter focuses on some of these methods.

Object Editing, Transforms, and Modifiers

Creating basic objects in MAX is alone a fairly powerful capability. But you can even edit all objects that you create in MAX, or even import into MAX, to change their shape, location, or any of a variety of other properties. These editing capabilities provide you with the tools necessary to become a master modeler so that you can more fully explore your imagination.

This chapter focuses on the basics of editing objects in MAX. In particular, you look at the following aspects of editing existing objects:

▲ Object properties

▲ Transforms versus modifiers

▲ Accessing transforms with the right mouse button

▲ Controlling transform pivot points

▲ Using selection transforms

▲ Modifiers

▲ The stack

Before you look at the editing commands in MAX, however, you need to understand a few basics about objects and editing in MAX. Once you understand these basic concepts, you can more effectively learn some of the editing commands in MAX. These basics include

▲ Editing object parameters

▲ Making copies, instances, and references

Editing Object Parameters

When you create an object in MAX, a Parameters rollout appears in the Create command panel. Through this rollout and others, you can precisely control the creation of the object you are working on. You also can access each of these parameters at any time by selecting the object and clicking on the Modify command panel. The editable object parameters appear in a rollout. This fact alone enables you to have complete control over the object at all times. Figure 8.1 shows the Modify command panel for a basic sphere.

Below the Modify commands is the Modifier Stack. All objects have a stack that keeps track of all the changes in an object. (See "The Stack" later in this chapter for more information on this important topic.)

Below the Modifier Stack rollout is the Parameters rollout for the Sphere. This rollout is an exact duplicate of the Creation rollout. Every object shows some sort of Parameters rollout here. This rollout enables you to go back and change any object days, weeks, months, or even years later.

This flexibility in modifying creation parameters enables you to explore your creative instincts to any degree you want. You don't have to worry about being very accurate when creating objects. You can always come back and add accuracy later by adjusting the original creation parameters. These creation parameters, as you see later, can also be animated over time.

Making Copies, Instances, and References

Many of the editing operations in MAX and a couple of the creation operations in MAX create different types of MAX objects, such as Copies, Instances, and References. The Copy command, for example, can create all three types of objects. Each object type is explained in the following list:

Figure 8.1

The Modify panel for a sphere.

▲ **Copy**. A copy of an object is an exact independent duplicate of the object. The only difference between the copy and the original is the name of the object.

▲ **Instance**. An instance is a copy of an object with a unique property. An instance is not a complete copy of an object, but rather a placeholder for the second copy of the object. The copy is exact, except for the transforms (position, rotation, and scale) of the instanced object. If you create a box, for example, and make a second copy of the box that is an instance, only one defined box exists in the scene. The second copy is a placeholder telling MAX to make another copy of the box at this location. If any instance of an object is changed, all other instances of the object and the original are changed. Many different types of objects in MAX can be instanced from animation to objects to materials.

▲ **Reference**. A reference is similar to an instance except for one key difference. In a reference, if the original object is changed, all the references are affected. But if a reference is changed, it does not affect the other references of the same object or the original object. If you make a reference copy of a box and change the reference, for example, the original box remains the same. Like instances, references are used in many different places in MAX. When working with objects that involve a modifier stack, this will only be true of modifiers added to the stack after the point where the object was referenced. (See Chapter 9, "Editing 2D Shapes and Loft Objects," for more on the Stack.)

Instances and references are powerful tools because they can end up saving a lot of time as well as a lot of memory. Say, for example, you have a room with 100 chairs in it. You can create 100 copies of the chairs or 100 instances of the chair. With 100 copies, if you have to change the chair, you must delete and recopy all 100. With instances, all you have to do is change one chair and all the rest update automatically. As an added bonus, instead of having 100 different copies of the same chair in memory, you have one with location markers telling MAX to repeat the chair at specific points. In this way, instances can save a lot of memory.

As mentioned previously, instances and references appear through many of the operations in MAX. You should make sure that you are familiar with the concept of instances and references before moving on.

Transforms versus Modifiers

MAX has two basic forms of editing besides creation parameters: transforms and modifiers. A *transform* is any operation that changes the size, rotation, or position of an object by essentially transforming it. A *modifier*, on the other hand, is a method of changing the internal structure of a piece of geometry. Twisting a cylinder is an example of applying a modifier whereby the end vertices of a cylinder are rotated from the start vertices, producing a twisted look in the cylinder.

Whenever a modifier is applied to an object, it is placed on the Objects Modifier Stack. Then you can come back at any time and modify the modifier in the stack and change how you use it. You can, for example, create a box with a twist and a bend modifier. Then you add a little more twist. Normally, adding more twist would mean starting over, or twisting the object after bending it, which may not yield the results you are looking for. With the stack, you can go back to the twist modifier and adjust how it is used, and the resulting geometry is also changed. (See "The Stack" later in this chapter for more information.)

Because transforms are the easiest editing tools to apply to one or more objects, they are discussed first.

Accessing Transforms

The easiest way to use a transform is to use the Select object button and select one or more objects. After you select the object(s), right-click on the object(s). A small pop-up menu (the object transform menu) appears so that you can access some of the transformation commands (see fig. 8.2).

The first three options of this menu—Move, Rotate, and Scale—are transforms. If you select Move, it is checked and a new black, four-arrow icon appears. You can then simply click on an object and drag it to a new location. By doing so, you have transformed the object.

Rotate works in a similar fashion, but has a circular icon to indicate the current transformation command. When you choose Rotate, though, you must move the mouse cursor up and down on the screen. As you move the mouse cursor toward the top of the screen, the object rotates in a clockwise fashion. If you move the mouse cursor toward the bottom of the screen, the object rotates in a counterclockwise fashion.

Scale also works in a similar way. When you choose scale, a different scale icon appears, enabling you to scale the object. After you click on and drag the object, moving the mouse cursor toward the top of the screen scales the object up, and moving the mouse cursor toward the bottom of the screen scales the object down. This movement works in a uniform scale that affects all axes of the object equally.

You can apply these transforms to a single object or a selection set. Selection sets present some unique problems for the Scale and Rotate commands. Scale, Rotate, and Move all use transform points around which the operation is performed. For the Move command, the transform point is not very critical. But for Scale and Rotate, the location of the transform point directly affects how the transform works. The Rotate command, for example, works great on a box in which the transform point is the center of the box. But you might want to rotate the box around a different point. So, you have to change the transform point. The need to use different centers of rotation or transform points becomes even more apparent in selection sets where transform points are calculated based on the center of the selection set.

Controlling Transform Center Points

In MAX, you can control the transform point of a selection set through the use of several tools. Using these tools you can define the location of the transform point based on the objects in the selection set. For controlling pivot points in a single object, see Chapter 20, "Linking and IK," for more information.

When you are executing a rotate or scale transform, the transform point appears as an axis tripod, so you know exactly where it is. You can have the transform point in basically three different locations. You can access these commands by choosing the Transform Center button to access the flyout. This flyout is shown in figure 8.3.

Figure 8.3

The Transform Center flyout is accessed by pressing the Transform Center button.

Each option is described in the following list:

- **Pivot Point Center**. The Pivot Point Center option uses the center of the select object or objects for the rotation and scale transform points.

- **Use Selection Center**. This option uses the center of a selection set of two or more objects. When a single object is selected, the center of the single object is used.

Transform Coordinate Center. This option uses the center of the coordinate system. In MAX, you can choose from one of seven different coordinate systems to work with. Depending upon the coordinate system you work with, the transform center is based on the center of the coordinate system. The default coordinate system is the View coordinate system where the center of the view is the transform center. If you are using a Grid object, it is the center of the Grid object.

The following exercise shows you how these options work:

USING DIFFERENT PIVOT POINTS

1. Load the file CH8A.MAX from \exercises\ch8 on the accompanying CD-ROM.

2. Use Select Objects and select both objects in the scene.

3. Right-click on the objects.

4. Choose Rotate from the Object Transform pop-up menu.

5. Choose Pivot Point Center from the Transform Center flyout.

6. Select Local as the axis type from the Reference Coordinate System drop-down menu.

7. Click on one of the objects and drag it toward the top of the screen. Rotate the object 45 degrees. You can use an angle snap to make your life easier. Notice how both objects rotate around their own axes.

8. Click on the Undo button.

9. Choose Use Selection Center from the Transform Center flyout. Notice the axis move to a central location between the two objects.

10. Repeat the Rotate command. Notice how the object rotates around the center point now.

11. Click on Undo again.

12. Choose Use Transform Coordinate Center from the Pivot flyout. The axis tripod moves to 0,0.

13. Repeat the Rotate command again.

Transform Axis Restriction

The ability to change the pivot point provides you with some degree of control over the transforms of objects. But you can also restrict the axis of motion. This capability gives you a very high degree of control. Many times you will want to move objects in one axis only. You might, for example, want to move an object vertically in space, but not in any other direction. By restricting the movement of the object to one axis you can accomplish this. When you combine this capability with the use of snaps, you can be as accurate and precise as you want because you have total control over the precision of the transformation of the object.

The transform axis restriction controls are located on the main toolbar (see fig. 8.4). The default restriction is XY or free movement in both X and Y directions.

Figure 8.4

The Transform Restriction buttons, located on the main toolbar.

Each button restricts all transforms to its associated axis or axes. When you activate an axis restriction, the transformation axis tripod highlights in red the axis to which you are restricted. The other axes are gray.

The transform axis restriction buttons rely on the reference coordinate system that you are currently using. The coordinate system determines the location and orientation of the axis tripod, and hence, the orientation of the axes. You can control the location and direction of the axes under the reference coordinate system drop-down list (see fig. 8.5).

Figure 8.5

The Reference Coordinate System drop-down list enables you to control the location and direction of the axes.

Each option of this drop-down list is described in the following list:

▲ **View.** This option uses the axis from the current viewport. It is the default setting. All viewports use the same view axis, where X points right, Y points up, and Z comes out of the screen toward you. When you use a non-orthographic (Camera, User, Perspective) viewport, the world coordinate system is used.

▲ **Screen.** With this option, the local axis of the active viewport is used. Therefore, X points to the right, Y points to the top, and Z comes toward you out of the screen.

▲ **World.** With this option, the world coordinate system appears around 0,0,0. In the Top viewport, X points to the right, Y points to the top of the screen, and Z comes toward you. These directions change for each viewport.

▲ **Parent.** This option uses the local axis of the parent object, if the object is linked to another. (See Chapter 20, "Linking and IK," for more information on linking.)

▲ **Local.** This option uses the local coordinate system of the selected object.

▲ **Grid.** This option uses the coordinates system of the currently active grid object. If none is active, the home grid is used.

▲ **Pick.** This option uses the coordinate system of any object that you choose on the screen. The object name is then added to the bottom of the transformation coordinate system drop-down list.

The following exercise shows you how to use these coordinate transforms in combination with axis restrictions:

AXIS RESTRICTIONS AND TRANSFORM COORDINATES

1. Load the file CH8A.MAX from the CD-ROM.

2. Select the sphere using select objects.

3. Right-click on the selected sphere to access the object transform pop-up menu and choose Move.

4. Click on the X-axis restriction button.

5. Click on the sphere and move it to a new location. You can move it only in the X axis on the screen.

6. Click on the Y-axis restriction and move the sphere again.

7. Choose Edit, Select None.

8. Select the text object.

9. Right-click on the Text object and select rotate. Rotate the text 30 degrees. Make sure that you are using a Z-axis restriction on the rotation.

10. Select the sphere.

11. Right-click on the sphere to access the object transform menu and choose Move.

12. Click on the Transform Coordinate drop-down list and choose Pick.

13. Click on the text object.

14. Turn on X-axis restriction.

15. Move the sphere. It moves only at a 30-degree angle because of the rotation of the text object. Here, you used the rotate transform coordinates to influence the sphere.

Using Selection Transforms

Many of the transforms in MAX are combined with selection commands, enabling you to execute two commands at the same time. The three most important selections transforms are

▲ Select and Move

▲ Select and Rotate

▲ Select and Scale

The Select and Scale transform enables you to use two additional types of transforms: non-uniform and squash.

Select and Move

Select and Move enables you to select and move an object all in one command. When you choose this command, you can select an object, just like you would with a Select Objects command. The difference is that if you hold down the mouse button, the cursor turns into a black cross of four arrows, and you can drag the mouse cursor around to reposition the object. This command works with single or selection sets of objects, just like the Select Objects command.

Select and Rotate

Select and Rotate works just like Select and Move, except that a black circle with an arrow appears when you select this command, and you can rotate the object around its center point. The rotation command works by moving the mouse cursor toward the top or bottom of the screen. Moving toward the top rotates the object in a clockwise fashion, whereas moving toward the bottom rotates the object in a counterclockwise fashion.

Select and Scale

The Select and Scale command is made up of three options. Each option performs the scale command in a slightly different way. The options are Uniform, Non-uniform, and Squash. You access them through a flyout on the Select and Scale button (see fig. 8.6).

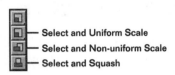

— Select and Uniform Scale
— Select and Non-uniform Scale
— Select and Squash

Figure 8.6

The Select and Scale flyout has three options: Uniform, Non-uniform, and Squash.

Each of these flyout options is described in the following list:

▲ **Uniform Scale**. This option works by scaling the object equally in all axes around the transform center. When you choose this option, you click on the object to select it and drag it toward the top or bottom of the screen. As you drag toward the top, the object scales up. Dragging toward the bottom scales down the object.

▲ **Non-uniform Scale**. This option works by non-uniformly scaling the selected object along an axis that is defined by the axis restriction buttons. If you turn on X-axis restriction and non-uniformly scale an object, for example, the object scales along the X-axis but no others.

▲ **Squash**. Squash is similar to Non-uniform Scale in that it uses axis restrictions. But Squash works in all three axes, not just one, to squash the object.

The transform options in MAX provide you with a high degree of control over the position, rotation, and scale of all objects in MAX. By using snaps and axis restrictions, you can effectively place an object as accurately as you need to in 3D space.

Modifiers

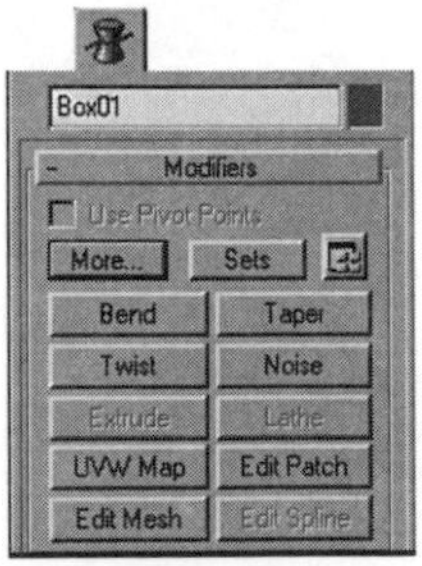

As mentioned previously, modifiers change the structure of the geometry of an object. You can apply a bend modifier to an object, for example, and it is bent depending on the parameters you set in the bend modifier. All the modifier commands are located in the Modify command panel (see fig. 8.7).

Figure 8.7

All the modifier commands are located in the Modify command panel.

To access any modifier in the Modify command panel, you must first select the object to which you want to apply the modifier. After you select the object, the modifiers that can be applied to the object show up with black text. Modifiers that cannot affect the selected object appear as grayed-out buttons.

Twist

You use the Twist modifier to twist an object around any axis. If you select an object and choose the Twist modifier, the Twist rollout appears (see fig. 8.8).

The Twist rollout is made up of three sections: Twist, Twist Axis, and Limits. Twist controls how much twist, in degrees, and the Bias of the twist. Like a helix, the Bias controls how close to the top or bottom of the object the twist occurs. The Twist Axis enables you to select the axis around which the twist is applied. In the Limits section, you can limit the Restrict the Twist modifier to vertices that lie between the upper and lower limits.

Some of the modifiers use a special object called a *gizmo* to apply the modifier (see fig. 8.9). This object appears as an orange box around the outside of your geometry. By rotating, moving, and scaling the gizmo, you can affect how MAX applies the modifier to the geometry. The limit effects change the location of the top and bottom of the gizmo around the Z axis of the gizmo. If both the upper and lower limit are equal, the result is the same as not limiting the effect. Of course, this varies a little from modifier to modifier.

You can modify the gizmo by clicking on the Sub-Object button under the Modifier stack rollout. Then, the gizmo is treated like any other box and can be moved, rotated, and scaled as long as the Sub-Object button is active. Because it is treated as a separate object, the gizmo also has a transform center, which is the pivot point of the object, but might not be the same as the center of the object. When you are done, click on Sub-Object again to deselect the gizmo.

Figure 8.8

The Twist Modifier rollout is made up of three sections: Twist, Twist Axis, and Limits.

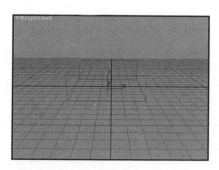

Figure 8.9

The gizmo, which can affect how MAX applies certain modifiers to the geometry.

Note

> Because other modifiers make use of the gizmo object, it is not discussed after this point. Further exercises in the book make the use of the gizmo more apparent. Make sure that you are conceptually familiar with what it does before moving on.

Some modifiers, like the twist modifier, work better with more complex geometry. If you create a box with 1 segment on each side, for example, the twist modifier has some effect but not a lot. With a more complex box of 15 segments on each side, the twist modifier's effect is much more pronounced and accurate. If you are not getting the desired effect, try increasing the complexity of the selected object. Figure 8.10 shows this difference.

Figure 8.10

A 1-segment box twisted versus a 15-segment box twisted.

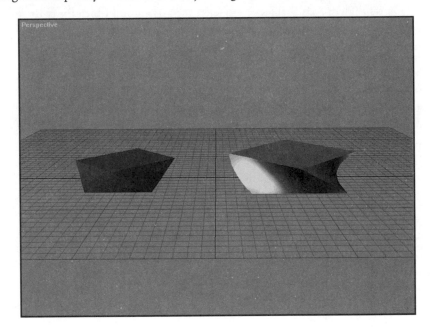

Figure 8.11

The Bend rollout.

Bend

The Bend modifier bends a selected object around a chosen axis. When you select an object and choose the Bend button on the Modify command panel, the Bend rollout appears (see fig. 8.11).

Like Twist, Bend has Bend, Bend Axis, and Limits sections. The only difference here is the Direction field under Bend. After you bend an object, you can also apply the bend in a different direction. Figure 8.12 shows a bent object, and figure 8.13 shows the same object with a direction angle applied.

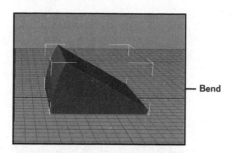

— Bend

Figure 8.12

A box that is bent around the Y-Axis using the Bend modifier.

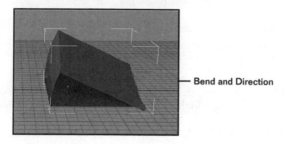

— Bend and Direction

Figure 8.13

The same bent box, but with a twist applied around the X-axis.

Taper

The Taper modifier tapers an object from one end to another. When you select an object and choose the Taper button, the Taper rollout appears (see fig. 8.14).

Again, Taper has sections similar to Bend and Twist. Under the Taper section of the rollout is a Curve field that enables you to apply a curve to the taper. Under Taper Axis, you can taper the object in more than one axis at a time, so you have two rows of axis settings. Figure 8.15 shows a tapered object.

Noise

The noise modifier applies random variations to the geometry to produce an organic-looking object. If you select an object and choose the Noise button, the Noise rollout appears (see fig. 8.16). The Noise function that is used in this modifier is used in many other places in MAX as well.

Figure 8.14

The Taper rollout appears after selecting the Taper button.

169

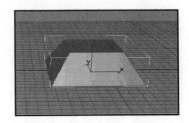

A box with a 41 degree taper applied in the XY axis.

Figure 8.16

The Noise rollout appears after selecting the Noise button.

Because the noise routine is used so much in MAX, each parameter of the noise routine is described in the following list:

▲ **Seed**. This parameter gives a starting point to the random number generator for the noise function. This can be any numerical number. By altering the seed, you change the pattern of random numbers.

▲ **Scale**. This enables you to set the overall size of that noise. Larger values provide rougher looking noise, while smaller values provide smoother noise.

▲ **Fractal**. This parameter enables you to use fractal algorithms that generate the noise. Fractals are a form of mathematics that are great at emulating complex natural looking forms.

▲ **Roughness**. Roughness enables you to control the fractal dimension, or overall roughness of the curve. Values are from 0 to 1 with 1 being the roughest.

▲ **Iterations**. This determines how many calculations the fractal function will take to generate the noise. Higher numbers result in a more accurate fractal noise, but take longer to generate.

▲ **Strength**. The overall strength or size of the noise is a particular axis. The scale parameter affects how large the noise is along the surface, whereas the strength affects the size perpendicular to the surface.

▲ **Animation**. This parameter enables you to turn on animation capabilities for the noise function so that it works over time.

▲ **Frequency**. This enables you to define the overall speed of the noise. Higher values make the object quiver faster.

▲ **Phase**. Phase enables you to control animation of the noise. Different values result in different animations of the noise parameter.

Figure 8.17 shows an object with a noise modifier applied to it.

Figure 8.17

The noise modifier applied to a box.

The Stack

When you apply a modifier to an object, it is added to the object's stack. The stack is a list of all the modifiers that you apply to an object, in the order in which you apply them. You can apply as many modifiers to an object as you like.

The stack is a rather unique and powerful tool in MAX. MAX takes the original geometry and applies each modifier in the order it appears in the stack. Every time you load the geometry into MAX, it is regenerated. This capability is powerful because you can go back into the stack and change any modifier. But it does have its drawbacks. Any change to a modifier affects all modifiers above it in the stack.

Say, for example, you create a box and apply a twist modifier, a UVW mapping modifier, and an edit mesh modifier to the box. If you use the edit mesh modifier to attach another object to the box, the attached object does not have any mapping applied to it because the mapping modifier appears in the stack before the object is attached to the box.

The Modifier Stack appears as a rollout above each Modifier rollout, as shown in figure 8.18.

Figure 8.18

The Modifier Stack rollout.

The drop-down list in the Modifier Stack rollout shows a list of the modifiers that have been applied to the currently selected object. You can select any modifier from the stack list. The parameters for that modifier then appear in a rollout below the Modifier Stack rollout. Figure 8.19 shows the stack drop-down list.

Figure 8.19

The stack drop-down list with a list of modifiers being applied to the current object.

In the list shown in figure 8.19, you see a box object that has a noise modifier applied and then a taper modifier. Figure 8.20 shows the object using this stack.

Figure 8.20

The current object using the stack.

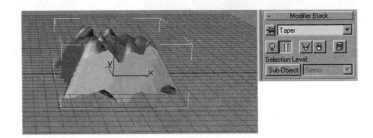

Below the stack drop-down list are several buttons to help you control and manipulate the stack. Figure 8.21 shows these buttons.

Figure 8.21

The Modifier Stack buttons that help control and manipulate the stack.

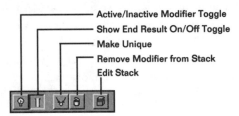

Each button is described in the following list:

▲ **Active Inactive Modifier Toggle.** This button deactivates the current modifier in the stack. This tool is handy if you want to see what the object would look like without this modifier being applied to it.

▲ **Show End Result On/Off Toggle.** This button is on by default and tells MAX to show you the object that is left over after applying the modifiers. When the button is off, the effects of all modifiers above the current modifier are not shown.

▲ **Make Unique.** If you select multiple objects and apply a modifier to the selection set, instances of the modifier are placed on each object's stack. This button converts that instance to a copy of the modifier.

▲ **Remove Modifier from Stack.** This button removes the current modifier from the stack. If you apply a modifier and do not like the end result, you can simply remove the modifier from the stack.

▲ **Edit Stack.** This button displays the Edit Modifier Stack dialog box where you can edit the stack (see fig. 8.22).

Figure 8.22

You can edit the stack in the Edit Modifier Stack dialog box.

In the Edit Modifier Stack dialog box, you can select modifiers and remove or collapse them. You can also make the object unique the same way by choosing the Make Unique button in the Modifier Stack rollout in the command panel. This dialog box is very useful when you have an object that has many modifiers applied to it.

The following exercise shows you how to use modifiers and the stack:

USING THE STACK AND MODIFIERS

1. Create a box that is 40 units cubed. Set the length, width, and height segments to 20 each.

2. Click on the Modify tab of the command panel.

3. Choose the Taper button.

4. In the Parameters rollout, set the Taper Amount to 2. Figure 8.23 shows the resulting object.

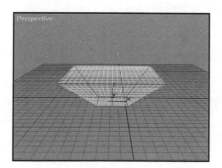

Figure 8.23

The box with a Taper amount of 2.0.

5. Click on the Twist button to apply a twist modifier.

6. Set the twist angle to 140.0. Figure 8.24 shows the resulting object.

The box with a 140-degree twist.

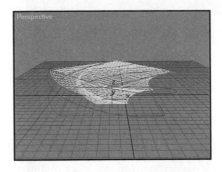

7. Click on the stack drop-down list and select the Taper modifier from the list.

8. Change the Twist amount to –0.50. Figure 8.25 shows the resulting object. Notice that the twist is still there, even though you just adjusted the Taper.

Figure 8.25

The box with a new Taper value.

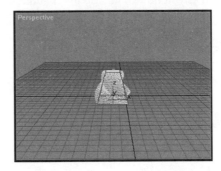

9. Click on the Edit Stack button to display the Edit Modifier Stack dialog box.

10. Choose Collapse All.

11. Choose OK to the warning message. Now you have removed the modifiers in the stack and are left with a static object that cannot be changed unless another modifier is applied to it.

The Modifier Stack is a powerful tool that enables you to parametrically edit any modifier of an object at any time. Take your time and experiment with it. You should be able to get the handle of it fairly quickly.

Summary

The capability to edit modifier geometry quickly and easily in MAX is a powerful feature. This feature is made even more powerful through the use of the stack where you can view and change any modifiers that you have applied to the object.

Modifying and transforming basic objects produce some very good results. But to really increase your arsenal of modeling capabilities, you need to be able to manipulate 2D shapes and loft objects as well.

The next chapter focuses on how to edit 2D shapes as well as 3D loft objects by applying deformations to the loft process.

Editing 2D Shapes and Loft Objects

Modifying and editing 3D primitives provides you with a wide variety of modeling capabilities. By modifying and editing shapes and 3D loft objects, however, you can expand your modeling skills to the point where you can model just about anything you want.

This chapter introduces you to the concepts of editing shapes and 3D loft objects. In particular, this chapter covers the following topics:

▲ Editing shapes

▲ Editing loft objects

▲ Working with deformation curves

Editing Shapes

In Chapter 6, you learned how to create basic shapes such as lines, arcs, and circles, and make 3D loft objects from these objects. Now, you learn how to apply a modifier to the shape and produce a 3D object that is not a loft object. You can use two modifiers to accomplish this task in MAX:

▲ Extrude

▲ Lathe

Figure 9.1

The Extrude command rollout.

Extrude

You use the Extrude modifier to extrude a shape into a 3D object. You can create some text, for example, and then apply an extrude modifier to the text and create 3D text with thickness. You can further modify the text by then applying a bend modifier to give the text a beveled appearance.

To use the Extrude modifier, you must first create a shape. After you select the shape, you can choose the Extrude button from the Modify command panel to give the shape some thickness. When you choose this button, the Extrude command rollout appears (see fig. 9.1).

In the Parameters section of the Extrude command rollout, you find all the options of the Extrude function that you can control. First is the Amount setting, which controls how tall the extrusion of the selected shape will be. You can control the number of segments in the extruded shape with the Segments setting. This capability is helpful if you need to create a more complex shape for use with another modifier, such as bend or twist, at a later time.

The Capping options control whether a closed shape has a top and bottom on it when the shape is extruded. You can control whether this cap is a morph cap or a grid cap as well. A morph cap is used whenever you are going to use this object either as a morph or a morph target. (See Chapter 23, "Special Effects Fundamentals," for more on morphing.) A grid cap is a standard way of capping an extruded object, even though MAX defaults to the morph cap.

Finally, you can control whether the resulting 3D object is a patch object or a mesh object. If it is a patch object, control points appear on the screen, and you can modify the object like a quad or tri patch. (See Chapter 10 for more information on editing control points.)

The following exercise shows you how to use the extrude modifier to create a 3D object.

USING THE EXTRUDE MODIFIER

1. Load the file CH9A.MAX from the accompanying CD-ROM. Figure 9.2 shows the contents of the file.

2. Select the shapes using the Select Objects button.

3. Click on the Modify tab of the command panel.

4. Choose the Extrude button.

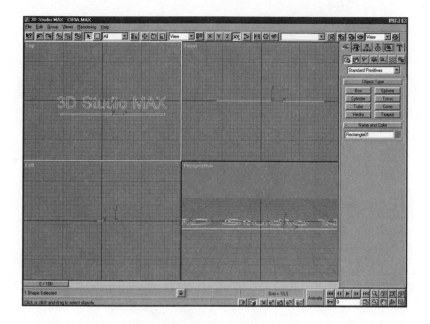

Figure 9.2

The CH9A.MAX file.

5. In the Parameters section of the command panel, set the Amount to 10 and the number of Segments to 4.

6. Make sure that both Cap Start and Cap End are turned on in the Capping section of the rollout. Figure 9.3 shows the resulting object.

Figure 9.3

The extruded object.

7. On your own, try applying a twist, bend, or taper modifier to the extruded object to see what the results are. After you apply the twist or bend modifier, use the Modifier Stack to return to the extrude modifier and change some of its parameters.

Lathe

The lathe modifier takes a shape and revolves it around one of three axes related to the shape. You could draw the profile of a wine glass, for example, and then apply a lathe modifier to the wine glass profile to create the full 3D wine glass object.

Like the extrude modifier, the lathe modifier works with a selected shape. After you select the shape, you can choose the Lathe button from the Modify command panel. The Lathe command rollout then appears, as shown in figure 9.4.

In the Lathe command rollout, three areas are worth a look. First are the actual lathe parameters. You can set the angle of rotation for the lathe anywhere from 0 to 360 degrees. If you rotate a shape the full 360 degrees, the shape will rotate around itself. The Weld Core option welds all the resulting coincident vertices in the center of the lathed object. You can also set the number of segments in the rotated object.

Like extrude, the Lathe command rollout offers the Capping and Output options. This rollout also includes a set of Direction buttons. Here, you can define the direction in which the lathe occurs, based on the world coordinate system.

Finally, you can define the alignment of the shape in this rollout. The alignment determines where the center of rotation for the shape is. Min aligns the rotation to the farthest left point of the shape. Center rotates the shape around its center. Max aligns the rotation around the farthest right point. Figures 9.5 through 9.8 show shapes with the various alignment options.

Figure 9.4

The Lathe command rollout.

Figure 9.5

The shape in the original position.

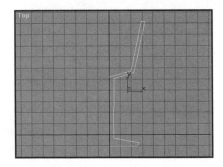

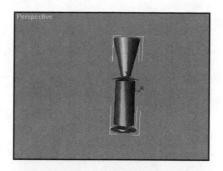

Figure 9.6

The shape as it is rotated around its center.

Figure 9.7

The shape as it is rotated around its min axis.

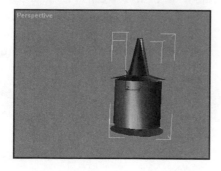

Figure 9.8

The shape as it is rotated around its max axis.

Figures 9.6 through 9.8 show that you can create several radically different 3D shapes from the same lathe operation of a shape.

The following exercise shows you how to create a lathe object using an existing shape.

USING THE LATHE MODIFIER

1. Open the file CH9B.MAX, which is located on the accompanying CD-ROM.

2. Select the shape using Select Objects.

3. Click on the Modify tab of the command panel.

4. Choose the Lathe button.

5. In the Align section, choose the Min button to align the rotation axis to the left side of the shape.

6. After the goblet appears, set the Degrees spinner to 180 in the Parameters section.

7. Now, you have half a goblet. Try experimenting with the axis buttons and the other alignment buttons to see how you can adjust the shape to make different 3D objects.

Editing Lofted Objects

In Chapter 6, you learned how to create a basic lofted shape. At this point, you can create a shape that is lofted along a path. The real power of lofted objects, though, is in the ability to deform the shape as it travels along the path. You can loft a shape along a straight line, for example, and as the shape is lofted, you can scale it down to produce a tapered shape. For example, by adjusting just the scale of a circular shape as it is lofted along a straight path, you could create a rather nice bottle that would otherwise be a little more difficult to create.

MAX provides the following five deformation tools:

▲ Scale

▲ Twist

▲ Teeter

▲ Bevel

▲ Fit

You can use each of these tools to deform the shape as it is lofted. You can apply one, more than one, or all these modifiers at any time. If you have used the DOS version of 3D Studio, this technique should be familiar to you. Note one key difference here: Deformations are applied after the loft shape is created. Applying them this way enables you to adjust the deformations and interactively see how the deformation affects the 3D object.

In the DOS version of 3D Studio, you have to apply the deformation as you loft the object, which means lofting the object, going to the 3D editor to see the result, and then returning to the 3D Lofter to make any necessary changes. In short, the process is a lot more time consuming and difficult to work with in DOS.

You can access the deformation tools by selecting the loft object and choosing the Modify tab of the command panel. At the bottom of the resulting rollout is a section titled Deformations (see fig. 9.9).

You can set a deformation simply by choosing the appropriate button. Each deformation type also has a button to the right of the deformation button. This button indicates whether the deformation is active. As mentioned previously, you can have as many deformations active at one time as you want. Simply check the ones you want. When the button is active, it looks like a lit lightbulb. Otherwise, it looks like a dark lightbulb.

Deformation tools enable you to create many unique and interesting objects. You should strive to become as familiar with these tools as you can.

Deformation Curves

A deformation is applied as a modifier to a lofted object. When you apply a deformation, you use a deformation curve to control how the deformation affects the object. Figure 9.10 shows the Scale deformation curve, which is a good example of a standard curve deformation dialog box.

Figure 9.9

The Deformations rollout.

Figure 9.10

The scale deformation curve.

In the deformation grid itself, a red line appears. This red line (called the deformation line) is representative of the length of the loft path of the loft object and the amount of deformation applied to the loft shape. By default, the line has two end vertices called *control points.* The location of the control points determines the amount of deformation at any given point along the deformation line. You can add or delete as many control points as necessary to change the shape of the line to match your needs. Control points can be moved at anytime by using the controls on the toolbar in the dialog box. (The exact controls are discussed later in this section.) The deformation line then becomes the key to controlling the exact modification of the final 3D object.

At the left of the deformation grid is a scale. This scale varies from deformation to deformation and measures the amount of deformation you are applying to the shape at any given point along the loft path. On a scale deformation (shown in figure 9.10), for example, the scale at the left goes from 100 percent to –100 percent or more. When a control point is moved up or down to a scale other than 100 percent, the scale of the loft shape changes at that point on the loft path to match the scale on the grid. If you moved the first control point on the left to 200 percent, the object would be twice as large at the start of the path, then gradually decrease in size to 100 percent at the other end. On a twist deformation, it may read 180 degrees to –180 degrees.

Figure 9.11 shows a scale deformation. Figure 9.12 shows you an adjusted scale deformation. Figures 9.13 and 9.14 show you the resulting object for both scale deformations.

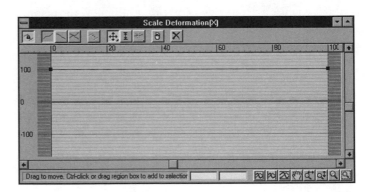

Figure 9.11

The scale deformation curve before adjustment.

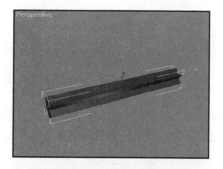

Figure 9.12

The object using the scale deformation curve before adjustment.

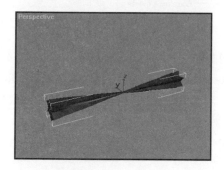

Figure 9.13

The adjusted scale deformation curve.

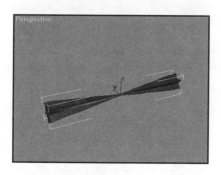

Figure 9.14

The object using the adjusted deformation curve.

In the Deformation dialog box, two sets of buttons are worth exploring. The first set, which is located across the top of the dialog box, is shown in figure 9.15. Additionally, at the bottom of the dialog box are two coordinate readouts to represent the location of the currently selected control point, on the deformation grid.

Figure 9.15

The Deformation buttons.

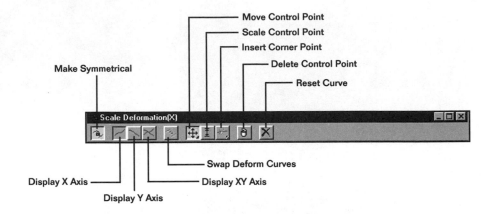

Each of the buttons shown in figure 9.16 is described in the following list:

- **Make Symmetrical**. Many of the deformation tools in MAX can affect both the X and Y axes of the lofted shape. This button forces both axes to use the same deformation curve.

- **Display X Axis**. When this button is active, the X-axis deformation curve is displayed in the grid window. This curve appears as a red line.

- **Display Y Axis**. When this button is active, the Y-axis deformation curve is displayed in the grid window. This curve appears as a green line.

- **Display XY Axis**. When this button is active, both the X and Y axes curves appear in the grid window at the same time. The X axis appears red, and the Y axis appears green.

- **Swap Deform Curves**. When you choose this button, the X and Y axes deformation curves are swapped. This button is active only if the Make Symmetrical button is disabled.

- **Move Control Point**. This button enables you to move a control point to a new location in the deformation grid. This button also contains a flyout of two other Move Control Point buttons (see fig. 9.17). The other two buttons restrict the movement of the control point to horizontal or vertical movement only.

Figure 9.17

The Move Control Point flyout buttons.

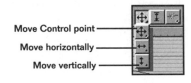

Scale Control Point. This button enables you to control the scale of a control point. This process has the effect of moving the control point up and down the grid at precise scale values.

Insert Corner Point. This button enables you to insert a new corner point at any point along the deformation curve. This button also has a flyout that enables you to insert a Bézier control point as well (see fig. 9.18). A Bézier control point enables you to control the curvature of the deformation line as it enters and leaves the control point.

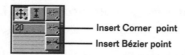
— Insert Corner point
— Insert Bézier point

Figure 9.18

The Insert Control Point flyout buttons.

Delete Control Point. This button enables you to remove any control points that you have inserted. You must select the control point first and then choose this button to delete it. You cannot delete the first or last control point in the line.

Reset Curve. This button resets the deformation curve to the default curve shown in figure 9.10.

You use the second set of buttons in the Deformation dialog box to control the view of the deformation curve. These buttons are shown figure 9.19.

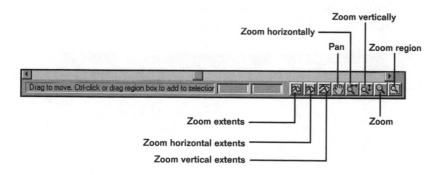

Zoom horizontally
Zoom vertically
Pan
Zoom region
Drag to move. Ctrl-click or drag region box to add to selection
Zoom extents
Zoom horizontal extents
Zoom vertical extents
Zoom

Figure 9.19

The Deformation View Control buttons.

Each button shown in figure 9.19 is described in the following list:

Zoom Extents. This button maximizes the view of the deformation line in the grid window.

Zoom Horizontal Extents. This button changes the view to display the endpoints of the deformation line at a maximum size in the grid window.

Zoom Vertical Extents. This button changes the view to display any vertical control points at a maximum size in the grid window.

Pan. This button works just like the Pan button in a regular MAX viewport. It enables you to move around the deformation grid without changing zoom scales.

Zoom Horizontally. This button enables you to stretch the grid horizontally to make more or less of the deformation grid appear. You click and drag horizontally to scale the grid.

Zoom Vertically. This button enables you to stretch the grid vertically to make more or less of the deformation grid appear. You click and drag vertically to scale the grid.

Zoom. This button works just like the Zoom button in a regular MAX viewport. You click and drag vertically to zoom in and out of the deformation grid.

Zoom Region. This button works just like the Zoom Region button in a regular MAX viewport. You simply define two opposite corners on which you can zoom in.

For each deformation tool these view control buttons will remain the same. As you explore each deformation tool, covered in the following sections, you are given the opportunity to use these buttons in exercises.

Scale

The scale deformation tool changes the scale of the shape as it travels along the loft path. You access the scale deformation tool by selecting the loft object and choosing the Scale button from the Deformations rollout. The Scale Deformation dialog box then appears, as shown in figure 9.20.

Figure 9.20

The Scale Deformation dialog box.

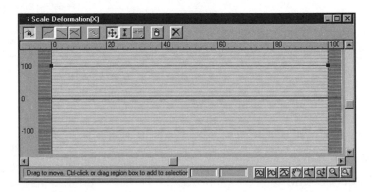

The following exercise shows you how to use the scale deformation grid:

USING A SCALE DEFORMATION

1. Load the file CH9C.MAX from the accompanying CD-ROM. (This file is used for the next three exercises in this chapter.)

2. Choose Select Objects and click on the loft object.

3. Click on the Modify tab of the command panel.

4. Click on the Deformations rollout to expand it.

5. In the rollout, choose the Scale button.

6. When the Scale Deformation dialog box appears, choose Insert Control Point from its toolbar.

7. Click on the red deformation line at approximately the midpoint. A new control point appears, as shown in figure 9.21.

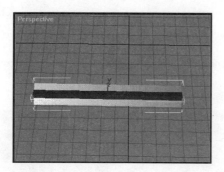

Figure 9.21

The scale deformation line with a new control point.

8. Choose Move Control Point from the dialog box toolbar.

9. Click on the new control point and move it vertically to a scale value of 25. (Watch the right coordinate readout at the bottom of the dialog box.) Move the coordinate to the left or right until the left coordinate reads approximately 50. (Alternatively, you can click in each coordinate readout box and type in the correct value when the control point is highlighted.) Figure 9.22 shows the resulting deformation curve and object.

Figure 9.22

*The deformation curve
and object.*

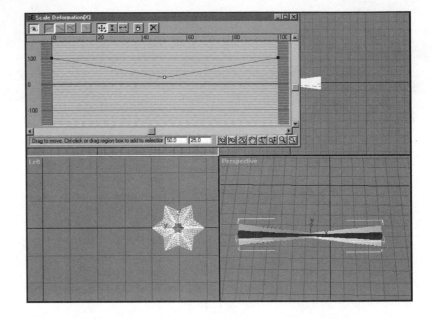

10. Click on the Make Symmetrical button to turn off symmetrical deformation

11. Click on the Display Y Axis button to show the Y axis.

12. Move the center control point to 50,150. Figure 9.23 shows the curve and resulting object.

Figure 9.23

*The new curve and
resulting object.*

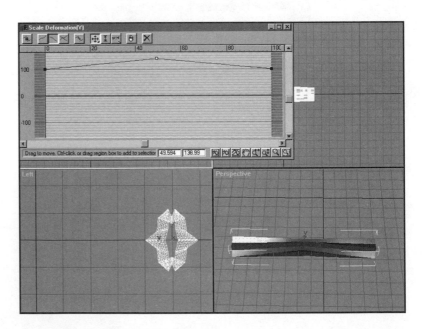

13. Choose the Reset Curve button.

14. Turn symmetry back on.

15. Choose the Insert Bézier Control Point button from the Insert Control Point flyout.

16. Click on the deformation curve at approximately the midpoint. A new control point with two new endpoints appears, as shown in figure 9.24.

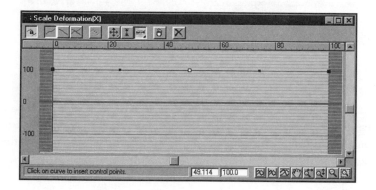

Figure 9.24

The Bézier control point.

17. Choose the Move Control Point button.

18. Click on the far right Bézier control point and move it vertically to a value of –100.

19. Choose Zoom Extents. Figure 9.25 shows the resulting curve and object.

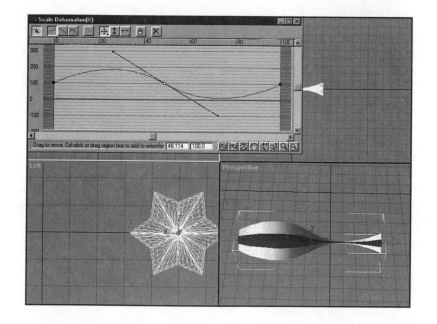

Figure 9.25

The Bézier deformation curve and resulting object.

20. Choose File, Reset to reset the system when you are finished. You may save the file if you want to, but it is not necessary for later exercises

Note

> The preceding exercise shows how to use both Bézier and corner control points in the deformation curves. The rest of the exercises in this chapter focus on how to use a particular deformation curve only. Feel free, however, to use either type of control point at any time.

Twist

The twist deformation tool rotates the shape around the loft axis as it is lofted. You access the twist deformation tool by selecting the loft object and choosing the Twist button from the Deformations rollout in the command panel. The Twist Deformation dialog box then appears, as shown in figure 9.26. Because a twist can act in one way only, the symmetry buttons are disabled in this dialog box.

Figure 9.26

The Twist Deformation dialog box.

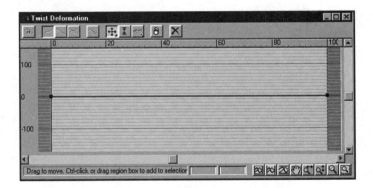

The following exercise shows you how to use the twist deformation grid:

USING A TWIST DEFORMATION

1. Load the CH9C.MAX file from the accompanying CD-ROM. (If you are continuing from the preceding exercise, reload the original file.)

2. Select the object by choosing Select Objects and then clicking on the object.

3. Choose Twist from the Deformations rollout in the command panel.

4. When the Twist Deformation dialog box appears, choose the Move Control Point Vertically button from the toolbar flyout.

5. Move the end control point to a value of 100. Figure 9.27 shows the resulting curve and object.

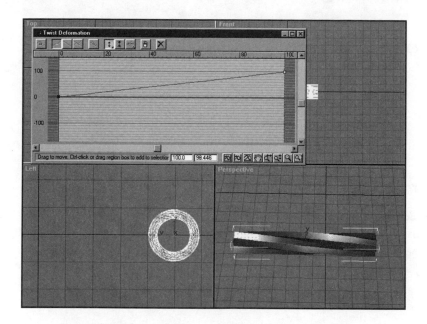

Figure 9.27

The twist deformation curve and resulting object.

6. Choose the Insert Corner Point button.

7. Click on the deformation line at the midpoint.

8. Choose the Move Control Point Vertically button.

9. Move the new control point to a value of –100. Figure 9.28 shows the resulting curve and object.

10. When you are done, Choose File, Reset to reset the system. You do not need to save any changes to this file unless you want to.

Figure 9.28

The new twist curve and resulting object.

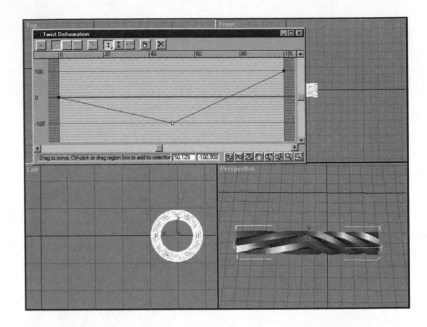

Teeter

The teeter deformation tool rotates the loft shape around an axis that is perpendicular to the loft axis. You access the teeter deformation tool by selecting the loft object and choosing the Teeter button from the Deformations rollout in the command panel. The Teeter Deformation dialog box then appears, as shown in figure 9.29.

Figure 9.29

The Teeter Deformation dialog box.

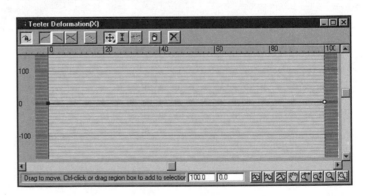

The following exercise shows you how to use the teeter deformation grid:

USING A TEETER DEFORMATION

1. Load the CH9C.MAX file from the accompanying CD-ROM. (If you are continuing from the preceding exercise, reload the original file.)

2. Select the loft object using Select Objects.

3. Choose Teeter from the Deformation rollout in the command panel.

4. When the Teeter Deformation dialog box appears, choose the Move Control Point Vertically button from the toolbar flyout.

5. Move the end control point to a value of –45. Figure 9.30 shows the resulting curve and object.

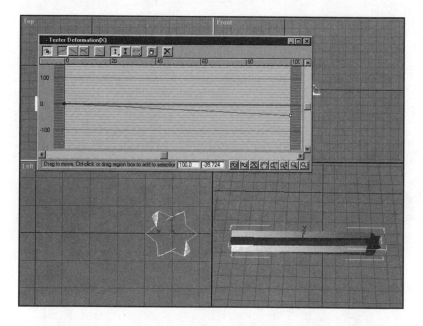

Figure 9.30

The teeter deformation curve and resulting object.

6. When you are finished, choose File, Reset to reset the system. You do not need to save the changes.

Bevel

The bevel deformation tool is similar to the scale tool in the fact that it changes the scale of the shape as it travels along the loft path. A bevel, however, correctly deforms complex objects such as text that have nested openings. If you loft the letter *P* and apply a scale deformation to it, for example, the *P* is equally scaled. A bevel scales the inside of the *P* differently from the outside, however, to produce a correct bevel. Figures 9.31 and 9.32 illustrate this difference.

Figure 9.31

The letter P scale deformed.

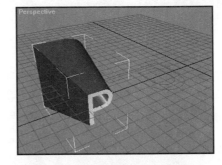

Figure 9.32

The letter P bevel deformed.

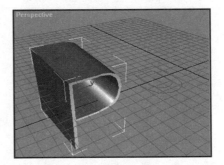

You access the bevel deformation tool by selecting the loft object and choosing the Bevel button from the Deformations rollout in the command panel. The Bevel Deformation dialog box then appears, as shown in figure 9.33.

Figure 9.33

The Bevel Deformation dialog box.

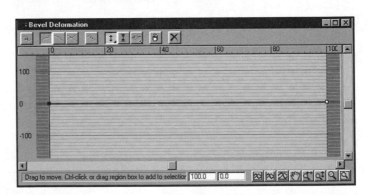

The following exercise shows you how to use the bevel deformation grid:

USING A BEVEL DEFORMATION

1. Load the file CH9D.MAX from the accompanying CD-ROM.

2. Select the loft object using Select Objects.

3. Choose the Modify tab of the command panel.

4. Choose the Bevel button from the Deformations rollout.

5. When the Bevel Deformation dialog box appears, choose the Move Control Point Vertically button from the toolbar flyout.

6. Move the end control point to a value of 20. Figure 9.34 shows the resulting object and deformation grid.

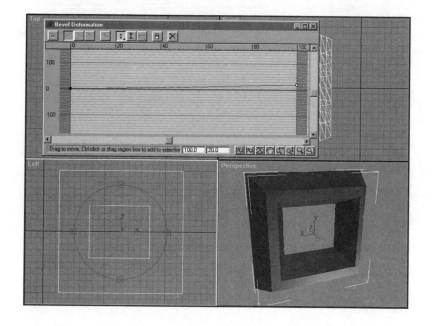

Figure 9.34

The bevel deformation grid and resulting object.

Fit

The fit deformation tool uses one or two profile shapes to deform the loft object. You can draw, for example, a side and top view of a phone handle. Then the lofted object is forced to match those profiles and create the phone handle. You access the fit deformation tool by selecting the loft object and choosing the Fit button from the Deformations rollout in the command panel. The Fit Deformation dialog box then appears, as shown in figure 9.35.

Figure 9.35

The Fit Deformation dialog box.

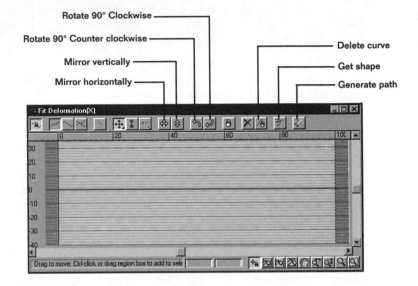

The Fit Deformation dialog box contains several new buttons that you need to be familiar with before looking at this tool in an exercise. Each new button is described in the following list:

Mirror Horizontally. This button mirrors the profile shape horizontally.

Mirror Vertically. This button mirrors the profile shape vertically.

Rotate 90 CCW. This button rotates the profile shape 90 degrees counterclockwise.

Rotate 90 CW. This button rotates the profile shape 90 degrees clockwise.

Delete Curve. This button deletes the selected profile shape curve.

Get Shape. This button enables you to load a shape as a profile for the loft object. You may have a different shape for both the X and Y axes. Any shape that is used for a profile must be a closed shape.

Generate Path. This button generates a new path that better matches the control points of the profile shape.

▲ **Lock Aspect.** When a shape is loaded as a fit shape, the deformation grid's vertical axis values correspond to the absolute size of the shape, and the horizontal axis values correspond to the percentage along the loft path. If a zoom extents is performed, the views for both the X and Y axis are maximized. A result of this, however, is that the shape's aspect ratio in the deformation grid is different than it is in the scene. When this button is on, the grid display is controlled such that the correct aspect ratio of the shape is maintained in the deformation grid during zoom operations.

The following exercise shows you how to use the fit deformation grid:

USING A FIT DEFORMATION

1. Load the file CH9C.MAX from the accompanying CD-ROM.

2. Choose Select Objects and select the loft object.

3. Click on the Modify tab of the command panel.

4. Expand the Deformations rollout.

5. Choose the Fit button.

6. When the Fit Deformation dialog box appears, choose the Get Shape button from the toolbar.

7. Click on the star shape in the Top viewport. The loft object is immediately deformed to match the new profile. Figure 9.36 shows the deformation curve and resulting object.

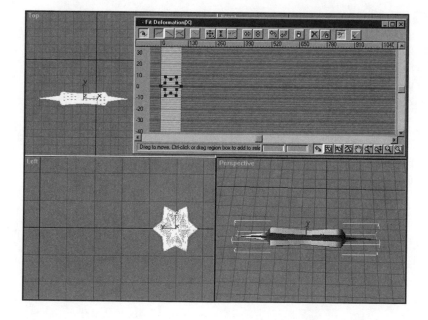

Figure 9.36

The fit deformation curve and resulting object.

8. Choose the Generate Path button to generate a new loft path based on the fit shapes. Figure 9.37 shows the resulting object.

Figure 9.37

The object with a new loft path.

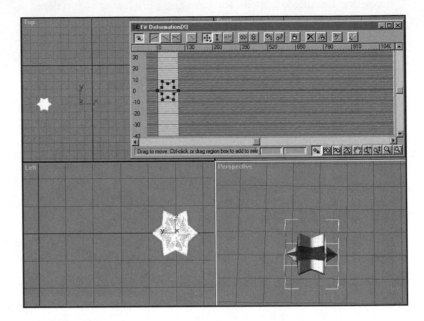

Summary

By editing and manipulating objects and 3D loft objects, you can create any of a wide variety of 3D objects. The deformations tools for 3D loft objects are particularly powerful for creating unique and interesting objects. This is especially true of the fit deformation tool where you can use one or two profile shapes to create a 3D object.

Beyond editing shapes and 3D loft objects, you can also edit objects at a variety of levels, depending on the type of object you are editing. A box can be edited, for example, at a face, vertex, or edge level if you use a special modifier called Edit Mesh. Three such special modifiers—Edit Mesh, Edit Spline, and Edit Patch—are the subject of the next chapter.

Modifying Objects at Different Levels

Up to this point, you have seen many ways to create and edit a variety of 2D and 3D objects in MAX. Now it is time to look at editing those objects at a higher level of detail. All objects in MAX are composed of component parts. A box, for example, is composed of vertices, faces, and edges. The ability to edit any of these component parts is extremely powerful.

You can edit objects at these various component levels using one of three special modifiers:

▲ Edit Mesh

▲ Edit Patch

▲ Edit Spline

Each works with the associated specific type of geometry. Edit Mesh, for example, works only with geometry that is some sort of mesh. Edit Patch works only with Bézier patches, and Edit Spline only works with splines. Each of these modifiers provides many powerful controls to edit existing corresponding geometry.

This chapter explores how to use the Edit Mesh, Edit Patch, and Edit Spline modifiers to edit the component parts of 2D and 3D objects. This chapter also covers the editing of Boolean objects because they also contain sub elements (called operands) that can be edited independent of the larger object.

Edit Mesh

The Edit Mesh modifier enables you to edit existing mesh geometry at three different sub-object levels. Each of these levels is defined in the following list:

▲ **Vertex**. A vertex is the most basic building block of geometry. It is a point in space through which geometry intersects. A line, for example, has two vertices, a start vertex and an end vertex. A box has eight vertices, and so on. Figure 10.1 shows the Edit Mesh Vertex rollout.

▲ **Face**. A face is a three-dimensional surface comprised of three vertices forming a triangle. Because a face is a flat surface, it is difficult to tell which side of the surface is up or down. A vector is drawn from the center of the face perpendicular into space. This vector, called a *normal*, determines which side of the face is up. Figure 10.16 later in this chapter shows you a good example of face normals. Figure 10.2 shows the Edit Mesh Face rollout.

Figure 10.1

The Edit Mesh Vertex rollout.

Figure 10.2

The Edit Mesh Face rollout.

▲ **Edge**. An edge is the line created when a face is formed. An edge occurs between two vertices or between two faces and appears as a solid line or is transparent. Figure 10.3 shows the Edit Mesh Edge rollout.

In addition to the different levels of editing that Edit Mesh allows you, you can also attach one object to another to form a larger, more complex object.

You can apply an Edit Mesh modifier simply by selecting the object you want to edit and then choosing Edit Mesh from the Modify command panel. Under the Modifier Stack section of the rollout, you can choose the level at which you want to work, to display the three rollouts shown in figures 10.2 and 10.3. Figure 10.4 shows the Selection Level controls.

The Sub-Object button enables you to work at a level below an object. The drop-down list to the right of the Sub-Object button enables you to select the level at which you want to work. Three basic levels are available for you to work at: Vertex, Face, and Element. Each is covered in the following sections.

Vertex

Vertex-level editing enables you to manipulate any object at lowest common denominator of the geometry, the vertex. With vertex-level editing, you can edit a single point or group of points to any degree you feel necessary. You can edit an object at this level by simply selecting the object and choosing Edit Mesh from the Modify command panel. By default, the Sub-Object level is set to Vertex.

When the Edit Mesh modifier is loaded, a series of ticks appears on the screen to indicate the location of the vertices of the object. Figure 10.5 shows an example of these ticks.

To actually edit a vertex, you must make another selection. If you choose Select Objects again and click on one or more of the vertices, they turn red to indicate that they have been selected for further editing. Figure 10.6 shows the sphere with selected vertices. You can use any selection method to select the vertices.

At this point, with the selected vertices, you can apply any transforms such as move or rotate. You can do so using either the select and transform tools, or by right-clicking on any selected vertex and selecting the appropriate option from the resulting pop-up menu.

The Edit Vertex rollout is broken down into three separate areas: Weld, Affect Region, and Miscellaneous.

Figure 10.3

The Edit Mesh Edge rollout.

Figure 10.4

The Selection Level controls.

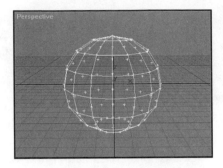

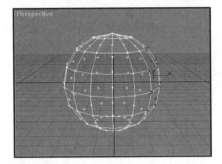

Weld

The Weld section of this rollout enables you to weld two vertices together into a single vertex. You can choose from two buttons here: Target and Selected. First, you must select the vertex that you want to weld to another vertex. Then you can choose the Target button and select the vertex to which you want to weld the selected vertex. If the vertices are within the weld threshold range, they are welded together. The weld threshold range specifies a sphere with a radius matching the range. If the two vertices lie together within that sphere, they are welded together. The default range is .001 unit.

Affect Region

The Affect Region section of the rollout enables you to affect a portion of the object when you move one or more vertices. Without Affect Region, only the vertices that you move are affected. Figure 10.7 shows a sphere with a vertex moved without using Affect Region. Figure 10.8 shows the same vertex moved with Affect Region.

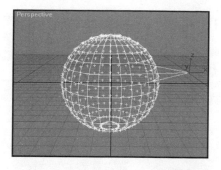

Figure 10.7

A vertex moved without Affect Region.

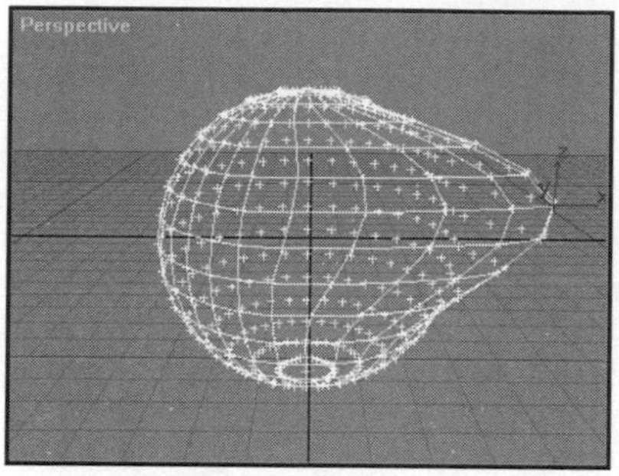

Figure 10.8

A vertex moved with Affect Region.

Choosing Affect Region enables the Ignore Backfacing check box. Ignore Backfacing tells MAX to ignore any faces in the affected region that are facing away from the viewport. The last option in this section of the rollout is the Edit Curve button. This button enables you to control how the affect region works on the object. When you choose this button, the Edit Affect Region Curve dialog box appears (see fig. 10.9).

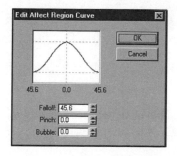

Figure 10.9

The Edit Affect Region Curve dialog box.

In the window of the Edit Affect Region Curve dialog box is a curve that is representative of the region that will be affected. Three values affect this curve: Falloff, Pinch, and Bubble. The Falloff determines the overall size of the region that is affected. The Pinch determines the shape of the curve and how it affects the region. The Bubble affects the curvature of the curve by making it more or less sloped.

The following exercise shows you an example of how to use Affect Region.

USING AFFECT REGION

1. Create a sphere with 32 segments at 0,0 with a radius of approximately 50 units.

2. Choose the Modify tab of the command panel.

3. Choose Edit Mesh.

4. Choose Select Objects.

5. In the Front viewport, click on the vertex that is farthest to the right on the equator of the sphere. Figure 10.10 shows this selection.

Figure 10.10

The sphere with the selected vertex.

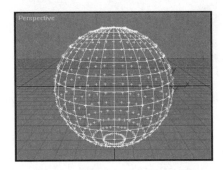

6. Turn on the Affect Region checkbox in the rollout. Turn off Ignore Backfacing.

7. Choose the Edit Curve button.

8. When the Edit Affect Region Curve dialog box appears, set the Falloff to 50. Set the Pinch to –2.0. Leave Bubble set at 0.

9. Choose OK to close the dialog box and return to MAX.

10. Choose Select and Move from the main toolbar.

11. In the Front viewport, click and drag the selected vertex to the right about 40 to 50 units. Figure 10.11 shows the resulting object, which is a pear in this case.

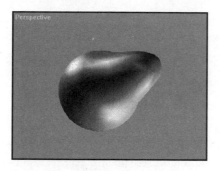

Figure 10.11

A pear created from an Affect Region move of a single vertex.

Miscellaneous

The last section of the Edit Vertex rollout contains some miscellaneous commands. Each is described in the following list:

▲ **Create**. This command enables you to create a vertex anywhere in space that is a part of this object. You create a vertex for use with the Build Face option, which is discussed later in this chapter.

▲ **Delete**. This command enables you to delete any selected vertex. When you delete a vertex, any faces that share the deleted vertex are also deleted.

▲ **Collapse**. This command enables you to collapse a group of selected vertices. When you do, all vertices collapse into a single vertex that is located in the center of all the selected vertices.

▲ **Detach**. This command enables you to detach any selected vertices into a separate object. If these vertices have faces attached to them, the faces are also detached.

▲ **Hide**. This command enables you to hide the selected vertices. When a vertex is hidden, you cannot edit it. This command does not affect any attached faces.

▲ **Unhide All**. This command unhides all hidden vertices so that you can edit them.

Faces

Face editing is probably the most powerful aspect of the Edit Mesh modifier. You can really control and manipulate the shape and form of the object using face editing. You apply face editing just like vertex editing, except that you choose the Face option from the Sub-Object drop-down list in the Modifier Stack.

Figure 10.12

The Selection rollout for Edit Face.

The Edit Mesh Face option has two separate rollouts: Edit Face and Edit Surface. Edit Face contains all the face-level editing commands, and Edit Surface contains commands related to surface normals and smoothing. These rollouts are covered in the following sections.

Edit Face

The Edit Face rollout is made up of five sections: Selection, Extrusion, Tessellation, Explode, and Miscellaneous. The Selection rollout is shown in figure 10.12.

As you do when editing vertices, you must select the faces on the selected object before you can edit them. In the Selection rollout, you can control how you select the faces. Three buttons control what you select with the Select Objects commands. The first button is Face, which selects an individual face. The second button is Polygon, which selects all coplanar faces. The last button is Element. If you attach any objects, the attached objects become elements of the larger object. You can select the whole element in one click by using this option.

The By Vertex checkbox to the right of the selection buttons sets the selection to work only off a vertex. With this option turned off, for example, you can click on the face or anywhere inside the face. With By Vertex turned on, you must click on a vertex of the face to select it. Finally, you have a planar threshold. This threshold determines whether a set of faces forms a coplanar polygon.

The Extrusion section of the Edit Face rollout enables you to extrude the selected faces, much like you would with the Extrude modifier. All you have to do is select the faces, click on the Extrude button, and then define a height for the extrusion in the Amount spinner field.

You use the Tessellation section of the rollout to increase the complexity of the selected faces by subdividing the faces into smaller ones. The two radio buttons in the Tessellation section determine the method that you use to create the tessellated faces. The Tension value determines how much tension is in the tessellated faces. Positive values cause a convex effect as the vertices are pushed outward. Negative values result in a concave effect.

You use the Explode section of the rollout to detach the selected faces into one or more smaller objects. The Angle Threshold determines which faces are split into separate objects. Any two faces that are a greater angle apart than the threshold value are split into two different objects. Lastly, you can choose whether the face is exploded into objects or into elements by choosing the appropriate radio button.

The last part of the Edit Faces rollout is the Miscellaneous section. Each of the buttons is described in the following list:

▲ **Detach**. This command detaches the selected faces into a separate object.

▲ **Collapse**. This command collapses the selected faces by welding all their vertices into a central vertex.

▲ **Make Planar**. This command makes the selected faces coplanar.

▲ **Build Face**. This command enables you to build a face by choosing points on existing vertices of the same object.

▲ **Delete**. This command deletes the selected faces.

▲ **Hide**. This command hides the selected faces so that you cannot edit them.

▲ **Unhide All**. This command unhides all hidden faces.

Edit Surface

The Edit Surface rollout is made up of three sections: Material, Smoothing Groups, and Normals. The Material section is intended for use on objects that have a multi/sub-object material assigned to them. Each different set of faces in the object that is going to have a different material must have its own material ID. You use the spinner field to change the material ID of the selected faces. The Select by ID button enables you to select the faces in an object that have a specific material ID. Choosing this button opens the Select By Material ID dialog box shown in figure 10.13.

In this dialog box, you can choose the material ID. The checkbox titled Clear Selection tells MAX to deselect all faces before selecting faces by their material ID. When you choose OK, the selection is made.

In the Smoothing Groups section of the Edit Surface rollout, you can assign smoothing for use during rendering. If an object such as a sphere does not have smoothing applied to it, the object renders faceted, like a diamond or other type of jewel. You can choose to assign a specific smoothing group to an object, or you can choose the Auto Smooth button. If you choose Auto Smooth, you have to use the Threshold spinner to define the angle between faces where smoothing will occur. If two faces are greater than the threshold value apart, they render faceted. As you can with the Material ID option, you can also select faces based on their smoothing group assignment by choosing the Select By Smooth Group button. Figure 10.14 shows the Select by Smooth Groups dialog box that appears when you choose this button.

Figure 10.13

The Select By Material ID dialog box.

Figure 10.14

The Select by Smooth Groups dialog box.

This dialog box uses the smoothing group number that is currently selected in the rollout to select the faces. You also can choose the Clear Selection check box.

The last section of the Edit Surface rollout is the Normals section. Here, you can control the direction of the surface normal of a face. Remember, the surface normal determines which side of the face is up. When you're rendering, the assigned material appears only on the normal side of the face. The Show Normals option is very important when you import geometry from other programs such as AutoCAD or Microstation. Many times, the geometry imported from these programs has flipped surface normals because AutoCAD and Microstation are not required to keep track of surface normals.

The Show Normals checkbox forces a blue line that changes color to white to appear in the center of all selected faces. The white end of the blue line represents the direction that the surface normal is pointing. Figure 10.15 shows the pear object with all the surface normals showing.

Figure 10.15

The pear with surface normals showing.

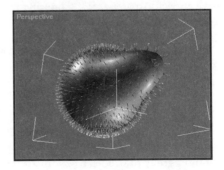

The Flip button in the Normals section reverses the directions of the surface normals on all selected faces. The Unify button forces all normals in a selection set to point in the same direction. You can use the Scale spinner to determine how large the white and blue surface normal line appears when the surface normals are showing.

The following exercise shows you how to use the Edit Mesh Face option to perform some general editing on a sphere.

USING EDIT MESH FACE

1. Create a sphere at 0,0 with a radius of 50.

2. Choose the Modify tab of the command panel.

3. Choose Edit Mesh.

4. Choose Face from the Sub-Object drop-down list.

5. With the polygon selection type chosen, click on a face to select the face and any associated faces.

6. Choose the Extrude button in the rollout and set the Amount spinner to 20. Figure 10.16 shows the resulting object.

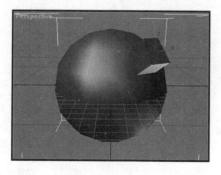

Figure 10.16

A sphere with an extruded face.

7. Choose the Undo button from the main toolbar.

8. In the Normals section of the Edit Mesh rollout, choose the Show Normals checkbox.

9. Switch your perspective view to a shaded view with highlights. You then see the selected face's surface normals appear.

10. Choose Flip in the Normals section. The normals are flipped, and the surface appears to disappear (see fig. 10.17.) The surface is there, just facing away from you.

Figure 10.17

The sphere with a flipped normal face.

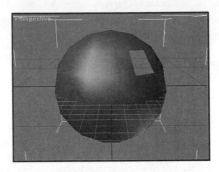

11. Choose Undo to remove the flipped surface.

12. Select all the faces on the right half of the sphere using a crossing window selection set. Figure 10.18 shows the selection set.

Figure 10.18

The correct selected faces on the sphere.

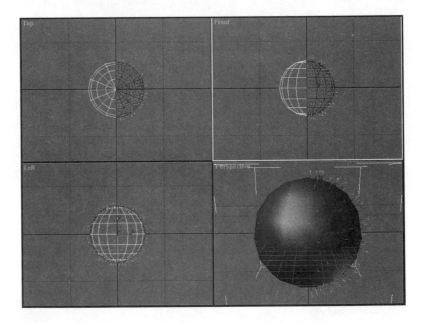

13. Choose Make Planer from the Miscellaneous section of the rollout. Figure 10.19 shows the resulting object.

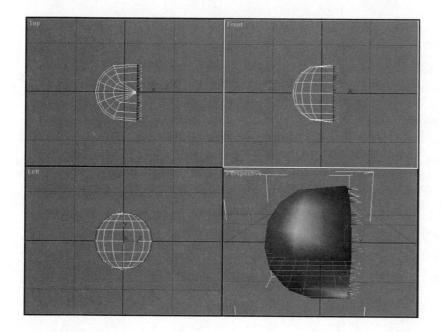

Figure 10.19

The sphere with planar faces.

Edges

As you can do with vertex and face, you can also edit objects at the edge level. An *edge* is defined as the side of a face or the shared line between two faces. You can apply edge-level editing like vertex- or face-level editing by simply choosing the Edge Sub-Object option from the Sub-Object drop-down list in the Edit Mesh Rollout.

The Edge rollout is made up of three basic areas: Extrude, Visibility, and Miscellaneous. The Extrude options work just like they do in the Face rollout, with one exception. The face is extruded perpendicular to the face normal. The edge is extruded in the world Z axis.

Visibility affects whether you can see an edge. Many times, you do not want to see an edge, simply to make the geometry easier to read. This section contains three buttons: Visible, Invisible, and Auto Edge. Visible and Invisible simply make the selected edge or edges visible or invisible. With Auto Edge, on the other hand, you have to use the Angle Threshold spinner to determine the maximum angle between two faces. If the angle between two faces is less than the threshold, the shared edge is made invisible.

Tip

> If you import geometry from AutoCAD or Microstation, all edges show by default. Select all the edges in the scene and apply an Auto Edge with a threshold of 1 degree. Doing so makes all coplanar faces have invisible edges and cleans up the drawing considerably. This change has no affect on rendering, only redraw speeds.

Each of the Miscellaneous buttons is described in the following list:

▲ **Divide**. When this button is turned on, you can click on any edge in the selected object. The edge is divided into two edges at the point you select.

▲ **Turn**. This button rotates the selected edge 90 degrees.

▲ **Delete**. This button deletes the selected edge.

▲ **Collapse**. This button deletes the selected edge and welds the edge endpoints together.

The following exercise shows you how to use the Edit Mesh Edge option.

USING EDIT MESH EDGE

1. Create a cone at 0,0.

2. Click on the Modify tab of the command panel.

3. Choose Edit Mesh.

4. Choose Edge from the Sub-Object drop-down list.

5. Select an edge using Select Objects.

6. Click on the Invisible button. The edge disappears. The faces are still correctly oriented and act as a solid surface, but you cannot see the shared edge.

7. Choose the Divide button and click on another edge. The surface is divided at that edge.

Attach Object

The last option of Edit Mesh is the ability to attach one object to another to form a larger object. The smaller objects become elements of the larger objects. You accomplish this task by first selecting the object to which you want to attach another object. Then choose Edit

Mesh in the command panel. Make sure that the Sub-Object button is turned off, and the Edit Object rollout appears (see fig. 10.20). Then choose the Attach button and select all the objects that you want to attach to the selected object.

Figure 10.20

The Edit Object rollout.

Edit Mesh is a powerful tool for editing objects at a variety of levels. It is extremely useful when you're dealing with imported files from AutoCAD or Microstation. You should learn and explore this modifier by creating objects and modifying them using this modifier. Do this because the Edit Mesh modifier is one of the most important modifiers you will use.

Edit Patch

The Edit Patch modifier is designed to work with the Quad and Tri Patch Bézier surfaces that you can create. Additionally, when you apply an Edit Patch modifier to an object such as a sphere, that object automatically is converted to a patch surface.

A *patch surface* is a Bézier surface that is controlled by a structured lattice. As you adjust the lattice, the underlying geometry is adjusted. Figures 10.21 and 10.22 show a patch sphere and its lattice, respectively.

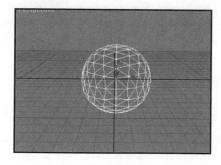

Figure 10.21

A patch sphere.

Figure 10.22

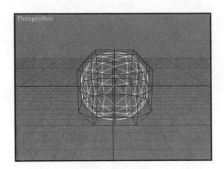

The control lattice for a patch sphere.

You can edit a patch object at four levels: Vertex, Edge, Patch, and Edit Object. Like the Edit Mesh modifier, these commands are accessed by selecting an object and applying the Edit Patch modifier. When you do, the mesh is converted to a patch, and you have the option of choosing the level within which you want to edit the patch surface.

Vertex

When you select an object and apply the Edit Patch modifier, the command panel rollout changes to that shown in figure 10.23. Note that the Vertex sub-object is the default level at which you can edit the object.

When the Edit Patch modifier is applied to an object, a lattice appears, and yellow boxes appear on the lattice to represent the vertices of the lattice. You can edit these vertices using any of the standard transform tools.

Additionally, you can choose certain points on the mesh itself where you can edit vertices. A sphere, for example, has six points on the patch surface where you can choose a vertex to edit. The number and location of the patch surface vertices vary from object type to object type. When you choose a vertex to edit, a series of four green control vertices appear (see fig. 10.24). These green vertices represent vectors for controlling the direction of the surface. You can also apply transform to the green vertices.

The green control vectors on the patch surface have two special transform options. If you right-click on the intersection point of the green vectors, you see a slightly different pop-up menu than the standard object transform pop-up menu shown earlier in the book (see fig. 10.25).

Figure 10.23

The Edit Vertex rollout.

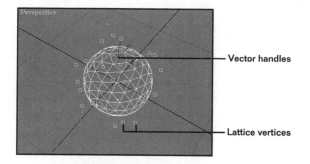

Vector handles

Lattice vertices

Figure 10.24

A patch surface vector with lattice vertices.

Figure 10.25

The Edit Patch Vector pop-up menu.

Two special options are located at the bottom of this menu: Coplanar and Corner. When you choose Coplanar, if you move one of the four green control vertices and vectors, the other three move in relation to the first. When you choose Corner, the selected green vertex and vector move independently of the other three. Figures 10.26 and 10.27 show this difference.

Editing a patch using transforms alone is a fairly powerful process. But you can also use the three sets of tools found under the Edit Vertex rollout: Topology, Display, and Filter.

Under the Topology section, you can control how you can edit the patch vertices. The Lock Handles checkbox enables you to edit the green control vertices while maintaining the tangents between them. The Weld button welds any selected vertices together, provided that they exist within the weld threshold distance. Lastly, you can delete any patch vertices by choosing the Delete button.

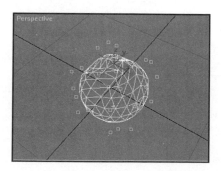

Figure 10.26

An edited sphere using Coplanar.

Figure 10.27

An edited sphere using Corner.

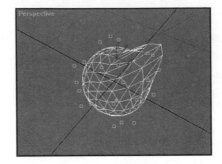

Warning

> Be careful using the Delete button under the Edit Vertex section of the Edit Patch rollout. If you choose this button, you delete a control point and, hence, any patches using that control point. You may end up deleting a lot more of the patch than you expect.

The Display options of the Edit Vertex rollout enable you to control the display of the lattice or the patch. Often, it is nice to turn off the patch and edit the lattice, or vice versa.

In the Filter section of the rollout, you have two sets of filters: Vertices and Vectors. When these boxes are checked, you can edit these types of patch controls. But if you uncheck one or both, you can no longer edit that control type.

The following exercise shows you how to use vertex-level patch editing.

Using Edit Patch Vertex

1. Create a sphere with a radius of 50 at 0,0 in the Top Viewport.

2. Choose the Modify tab of the command panel.

3. Choose Edit Patch.

4. Choose Select and Move.

5. Click on any yellow vertex and move it to a new position.

6. Choose Undo.

7. Move the mouse cursor over the front of the sphere in the Perspective viewport until you see the cross cursor. Click to select the patch surface control points. Four green vertices appear.

8. In the Display section of the Edit Vertex rollout, turn off the Lattice check box.

9. Choose Select and Move from the main toolbar, and click on one of the green vertices. Move the vertex to a new location. Notice how the other three green vertices act.

10. Choose Undo.

11. Right-click on the intersection of the green vertices.

12. When the Edit Patch Vector pop-up menu appears, choose Corner.

13. Repeat step 9. Notice how the other green vertices react now.

14. Choose the Delete button under the Topology section of the Edit Vertex rollout. Because you're working with a sphere, four patches share the same control point. When you delete them, you are left with a hemisphere.

Edge

When you're edge editing a patch, you're working with the edges of the control lattice, not the patch surface itself. When you choose the Edge option from the Sub-Object drop-down list in the command panel, the Edit Edge rollout appears (see fig. 10.28).

You can select any editable edge by clicking on it. The selected edge turns red. Not all edges in the lattice are editable. You can determine which ones are editable by watching your mouse cursor as you move it over the lattice. When it turns into a crosshairs, you are over an edge that you can edit. Figure 10.29 shows a lattice with a selected edge.

Figure 10.28

The Edit Edge rollout.

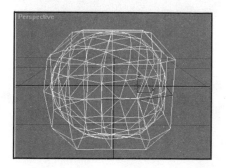

Figure 10.29

The lattice with a selected edge.

After you select an edge, you can apply any transform to that edge, as usual. When you do, the underlying patch surface is adjusted. Edge editing affects a much larger area of the patch surface than does vertex editing.

The Edit Edge rollout contains three sections: Subdivision, Add Patch, and Display.

The Subdivision section enables you to control the complexity of the patch object. A more complex patch provides you with finer control over the surface. The Propagate button determines how large an area the Subdivide button affects. When the option is active, the Subdivide button affects all adjoining patch surfaces in the object. Otherwise, the Subdivide button affects only the patch surfaces that are controlled by the currently selected edge. Figures 10.30 and 10.31 show the difference between a propagated subdivide and one that is not.

Figure 10.30

A sphere subdivided with Propagate turned on.

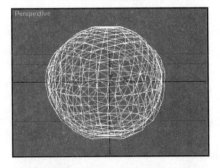

Figure 10.31

A sphere subdivided with Propagate turned off.

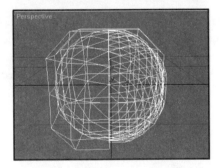

The Add Patch section of the Edit Edge rollout enables you to add either a Tri or a Quad patch to the selected edge. The Display section enables you to view or hide the lattice and surface.

Patch

Patch objects are composed of combinations of patch surfaces. When you edit an object at a patch level, you can select the section of the lattice that controls one of the patch surfaces. Figure 10.32 shows a selected patch level surface.

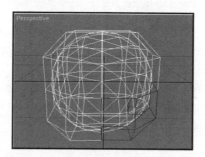

Figure 10.32

A lattice selected with patch-level editing.

As you can do with a vertex and edge, you can right-click on the selected section of the lattice and apply any transform to the selected area. But when you do right-click, the resulting pop-up menu has two additional options worth mention (see fig. 10.33).

Figure 10.33

The Edit Patch at a Patch Level pop-up menu.

The two new options are Auto Interior and Manual Interior. These options define how the lattice can be transformed. When you activate Manual Interior, the center of the selected lattice area does not transform, but the rest of the selected area does. When you activate Auto Interior, the complete selected area of the lattice is transformed.

Choosing the Patch sub-object option displays the Edit Patch rollout in the command panel (see fig. 10.34). Under the Edit Patch rollout are three sections. Two of these sections, Display and Subdivision, are the same as the ones mentioned earlier. The other section, Topology, deserves a little more attention.

Under the Topology section, you can choose the Detach button to detach the currently selected patch surface into a separate patch object. The Reorient and Copy buttons affect how the patch surface is detached. When reorient is active, the detached surface is moved to the origin, and its normal is reoriented to the angle of the current construction plane. When Copy is active, a copy of the selected surface is created as a separate patch object. Lastly, the Delete button enables you to delete the selected patch object.

Edit Object

The last option of the Edit Patch modifier occurs when no sub-object levels are selected in the command panel. In this case, the Edit Object rollout appears, as shown in figure 10.35.

Figure 10.34

The Edit Patch rollout.

Figure 10.35

The Edit Object rollout.

Two sections appear in this rollout. The first, Display, is the same as the Display sections in other rollouts. In the second section, Topology, you can increase the number of steps for the patch surface by setting the Steps spinner. Increasing the number of steps increases the complexity of every surface in the patch object.

Lastly, you can attach another patch object to the currently selected object by choosing the Attach button. The Reorient checkbox forces the attached patch object to reorient its normal to the current construction plane at the origin.

The Edit Patch modifier is a powerful method for editing Bézier patch surfaces. If you work a lot with Bézier patch surfaces, such as Tri or Quad patches, you should learn how to use this modifier as well. Additionally, if you want to convert a mesh to patch, simply apply this modifier with no options, and it will convert the selected mesh.

Edit Spline

You use the Edit Spline modifier to edit any 2D spline object. It is not available unless a 2D spline object is selected. When one is selected, the Edit Spline rollout appears, as shown in figure 10.36.

You can edit a 2D spline at four different levels: Vertex, Segment, Spline, and Edit Object. These editing levels are covered in the following sections.

Vertex

If you choose the Sub-Object button in the command panel and then select Vertex from the Sub-Object drop-down list, the Edit Vertex rollout appears (see fig. 10.37). When you choose the Vertex option, the vertices of the selected 2D spline appear as small white crosses on the screen. A single vertex is marked with a white box, which indicates the position of the first or start vertex of the spline.

At this point, you can click on any vertex. The vertex turns red to indicate that it has been selected. Then you can apply any transform you want to the vertex. Also, if you right-click on the vertex, a pop-up menu appears (see fig. 10.38). Four new options in this menu affect how the spline enters and leaves the selected vertex.

Each of the new pop-up menu options is described in the following list:

Figure 10.36

The Edit Spline rollout.

Figure 10.37

The Edit Vertex rollout.

Figure 10.38

The Edit Spline Vertex pop-up menu.

▲ **Smooth**. If you choose this option, the spline around the selected vertex becomes a smooth curved spline instead of a corner.

▲ **Corner**. This option converts the splines around the selected vertex to straight lines.

▲ **Bézier**. If you choose this option, the splines around the vertex are converted to curved splines, and a line with two green handles appears to enable you to adjust the curvature of the splines as they enter and leave the vertex (see fig. 10.39). You can adjust these handles using any standard transform technique.

▲ **Bézier Corner**. A Bézier corner is similar to a Bézier vertex, but you can adjust the handles of the curvature adjustment line independently of each other by choosing this option. When you move one handle in a Bézier vertex, the other handle moves as well.

Figure 10.39

The Bézier vertex handles.

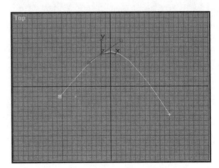

These four commands correspond to the same corner types that are available when you create a 2D spline. These commands enable you to adjust or change any corner type of any 2D spline at any time.

The Edit Vertex rollout contains several options. Each is described in the following list:

▲ **Connect**. This button enables you to connect to vertices with a straight line segment. When you choose this button, you click on the first vertex and drag to the second vertex. When the mouse cursor is over the second vertex, the cursor changes to two parallel lines to indicate that you want to connect these vertices. When you let go of the mouse button, the line is created.

▲ **Break**. This button enables you to break a vertex in the middle of a line. When you do, the vertex becomes two coincident vertices. This process has the same effect as breaking the spline into two. This option does not affect start and endpoint vertices.

▲ **Refine**. This button enables you to place a vertex anywhere in the spline without changing the shape of the spline.

▲ **Insert**. This button enables you to place a vertex anywhere in the selected spline and then reposition that vertex in a new location. After you place the first vertex, you can keep placing vertices. To get out of the command, you must right-click.

▲ **Make First**. This button enables you to make a selected endpoint the first vertex of the line. The endpoint must be selected before you can use this option. This option does not work with vertices in the middle of splines, or on closed splines.

▲ **Weld**. This button enables you to weld two coincident vertices together into one. Both vertices must reside within the weld threshold distance of each other.

▲ **Delete**. This button enables you to delete a vertex. When you do, all segments that intersect the vertex are deleted as well.

▲ **Lock Handles**. If this checkbox is turned on, when you select two or more vertices at the same time that have smoothing applied to them, such as a Bézier curve vertex, two green handles appear. If you transform one of the handles with the Lock Handles check box turned off, it transforms independently. With Lock Handles turned on and the Alike radio button chosen, the same handle on each selected vertex is transformed equally. With the All radio button chosen, all vertex handles change when you are transforming one vertex handle.

The following exercise shows you how to use Edit Spline Vertex to edit an existing 2D spline.

USING EDIT SPLINE VERTEX

1. Load the file CH10A.MAX from the accompanying CD-ROM.

2. Select the 2D spline.

3. Click on the Modify tab of the command panel.

4. Choose Edit Spline. Make sure that Vertex is chosen in the Sub-Object drop-down list.

5. Click on the center vertex in the Top viewport to select it.

6. Right-click on the vertex and choose Smooth from the resulting pop-up menu. Figure 10.40 shows the resulting spline.

Figure 10.40

*The vertex using a
smooth corner.*

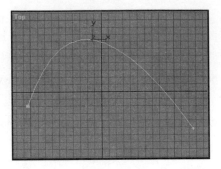

7. Choose Undo.

8. Right-click on the vertex and choose Bézier for the corner type from the resulting pop-up menu. The handles appear with green vertices.

9. Choose Select and Move, and click on one of the green vertices and move it around. Notice how the other vertex reacts.

10. Choose Undo until you are back to the original spline.

11. Right-click and choose Bézier Curve from the pop-up menu this time.

12. Again, choose Select and Move, and move one of the vertices. Notice that both vertices react.

13. Turn off Lock Handles in the Edit Vertex rollout.

14. Move one of the vertices again. Notice that it is now independent.

15. Choose the Connect button from the Edit Vertex rollout.

16. Click on one endpoint and drag to the other endpoint. A line forms to close the shape.

Segment

As you can do with vertex, you can also edit splines at the segment level. A *segment* is defined as a spline between two vertices. All 2D splines have at least one segment. You can edit splines at the segment level by choosing Segment from the Sub-Object drop-down list in the command panel. The Edit Segment rollout then appears, as shown in figure 10.41.

The four options for editing a spline at the segment level are described in the following list:

▲ **Break**. This button enables you to split a spline into two separate splines by adding a vertex at the point you click on the spline.

▲ **Refine**. This button enables you to add a vertex to a spline without breaking the spline into two.

▲ **Detach**. This button enables you to detach a spline segment into a separate segment. You must first select the segment you want to detach Also, you can choose to reorient or copy the segment, much like you can a detached patch surface.

▲ **Delete.** This button enables you to delete the currently selected segment.

Spline

As you can do with segment and vertex, you can also edit a spline at the spline level. If you choose Spline from the Sub-Object drop-down list in the command panel, the Edit Spline rollout appears, as shown in figure 10.42.

Figure 10.41

The Edit Segment rollout.

Figure 10.42

The Edit Spline rollout.

The Edit Spline rollout options are described in the following list:

▲ **Close**. This button enables you to close any open 2D splines by connecting the start and endpoints with a line segment.

▲ **Outline**. This button enables you to create a parallel version of the spline by specifying an outline width. When you choose the button, you can click on the spline and drag to create the outline, or simply select the spline and adjust the Outline Width spinner. The Center check box creates the outline using the original spline as the center. Otherwise, the outline is created above the original spline. Figure 10.43 shows a spline and an outline version of the spline.

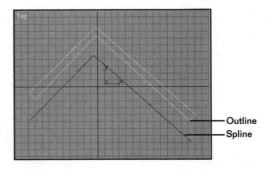

▲ **Boolean**. This button enables you to combine two separate closed splines into one of three combinations: Intersection, Union, and Subtraction. For this option to work, the two splines must be a part of the same shape. They cannot be two different shapes. Simply select the first shape and choose the Boolean type. Click on the Boolean button and then choose the second shape. The Boolean shape is immediately created.

▲ **Mirror**. This button enables you to mirror the currently selected spline. You can mirror horizontally, vertically, or both. The Copy checkbox enables you to make a copy of the spline as it is mirrored.

▲ **Detach**. As you can do with vertex and segment, you can detach a spline into a separate shape using this button. You can also reorient or copy the spline as you detach it by choosing either the Reorient or Copy checkboxes.

▲ **Delete**. This button enables you to delete the selected spline.

The following exercise shows you how to use spline-level editing.

USING EDIT SPLINE AT A SPLINE LEVEL

1. Load the file CH10B.MAX from the accompanying CD-ROM.

2. Select the shape. (All three circles are created as one shape.)

3. Choose the Modify tab of the command panel.

4. Click on Edit Spline.

5. Choose Spline as your editing level in the Sub-Object drop-down list.

6. Select the upper right circle by clicking on it.

7. Choose the Outline button in the Edit Spline rollout. Set the width to 10.

8. Select the large circle in the lower right.

9. Choose Boolean from the rollout and select Union as the type.

10. Click on the farthest left circle. The two circles are joined together.

11. Click on the Mirror button in the rollout. The shapes are mirrored horizontally.

12. Turn on the Copy checkbox and click Mirror again. A second version appears mirrored from the first.

Edit Object

Lastly, you can edit the spline at any object level. You can access this level by turning off Sub-Object in the command panel. Figure 10.44 shows the resulting Edit Object rollout.

As you can the other Edit Object modifiers mentioned in this chapter, you can attach a spline to the selected spline by choosing the Attach button. Additionally, you can choose the Create Line button as a shortcut to add more line segments to the existing spline without having to go back to the Create command panel.

Edit Spline is powerful for editing 2D shapes. Understanding how to use this modifier is necessary, especially if you work a lot with loft objects.

Figure 10.44

The Edit Object rollout.

Figure 10.45

*The Modify command
panel for Boolean
objects.*

Editing Boolean Objects

Editing Boolean objects at different levels only means one thing: you have the capability to edit the operands that you originally created the Boolean object from. Remember, the operands are the original objects. If you select a Boolean object, you can access the Boolean parameters for that object in the Modify command panel (see fig. 10.45).

Under the Display section of the rollout, you can turn on the display of the operands. Once you do this, all you have to do is turn on Sub-Object selection under the Modifier stack rollout. When you do, you may select and edit any operand of the Boolean object, as if it were a separate object. When you are finished, the Boolean object will be modified.

The following exercise briefly illustrates how easy this is:

MODIFYING A BOOLEAN OBJECT

1. Load the file CH10C.MAX from the accompanying CD.

2. Select the Object in the scene.

3. Click on the Modify command panel tab.

4. Select Operands under the display section of the rollout.

5. Click on Sub-Object under the Modifier Stack rollout.

6. Choose Select and Move.

7. Click on the smaller box and move it to a new position.

8. Click on Result button under Display to see the result of this move.

Summary

You use the three main modifiers—Edit Mesh, Edit Patch, and Edit Spline—to edit a variety of objects at different levels. Although using these modifier may be sometimes tedious, it is a very powerful method for creating some unique and interesting objects.

As you will see later in this book, some functions in MAX require you to have the ability to edit objects at different levels. To use a Multi/Sub-object material correctly, for example, you need to be able to edit an object at a face level to set up the material IDs for the Multi/Sub-object material.

Now that you have a good start with the modeling features of MAX, you're ready to move on to composition and rendering fundamentals. The next chapter shows you how to create lights and cameras so that you can illuminate and view your scene correctly.

PART *IV*

COMPOSITION AND RENDERING FUNDAMENTALS

Composition Basics: Lights and Cameras

When you are creating a scene in 3D Studio MAX, composing the scene is an important factor in expressing your intent. The composition of a scene consists of three items: Lights, Cameras, and Materials.

Composition is a fundamental key to a good rendering or animation. Good composition is a combination of creating the correct viewing position with the camera, adding correct lighting, and rendering it with the correct materials or special effects. By combining all these elements together, you create a scene that has a high impact on the viewer. If any element is incorrect, such as a light in the wrong place, the scene will have much less impact.

This chapter focuses on the five primary steps to correctly view and light a scene in MAX. These steps consist of the following:

▲ Viewing a scene

▲ Cameras in MAX

▲ Illumination

▲ Lighting in the Interactive Renderer

▲ Lights in MAX

Viewing a Scene

When you create a scene, the way you view the scene is critical to expressing the content of the scene to the viewer. You can view the scene from an orthographic or a perspective view. Obviously, an orthographic view is not as realistic as a perspective or camera view, and hence, detracts from the realism of the scene. In MAX, you can render any viewport—Front, Left, Right, Top, Bottom, Back, and User—except a Track View viewport (Track View is discussed in Chapter 18).

But these are all orthogonal viewports that, although they may express information, do not express the way your eyes view the world. Humans always see the world in a perspective view (in which depth of field is easy to determine because objects that are farther from the viewpoint are smaller than those that are closer).

MAX provides two types of perspective viewports: perspective and camera. There are several differences between a perspective view and a camera view. A *camera view* has an icon that appears in the scene and has controllable parameters, such as Field of View and lens lengths. A *perspective view* (see fig. 11.1) works just like an orthogonal view, except that you can adjust its Field of View, or width.

Figure 11.1

A Perspective viewport showing a perspective view of the model.

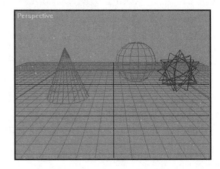

Using a perspective view to look at your scene is effective and realistic looking, but a camera view is much more powerful because you can control many other aspects that you cannot control in a perspective view. In the next section, you learn more about MAX's cameras.

Working with Cameras in MAX

MAX bases a camera view on principles involved in photography. For example, a 35mm camera uses different lenses to capture scenes at different sizes. Also, two points are always associated with a 35mm camera: the point where you are standing, holding the camera (called the *camera point*) and the point at which you are pointing the camera (called the *target point*). Using these connotations, you can create a camera view with precise view locations.

MAX provides two types of cameras that you can use to view a scene: target cameras and free cameras. You can access the camera creation commands by choosing the Camera button from the create types buttons under the Create command panel, thus displaying the camera rollouts shown in figure 11.2.

Figure 11.2

The Create Command panel for cameras where you can set the camera parameters.

Target Cameras

A target camera has both a camera point and a target point, each of which can be assigned a unique name to make them easily accessible and selectable. When both points are not hidden, they appear as an icon in all orthogonal views.

Figure 11.3 shows you a camera icon in the Top viewport. This icon is composed of three parts: the camera, the target, and the cone. The cone is present to show you how wide the field of view is for the camera. Both the camera and target points of the icon may be transformed by using any standard transform method, such as select and move.

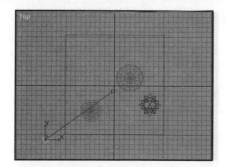

Figure 11.3

A Target Camera icon showing the different parts of a target camera.

To create a target camera, you first choose the Target button on the Cameras Create command panel. A rollout of all the target camera parameters appears, as shown in figure 11.4.

Figure 11.4

The Camera Parameters rollout where you can set the parameters for a camera.

Figure 11.5

The View pop-up menu with the Fundamentals 1 viewport showing.

Having chosen the Target button, all you have to do to create the camera is click at any point in any orthographic view to choose the camera location in any viewport and drag to place the target. After the icon is created, you can switch any view over to the camera view by right-clicking on any viewport, selecting the views fly-out from the pop-up menu, and choosing the camera name from this list. In figure 11.5, the name of the camera is Fundamentals 1.

Alternatively, when the camera viewport is active, you can switch the view to a camera view by pressing the C key. Some scenes may have more than one camera defined. If a camera is selected when the C key is pressed, the viewport will display the view from the selected camera. Otherwise, if no camera is selected, a list of cameras in the scene will appear for you to choose the camera from. Figure 11.6 shows you this list.

Because the camera and target of the camera icon are treated as standard objects in MAX, you can use standard transforms to precisely position the camera in 3D space, using the camera view as a guide.

When you create the camera, you have the option of controlling any of the camera parameters displayed in the rollout. Alternatively, you can change any of these parameters at any time by using the Modify command panel or the viewport control buttons (discussed later in this section).

When you create a camera you can control many of its parameters. Brief descriptions of these parameters follow:

▲ **Lens**. Enables you to control the length of the camera lens. Using this spinner, you can set lens lengths (accurate to three decimal places) from 0.001 up to any positive value you like. The higher the number, the greater the magnification in the lens view.

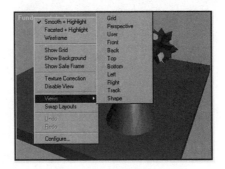

▲ **FOV.** Enables you to control the Field of View for the camera. This value is tied directly to the lens length. As the lens length gets longer, the field of view gets narrower, and vice versa.

▲ **Stock Lenses.** Enables you to choose predefined lens lengths and FOVs. These buttons correspond closely to the 35mm camera lenses you can purchase. By choosing one of these buttons you enter predefined values in both the Lens and FOV spinners.

▲ **Show Cone.** Enables you to show the FOV cone in all viewports except the camera viewport.

▲ **Show Horizon.** Enables you to view the horizon line for the camera position (see fig. 11.7). This feature is necessary for matching perspective on a photographic background. You can view the background in the viewport and match the horizon line to the horizon in the photo, thus ensuring that the scene's perspective is matched.

Figure 11.6

The Select Camera dialog box where you can select a camera when there is more than one camera in the scene.

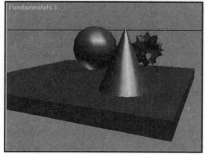

Figure 11.7

The horizon line in a camera viewport showing the horizon for the current view.

▲ **Environment Ranges.** Enables you to control where environmental effects, such as fog, start and stop. Fog and other environmental effects are based on distances from the camera. Use Near Range to define the start of the effect, and Far Range to define its end. (For more information, see Chapter 21, "Rendering Animations.") The Show button shows two spheres that represent the near and far ranges (see fig. 11.8). The near sphere is a flesh color; the far sphere, a dark brown. Environmental effects will occur only between these two spheres.

Figure 11.8

The environmental ranges spheres of a camera define where environmental effects can occur.

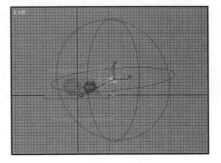

▲ **Clipping Planes**. Enables you to clip the scene at a set distance away from the camera. When you want to see inside some geometry, for example, you can set a clipping plane to cut that geometry. The Clip Manually button must be enabled for you to control the near and far clipping distances, which work very much like environment ranges. In the scene shown in figure 11.9, near clipping is on and the cone is clipped.

Figure 11.9

A clipped viewport showing how a camera can clip objects.

Warning

Due to the way the Interactive Renderer works, some camera viewports may appear to clip, even though you do not have camera clipping enabled. If this occurs, enable your camera clipping and set Near Clip to 0 and Far Clip to a value high enough to show all of the scene. Enabling this option overrides any clipping done by the Interactive Renderer.

An alternative way to adjust the camera viewport is to use the viewport control buttons. The camera viewport control buttons are available when the camera viewport is active (see fig. 11.10.)

Perspective ———— Roll camera
Dolly camera ———— Zoom Extents All
FOV ———— Min/Max toggle
Pan ———— Orbit camera

A brief description of each button follows:

Dolly Camera. Enables you to move the camera closer to or farther from the target without changing the field of view or lens length. Works by clicking and dragging vertically in the camera viewport.

Perspective. Enables you to change the distance between the camera and target without changing the location of the target. The FOV changes accordingly. Works by clicking and dragging vertically in the camera viewport.

Roll Camera. Enables you to rotate the camera around the axis of the cone. Works by clicking and dragging vertically in the camera viewport.

Zoom Extents All. Zooms out to the maximum extents of the scene in all viewports. Affects all views except camera view.

FOV. Enables you to change the field of vision without changing the location of the camera or the target. Works by clicking and dragging vertically.

Pan. Enables you to pan around the scene by clicking in the scene and dragging to a new location. The scene will pan relative to the two points you selected. Works in all viewports.

Orbit Camera. Enables you to change the position of the camera in 3D space by clicking and dragging in any direction in the camera viewport. The FOV does not change.

Min/Max Toggle. Enables you to maximize or minimize the current viewport. Selecting this button maximizes the current viewport so it takes up all of the screen. If a viewport is already full size, it reduces the viewport back to its original size.

The following exercise shows you how to create a camera and adjust some parameters.

CREATING AND USING A TARGET CAMERA

1. Load the file CH11A.MAX from the accompanying CD. (This file will be used for many of the exercises in this and the next three chapters.)

2. Click on the Camera button in the Create command panel.

3. Choose the Target button.

4. In the Top viewport, click at –120,–120, drag to 0,0 and let go. The camera is created on the current construction plane, in this case, the home grid. The camera icon appears as shown in figure 11.11.

Figure 11.11

The Camera as it is used in the scene.

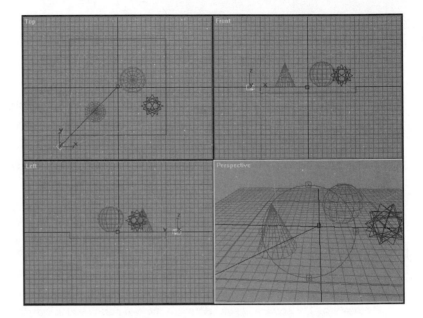

5. Right-click on the camera in the Front viewport. Choose Move from the list on the Object Transform pop-up menu.

6. Move the camera vertically 80 units.

7. Click on the Perspective viewport name to activate it.

8. Press the C key to change the Perspective viewport to the Camera viewport.

9. The perspective is a little close. Choose the Modify command panel tab.

10. Choose 35mm in the Stock Lenses section of the parameters rollout.

11. Switch the camera view to a shaded view by right-clicking on the viewport name and choosing Smooth + Highlights. Figure 11.12 shows you the camera view at this point.

12. Save the scene as CH11B.MAX for use in an exercise later in this chapter.

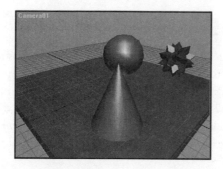

Figure 11.12

The shaded camera view showing the final view.

Free Cameras

A free camera is the same as a target camera, but with one difference—a free camera does not have a target. Free cameras are intended for use in animations in which the camera is attached to a motion path or a trajectory. (See Chapter 19 for more information about trajectories.) You can control the direction of the free camera by using any standard transform on the free camera icon. When you create and place a free camera, it appears perpendicular to the current construction plane and must be transformed to the correct position. Figure 11.13 shows you a free camera.

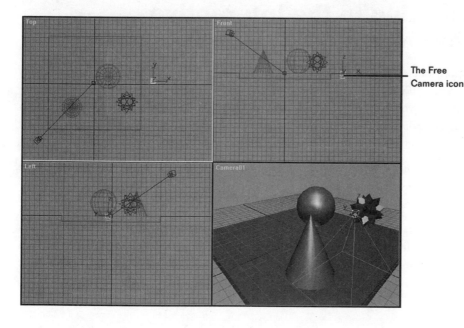

The Free Camera icon

Figure 11.13

The Free Camera icon appears perpendicular to the construction plane when it is placed.

Illuminating a Scene in MAX

Viewing a scene correctly is important, but not nearly as important as illuminating the scene correctly. *Illumination* is the process of lighting a scene accurately to match the lighting situation you are seeking. For example, interior architectural lighting is fairly complex and involves the use of many lights for special highlights. Without correct lighting, an architectural scene loses much of its realism and impact. Exterior architectural rendering, on the other hand is very easy to illuminate. All you need is one light that represents the sun.

The point is, illumination is probably the most important aspect of realism in a rendering. Without proper illumination, you cannot create a good rendering. The tools presented in the rest of this chapter should help you understand how to best illuminate your scenes. But to understand how to illuminate your scenes correctly, you need to analyze how lighting works in real life. And to do so you need one thing: experience. The more renderings you do, the more you will understand lighting and how it works in a scene. If your lighting is not quite correct at first, don't be discouraged. Keep working with the lighting until you get it right.

Lighting in the Interactive Renderer

Before looking at the types of lights available in MAX, a brief word about the interactive renderer. When you view a scene in shaded mode, lighting is approximated to give you a sense of what the final rendered scene will look like. MAX uses two default lights to illuminate objects in the interactive renderer until you create a light. When you create a light, the default lights are turned off and the scene is illuminated with the new light.

The scene shown in figure 11.14 is illuminated with default lighting in the interactive renderer. Figure 11.15 shows you a scene illuminated with a single spot light in the interactive render.

Just remember, the lighting in the interactive renderer is a preview, and only approximates the lighting in the final rendering. You should always render the scene to view the full effect of the lighting.

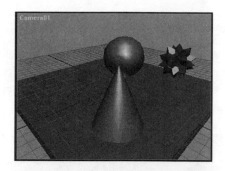

Figure 11.14

The handling of the default lighting in the interactive renderer.

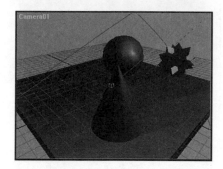

Figure 11.15

The handling of user-created lighting in the interactive renderer.

Lights

MAX provides you with the following five types of lights for illuminating a scene:

▲ Ambient

▲ Omni

▲ Directional

▲ Target Spot

▲ Free Spot

These light types are described next.

Ambient Lighting

Ambient lighting is a general, even illumination that occurs on every surface in the scene. The higher the ambient lighting, the brighter the surfaces become. You can access the ambient lighting controls by choosing Rendering, Environment from the pull-down menus. Figure 11.16 shows you this dialog box.

Figure 11.16

The Environment dialog box where you can set the ambient light levels for the scene.

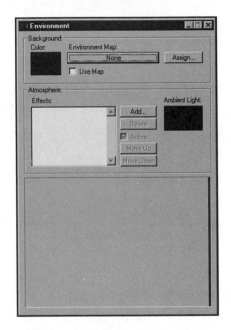

In the Atmosphere section of this dialog box, a dark color swatch represents the ambient light. You can control the intensity of the ambient light by clicking on this color swatch and then using the Color Selector: Ambient Light dialog box shown in figure 11.17.

Figure 11.17

The Color Selector: Ambient Light dialog box where you can select the color of the ambient lighting.

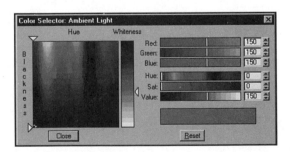

By sliding the Whiteness slider up and down, you can control the intensity of the ambient light. The scene shown in figure 11.18 was rendered with an ambient light setting of 11 (the default intensity). Figure 11.19 shows the same scene rendered with an ambient light setting of 150.

Figure 11.18

A scene with ambient lighting of 11, which is the default ambient lighting.

Figure 11.19

A scene with ambient lighting of 150, which considerably brightens up the surfaces in the scene.

Only under special circumstances will you need to adjust the ambient lighting. Generally, you can use the default setting of 11.

Omni Lights

An *omni light* is a special type of light that casts light from a single point equally in every direction. An omni cannot cast shadows and is used to provide general illumination for a scene.

To create an omni light, choose the Lights button on the Create command panel, then select the Omni button on the lights rollout shown in figure 11.20.

Figure 11.20

The Lights rollout where you can select the light type.

Then use the Omni lights rollout (see fig. 11.21) to place the omni light and adjust its parameters. The icon for an omni light is a simple pyramid. Be sure to give each light a name (as with all other objects in MAX). In this figure, the omni light is named Omni01.

Note

All the parameters discussed here are common to all light types in MAX. Refer to this section whenever you need to review information about light parameters.

The following descriptions of general lighting parameters apply not only to omni lights but also to the other light types:

▲ **On**. Enables you to turn the light on and off. When the light is off, it has no influence on the scene.

▲ **Exclude**. Enables you to exclude or include objects from the influence of a light. For example, if you want to add extra illumination to a single object in the scene, you can either include just that object or exclude all objects

Figure 11.21

The Omni Lights rollout where you can set the omni light parameters.

except the one you want to illuminate. When you choose this option, the Exclude/Include dialog box shown in figure 11.22 is displayed.

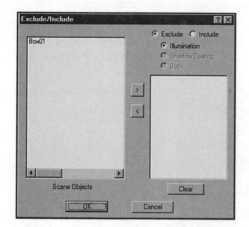

Figure 11.22

The Exclude/Include dialog box where you can define what objects in the scene are under the influence of the light.

At the top of the box, you can choose to exclude or include objects. The objects in the scene are in the list on the left; those in the list on the right are objects that are excluded or included. Because omni lights cannot cast shadows, the exclusion for shadow casting option is grayed out.

▲ **Color**. Enables you to control the color of the light. You access the color selector by clicking on the color swatch next to the On radio button. When you set the color of a light, that color directly affects the color of materials in the scene. (See Chapters 12, "Basic Materials" and 13, "Mapped Materials" for more information on materials.) You can set the color by using HSV or RGB methods of choosing colors. (Refer to Chapter 4, "3D Objects" for more information on color systems.)

▲ **Multiplier**. Enables you to define the overall strength of the light. Higher values make the light and all the surfaces it influences brighter.

▲ **Attenuation**. Enables you to control the distance from the light source at which the light still has effect. Most lights in real life lose intensity the farther away from the light source you get. Attenuation works just like the camera's environment ranges, with a start and end range. To enable attenuation, choose Use; choose Show to see the attenuation spheres.

Directional Lights

A *directional light* casts parallel light rays an infinite distance from a single point. (The sun is an example of a directional light.) A directional light, unlike an omni light, can cast shadows. You can create a directional light by choosing the Directional button from the Lights Create command panel. Figure 11.23 shows the directional light rollout.

Figure 11.23

The Directional Lights rollout where you can control the settings of the directional lights.

After you select the directional light option, you place the light by clicking anywhere in the scene. (The light is placed perpendicular to the view.) Then use standard transforms on the light to position it correctly.

Because a directional light has shadows, many parameters (in addition to the previously described general ones) are involved. Descriptions of these directional parameters follow:

▲ **Hotspot**. A defined area around the light in which the light is brightest and constant. A directional light casts parallel rays from this broad area.

▲ **Falloff**. A secondary area outside the hotspot, where the light falls off from brightest intensity to nothing. When the hotspot and falloff are close together, you get a crisp edge shadow. When they are far apart, you get a soft shadow.

▲ **Overshoot**. Forces the directional light to act as an omni light, but still cast shadows in the hotspot and falloff regions.

▲ **Circle/Rectangle**. Defines whether the hotspot and falloff areas are circular or rectangular. If rectangular, you can adjust the aspect ratio of the light to change the shape of the rectangle.

▲ **Projector**. Enables you to use the light as you would use a film projector. You can assign a bitmap to be projected. (See Chapter 23, "Special Effects Fundamentals" for more information on this feature.)

▲ **Cast Shadows**. Forces the light to cast shadows. By default this option is off. When the option is enabled, the light casts shadows by using either shadow maps or ray-traced shadows. (Turning on this option causes rendering to slow down dramatically.)

▲ **Shadow Maps**. Sets the shadow type to use shadow maps instead of ray-traced shadows. When this option is enabled, MAX generates a map of the shadow and uses it to render the shadow. Shadow maps render much faster than ray-traced maps, but are less accurate. Shadow maps have four options: Map Bias, Size, Sample (Smp) Range, and Absolute Map Bias. Map Bias determines how far beyond the shadow-casting object the shadow will appear. The default is 4. For crisp close shadows, set this option to 1. Map Size determines how large the shadow map is. The larger the map, the more accurate the shadow (but the more memory used by the shadow map). The Sample Range affects how much of the shadow map is averaged. This option directly affects the edge of the shadow, determining how soft it is. When the last option, Absolute Map Bias, is enabled, the shadow map bias is determined on an object-by-object basis; otherwise, it is based on the scene as a whole.

▲ **Ray-Traced Shadows**. Sets the shadow type to ray-traced shadows. A ray-traced shadow uses a computationally intensive technique, called *ray tracing*, to physically trace the edge of each shadow. This option is great for crisp, clean shadows and is very accurate. But ray-traced shadows dramatically increase rendering time. The only option for ray tracing is Ray Trace Bias. This option, like its shadow map counterpart, affects how far beyond the shadow-casting object the shadow will appear.

Now for a look at the two types of spotlight—target and free—available in MAX.

Note

Because both types of spotlight use the same parameters as a directional light, these parameters are not covered in the following sections. Refer to this section for a review, if you need to.

Target Spot

A *target spot* is similar to a directional light, except that the light rays are not parallel (rather, they originate from a single point) and a spotlight can make use of attenuation. You create a spotlight in much the same way you create a camera, by choosing a light point and dragging to a target point after you choose Target Spot from the Lights Create command panel shown in figure 11.24.

Figure 11.24

The Target Spot Light rollout where you can control the settings of a target spot light.

Target spotlights are commonly used for casting shadows in scenes, particularly interior scenes. Whenever you need a shadow-casting light, use either a free or a target spotlight, as they are the only light types that can cast shadows that are easily controllable. Distant lights should only be used in instances such as the sun.

Free Spot

A free spotlight is very much like a free camera. It has no target, but is exactly like a target spot in every other way.

The following exercise shows you how to use some of these light types to illuminate a simple scene.

ILLUMINATING A SCENE

1. Load the scene CH11B.MAX that you created earlier.

2. Choose the Lights button on the Create command panel.

3. Choose Target Spot.

4. Click at 0,–150 and drag to 0,0.

5. In the command panel, turn on Cast Shadows. Set the hotspot to 50 and the falloff to 90 to create a soft shadow.

6. In the front viewport, move the light vertically 100 units. When you do, MAX updates the interactive renderer display (see fig. 11.25).

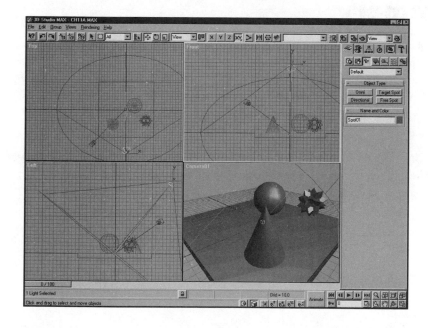

Figure 11.25

The scene with the correct spotlight.

7. Choose the Render Scene button from the main toolbar. (Rendering is covered in Chapter 14. Don't worry if you don't quite understand the next two or three steps.)

8. Click on the 640×480 button to set the rendering resolution.

9. Choose Render. (Figure 11.26 shows the rendered scene.)

10. Close the Render window when you finish viewing the rendering.

Figure 11.26

The rendering of the scene with correct lighting.

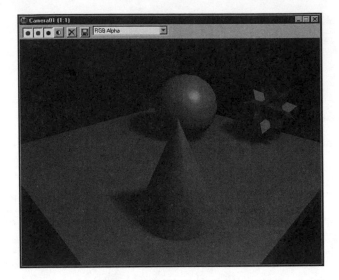

Summary

There are several components that must be executed well to produce a good scene in MAX. These components included viewing and lighting a scene. Without proper viewing (Cameras and Perspective Views), the scene might not look correct. Without proper lighting (Omni, Ambient, Distant, Spot, and/or Target Lights), the scene definitely will not look correct. The combination of these two items is critical to creating a realistic and powerful scene.

The next chapter introduces you to materials and how to create and assign them to an object. When you add materials, you have the last elements necessary for rendering still-frame images.

Basic Materials

Lighting and composition, discussed in Chapter 11, "Composition Basics: Lights and Cameras," are two important elements to rendering. The third important element is materials. By creating and assigning materials to surfaces in MAX, you can emulate real-world materials such as wood, steel, and plastic. And by applying such materials to your objects, you can add a great deal of realism to an otherwise artificial-looking scene.

This chapter explores the basic material capabilities in MAX. Chapter 14, "Advanced Materials," focuses on advanced materials in MAX. In particular, this chapter focuses on the following:

▲ The Material Editor interface

▲ The Material/Map Browser

▲ Standard materials

▲ Basic standard material parameters

▲ Extended standard material parameters

A *material* is a defined set of parameters that is assigned to a surface to give the surface a realistic quality when rendered using any of a number of rendering methods. In MAX, you can find two basic types of materials: standard and mapped. A standard material uses colors, shininess, and transparency values to define the material. A mapped material uses some sort of bitmap, such as a GIF or TIF file, and applies the map to the surface of the object in a variety of ways. A mapped material requires mapping coordinates to tell the renderer how to place the bitmap.

You can combine standard and mapped materials in hundreds of different ways to create just about any material that you can find in the real world. In MAX, you use the Material Editor to create and assign materials to objects.

The Material Editor Interface

The Material Editor is a powerful interface in MAX for creating and editing materials. You can access the Material Editor by clicking on the Material Editor button on the toolbar, or by choosing Edit, Material Editor. The Material Editor then appears, as shown in figure 12.1.

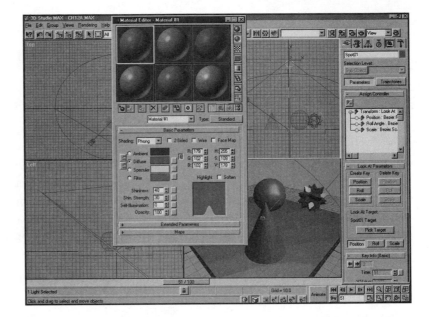

The Material Editor

The Material Editor is a single window broken down into three different areas: the sample windows, the Material Editor controls, and the Parameters rollout.

The sample windows provide you with previews of how the material is going to look when rendered in the scene. The Material Editor contains a total of six windows. The active window has a white border around it. When a material is assigned to an object in the scene, four white triangles appear in the corners of the sample window (see fig. 12.2). These triangles indicate that the material is now "hot." A hot material is instanced to the material assigned in the scene. In other words, when you change any parameters on a hot material in the Material Editor, the changes are automatically reflected in the scene.

Figure 12.2

A "hot" material is indicated by white triangles in the corners of the sample window.

If you want to work on a material without it being hot, you can click and drag the sample window and drop it on another window. The material is then copied to the new window. The original is still hot, and the copy is not.

The sample windows are surrounded by a series of buttons, as shown in figure 12.3. These buttons are the controls for the Material Editor.

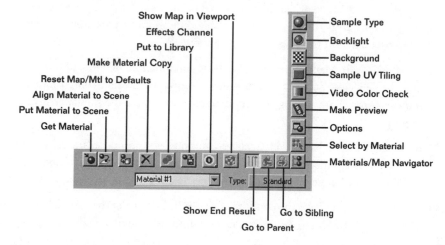

Figure 12.3

The Material Editor controls.

Each button is described in the following list:

Get Material. This button enables you to load a material or create a new material. Choosing this button displays the Material/Map Browser. (See the following section for an in-depth discussion of the Material/Map Browser.)

Put Material to Scene. This button enables you to update the definition of a material in the scene with the current material in the Material Editor or save a material definition to the scene.

Assign Material to Selection. This button enables you to assign the current material to all selected objects in the scene. Objects must be selected before you choose this button. Fortunately, you can select objects while the Material Editor is open.

Reset Map/Mtl to Default Settings. This button resets the current sample window to the default material settings.

Make Material Copy. Using this button, you can make a copy of a hot material. The copy is placed in the current sample window. This capability is helpful if you don't want to use another sample window to work with the material.

Put to Library. This button saves the current material to a material library. You must then save this library to disk by using the Material/Map Browser.

Material Effects Channel. Using this button, you can assign the material to one of nine effects channels for use in the video post. (See Chapter 21, "Rendering Animations," for more information on the video post.)

Show Map in Viewport. This button enables you to show the current bitmap used in the material in the current shaded viewport. This method for working with mapping in MAX is powerful. This button is available only when you are working with the bitmap parameters of the map you want to show.

Show End Result. Many materials in MAX are combinations of standard and mapped materials. The Show End Result button always shows you the final composition in the sample window. Turning this option off enables you to see the submaterial you are currently working on.

Go to Parent. Materials in MAX can be combined to form other materials; in this system, a *parent* is a material composed of one or more other materials. Choosing this button takes you to the parent material when you are working on a sibling.

Go to Sibling. A *sibling* is the opposite of a parent. It is one of the materials a parent is composed of. Choosing this button takes you to the nearest sibling.

Materials/Map Navigator. This button enables you to view the Map Navigator (see fig. 12.4). Using the Map Navigator is a quick and easy way to find out which bitmaps are being used in the scene and what materials are defined in the scene.

Select by Material. This button enables you to select objects in the scene based on the material assigned to them. When you choose this button, a Select Entities dialog box appears, as shown in figure 12.5. All objects using the current material are highlighted in the list in the dialog box.

Options. This button enables you to set the options for the Material Editor. The resulting dialog box is shown in figure 12.6.

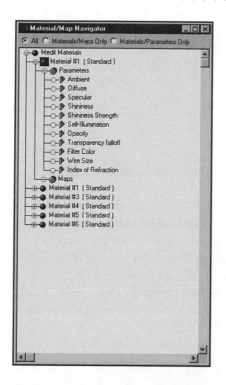

Figure 12.4

The Material/Map Navigator.

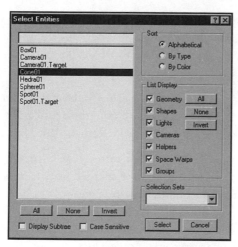

Figure 12.5

The Select Entities dialog box.

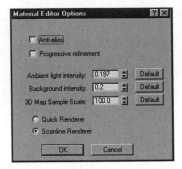

Figure 12.6

*The Material Editor
Options dialog box.*

The Anti-alias check box of the Material Editor Options dialog box forces the sample window preview to be anti-aliased. Anti-aliasing produces smooth edges but slows down the redraw of the sample window. The Progressive Refinement checkbox tells MAX to use this type of rendering algorithm to create the sample windows. Progressive Refinement gradually renders the sample until it is complete. This capability is handy on slow systems. The three spinner fields enable you to set the ambient light and background color intensities for the sample window, as well as the map sample size when you're using 3D maps such as bump maps. You also can choose how MAX renders the sample windows by selecting one of the two radio buttons. Scanline rendering is slowest but produces the highest quality preview. Quick is faster but not as high in quality.

 Make Preview. One type of material that you can create in MAX is an animated material. This button enables you to make a preview of the animated material so that you can see how it looks. This button also has two flyout buttons for viewing a preview that has already been made and for renaming a preview.

Video Color Check. This button checks the colors in the material versus NTSC and PAL video color standards. Any colors that are outside these standards are either flagged or corrected depending on the settings in the Preferences dialog box.

Sample UV Tiling. If you create a mapped material, the material may be copied repeatedly across the surface of the material. A mapped material uses a bitmap as its colors. Under some circumstances, this bitmap might need to be applied at a scale smaller than the object, resulting in tiled copies of the bitmap across the surface of the object. Sometimes this repeating of the bitmap in the material results in seams. This button enables you to see the material at various tiling ratios on the sample object.

Background. This button enables you to choose the type of background the sample window uses. The default is black, which is difficult to use with glass or transparent materials. The other option is a checkered background that appears when this button is enabled. Figure 12.7 shows the sample windows with a checkered background.

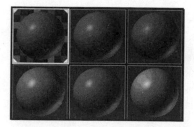

Figure 12.7

The checkered background sample window.

Backlight. This button places a light behind the sample object to give backlighting to the material. Backlighting makes the material easier to see in the sample window.

Sample Type. Using this button, you can choose the type of sample object. From the flyout that appears, you can simply choose the option you want. The three choices are sphere, cylinder, and box.

Below the Material Editor control buttons are the material name drop-down list and the Type button. Choosing the Type button also opens the Material/Map Browser.

Below the material name drop-down list are the three Parameter rollouts: Basic, Extended, and Maps. Depending on the type of material you are creating, you will use one or more of these rollouts to control that material.

The Material/Map Browser

You use the Material/Map Browser to load existing materials or bitmaps, or create new materials from a standard set of template materials. You can access this dialog box by choosing the Get Material button in the Material Editor (see fig. 12.8).

On the left side of the dialog box are the material browser controls. They are broken down into four different areas: Browse From, Method, File, and Show. On the right side of the dialog box is the browser window itself. It shows a list of materials and maps. Materials are listed with a blue dot and maps are listed with a green parallelogram.

The Browse From section of the dialog box lists five different ways that you can browse materials and maps. Each method is described in the following list:

▲ **Material Library**. This radio button enables you to browse maps and materials contained in the current material library. When you choose this option, the File section of the dialog box becomes available so that you can load and save libraries of materials. MAX saves materials definitions within each MAX scene. You use libraries to create predefined sets of materials that can be loaded into any scene and assigned to any object.

Figure 12.8

The Material/Map Browser.

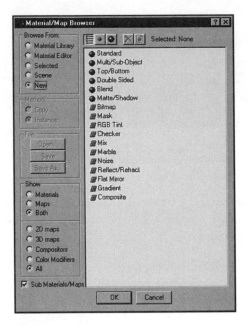

▲ **Material Editor.** This radio button enables you to browse maps and materials from the currently defined materials in the Material Editor. Only six materials are listed because the Material Editor has only six windows.

▲ **Selected.** This radio button enables you to browse maps and materials from all selected objects in the scene.

▲ **Scene.** This radio button enables you to browse maps and materials that are currently being used in the scene, regardless of where the materials are saved.

▲ **New.** This radio button enables you to browse the map and material templates that you can use to create new materials. Figure 12.8 shows this layout.

The Method section of the dialog box enables you to choose the method that MAX uses to place a material or map in a submaterial slot. Some materials are composed of smaller submaterials. You can elect to use instances or copies of a map or material in a submaterial.

The File section of the dialog box is used exclusively in conjunction with the Material Library radio button in the Browse From section. Here, you can open and save material libraries. A *material library* is a collection of parameters that defines materials. A material library may contain as many materials as you need. Material libraries are saved with a .MAT file extension.

The Show section of the dialog box determines what types of maps and materials show in the browser window. You can elect to show maps, materials, or both. When you are creating a new material, you can also choose the type of bitmaps that are available for use. You can choose only bitmaps that are 2D maps, for example, or bitmaps that are compositors. Below the Show section is a check box that enables the display of materials and submaterials and maps. Figure 12.9 shows an example of this type of display.

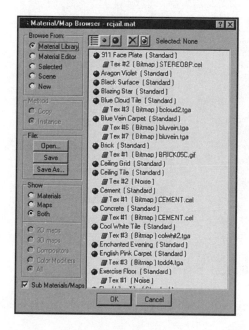

Figure 12.9

The Sub Materials/Maps Display.

At the top of the Material/Map Browser window is a set of buttons to control the display of materials. Each button is described in the following list:

▲ **View List**. This button enables the display of materials and maps as a list, as shown in figure 12.9.

▲ **View Small Icons**. This button enables the display of materials and maps as miniature spheres of the material.

▲ **View Large Icons**. This button enables the display of materials and maps as larger spheres that are easy to read. This view provides a great sample of what the materials look like. Figure 12.10 shows the list from 12.9 as large icons.

Figure 12.10

The material list as large icons.

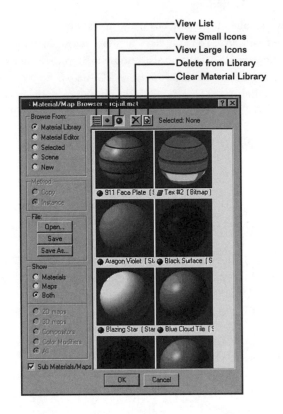

▲ **Delete from Library**. This button enables you to delete the currently selected material from the material library.

▲ **Clear Material Library**. Using this button, you can delete all materials from the current material library.

The Material/Map Browser is a key element to the creation and use of materials. As you explore and create new materials in this chapter and Chapter 14, "Advanced Materials," you get a lot of practice using this dialog box. Now, you're ready to look at materials and how to create and use them.

Standard Materials

A *standard material* does not use bitmaps and is not a combination of other materials. You use standard materials to create real-world materials such as paint, plastic, metal, and glass. These materials are simply a combination of colors, transparency, and reflectivity.

Two sections of the Material Editor enable you to create and control the parameters of a standard material: the Basic Parameters rollout and the Extended Parameters rollout.

Basic Parameters

When you open the Material Editor, the Basic Parameters rollout appears by default (see fig. 12.11).

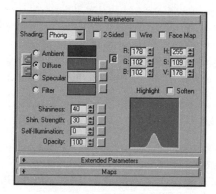

Figure 12.11

The Basic Parameters rollout.

A standard material is composed of many parameters that combine to form the material. Each of the basic parameters is described in the following list:

- ▲ **Shading**. Using this spinner, you can select the method that MAX uses to render the material. You have three choices: Constant, Phong, and Metal. Constant provides a flat shading. Phong provides materials, reflection, and so on. Metal provides a brighter highlight and deeper reflections. You can also select the rendering method when you render the scene.

- ▲ **2-Sided**. This checkbox enables you to render materials as two-sided materials. Glass should be two-sided, for example, because you can always see through the material to the other side. With 2-Sided turned on, when you render the scene, you can also select two-sided rendering so that you can see the material correctly on both sides of any face.

- ▲ **Wire**. This checkbox enables you to force MAX to render the objects with this material as a wireframe.

- ▲ **Face Map**. This checkbox enables you to force MAX to map the material to each face on the object to which the material is assigned. This option is generally used only with mapped materials.

- ▲ **Ambient**. This radio button enables you to define the color of the material when it is in shade and shadow. You can use the RGB and HSV color sliders to adjust the color. Alternatively, you can click on the color swatch to the right of the Ambient label.

Clicking on this swatch opens the standard MAX color selector in which you can also select the color. To the left of the Ambient radio button is a Lock button. You can lock the Ambient color to the diffuse color. If you do, when you change the ambient color, the diffuse changes as well.

▲ **Diffuse**. This radio button enables you to define the general overall color of the material. You can lock this color to the ambient, specular, or both colors. To the right of the Diffuse Color swatch is a blank button. Choosing this button opens the Material/ Map Browser. You can select a map to apply to the diffuse color if you like. (See Chapter 13, "Mapped Materials," for more information on this capability.)

▲ **Specular**. This radio button enables you to define the color of any specular highlights or bright spots on a material.

▲ **Filter**. This radio button enables you to define colors that are transmitted by the material. If you create a blue glass bottle and render it in a scene with a raytraced light, for example, the shadow of the glass is the color of the blue glass. Filter enables you to control how that shadow color looks.

▲ **Shininess**. Using this spinner, you can define how large the specular highlight is on the material. The larger the value, the smaller the highlight, and the shinier the material is.

▲ **Shin Strength**. Using this spinner, you can define how bright the specular highlight is on the material. Both shininess and shininess strength affect the bell-shaped curve to the right of the spinners. This highlight curve gives you a graphical representation of the two sliders. Again, you can apply maps to shininess and shininess strength.

▲ **Self-Illumination**. Using this spinner, you can define how bright a material is. Self-Illumination makes the material appear to have its own light source. A neon light, for example, makes a great self-illuminated material.

▲ **Opacity**. Using this spinner, you can define how transparent the material is. At 100, the material is opaque, or solid. At 0, it is completely transparent. Glass, for example, is somewhere between 5 and 50, depending on how dark you want it to be.

▲ **Soften**. This checkbox enables you to soften the highlight on a material. Softening makes the material look less bright.

The following exercise shows you how to create a standard material and assign it to an object in a scene.

CREATING AND USING A STANDARD MATERIAL

1. Load the file CH12A.MAX from the accompanying CD-ROM.

2. Click on the Camera viewport name to make it active, if it is not already active.

3. Change the shading mode in the Camera viewport to Smooth + Highlights.

4. Choose the Render View button from the main toolbar. The Render dialog box then appears.

5. Choose the 640×480 button under Output size.

6. Choose Render. Figure 12.12 shows the rendered scene. As you can see, no materials appear in this figure. The objects are rendered with their object colors.

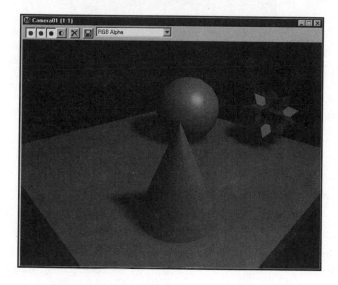

Figure 12.12

The rendered scene before any materials.

7. Close the render window after it is finished rendering.

8. Choose Select Objects from the main toolbar.

9. Click on the cone in the viewport to select it.

10. Choose the Material Editor button from the main toolbar.

11. In the Material Editor, click in the material name drop-down list and change the name of the current material from Material#1 to Cone.

12. In the Parameters rollout, set the shading method to Metal.

13. Click on the color swatch next to the Diffuse radio button.

14. Select a medium yellow from the Hue box. You can do this by clicking on the color you want.

15. Set the Shininess spinner to 60 and the Shininess Strength spinner to 100. Figure 12.13 shows the material at this point.

Figure 12.13

The cone material.

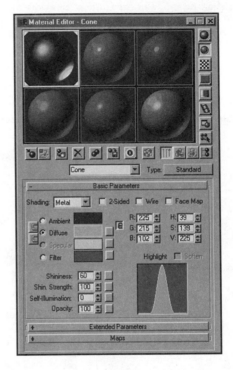

16. Choose the Assign Material to Selection button in the Material Editor to assign the material to the cone. In a shaded view, you should see the cone change to a shade of yellow.

17. Choose the Render Last button from the main toolbar. The scene is rerendered with the new material (see fig. 12.14).

18. Close the render window again.

19. Choose the Put to Library button in the Material Editor. A dialog box appears asking you the name for the material when it is saved into the current material library.

20. Choose OK to accept the name you gave it earlier and close the dialog box.

21. Choose the Get Material button to access the Material/Map Browser.

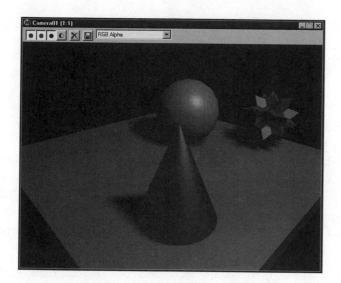

Figure 12.14

The cone rendered with the new material.

22. In the Material/Map Browser, choose Material Library in the Browse From section. You should see the Cone material listed. The material is now saved to the library, but the library has not yet been saved to disk.

23. Choose the Save As button in the File section.

24. In the File Save dialog box, name the material library **FUND.MAT**. Save the library someplace on your hard drive where you can access it again at a later time. Throughout the course of this book, you will add materials to the library.

25. Choose Save to save the file to disk.

26. Close the Material/Map Browser.

27. Choose Select Objects from the main toolbar. Select the sphere in the scene. Create a new material named **sphere** and assign it to the object. Save this material to the library.

28. Repeat step 27 for the ground and star objects. Experiment with some of the different material settings. Use Render Last to check the material on the object in the scene. Also, make sure that you save all materials to the library.

Extended Parameters

Beyond the basic parameters of a standard material are several extended parameters that affect how the material appears in your scenes. You can access these parameters by expanding the Extended Parameters rollout in the Material Editor. Figure 12.15 shows this rollout.

Figure 12.15

*The Extended
Parameters Rollout.*

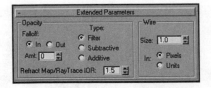

The extended material parameters affect two aspects of a material: opacity and wireframe. Under the Opacity section of the rollout, you can set three options: Falloff, Type, and Refraction IOR. The Falloff controls how a material's opacity is translated. You can choose two ways: In and Out. When Falloff is set to In, the transparency of the material increases toward the center of the object, like glass. When Falloff is set to Out, the transparency of the material increases toward the edge of the object, like clouds, smoke, or fog. The Amount slider determines how much transparency the object has at the outer or inner edge.

You can determine the colors of the transparent material in three ways by choosing one of the three radio buttons in this section. Because a material is transparent, colors of objects behind the transparent object show through, affecting the color of the transparent material. Filter uses the filter color assigned in the Basic Parameters rollout and multiplies it by the color of the material behind the transparent object. Subtractive subtracts the filter color from the colors behind the object. Additive adds those colors. Each radio button provides a slightly different effect for transparent materials.

The Refract Map/Raytrace IOR is the Index of Refraction. *Refraction* is the bending of light as it passes through a material such as glass or water. If you stick a pencil in a glass of water and look at it from the side, it looks broken. This appearance is a property of refraction. Some materials such as refraction mapped or transparent materials exhibit this effect. Using the spinner, you can enter the IOR for the material. Air has an IOR of 1, for example, and glass has an IOR of 1.5. The higher the number, the more refraction.

For the wire parameters, you can determine the size of the wires in the wireframe when you render an object with a material with wire turned on. You can set the size either in pixels or in units. Larger values result in larger wire sizes in the wireframe object.

The following exercise shows you how to use some of the extended material parameters to control a material.

USING EXTENDED MATERIAL PARAMETERS

1. Load the Material Editor.

2. Change the diffuse color to a light blue.

3. Turn on the Wire checkbox under the basic parameters.

4. Click on Extended Parameters to display this rollout.

5. Set the Wire Size to 4 pixels. Figure 12.16 shows you the material preview at this point.

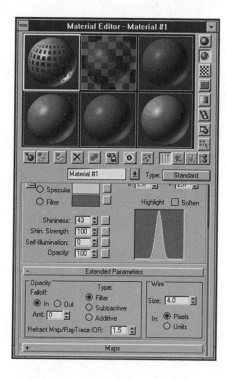

Figure 12.16

A wire material using thicker wires set under Extended Material parameters.

6. Click on the second sample material window to make it active.

7. Click on the Background button in the Material Editor to change the background of the sample window to checkered.

8. Set the opacity of the material to 55.

9. Under Extended parameters, set the type to Subtractive and watch the material preview.

10. Set the type to Additive and watch the material preview. Figure 12.17 shows you the three different opacity types.

Figure 12.17

Viewing the opacity types: Filter, Subtractive, and Additive.

Summary

Many little parameters can affect how a basic material looks and acts. Careful adjustment and application of these materials add a great deal of realism to your scene. Through the adjustment of the material parameters, you can create materials such as paint, metal, glass, and plastic. These materials can then be saved to material libraries so you do not have to recreate them.

While there are many options you have with basic materials, they are somewhat limited. Fortunately, in MAX you can create more materials by using mapped materials. Mapped materials are the subject of the next chapter.

Mapped Materials

By using the standard and extended material controls, you can create a broad spectrum of materials. But these materials are very limited in what you can create. Creating a surface such as marble, for example, is impossible using a standard material. To accomplish this task, you must use a different material type called a *mapped material*.

This chapter focuses on how to create and use mapped materials. In particular, this chapter focuses on the following topics:

▲ Creating a mapped material

▲ The Bitmap Material rollouts

▲ UVW mapping coordinates

▲ Mapping coordinate types

A mapped material uses a bitmap to apply any of a number of effects to the material. A *bitmap* is usually a scanned photograph of a real-world material. This bitmap is then mapped across the surface of the material in a variety of different ways, depending on the geometry and the effect you want.

Creating a Mapped Material

You can access the mapped material controls under the Maps rollout in the Material Editor. Figure 13.1 shows this rollout.

Figure 13.1

The Maps rollout.

You can apply a map to a material simply by clicking on the None button next to the map type that you want. This enables you to select a map type to apply to the material. For starters, this map will be called Tex #X where X is a number that is assigned to each bitmap as it is loaded. You will be able to change this name at any time. When you click on the button, a shortened version of the Material/Map Browser appears, as shown in figure 13.2.

Figure 13.2

The Bitmap Material/ Map Browser.

In this version of the Material/Map Browser, only bitmaps are listed. You can choose any of 11 different types of bitmaps for use in the mapped material. For the purposes of this chapter, only the Bitmap type is used. This type applies a standard bitmap to the mapped material. The others are discussed in Chapter 14, "Advanced Materials."

If you double-click on the bitmap icon in the browser list, you go back to the Material Editor, but it contains a new set of rollouts that enable you to load and control how the bitmap is used by the material. Figure 13.3 shows these rollouts.

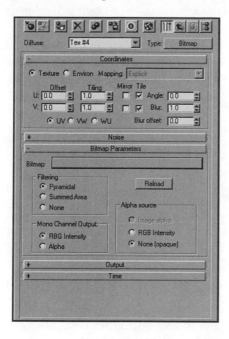

Figure 13.3

The Bitmap Material Control rollouts.

At this point, you are working with a submaterial (or sibling) of the material shown in the sample window. It is indicated in the material name drop-down list, which now reads Tex #4. This name indicates that this texture is the fourth one to be used. (The number simply indicates how many bitmaps have been used at one point or another in the material. It does not reflect that four bitmaps are currently being used.) You can access the basic parameters of the material again by either clicking on the drop-down list and choosing the name of the material (it will appear above the Tex #4) or choosing the Go To Parent button because you're using a sibling material.

The Bitmap Material Rollouts

After you choose the bitmap you are going to use in the material, the Material Editor displays five rollouts that you can use to control the bitmap and how it is translated: Coordinates, Noise, Bitmap Parameters, Output, and Time. These same five rollouts apply to any type of bitmap that is used as a material. These rollouts are discussed in the following sections.

The Coordinates Rollout

You use the Coordinates rollout of the Material Editor (refer to figure 13.3) to control how the bitmap is applied to the mapping coordinates. Mapping coordinates (discussed later in this chapter) tell MAX how to apply the material to the object in the scene, using any of a variety of methods. MAX applies the mapping coordinates using a mapping icon. Planar mapping, for example, uses a rectangle as its mapping icon. The rectangle represents one copy of the bitmap as it is applied to the surface. Figure 13.4 shows a planar mapping icon applied to an object. This icon is repeated across the surface of the object to apply the bitmap.

Figure 13.4

The planar mapping icon on an object.

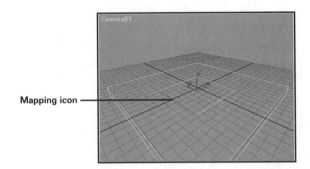

Mapping icon

You can choose from two types of coordinates: texture and environment. Texture coordinates are used in all types of materials. Environment coordinates are used only when the material is being used for environmental effects, such as a realistic backdrop. Environmental effects are discussed in Chapter 16, "Environmental Effects." Texture coordinates, on the other hand, are used for all materials that use any type of bitmap, and define how the bitmap is applied to the mapping icon. This capability provides you with two levels of control over bitmap scaling in mapped materials. You can control the scale at the mapping level by adjusting the icon or at a material level by adjusting the texture coordinates.

The first type of texture coordinates that you can control are the offset coordinates. Offset coordinates enable you to define the location of the bitmap within the mapping icon. They are defined as U and V (so that you don't confuse them with the world coordinates of X and Y). The offset values enable you to adjust where the bitmap appears in the mapping icon. When the values are set to 0,0, the bitmap appears in the lower-left corner of the icon. The tiling texture coordinates determine how many copies of a bitmap appear in the mapping icon. Figure 13.5 shows a material applied with tiling set to 1. Figure 13.6 shows the same material with tiling set to 4.

Figure 13.5

A material with tiling set to 1.

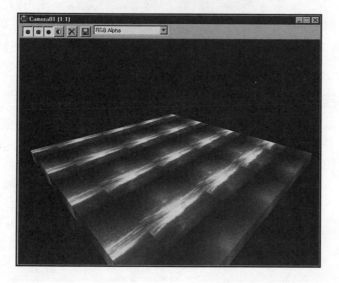

Figure 13.6

A material with tiling set to 4.

The Mirror option in the Coordinates rollout enables you to mirror the coordinates, which in turn mirrors the bitmap. You also have the option of enabling and disabling tiling by selecting the check boxes under Tile. On the right side of the rollout, you can control the rotate angle of the bitmap as well as the amount of blur. You can use the Blur spinner to make some unique blurry materials for special effects such as warping materials. Lastly, the blur offset enables you to blur the bitmap without regards to the distance from the viewpoint. Blur itself gives the bitmap a general blur. As you get farther away from the bitmap, it appears more and more blurry.

The bitmap coordinates are applied as UV, but in reality, you have UVW coordinates for mapping types such as box or shrink-wrap mapping. At the bottom of the Coordinates rollout, you can select which two of the three UVW coordinates you want to work with in the fields and spinners in this rollout.

The Noise Rollout

The Noise rollout of the Material Editor enables you to apply some "noise," or some imperfections, in the bitmap to make it look more realistic. If you use a bitmap of marble, for example, it may look too perfect in the rendering. Adding a little noise, however, makes it less perfect and more realistic. Figure 13.7 shows you a rendering of a bitmap applied to a surface with no noise. Figure 13.8 shows you the same figure with noise applied. The Noise rollout is shown in figure 13.9.

A 3DS map applied to a box with no noise.

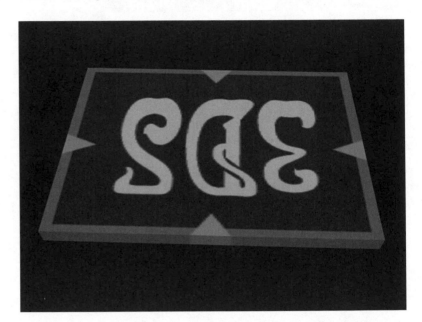

The six controls in the Noise rollout are described in the following list:

▲ **On**. This check box enables you to control whether noise is applied to the bitmap.

▲ **Amount**. Using this spinner, you can define how much noise appears in the bitmap. You can set it anywhere from 0 to 1, where 1 is full noise and 0 is no noise.

▲ **Levels**. Using this spinner, you can define how much fractal calculations are used in the noise. Fractals are a special form of mathematics that are good for modeling organic items.

▲ **Size**. This spinner enables you to define how large the noise is.

▲ **Animate**. This check box enables you to animate the noise over time.

▲ **Phase**. Using this spinner, you can control the speed of the noise animation.

Figure 13.8

A 3DS map applied to a box with noise.

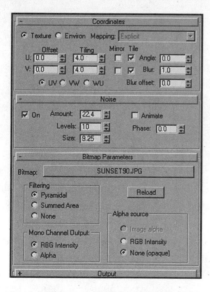

Figure 13.9

The Noise rollout in the Material Editor.

The Bitmap Parameters Rollout

Probably the most important bitmap rollout in the Material Editor is the Bitmap Parameters rollout, as shown in figure 13.10. In this rollout, you load the actual bitmap for use and set up any parameters for the use of this bitmap.

Figure 13.10

*The Bitmap Parameters
rollout.*

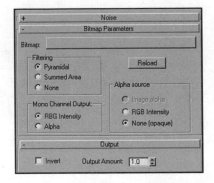

At the top of the rollout is a field titled Bitmap, with a long button to the right. This button enables you to load a bitmap into MAX. If you click on this button, the select bitmap image file dialog box appears (see fig. 13.11).

Figure 13.11

*You can select the
bitmap you are going to
use in the material in
the Select Bitmap
Image File dialog box.*

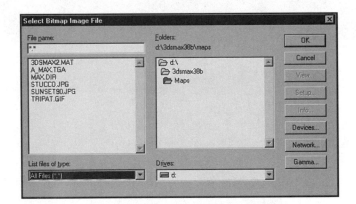

From this dialog box, you can load any of a variety of bitmaps for use in the material as any type of mapping such as diffuse or bump mapping. You can also load animated bitmaps for use as animated materials. When you load a file into MAX, it is loaded using the *universal naming convention* (UNC). This convention makes it easy to share bitmaps across the network. Say, for example, you have a machine named DARKSTAR on your network, and it contains all your map files in a directory called MAPS. Under UNC, this directory is referred to as \\DARKSTAR\MAPS. No drive letters are used because they can change with different drive mappings across the network. To select the bitmap file, simply navigate to the correct directory and double-click on the file, or select the file and choose OK. In either case, you will be returned to the bitmap rollouts and the name of the bitmap file will appear on the bitmap button.

Bitmaps must be located in a *bitmap map path* so that you can use them when you're rendering in MAX. You can define as many bitmap map paths as you like by choosing File,

Configure Paths and then choosing the Bitmaps tab in the Configure Paths dialog box (see fig. 13.12). You generally will define your bitmap paths right after you install MAX. You can, of course, change or add paths to your bitmap paths at any time when you are working with MAX. Any changes that you make will immediately take effect.

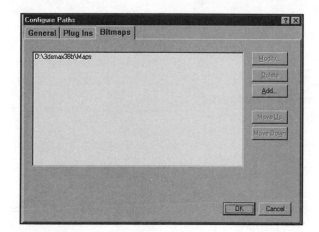

Figure 13.12

The Configure Paths dialog box.

By choosing the Add button, you can access a standard file open dialog box named Choose New Bitmap Path (see fig. 13.13). In this dialog box, all you have to do is navigate to the new directory and choose the Use Path button. At this point, you return to the Bitmaps tab of the Configure Paths dialog box.

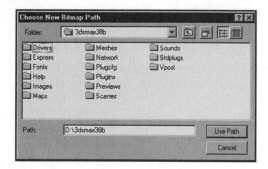

Figure 13.13

The Choose New Bitmap Path dialog box.

After you add your bitmap paths, you can choose OK in the Configure Paths dialog box to return to MAX. Now, the renderer can load the bitmaps correctly.

You can select the type of bitmap file to load by displaying the List Files of Type drop-down list in the lower left corner of the dialog box. This list, shown in figure 13.14, shows all the file types that you can load as a bitmap in MAX. After you choose the type of bitmap file you want, choose OK to close the Select Bitmap Image File dialog box and return to the Material Editor.

Figure 13.14

The List Files of Type drop-down list in the Select Bitmap Image File dialog box.

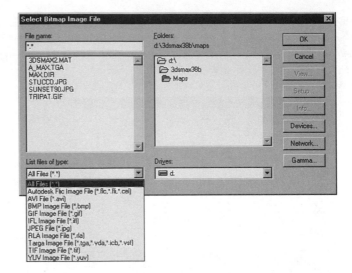

Below the Bitmap button in the Bitmap Parameters rollout are several bitmap parameters that you can control. They are divided into three categories: Filtering, Mono Channel Output, and Alpha Source.

In the Filtering section, you can select the method used to anti-alias the bitmap. Aliasing generally occurs on straight lines that are at an angle in the image, forcing a stair step look. *Anti-aliasing* is the process of smoothing out the stair step lines in an image by balancing the color of pixels near the aliased line. This results in a slightly blurrier image, but a much smoother one. In MAX, you have three choices here: Pyramidal, Summed Area, and None. These choices simply define three different ways of mathematically handling anti-aliasing. In general, Summed Area is the best, but it takes up four times more memory than Pyramidal. For most purposes, Pyramidal should be good enough. As always, you can choose none so you do not have any anti-aliasing of your bitmaps.

In the Mono Channel Output section, you can determine which color channels of the bitmap are used for certain mapping types. A bump map, for example, gives the surface of the material the appearance of 3D bumps. These bumps are created by using the monochrome output of a bitmap, where black is no bump and white is a bump. You can have the monochrome output of a bitmap determined from two sources: the RGB channels or the Alpha channel. Using the RGB channels is most common because the intensity of the RGB colors can easily be translated into the bump map values. Also, most maps that you will use will not have an alpha channel. This is because alpha channels are generated when an image is rendered. Most maps are scanned images, which cannot have an alpha channel. The Alpha option is used only with bitmaps that contain an alpha channel. An *Alpha channel* is an extra 8 bits of color that are used to determine different levels of transparency in a bitmap. Alpha channel images are, generally speaking, 32-bit color images instead of 24-bit.

Lastly, you can determine the Alpha source. Because some bitmaps do not have an Alpha channel, the transparency of the bitmap must be determined in other ways. You have three choices: Image Alpha, RGB Intensity, and None. None produces an opaque or solid bitmap with no transparency values. Image Alpha uses the top left pixel of the bitmap as the transparent color. RGB Intensity takes the monochrome output of the bitmap and assigns transparency based on that information. Black is completely transparent, and white is completely opaque.

Note

> At this point, you may be a little confused about Alpha and RGB Intensity and so on. In later chapters, such as Chapter 22, "Video Post," you will learn how to use an Alpha channel to composite two images together into one using an Alpha Compositor video post filter.

The Output Rollout

The next rollout in the Material Editor that enables you to control a bitmap in MAX is the Output rollout, as shown in figure 13.15. Here you can control how strong the bitmap is in the material.

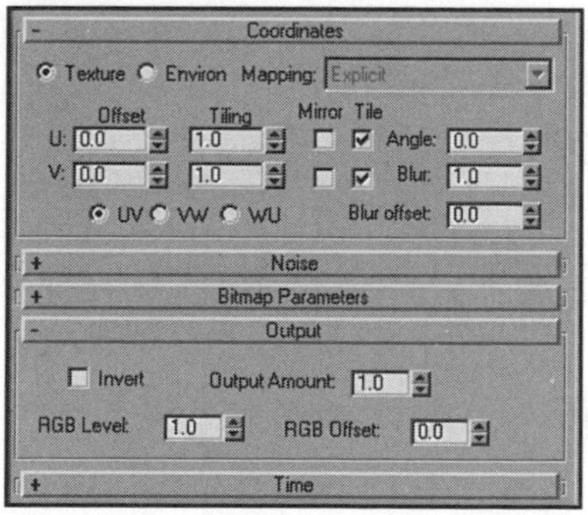

Figure 13.15

The Output rollout.

You can control four options here: Invert, Output Amount, RGB Level, and RGB Offset. Invert reverses the hues in the bitmap, giving the map the effect of being a negative. Output Amount controls how much of the bitmap is mixed in a composite material. (See Chapter 14 for more information on composite materials.) RGB Level controls how intense the hues of the bitmap are. Increasing this value increases the saturation of the colors in the bitmap, to the point where they become self-illuminated. Decreasing the value causes the colors to become more gray and dull. Using the RGB Offset spinner, you can adjust the colors in the bitmap. The number in the spinner is added to the RGB colors in the image; the higher the amount, the closer the bitmap comes to white.

The Time Rollout

As mentioned previously, you can use certain types of bitmaps, such as AVI or FLIC files, as animated bitmaps. You might create an animated bitmap material and apply it to the surface of a TV screen in your scene, to give the illusion that something is on TV. The Time rollout (see fig. 13.16) controls when and how MAX uses animated bitmaps in an animation.

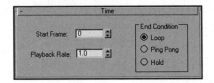

The time controls enable you to define how and when the animated file is played back in the material. First, you can define the start frame, in the Start spinner field. Then, you can define the playback speed. A value of 1.0 in the speed spinner field plays back the animation file at the speed which it was saved. Higher values play back faster and lower values slower. Lastly, you can define how to handle the animation file if it is shorter than the time segment in which it appears. You can either loop the file to make it play repeatedly, ping pong the file to make it play forwards, then backwards, or simply hold on the last frame.

As you can see, you can control many parameters of a bitmap that is used in a material. If you choose the Go To Parent button in the Material Editor, you can return to the main Material Editor rollouts. Here, you will see the Tex #4 bitmap appearing in the button next to the material map type that you chose earlier.

Map Types

MAX supports a variety of mapped material types, as shown earlier in figure 13.1. The following list describes these map types:

▲ **Ambient**. This option enables you to apply a map to the ambient color of a material. Generally, this setting is locked to the diffuse color and is not changed. If you change the ambient color of the material, you will tint the color of the bitmap, which might be something you do not intend to do. In fact, it is better to tint the color of the bitmap by either using a colored light or an RGB tint map that is discussed in Chapter 14.

▲ **Diffuse**. This option enables you to apply a map as the diffuse color. Remember, the diffuse color is the overall general color of the material. If you want a marble material, for example, you can apply a marble map as the diffuse color. Figure 13.17 shows an example.

Figure 13.17

A diffuse-mapped material showing how a map is applied to the surface to give the surface a sense of realism.

▲ **Specular**. This option enables you to apply a map to the specular highlight of a material. You do so to produce some randomness in the specular highlight. Figure 13.18 shows an example.

▲ **Shininess**. Using this option, you can apply a map to the shininess of an object. This option affects the colors of the shiny areas of the object. You can also use this setting to determine where the object is shiny and where it is not. Figure 13.19 shows an example.

▲ **Shin Strength**. This option enables you to apply a map to affect the strength of the shiny areas of the object. Figure 13.20 shows an example.

Figure 13.18

A specular-mapped material showing how a map is used to influence the specular highlights of the material.

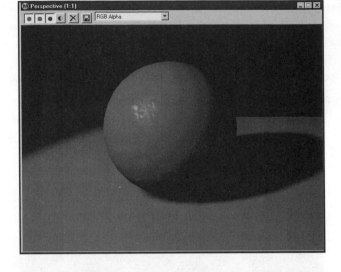

Figure 13.19

A shininess-mapped material showing how a map is used to disrupt the colors of the shiny areas of a shiny material.

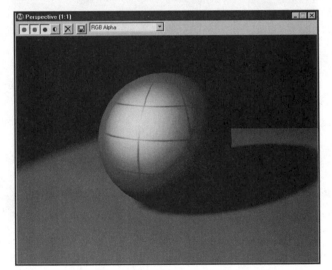

▲ **Self-Illumination**. Using this option, you can apply a map to control where an object is self-illuminated and where it is not. Figure 13.21 shows an example.

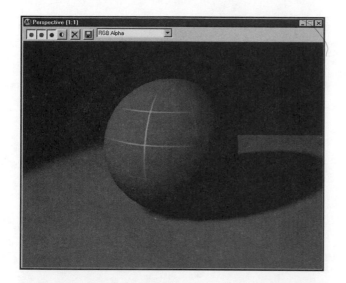

Figure 13.20

A shin strength-mapped material showing how a bitmap can be used to influence how strong the shiny areas are.

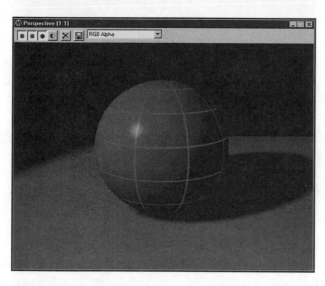

Figure 13.21

A self-illumination-mapped material showing how you can use a map to control where an object is self-illuminated.

▲ **Opacity**. Using this option, you can control where an object is opaque and where it is not. This option is very powerful for effects such as text on top of glass. Figure 13.22 shows an example.

Figure 13.22

An opacity-mapped material showing you how you can use a map to define opaque and transparent surfaces.

▲ **Filter Color**. This option enables you to apply a bitmap to change the colors of objects that appear behind transparent materials. The objects' colors are added to the bitmaps' colors. Figure 13.23 shows an example.

Figure 13.23

A filter color-mapped material shows you how you can use a map to change the color of objects behind a transparent material.

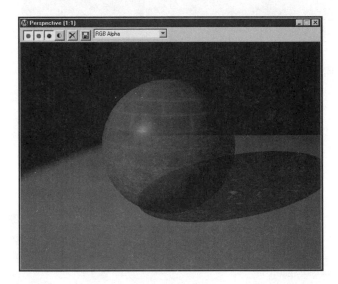

▲ **Bump**. This option enables you to apply a bitmap to give the illusion of a 3D surface on an object. Applying a brick map as a bump map, for example, gives the material the illusion of having 3D mortar joints, without your having to model them. Figure 13.24 shows an example.

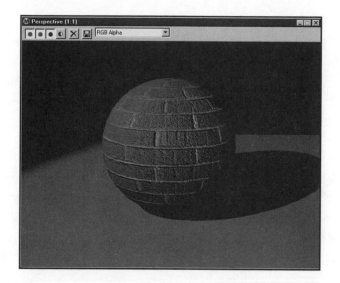

Figure 13.24

A bump-mapped material shows you how you can use a map to apply 3D surfacing to a material.

▲ **Reflection**. Using this option, you can apply a bitmap for use as a reflection on the surface of a material. You can also make use of automatic reflections if necessary. Figure 13.25 shows an example.

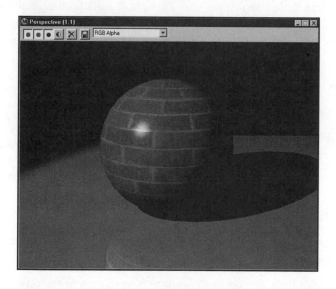

Figure 13.25

A reflection-mapped material shows you how you can use a map as a reflection on the surface of a material.

▲ **Refraction**. This option enables you to apply a bitmap to control the refraction of light in a transparent object. You must use this type of mapped material if you want to have a refractive effect. Figure 13.26 shows an example.

Figure 13.26

A refraction-mapped material shows you how you can use a map to create a refractive effect in transparent surfaces.

Each mapped material type has an on/off check box and an Amount spinner. You can combine as many of these mapping types as you like simply by defining the mapped material and turning it on. Using the Amount field, you can control how strong the mapped material type is. Reflection mapping, for example, is a subtle effect. It is usually applied in combination with a diffuse map to reflect the surrounding environment. Many times, its value is only around 10 or 20. At a strength of 100, it is like a mirror, and the diffuse map is lost.

The following exercise shows you how to create two types of mapped materials.

CREATING A DIFFUSE-MAPPED MATERIAL

1. Click on the Material Editor button on the main toolbar to open the Material Editor.

2. In the material name drop-down list, name the material **Fund2.**

3. Click on the Maps rollout to expand it.

4. Choose the None button to the right of the Diffuse option. The Material/Map Browser then appears.

5. In the Material/Map Browser, double-click on the Bitmap entry at the top of the list in the window. The Bitmap Parameters rollout then appears in the Material Editor.

6. Click on the long, blank button next to Bitmap.

7. Choose AGRAGATE.JPG from your \3DSMAX\MAPS directory.

8. Choose OK to close the Configure Paths dialog box and return to the Material Editor. The map is then loaded into MAX.

9. In the Material Editor, rename the texture from Tex #1 to Stones.

10. Choose the Go To Parent button. You can now assign the material to any object and save it to a material library.

CREATING A BUMP- AND DIFFUSE-MAPPED MATERIAL

1. In the Material Editor, click in the second sample window to make it active.

2. Repeat the first nine steps of "Creating a Diffuse-Mapped Material," but use file BRICKTAN.GIF from your \3DSMAX\MAPS directory instead.

3. Choose the Go To Parent button.

4. Because bump maps are generally the same as diffuse maps (so that the bumps match the diffuse pattern), you can easily create the bump map. An easy way to do this is to click on the diffuse map button that now reads BRICKTAN.GIF, and drag it down to the None button next to bump. A dialog box appears asking you if you want to make a copy, instance, or swap. Choose Copy and OK.

6. Using the Amount spinner next to Bump, set the bump strength to 225. You should now be able to see the effect of the bump map in the sample window.

7. In the material name drop-down list at the top of the Material Editor, rename the material to 3D Brick. You can now assign the material to any object or save it to a material library.

UVW Mapping Coordinates

Mapped materials are fairly powerful, but they are useless without mapping coordinates. *Mapping coordinates* tell MAX how to apply the bitmaps used in the material to the surface of the object. Mapping coordinates are applied based on the type of geometry you are using. You can apply seven types of mapping coordinates:

▲ Lofted

▲ Object Created

▲ Planar

▲ Spherical

▲ Box

▲ Cylindrical

▲ Shrink Wrap

You apply the first two, Lofted and Object Created, when you create the geometry. Back in Chapter 5, "Creating Lofted Objects," you had an option of applying mapping coordinates when you created the loft object. The same applies to any other type of geometry. Each type always has a generate mapping coordinate button somewhere in the rollouts to control the generation of mapping coordinates. You can opt to apply these types of coordinates or add your own coordinates at a later date.

Because the mapping coordinates are based on the geometry of the object, you must learn when you need to use what type of mapping coordinates. For example, when you map a material to a box, you can either use a box mapping type or a planar mapping type. Figure 13.27 shows the different mapping coordinates on their respective geometry types.

Figure 13.27

The different mapping types.

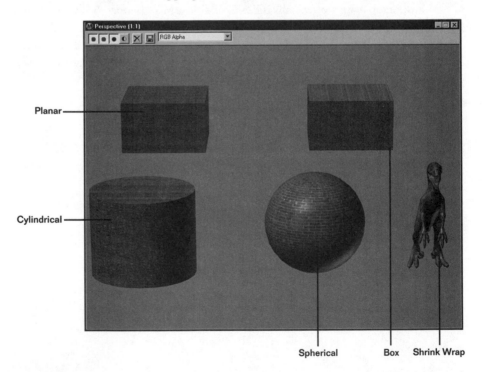

In this figure, two boxes are using two different types of mapping: planar and box mapping. As you can see, the planar mapping works on two of the six surfaces, whereas box works correctly on all six surfaces of the box. Which type of mapping is correct depends upon the scene that the object is being used in. Spherical mapping is generally used on any surface that is close to a sphere or hemisphere. Cylindrical is used on vertical curved surfaces. In instances where none of the previously mentioned mapping types work, shrink wrap mapping can be used. Shrink wrapping is very effective for organic shapes such as human, or in the case of figure 13.27, dinosaur figures. Only experience will help you determine which mapping coordinates are right for a given object. Until then, you have to experiment with the different mapping types using the information in this chapter as a guide.

You can apply mapping coordinates to any geometry simply by selecting the geometry and then applying a UVW Mapping modifier. Figure 13.28 shows the UVW Mapping modifier rollout in the Modify command panel.

The mapping controls are broken down into two sections: Mapping Types and Alignment. Each of the mapping types are discussed in the following list:

▲ **Planar**. This type of mapping applies the bitmap as a flat plane across the surface of the object (refer again to figure 13.27). As you can see, the map is planar, so when a face is perpendicular to the mapping coordinates, the map is severely stretched. To avoid the stretching, you can rotate the mapping icon into 3D space so that no surface of the object is perpendicular. Generally, you use planar mapping only on flat planar surfaces, but you can use it on any object.

▲ **Spherical**. This type of mapping is used to apply bitmaps to spheres or heavily curved objects. Figure 13.27 shows an example of spherical mapping applied to a sphere.

▲ **Box**. This type of mapping is applied to a rectangular three-dimensional box. If you use planar mapping, you always see some sort of stretching along one or more faces. Box mapping applies planar mapping equally to each of the six sides of the box.

▲ **Cylindrical**. This type of mapping is applied to a cylinder or other such object. You could use spherical mapping, but the caps on a cylinder are never mapped correctly, and the map appears stretched along the length of the cylinder. With cylindrical mapping, you avoid these problems.

▲ **Shrink wrap**. This type of coordinate mapping is kind of a catchall of mapping coordinates. You use shrink wrap on surfaces that are organic in form and do not work well with the other types of mapping. Figure 13.27 shows a raptor dinosaur that uses shrink wrap mapping. This type of mapping coordinate is powerful for mapping human, animal, and plant surfaces that are organic in form.

Figure 13.28

The UVW Mapping rollout.

The Alignment controls define where the mapping icon appears. The alignment controls are described in the following list:

▲ **Fit**. This button forces the mapping icon to fit the size and shape of the selected object.

▲ **Center**. This button centers the mapping icon in the center of the selected object or group of objects.

▲ **Bitmap Fit**. Using this button, you can force the aspect ratio of the mapping icon to match that of the bitmap being mapped. This eliminates stretching and warping in the bitmap. When you choose this button, a dialog box appears, enabling you to select the bitmap from which you want to take the aspect ratio. Generally, it is the same bitmap you are using in the material.

▲ **Normal Align**. This button aligns the mapping icon with the normal of the selected object or face.

▲ **Reset**. Using this button, you can reset the mapping icon to its original position and scale.

▲ **Acquire**. This button retrieves the mapping icon from an object that already has mapping applied to it. This capability is handy for copying mapping coordinates from one object to another.

All mapping coordinates are applied through the use of a mapping icon. The mapping icon is also called a *gizmo* and can be adjusted at a subobject level. When you apply a UVW Mapping modifier, under the Modifier Stack rollout, you can access the gizmo subobject. When you activate it, the gizmo turns bright yellow. After you have activated it, you can apply any standard transform to adjust the location, scale, and orientation of the mapping icon. This procedure is commonly used to control mapping.

You can make this process easier on yourself by isolating the object you are working on and hiding all others. Then switch your viewport over to a shaded view. When you are creating the material and are working with the bitmap, you should be able to choose the Show Bitmap in Viewport button in the Material Editor. You get an interactive textured view of the map on the object. Then, as you adjust the mapping icon, you can see the effect instantly.

For each type of mapping coordinates, you can also control the scale by setting the tiling in the Mapping section of the Parameters rollout. The tiling here is similar to the tiling in the Material Editor. Both cause more or less than one copy of the bitmap to appear in the area of the mapping icon. You can have more than one copy of the bitmap on the surface of the object if the mapping icon is smaller than the object. You can have less than one copy of the bitmap on the surface when the mapping icon is larger than the object it is mapped to. Part of the bitmap will always be cropped in this instance. You can also flip the bitmap here.

Note

The UVW Mapping modifier should be the last modifier you apply in the stack. Say, for example, you apply a UVW mapping modifier to an object. Then you come back later and use Edit Mesh to attach an object to the existing object. The newly attached object will not have the UVW mapping coordinates because it exists higher up in the stack.

The following exercise shows you how to apply mapping coordinates and a material to an object.

USING PLANAR MAPPING

1. Load the file CH13A.MAX.

2. Select the ground object.

3. Choose the Material Editor button from the main toolbar.

4. In the Material Editor, create a diffuse-mapped marble material. Turn on Show Map in Viewport button in the Materials Editor when you are creating the material.

5. Apply the marble material to the ground by choosing Apply Material to Selected Objects in the Materials Editor.

6. Choose the Modify tab of the command panel.

7. In the Modify Command panel, choose UVW Mapping to apply mapping coordinates to the ground.

8. In the Alignment section of the Parameters rollout, choose Bitmap Fit. Select the marble bitmap you used in the material in step 5.

9. Set your Top viewport to a shaded mode.

10. Choose Sub-Object from the Modifier Stack rollout above the UVW Modifier rollout.

11. Choose Select and Scale from the main toolbar.

12. In the Top viewport, click and drag on the yellow gizmo icon. You should be able to see the map scale up and down. Adjust the scale until you are comfortable with the object. The mapping and materials are now applied.

Summary

Mapped materials are powerful tools for adding realism to a rendering or animation. By using any of a variety of different mapped material types such as bump-mapped, diffuse-mapped, or even reflection-mapped, you can create photo-realistic scenes that match real world materials and effects. You are encouraged at this point to explore using different materials in different types of scenes to see how they work or affect the overall quality of the scene. For example, you could apply a diffuse- and bump-mapped brick material to a wall to add a high degree of realism. Or, you could use a specular-mapped material to give the surface of a shiny object the illusion that it is not perfectly flat.

But, for these images to become even more powerful, however, you can combine mapped and basic materials in various ways to create a whole slew of new materials. MAX provides you with five new material types that help you accomplish this. These new material types are the focus of the next chapter.

Advanced Materials

Basic and mapped materials provide you with a lot of power and flexibility. But MAX does not stop there. You can create many different combinations of the basic and mapped materials to create any material you could possibly ever want. MAX makes this easy by providing you with five complex material templates that you can use to combine basic and mapped materials with.

This chapter introduces you to these combination materials, as well as some advanced map types. In particular, this chapter explores the following types of complex materials:

▲ Multi/Sub-Object materials

▲ Top/bottom materials

▲ Double-sided materials

▲ Blend materials

▲ Matte/shadow materials

If you recall from Chapter 13, "Mapped Materials," you work with mapped materials in the Maps rollout section of the Material Editor. By clicking on the None button next to the mapped material type you want, you display a shortened version of the Material/Map Browser. It is from this browser that the Bitmap type is examined in Chapter 13, "Mapped Materials." For more complex maps, however, you need to consider the other map types in the Material/Map Browser.

Material Maps Other than Bitmaps

In the preceding chapter, you learned how to apply a bitmap as a mapped material for use in bump, diffuse, or other such mapped material. MAX provides you with 10 other map types that you can use instead of a standard bitmap. You can access these map types when you choose the None button next to the map type in the Maps rollout in the Material Editor. This is the same as creating a normal mapped material, but you choose a different type rather than the bitmap type that you used in the last chapter. The shortened Material/Map Browser then appears (see fig. 14.1).

Figure 14.1

The Material/Map Browser.

In all the cases in Chapter 13, "Mapped Materials," you chose Bitmap from the top of the window on the left side of the Material/Map Browser. In this chapter, you look at other options.

Mask

The Mask material enables you to block a section of one material with another. If you want to have text on a box but do not want to model the text, for example, you could create a bitmap of the text and then use it as a mask to mask out the underlying material. When you choose this option, the Mask Parameters rollout appears in the Material Editor, as shown in figure 14.2.

Figure 14.2

The Mask Parameters rollout, where you can choose the map to be used as the mask.

Here, you can choose the map to use as the mask or the map. The mask is the bitmap that blocks part or all of the map. The mask process uses the strengths of the colors in the bitmap to determine translucency.

When you choose the None button for either Mask or Map, you again go to the Material/ Map Browser. Here, you can again choose any type of map you like. So, you can effectively nest mask maps inside of mask maps if you want to. More than likely, you will probably go ahead and choose the bitmap type here. Then you can just set up the bitmap as you would normally. When you are done, you end up with a material something like the one shown in figure 14.3.

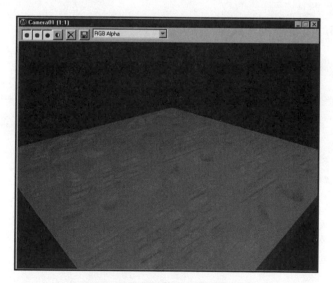

Figure 14.3

A mask-mapped material created by applying the A_MAX.TGA bitmap file to mask the underlying wood material.

The following exercise shows you how to create a mask-mapped material.

CREATING A MASK-MAPPED MATERIAL

1. Load the Material Editor.

2. Expand the Maps rollout.

3. Click on the None button next to Diffuse. The Material/Map Browser appears.

4. In the window on the left side of the Material/Map Browser, choose Mask as the map type. The Mask Parameters rollout then appears in the Material Editor.

5. In this rollout, click on the None button next to Map. The Material/Map Browser appears again.

6. In the window on the left side of the Material/Map Browser, choose Bitmap as your type this time. The Bitmap Parameters rollout then appears in the Material Editor.

7. In this rollout, click on the Bitmap button and choose ASHSEN_2.GIF from your 3DSMAX\MAPS directory as your bitmap.

8. Choose the Go To Parent button to return to the Mask controls.

9. Choose None next to Mask.

10. Choose Bitmap as your map type.

11. Click on the Bitmap button and choose TILERND.GIF from your 3DSMAX\MAP directory.

12. Choose the Go To Parent button twice.

13. Name the material **Mask1**. Save it to the Fund1 material library that you created in Chapter 12, "Basic Materials."

RGB Tint

An RGB Tint map type enables you to adjust the Red, Green, and Blue channels of a bitmap. If you want to change the blue tint of an image, for example, you can apply an RGB Tint to that bitmap. When you choose this option in the Material/Map Browser, the RGB Tint rollout appears in the Material Editor, as shown in figure 14.4.

Figure 14.4

The RGB Tint rollout.

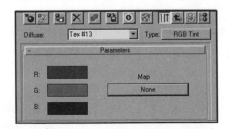

In this rollout, you see three color swatches. If you click on any of them, you get the standard color picker for MAX. You can use the color picker to select colors to tint the RGB channels. (See Chapter 5, "Creating Lofted Objects," for more information on the Color Picker if you need a refresher.) By changing one of these colors, you change the tint of the bitmap. If you click on the red channel and decreased the intensity of the red, for example, you remove some of the red from the image. You select the bitmap by choosing the None button under Map. Again, choosing None takes you back to the Material/Map Browser.

Checker

A Checker map type enables you to create a checkerboard out of two different materials. When you choose this option, the Checker rollout appears, as shown in figure 14.5.

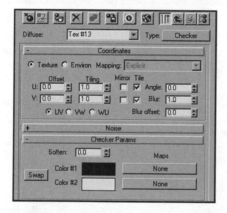

Figure 14.5

The Checker rollout.

Two additional rollouts, coordinates and noise, also appear for the checker map type. They work just like they do with standard bitmap map types.

The checkerboard is formed from two colors: black and white. You can change these colors by clicking on the Color #1 and #2 swatches in the Checker Params rollout. Alternatively, you can apply maps as either or both of the checkers. When you use maps, go to the Material/Map Browser, where you can choose a map type. The Swap button enables you to swap the position of both checkers. Figure 14.6 shows an example of a checker material.

Figure 14.6

*An example of the
checker material.*

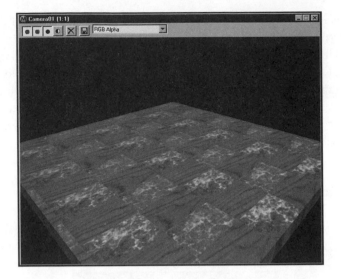

Figure 14.6

*An example of the
checker material.*

Using the Soften spinner of the Checker Params rollout, you can blur the edges between
the checkers. This control is very sensitive. Figure 14.7 shows the checkerboard originally
created in figure 14.6 with a soften of 0.5 applied.

Figure 14.7

*The checker material
with a soften value of
0.5.*

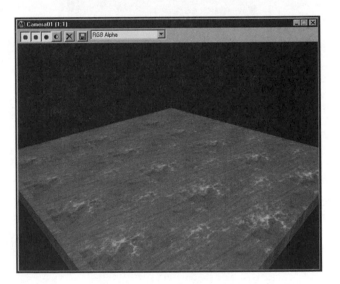

The following exercise shows you how to create a checker material.

CREATING A CHECKER MATERIAL

1. Start the Material Editor and click on Maps to extend the Maps rollout.

2. Click on None next to Diffuse. The Material/Map Browser appears.

3. In the window on the right side of the Material/Map Browser, choose Checker as your bitmap type. The Checker rollout then appears in the Material Editor.

4. In this rollout, click on None under Maps for Color #1. The Material/Map Browser appears again.

5. In the window on the right side of the Material/Map Browser, choose Bitmap as the map type and choose MARBTEA2.GIF.

6. Choose the Go To Parent button in the Material Editor.

7. Click on None under Maps for Color #2 in the Checker Parameters rollout.

8. In the Material/Map browser, Choose Bitmap as the map type. The bitmap rollouts appear again. Choose BENEDITI.JPG as the second material.

9. Choose the Go To Parent button in the Material Editor.

10. Set the Soften value to 0.05 in the checker parameters rollout.

11. Choose the Go To Parent button again in the Material Editor.

12. Name the material **Checker1** and save it to your material library.

Mix

The Mix map type enables you to mix two colors or bitmaps together to form a third. You can control the mix amount between the maps and/or colors. When you choose this option, the Mix Parameters rollout appears in the Material Editor, as shown in figure 14.8.

The mix materials work just like the checker materials do. You have Color #1 and Color #2 as well as Map options. All you have to do is specify the mix amount in the Mix Amount spinner. A mix amount of 1 gives Color #2 full control. A mix amount of 0 gives Color #1 full control. Alternatively, you can control the mix amount using the Mixing curve, which is a graphical representation of the mix amount versus the actual amount of the mixing of the two colors that will be applied to the material. The Mixing curve makes it easy to control the mix of materials over time.

Figure 14.8

The Mix Parameters rollout.

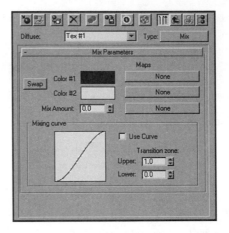

Marble

The Marble map type enables you to create a procedural material, which is defined by mathematical constraints instead of bitmaps. Procedural materials use less memory, but they also take longer to render. Procedural materials use very little memory because they are just a mathematical algorithm and not a bitmap that must be loaded. But, because they do use mathematical algorithms, procedural materials do take quite a bit longer to render than a bitmap. When you choose this option, the Marble Parameters rollout appears in the Material Editor, as shown in figure 14.9.

Figure 14.9

The Marble Parameters rollout.

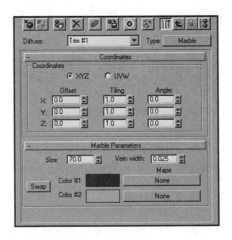

Again, you have a Coordinates section, but these coordinates control how the marble is used. You can choose either XYZ and UVW coordinates. XYZ locks the marble coordinates down to real-world coordinates, and UVW locks the coordinates down to the object. With XYZ, you can effectively Boolean subtract a section of the object, and it renders as if you cut the section out of solid marble.

In the Marble parameters rollout, you can control the vein colors, much like checker colors. You can also control their width and overall size. By adjusting these parameters, you can create just about any marble material that you like.

Noise

A Noise map type applies random areas of two colors. Noise is great for creating complex materials such as ceiling grid tile or grout walls. When you choose this option, the Noise rollouts appear in the Material Editor, as shown in figure 14.10.

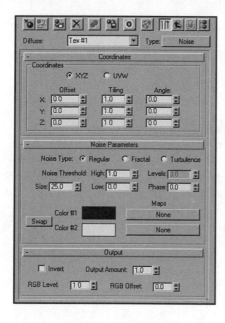

Figure 14.10

The Noise rollouts.

Again, for the Noise map type, you have coordinate controls in the Coordinates rollout that work just like the marble controls. Also, you have a set of output controls in the Output rollout that work just like the bitmap output controls.

You control the noise through the Noise Parameters rollout. You can choose from one of three different ways of creating noise: Regular, Fractal, and Turbulent. Each has a slightly different effect on the noise function. Figure 14.11 shows you three sample materials, each using a different form of noise.

Figure 14.11

The Noise Functions: Regular, Fractal, and Turbulent.

Below the noise types are the noise controls. Each controls a different aspect of the noise function. Each is listed below and briefly described:

▲ **Noise Threshold**. This control enables you to set a low and high threshold. By setting these values, you control the amount of discontinuity at the transition threshold.

▲ **Levels**. This control determines how much fractal energy is used in fractal and turbulence noise types.

▲ **Phase**. This control enables you to control the speed of the animation of the noise.

▲ **Size**. This control enables you to set the size of the noise in the map.

You also can assign different colors or maps to the noise function, much like you can with the checker controls.

Reflect/Refract

The Reflect/Refract map type enables you to apply a reflection or refraction map to the material. You should use this option on any material that you want to have a reflection or refraction. You should only use this type of map with the Reflection or Refraction map types in the Maps rollout, however. These map types are intended for use in those map types only and can produce unusual results when used as other maps. When you choose this option, the Reflect/Refract Parameters rollout appears, as shown in figure 14.12.

Figure 14.12

The Reflect/Refract Parameters rollout.

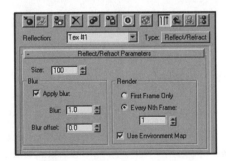

The Reflect/Refract map type works by rendering six views (front, back, left, right, top, and bottom) from the center of the object to which the reflection or refraction is applied. Then it maps those six views using spherical mapping coordinates to the object.

Using the Size spinner in this rollout, you can determine how large the reflection or refraction maps are. A value of 100 provides the greatest amount of detail; less than 100 loses detail. You can also apply a blur to the reflection to checking the Apply Blur check box. Most reflective and refractive surfaces are somewhat blurry anyway, so you should always apply a little blur. In this rollout, you also can define whether the reflection or refraction maps are generated in the first frame of an animation only or every Nth frame by choosing the appropriate radio button. Unless the object to which you assign the map type is moving or an object that will be seen in the reflection/refraction is moving, first frame should be fine. Otherwise, you might need to regenerate the reflection maps occasionally.

Flat Mirror

You apply a Flat Mirror map type to surfaces that are coplanar or flat, such as a mirror. Then a single reflection map is generated and applied to the coplanar surface. You should apply this map type as a reflection-mapped material because that is where it is intended to be used. Use in other mapping types can produce unusual results. Figure 14.13 shows the Flat Mirror Parameters rollout that appears when you choose this map type.

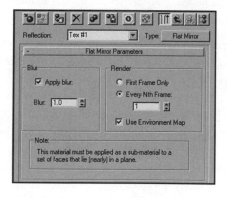

Figure 14.13

The Flat Mirror Parameters rollout.

The Flat Mirror Parameters rollout has the same controls as the Reflect/Refract Parameters rollout, and they work the same.

Gradient

The Gradient map type enables you to create gradient color fills for use as maps or as backgrounds. Figure 14.14 shows the Gradient rollouts that appear when you choose this option.

Figure 14.14

The Gradient rollouts.

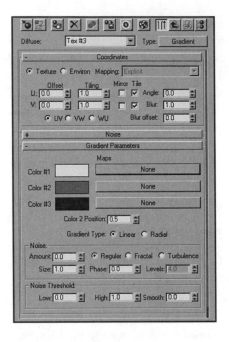

The Gradient rollouts Output, Noise, and Coordinates work like they do with other materials. In the Gradient Parameters rollout, you actually control the gradient.

A gradient is composed of three different colors or maps, labeled Color #1, Color #2, and Color #3 in the gradient parameters rollout. Clicking on a color swatch brings up the standard color picker where you can select any color you want. You define the gradient by determining the location of the second color with respect to the top and bottom of the gradient. This location affects how smooth the gradient is. A value of 1 places the second color at the top of the gradient and you cannot see the first color. The same happens with a value of 0 at the bottom of the gradient, except that you will not be able to see Color #3 in this case. If the location of the second color is 0.5, it is halfway between the first and third colors. Higher values move the second color closer to the top and give the third color more influence. You can use either colors or maps as your gradients. Then you can choose whether you want to use a linear or radial gradient.

If you want, you also can apply some noise to the gradient to make it less perfect. The Noise parameters in the Noise section of the Gradient Parameters rollout work just like the ones for the Noise map type.

Composite

The last new map type is Composite. Using the Composite Parameters rollout shown in figure 14.15, you can overlay as many submaterials on top of one another as you like.

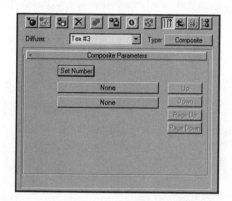

Figure 14.15

The Composite Parameters rollout.

First, you can set the number of maps by choosing the Set Number button. The default is two maps. Then you simply assign the maps you want. Each is overlaid on top of the other. MAX uses the bitmap's Alpha channel to perform the overlaying, so you should use only maps that have an Alpha channel in them.

Using MAX, you can view only two materials at a time when you're using this map type. If you have more than six materials, you can use the up and down buttons in the rollout to scroll up and down through the list.

The map types discussed in the previous sections can be used in any material or any place where you can access the Material/Map Browser. You can even nest map types within other map types to create very complex materials. But don't go overboard. You should try to keep your materials as simple as possible to achieve the effect you are looking for. Doing so not only saves you time and effort but also makes corrections later a lot easier.

Using Material Templates

Beyond the map types, MAX also provides five complete new material templates that use combinations of maps to create new materials:

▲ Multi/Sub-Object materials

▲ Top/bottom materials

▲ Double-sided materials

▲ Blend materials

▲ Matte/shadow materials

Whenever you create a new material in MAX, you can choose one of these templates in the Material/Map Browser to help you get started. Figure 14.16 shows you the Material Map browser showing you these material types. Alternatively, you can click on the Types button to change the material type to one of the templates. This displays a shortened version of the Material/Map browser shown in figure 14.16.

Figure 14.16

The Material/Map browser with new material types showing.

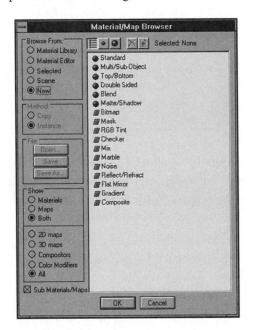

Multi/Sub-Object Materials

Multi/Sub-Object materials are used to assign different materials to different faces in the object. First, you must create the Multi/Sub-Object material and assign it to the object. Then you have to use Edit Mesh to assign the faces to specific materials in the Multi/Sub-Object material. You can access the Multi/Sub-Object controls by choosing Multi/Sub-Object from the Material/Map Browser when you start a new material. Choosing this option displays the Basic Parameters rollout in the Material Editor, as shown in figure 14.17.

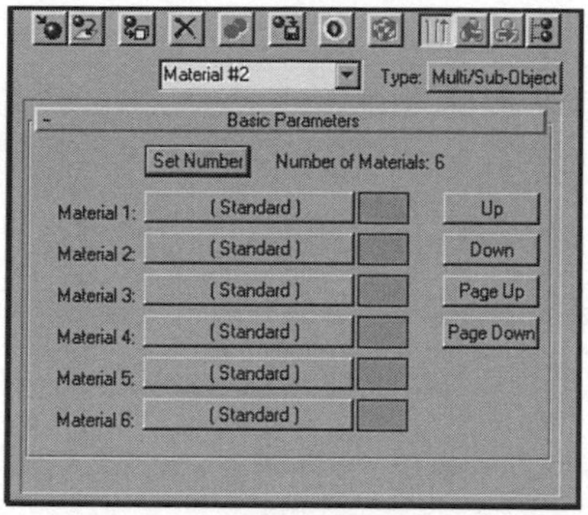

Figure 14.17

The Multi/Sub-Object Basic Parameters rollout.

You can have any number of sub-object materials. You can choose the Set Number button in this rollout to define how many sub-object materials you will have. You use the Page Up and Page Down buttons when you have more than six materials. MAX displays only six materials at a time, so you have to use these buttons to scroll up and down.

Each material is listed in a row with a material ID. Material 1, for example, has a material ID of 1. Material 2 has a material ID of 2. When you choose the button next to the material ID, a standard material rollout appears. Here, you can either start a new material or load an existing material for use with the Multi/Sub-Object material. Choose the Go To Parent button to return to the Multi/Sub-Object material.

After you create the material, you assign it to an object. Then you can apply an Edit Mesh modifier to the object in the Modify command panel. After you apply the modifier, turn on sub-object editing for faces and select the set of faces to which you want to apply one of the materials. Then scroll down to the Edit Surface rollout in the Edit Mesh Modify command panel and change the material ID for the selected faces to the material ID from the Multi/Sub-Object material that you want to assign to the selected faces (see fig. 14.18).

The following exercise shows you how to create a Multi/Sub-Object material and correctly assign it to different parts of an object.

Figure 14.18

The Edit Surface rollout.

CREATING AND USING A MULTI/SUB-OBJECT MATERIAL

1. Create a box in MAX.

2. Load the Material Editor.

3. Click on the Get Material button in the Material Editor.

4. Double-click on Multi/Sub-object in the Material/Map Browser.

5. Click on the Standard button in the Material 1 slot of the Basic Parameters rollout.

6. Name the submaterial Marble.

7. Expand the Maps rollout.

8. Choose None next to Diffuse in the Maps rollout.

9. Choose Bitmap as the map type in the Material/Map Browser.

10. Click on the Bitmap button in the Bitmap Parameters rollout to load a bitmap.

11. Load MARBTEA2.GIF from your 3DSMAX\MAPS directory and choose OK.

12. Choose the Go To Parent button in the Material Editor.

13. Choose the Go To Parent button again to return to the Multi/Sub-Object rollout.

14. Click on the Standard button slot 2.

15. Name the material Gold.

16. Set the diffuse color to a bright yellow, the shininess to 75, and the shininess strength to 85.

17. Choose the Go To Parent button in the main toolbar.

18. Choose Select Objects from the main toolbar.

19. Click on the box to select it, if it is not already selected.

20. Choose Assign Material to Selection in the Material Editor.

21. Close the Material Editor.

22. Choose the Modify command panel tab and choose Edit Mesh.

23. Choose Face from the Sub-Object drop-down list.

24. Choose the Face button under Selection to set your level of detail in working with faces.

25. Select all the faces in the box

26. Scroll down to the Edit Surface section of the rollout. Set the material ID for all faces to 1.

27. Click on the top surface of the box to select one of the faces.

28. Scroll down to the Edit Surface section of the rollout.

29. Set the Material ID to 2 for the selected face.

30. Scroll back up and choose UVW Mapping to apply some mapping to the surface.

31. Make the Perspective View active and choose Render View.

32. Set the resolution to 640×480 and choose Render. Figure 14.19 shows the result.

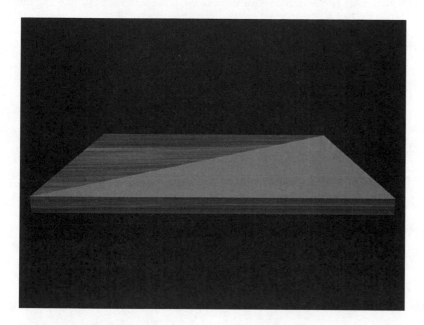

Figure 14.19

The rendering of a Multi/Sub-Object material.

Top/Bottom Materials

A top/bottom material assigns two different materials, one to the top and one to the bottom of the object. The top of an object is defined by its height in the Z axis. When you choose this option in the Material/Map Browser, the Top/Bottom Material Basic Parameters rollout appears, as shown in figure 14.20.

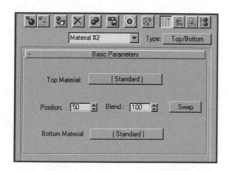

Figure 14.20

The Top/Bottom Material Basic Parameters rollout.

In the rollout, you can choose two buttons that enable you to either create or load existing materials. Between the two buttons are the controls for the top/bottom material. Position defines, as a percentage, where the break between the two materials appears on the object. A percentage of 75 places the top material on the top 25 percent of the object, and the other 75 percent is the bottom material. The Blend option controls how much blending, if any, exists between the two materials. You also can swap the materials by choosing the Swap button.

The following exercise shows you how to create and assign a top/bottom material.

CREATING AND USING A TOP/BOTTOM MATERIAL

1. Create a sphere.

2. Load the Material Editor and choose the Type button in the Material Editor.

3. Choose Top/Bottom from the Material/Map Browser.

4. Click on the Standard material for the top material.

5. Set the diffuse color to bright red, shininess to 70, and shininess strength to 20.

6. Name the material **Red1.**

7. Choose the Go To Parent button.

8. Set the blend to 25.

9. Choose Assign Material to Selection.

10. Render the Perspective viewport as in the preceding exercise.

Double Sided Materials

A double sided material is similar to two-sided rendering. Instead of having the same material appear on both sides of the face, however, you can now apply a different material to each side of a face. When you choose this option, the Double Sided Material rollout appears, as shown in figure 14.21.

The Double Sided Material rollout offers only two controls. First, you can choose what materials appear on each side of the face. The facing material is the one that shows on the side of the face with the normal. Then you can control the amount of translucency between the two sides of the face by setting the Translucency spinner. This amount determines how much of the back material you can see through the front material.

Figure 14.21

The Double Sided Material rollout.

Blend Materials

A blend material is similar to a mix map in the fact that it blends two materials together. A mix map can only blend maps. Otherwise, they function about the same. When you choose this option from the Material/Map Browser, the Blend Material rollout appears, as shown in figure 14.22.

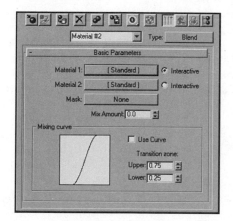

Figure 14.22

The Blend Material rollout.

The controls for blend materials are the same as for mix maps, except for two. First, you can add a mask map to help control the mixing between the two materials. The mixing is controlled by the intensities in the mask map. As the intensity of the colors in the mask map increase, the mixing between the two materials decreases until the point where no mixing occurs whatsoever. The opposite happens when the intensities of the mask map go down. Second, you can define which map is going to show in the interactive rendered by choosing the Interactive button.

Matte/Shadow Materials

A Matte/Shadow material is a special type of material that is used only for certain special effects. Hence, it is beyond the scope of the book and will not be discussed here. A matte shadow material is used to create a proxy object in a scene with a bitmap background. This proxy object is invisible and enables you to see the background behind it. You can use this proxy object for two purposes: to hide another object on top of the background, or to receive shadows on top of the background. Those are the only two uses for a matte/shadow material. It is recommended that you do not explore this material type until you understand environments, rendering, animation, and have more experience with shadow casting.

Summary

Complex materials round out your arsenal of materials so you can create any type of material you could ever need. For example, Multi/Sub-Object materials can be used to add different materials to different faces of the same object. Blend materials can be used to get rid of seams due to tiled materials, by blending two different versions of the same bitmap, each with different UV scaling and offset values. The more you explored these material types, the more uses you will find for them.

Up to this point, you have seen many different methods for creating and using materials. You may or may not have a need for all the different methods. With MAX, however, having all that flexibility is always nice. Knowing how to use materials, though, isn't that great unless you know how to render. Rendering is the focus of the next chapter.

Rendering a Scene

Now that you have seen how to model, compose, and set up a scene for rendering, it is time to learn the ins and outs of rendering. This chapter concentrates on the techniques associated with rendering a still image. In particular, this chapter focuses on the following topics:

▲ Rendering options

▲ Rendering parameters

▲ Multithreaded rendering

▲ Output options

At the end of this chapter, you will find a brief review exercise. This exercise is intended to help you review many of the commands and skills you have learned up to this point, before moving on to environments and animation. This exercise should help you to see where your skill set lies at this point and whether or not you need to review any material again.

Rendering Options

In MAX, you can render any active viewport, except for a Track View viewport. You can also render any *section* of a viewport. You can control what you are rendering by using three buttons and a drop-down list on the main toolbar (see fig. 15.1)

Figure 15.1

The Render buttons on the main toolbar where you can control what view or section of a view you are going to render.

A brief description of each button follows:

▲ **Render View**. Renders the active viewport, unless a different render type is chosen. Displays the Render Scene dialog box, in which you can set any rendering parameters.

▲ **Quick Render**. Renders the currently active viewport, but accepts the default settings and does not display the Render Scene dialog box.

▲ **Render Type**. Four options (View, Selected, Region, and Blowup) enable you to choose which part of the viewport to render. View renders the entire viewport. Selected renders only currently selected objects. Region renders a smaller area of the viewport that you define with a window. (The window, displayed as a black dashed line, can be resized or moved. After you set the size and position, you execute the rendering by choosing OK in the lower right corner of the viewport.) Blowup is the same as Region, except that the Blowup option renders the region at full size. Figure 15.2 shows you the Render Region and Blowup controls.

Figure 15.2

The Render Region, Blowup Marker box, and OK button where you can define the region you want to render.

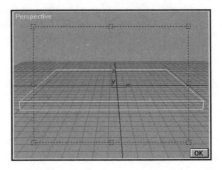

▲ **Render Last**. Renders the last view you rendered, with the same settings. Very helpful for creating test renders.

After you select what you are going to render, all you have to do is set the rendering parameters and let the system process the rendering. Depending upon the complexity of the scene, the speed of your processor, and the amount of memory in your system, rendering lasts a few seconds, several hours, even days.

To render a scene, first activate the viewport you want to render, and choose the Render View button from the main toolbar to display the Render Scene dialog box, shown in figure 15.3.

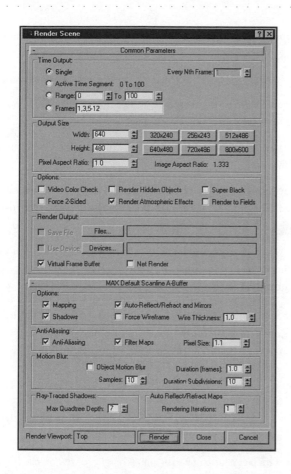

Figure 15.3

The Render dialog box where you can set up rendering parameters and actually execute the rendering process.

Rendering Parameters

Many of the Render command's parameters are of interest. The Render Scene dialog box parameters shown in figure 15.3 are described here, section by section.

Common Parameters

Although MAX is capable of using more than one rendering engine, all rendering engines have certain common parameters. Brief descriptions of these parameters, displayed in the Common Parameters rollout, follow.

You use the Time Output parameters to define which segment of an animation or still frame you are going to render, as follows:

▲ **Single**. Renders the current viewport at the current frame of the animation.

▲ **Active Time Segment**. Animations are based on time segments. This option renders the currently active time segment.

▲ **Range**. Enables you to render a series of frames. For example, you could render frames 20 to 50 as a test render.

▲ **Frames**. Enables you to pick individual frames from an animation. Just separate each frame with a comma. For example, 10-23,40-50 will render two segments of animation, one from frames 10 through 23 and the other from frame 40 to 50.

▲ **Every Nth Frame**. When you render ranges or active time segments, you can use this spinner to determine whether to render every frame, every other frame, and so on. Often you do this simply to test an animation.

Options in the Output Size section of the dialog box enable you to set the resolution of the final image. Resolutions are set as pixels. A *pixel* is a single dot in the image. The image is formed by combining enough dots at a small enough resolution. The higher the resolution the crisper the image, the longer the rendering time, and the larger the output file.

▲ **Width**. Enables you to set the width of the output image.

▲ **Height**. Enables you to set the height of the output image.

▲ **Pixel Aspect Ratio**. This is the ratio of width versus height for the pixels. It is calculated as a 4:3 ratio. The combination of the pixel aspect ratio and width and height should always result in an image aspect ratio of 1.33. So, if you set a width and height, you can adjust the pixel ratio until the image aspect reads 1.33.

MAX has a series of preset rendering resolutions and aspect ratios. For certain hardware output devices, you use a specific resolution and aspect ratio. You can plug in this information by simply right-clicking on a button to set it to a new value. Figure 15.4 shows the Configure Preset dialog box. After you set the width and height, the button will now read the new values.

In the Options section of the Common Parameters dialog box is a set of rendering options that are either enabled or disabled. Depending upon your preferences, these options will either be enabled or disabled by default. Descriptions of these options follow:

Figure 15.4

*The Configure Preset
Dialog Box where you
can set Preset Buttons
to rendering resolutions
and aspect ratios you
use commonly in your
work.*

▲ **Video Color Check**. Checks the colors of the output image versus accepted color standards for NTSC and PAL video outputs. Depending upon your preferences, MAX will either correct any colors that are unacceptable, or flag them with a color of your choice (usually black) to warn you.

▲ **Render Hidden Objects**. As you are working, you often will hide objects to make a scene easier to work on. By enabling this option, you can render the hidden objects without having to unhide them.

▲ **Super Black**. This option, which limits how dark an object can be, is used for compositing purposes when the object is on top of a pure black background. (Super black helps you to distinguish between the object and the background.) The value of super black is set in the preferences for MAX.

▲ **Force 2-Sided**. Forces the renderer to render both sides of a face, regardless of the surface normal. This is used a lot when you import geometry from other programs because most other modeling programs, such as AutoCAD do not track face normals, they usually import pointing in different directions. It is effective, but does increase rendering time by a few seconds for each frame of an animation. Don't use this option unless you have to, as 2-sided rendering may cause materials to look incorrect when rendered on the back side of a face.

▲ **Render Atmospheric Effects**. Fog and other such atmospheric effects are computationally intensive. This option enables you to disable the atmospheric effects to speed up test renders.

▲ **Render to Fields**. Applies only to animation and video output. See Chapter 21, "Rendering Animations," for information about using this option.

The Render Output section of the dialog box enables you to determine where the final rendered image goes. Descriptions of the options follow:

▲ **Files**. Enables you to specify a file name and location for the output file when you choose the Files button. Figure 15.5 shows the resulting dialog box. You specify the location and file name. The file type is set when you type the extension. When you do, you can set up the file type with the Setup button (see section "Output Options" later in this chapter).

Figure 15.5

The Render Output File dialog box where you can set the filename and file type for saving rendering images or animations.

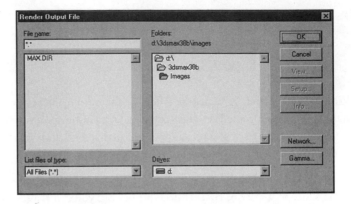

▲ **Devices**. Enables you to render the file(s) to a specific piece of hardware that requires a special driver. An ACCOM WSX video recorder is an example of this type of device.

▲ **Virtual Frame Buffer**. Renders the file to the virtual frame buffer as well as to the output file or device. The *frame buffer* is a simple window that enables you to watch the rendering as it is computed. Figure 15.6 shows you the frame buffer with a rendering.

Figure 15.6

The Virtual Frame Buffer where you can see rendered images as they are generated.

▲ **Net Render**. Enables you to use a network of machines to render off individual frames of an animation. See Chapter 21, "Rendering Animations," for more information on this feature.

MAX Default Scanline A-Buffer

These options are specific to the default rendering engine in MAX. If you have a plug-in rendering engine, you may see different settings here.

▲ **Mapping**. Enables or disables the use of maps in materials. Turn off this option when you want to render segments of an animation quickly so that you can check the motion.

▲ **Shadows**. Enables or disables the use of shadows and shadow casting. By disabling this option you can increase rendering speed dramatically and make it easy to check other aspects of the rendering.

▲ **Auto-Reflect/Refract and Mirrors**. Enables or disables the production of auto-reflected or refracted maps. As with the Shadows option, disabling this option speeds up rendering so that you can check other aspects of the rendering.

▲ **Force Wireframe**. Forces all geometry to be rendered as a wireframe, regardless of the material settings.

▲ **Wire Thickness**. Defines the thickness (in pixels) of the wires in wireframe rendering.

▲ **Anti-Aliasing**. *Anti-aliasing* is the process of smoothing out jagged or "aliased" lines in an image. When this option is disabled, rendering speeds up but the image quality suffers. Figures 15.7 and 15.8 show the same scene with and without anti-aliasing, respectively.

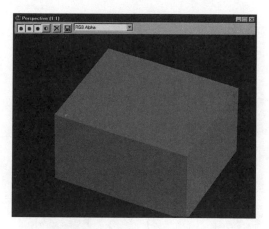

Figure 15.7

A scene with Anti-Aliasing turned on.

▲ **Filter Maps**. Enables or disables the filtering of bitmaps for smoothing or anti-aliasing. Without the filtering, the bitmaps used in the scene, whether in materials or as backgrounds, will have aliased lines and edges. This is a memory-intensive task that slows down rendering times. Generally, unless you are doing test renders, this should always be left on as it will produce the best looking materials that use bitmaps.

Figure 15.8

The same scene without Anti-Aliasing.

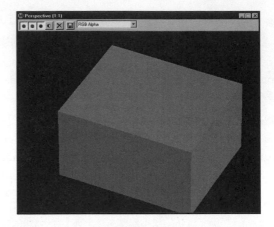

▲ **Pixel Size**. Enables extra smoothing in the wire lines in a scene to avoid ropiness in the pixels. Valid values are from 1 to 1.5. You should always set this to 1.5 for final renderings. Although this setting will increase render times, the quality will be much better. Figures 15.9 and 15.10 show renderings with a pixel size of 1.1 and 1.5, respectively.

Figure 15.9

In this scene, Pixel Size is set at 1.1.

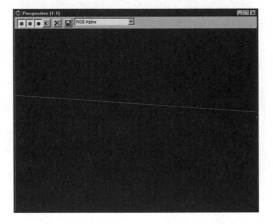

The Motion Blur parameters, which are specific to animation, are covered in Chapter 21, "Rendering Animations."

As its name indicates, the Ray-Traced Shadows section presents the following rendering parameters for ray-traced shadows:

▲ **Max Quadtree Depth**. Use this parameter to control the time versus memory requirements for ray-traced shadows. Higher values make the process of creating ray-traced shadows faster, but take much more RAM than lower values. The lower the value, the slower the ray-traced shadows are to create, but the less RAM you use.

Recommended values are between 4 and 8. Below 4, the quadtree gets too small and shadow quality suffers. Above 8, too much RAM will be used and the quality of the shadows does not increase proportionally.

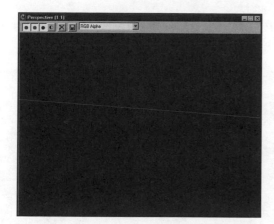

Figure 15.10

The same scene, with Pixel Size set at 1.5.

Use Auto Reflect/Refract Maps to control reflection and refraction mapping, as follows:

▲ **Rendering Iterations**. When rendering reflective surfaces, you may be able to see other reflective surfaces in the first reflective surface, and so on. For example, a group of silver balls shows multiple reflections of each other. This variable controls the number of levels of reflections you can see in a single surface.

The Render button executes the rendering process, using the settings you set in the dialog box. Figure 15.11 shows a rendering in progress.

The most important part of the Rendering Progress dialog box, besides the amount of time remaining, are the scene statistics at the bottom of the box. These tell you not only how many faces, objects, and lights are active in the scene, but also, and more important, how much memory you are using. This number is approximate, and can be used to guess the amount of memory you need.

For rendering speed, it is very important that you have enough RAM to run the rendering completely from RAM. The second you start swapping to disk, speed drops dramatically. For MAX, 32 MB of RAM is a minimum. For small to medium scenes, you should have 64 MB of RAM. For large scenes, greater than 300,000 faces, you should have more than 64 MB of RAM.

To see exactly how much memory MAX is using, you can use the NT Performance Monitor, which is located in the Administrative tools program group. (Consult your NT documentation on how to use the Performance Monitor.) Add a line to the chart that shows the Process/Private Bytes/_Total. This line shows you the exact amount of memory

NT thinks it is using for all running applications. Figure 15.12 shows you an example of the performance monitor showing private bytes usage for a typical MAX session. If this number is greater than the amount of RAM in your system, you need more RAM to get the most effective use of your hardware with MAX. Figure 15.12 shows that the system is currently using 33 MB of RAM. (For more information about the Performance Monitor, consult your NT documentation.)

Figure 15.11

A rendering in progress showing the virtual frame buffer and Rendering Stats dialog box.

Figure 15.12

The Performance Monitor showing Private Bytes memory usage for a typical MAX session.

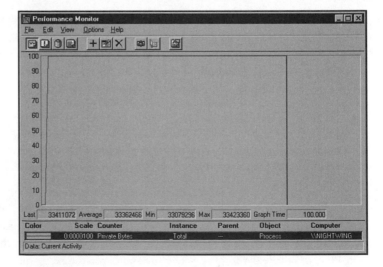

Multithreaded Rendering

One reason Kinetix decided to develop MAX for the Windows NT operating system was to take advantage of the multithreaded and multiprocessing capabilities. Multithreading breaks down program tasks into threads, which can then be executed on the next available processor. With the advent of the Pentium and Pentium Pro processors, single, dual, and quad-processor computers are increasingly common.

Without multithreading, running MAX on a dual-processor machine is no more effective than running it on a machine with a single processor (in fact, it may even be a little slower). But with multithreading, you will see rendering speeds that are between 1.6 and 1.9 times faster on still images, depending upon the complexity of the scene.

You can enable and disable multithreaded rendering in MAX through the Rendering section of the Preference Settings dialog box. Choose File, Preferences to display the Preference Settings dialog box, then click on the Rendering tab (see fig. 15.13) to display the rendering settings. The check box for multithreaded rendering is in the lower right corner, and is on by default. By late 1996, you should see several quad-processor machines that can really take advantage of this particular option!

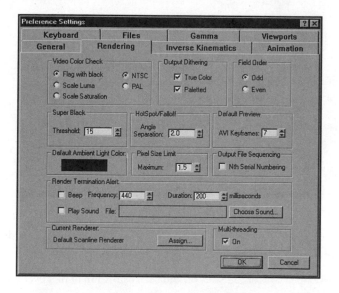

Figure 15.13

The Rendering Preferences dialog box where you can define the default settings for the default renderer.

The other preferences in this dialog box relate to various rendering aspects that are covered at various points throughout this book. You can study them on your own as you progress through the various chapters.

Output Options

The last group of rendering options to consider are the file output options. MAX can save to a variety of file types. You can set the file type by choosing the Files button in the Render Scene dialog box and then choosing a file type from the List files of type drop-down list shown in figure 15.14.

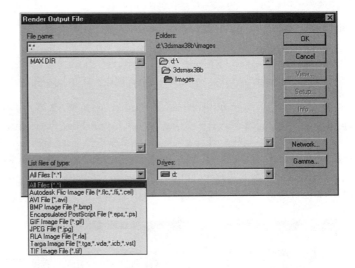

Brief descriptions of the file types follow:

▲ **Autodesk FLC**. A collection of animated file types such as FLC and FLI. CEL files, a still image format from the old days of Animator Pro, are also considered FLC files.

▲ **AVI**. Video for Windows **A**udio **V**ideo **I**nterleave format. This is a common online video playback format for animations and sound.

▲ **BMP**. Windows Bitmap file. Useful for importing images into some programs or as a background on your NT desktop.

▲ **Encapsulated PostScript**. PostScript output for use with PostScript printing devices or in desktop publishing programs.

▲ **GIF**. A format developed by CompuServe for quick transmission of files over modem. This format limits the image to 256 colors, and is very compact.

▲ **JPEG**. A special file format that uses a lossey algorithm to greatly compress images. The higher the compression, the smaller the file, and the worse it looks.

▲ **Targa**. The most common output format. This type of file is a full 24-bit color image and is commonly used with many output devices. Targa also supports alpha channels at 32 bits. If you are going to use alpha channels for compositing, you must render the files as 32-bit Targas.

▲ **Tiff**. Another popular 24-bit color image format. It is commonly used to import images into other programs.

Choose a file type according to the appropriate output device or destination. You can also set up parameters for most file types. Simply choose the file type from the drop-down list and select the Setup button in the Render Output File dialog box. Figure 15.15 shows the setup dialog box for a Targa image file. This dialog box is called the Targa Image Control dialog box. The image file setup will vary from file type to file type.

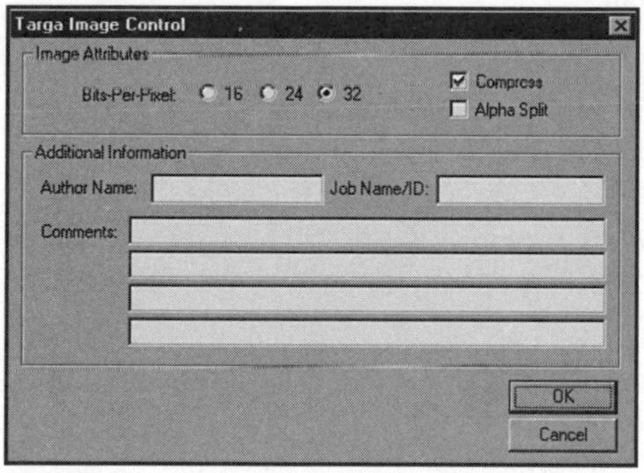

Figure 15.15

The Targa Image Control dialog box where you can set the targa image output options.

Before you save an image to a specific file type you can also correct the file's gamma. *Gamma* measures the contrast that affects the midtones of an image, and gamma correction affects the overall brightness of the image. For some output devices (such as video), gamma correction may be necessary for the image to look right. To correct the gamma, you choose the Gamma button and then change the settings in the Output Gamma Settings dialog box (see fig. 15.16).

Figure 15.16

Use the Output Gamma Settings dialog box to correct the file's gamma.

Gamma corrections are generally somewhere between 1.0 and 2.5. The higher the value, the brighter the image. You will have to experiment with your output equipment to see whether you need gamma correction at all. Alternatively, you can also set up gamma in the MAX preferences.

Review Exercise: Creating and Rendering a Scene

At this point, you should feel fairly comfortable rendering a still image and saving it to a file. Before moving on to other topics in MAX, it is time for a quick review. The following exercise reviews some of the topics covered up to this point, and should bring some of that information together for you.

This exercise creates a basic table scene with a teapot, light, camera, and materials. Feel free to embellish the exercise and get more practice by adding your own touches to the end.

CREATING A TABLE SCENE

1. Load MAX.

2. Choose Views, Unit Setup and select US Standard with Feet and Fractional inches. Choose OK.

3. Choose Views, Grid and Snap Settings.

4. Set the grid spacing to 6", and choose OK.

    At this point, you have created a basic setup and are now ready to begin modeling.

5. Turn on 2D Snap at the bottom of the screen.

6. Choose Box from the Create command panel.

7. Click at 0,0 and make the box 6" long by 6" wide, and 3' tall. Use the spinner to make any final adjustments. Name the box Leg1.

8. Choose Select and Move from the main toolbar.

9. Hold down the Shift key and click on the box in the top viewport.

10. Click on the box and drag it to the right 6'. This enables you to copy the box.

11. In the Clone Options dialog box, choose Copy as the option and choose OK.

12. Click and hold again on the leg, dragging it vertically 3' while holding down the Shift key.

13. Repeat step 12 for the other leg. Figure 15.17 shows the scene at this point.

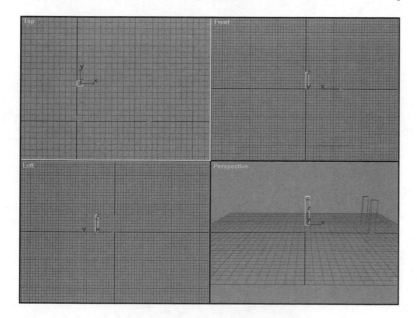

Figure 15.17

The Four Legs of the Table in their correct positions.

14. Create a box at –6",–6" by 6'6", 3'6" with a height of 3". Name the box **table top**.

15. Choose Select and move.

16. In the front viewport, click on the box and move it vertically until it sits on top of the legs.

You have completed the table. At this point you can either use Edit Mesh to join the five objects into a single object, or leave the objects as-is. For the exercise, you will join the objects.

17. With the table top highlighted, choose the Modify command panel tab.

18. Choose Edit Mesh.

19. Turn off Sub-object selection so you can attach another object to the selected object.

20. Choose the Attach button.

21. Click on each leg to attach it to the table top. Rename the object to Table.

22. Choose Attach again to turn it off.

23. Create a teapot and place it on the table.

24. Under the Create command panel, choose the Cameras button.

25. Choose the Target button to create a target camera.

26. Click at 10',–3' and drag to the center of the table to place the camera and target.

27. Choose Select and move.

28. Click on the camera in the front viewport and move it vertically 6'.

29. Repeat for the target, but move it up 3' so that you are looking at the table.

30. Click on the Perspective viewport name to activate it, then press C to switch to a camera view.

31. Right-click on the Camera viewport name and choose Smooth + Highlights. Figure 15.18 shows you the scene at this point.

Figure 15.18

The shaded scene from the camera view showing the table.

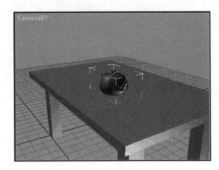

Now that you have created the camera view, it is time to create the lighting. For this scene, you will use a spotlight with a soft shadow.

32. On the Create command panel, choose the Lights button. Select Target Spot.

33. In the top viewport, click at 0,–5' and drag to the center of the table to place the spotlight and its target.

34. Choose Select and move, and move the light vertically 10' in the front viewport.

35. Repeat step 34 for the target of the light, but move it only 3' vertically.

36. Click on the Left viewport name to make the Left viewport active. Press the $ key to change this to a spotlight view.

37. Choose the Select objects button from the main toolbar.

38. Click on the light itself.

39. Choose the Modify command panel tab.

40. Set the hotspot to 30 and the falloff to 60. Turn Cast Shadows on. Figure 15.19 shows you the scene at this point.

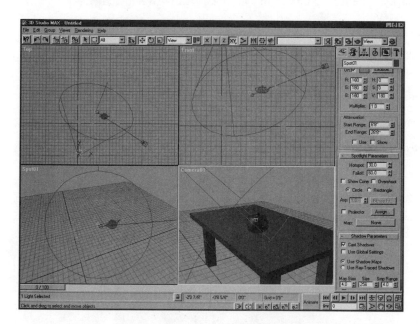

Figure 15.19

The scene showing you how the cameras and lights are placed.

You have set up and composed the scene. Now it is time to create the materials for the scene and render it. Before proceeding any further, however, choose File, Save and save the file as CH15A.MAX.

Applying Materials and Rendering the Table Scene

At this point, you have modeled a table scene, created lights, and created cameras. Now it is time to apply some materials to the scene and render it.

1. Choose Select Objects from the main toolbar.

2. Click on the table to select it.

3. Choose the Materials Editor button from the main toolbar.

4. Rename Material #1 Table.

5. Expand the Maps rollout, then select the None button next to diffuse.

6. Double-click on bitmap to select the map type.

7. Click on the bitmap load button to load the bitmap.

8. Select the file ASHSEN_2.GIF from your 3DSMAX\MAPS directory.

9. Choose Assign Material to Selection.

10. Choose Show Bitmap in Viewport. At this point, the table should turn white because it has no mapping yet.

11. Minimize the Materials Editor.

12. Click on the Modify command panel tab, and choose UVW Mapping.

13. Set the type of mapping to Box.

14. Choose Bitmap Fit.

15. Select the ASHSEN.GIF file again, and choose OK. Figure 15.20 shows you the scene with the material applied to the table. You may want to play with some sub-object gizmo adjustments at this point, to get used to how you control mapping coordinates.

Figure 15.20

The scene with wood applied to the table so it will render more realistically.

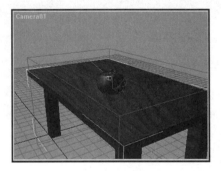

16. Save the file again.

17. Choose Select Objects from the main toolbar, and select the teapot.

18. Expand the Materials Editor again. (It should be minimized in the lower-left corner of the screen.)

19. Click in the second material slot to make it active. Rename the material, changing Material #2 to Teapot.

20. Set the Diffuse color to a bright yellow.

21. Lock the Ambient and Diffuse Colors. Choose OK in response to the warning about locking the colors.

Note

> Normally, the ambient and diffuse colors are separate. Locking them together forces both colors to be the same. Because this is not normal, MAX gives you a warning message to make sure you are aware of this.

22. Set the Shading Limit to Metal.

23. Set the shininess to 90 and the Shin strength to 30.

24. Expand the Maps rollout and choose the None button next to Reflection Mapping. This displays the Material/Map browser.

25. Choose Reflect/Refract in the Material/Map Browser.

26. Choose Go to Parent to return to the original material.

27. Choose Assign Material to Selection.

28. Save both materials to your material library, then close the Materials Editor.

29. Click on the Camera viewport name to activate it, and choose Render View.

30. Set the resolution to 640×480, and choose Render. Figure 15.21 shows the rendered scene.

31. When the rendering is finished, save the file.

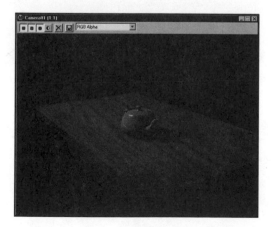

Figure 15.21

The final rendered scene showing materials, lighting, and composition elements.

At this point, you have the start of a good scene. On your own, add some fruit, some other dishes, a ground plane—perhaps even walls or other furniture to the scene. Get plenty of practice with this process before you move on to the next couple of chapters.

Note

The file for the preceding exercise is provided on the CD (the file name is CH15A.MAX). You can load and use this file if you wish, instead of starting from scratch. The file is provided so that if you get stuck you can look at it, see how it was created, and find your mistakes.

Summary

Rendering and output are fairly important issues in MAX. They will grow familiar as you work with MAX. In the next chapter you will look at one more topic, environmental effects, before moving on to animation.

CHAPTER 16

Environmental Effects

For many scenes you create, you will need to be able to simulate real-world environments so that you can create the realism and sense of space that are critical to a rendering. For example, a nighttime scene in the early spring or late fall, such as around Halloween, would greatly benefit from the usage of fog to create a sense of ambiance and mood. These environments may be earthly or alien, day, or night, but in all cases, careful use of environmental effects will greatly enhance the realism and the overall impact of the image or animation.

This chapter focuses on how to create environmental effects. In particular, you will learn how to work with the following:

▲ Volumetric lights

▲ Volumetric fog

▲ Fog

▲ Environment mapping

▲ Perspective matching

Environmental effects in MAX are accessed by choosing Environment from the Render pull-down menu. This displays the Environment dialog box, shown in figure 16.1. The dialog box is divided into two areas: Background and Atmosphere. Environment controls, such as mapping and perspective matching, are controlled from the Background section of the dialog box, and are covered later in this chapter.

Figure 16.1

*In the Environment
dialog box, you can
create many
environmental effects.*

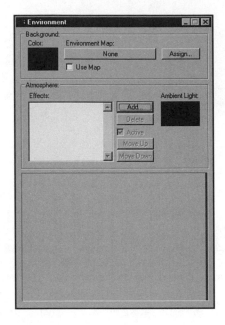

The Atmosphere section enables you to create and add three types of atmospheric events to your rendering: Fog, Volumetric Fog, and Volumetric Lights. Choosing the Add button in the Atmosphere section displays the Add Atmospheric Effect dialog box (see fig. 16.2), in which you can add one of these three atmospheric effects.

Figure 16.2

*The Add Atmospheric
Effect dialog box
enables you to add
volumetric lights and
fog, or regular fog.*

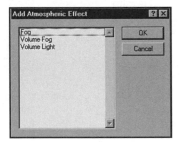

The first portion of this chapter, then, examines the atmospheric effects you can add in MAX. The first effect covered is volumetric lighting.

Volumetric Lights

A *volumetric light* is one that has the appearance of a spotlight shining through fog or steam. These types of lights are incredibly powerful for evoking mood or adding realism to both day- and nighttime renderings. For example, a volumetric light can be used to create a spotlight effect such as those found in the Batman movies. Figure 16.3 shows you a sample file using volume lights.

Figure 16.3

The Kinetix logo using volumetric lights.

Unfortunately, volumetric lights are computationally intensive and will dramatically slow down your renderings. This occurs because the rendering engine has to fill the light cone with a fog like effect, resulting in many more calculations that are necessary. This increases when objects cast shadows in the volumetric light. You should use them sparingly, only when you need to. On the plus side, because of the intensity of a volumetric light, dual-processor computers render faster when you use volumetric lights than when you use regular lights. This occurs simply because the more computationally intensive a scene is, the better a dual processor machine will process it.

Volumetric lights work with any existing light in a MAX scene, except ambient lighting. They don't work with ambient lighting because ambient lighting is a general illumination applied to all surfaces and does not manifest itself as a physical volume as the other light types do. When you select the Volume Light option from the Add Atmospheric Effect dialog box, the parameters rollout for a volumetric light is displayed (see fig. 16.4).

The first thing you must do to create the volume light is to choose the Pick Light button (at the top of the rollout, under Lights:). When the button turns green, indicating that it is active, all you have to do is select the light in the scene with the mouse light. Once the light is selected, it appears in the drop-down list to the right. This list includes all lights that are assigned as volume lights. You must do this because to create a volumetric light, you must use an existing light in the scene. (To convert any of these lights to a "regular" light, simply remove it from the list.)

Figure 16.4

The Volume Light Parameters rollout where you can set how a volumetric light works.

You first must select the light or lights to change to a volume light. Clicking on the Pick Light button in the Lights section enables you to pick lights directly from your scene. When you activate the Pick Light button, then click on a light in the scene, that light changes to a volume light, and its name appears in the drop-down list at the right of the Light section. This drop-down list shows all the lights that you have assigned as volume lights. To remove a light from the list and reassign it as a nonvolume light, simply select the light name and click on the Remove Light button.

Volumetric lights have many different controls. These controls are broken down into three main sections: Volume, Attenuation, and Noise.

With the Volume parameters, you can control the way the volumetric light is created. Descriptions of these parameters follow:

▲ **Fog Color**. Enables you to control the color of the fog. By clicking on the color swatch, you get the standard color picker. In this case, however, the fog color is mixed with the color of the light. If you want to control the color of the fog, it is recommended that you change the color of the light and leave the fog white.

▲ **Exponential**. When you are using transparent objects, fog can create a problem by exposing the objects. Exponential softens the fog to reduce this problem. The exponential option is an on/off toggle.

▲ **Density**. The higher the density, the more light reflected, and the brighter the fog. Densities of between 2 and 6 percent are recommended for realistic fog.

▲ **Max Light %**. As the fog gets farther from the light source, it becomes more and more dense, approaching white. This option enables you to limit, to a percentage of the maximum, how bright the fog will get. The default is 90 percent.

▲ **Min Light %**. Enables you to have foglike effects outside the cone of the light. Generally, you will not change this variable, unless you want to lose a little control over where the fog occurs in the scene. The default is 0 percent.

▲ **Filter Shadows**. Enables you to increase or decrease the quality of the volume fog by adjusting the sampling rate, but with the price of increased render time because the render must calculate more samples with higher sampling rates. Of the three preset options—Low, Medium, and High—you should use a setting of high for final renderings as it produces the most accurate shadows. The low setting should be used for all test renderings because it is faster. You can control the sampling by turning off the Auto feature and adjusting the Sample Volume % spinner.

Attenuation enables you to control how far away from the light the volumetric effects continue, based on the current ranges set for the light. In other words, as you get farther away from the light, the volumetric effects grow weaker and weaker. The ranges setting discussed in Chapter 11, "Composition Basics: Lights and Cameras," is used to control these distances. Brief descriptions of the options follow:

▲ **Start %**. Enables you to control where attenuation of the volume light begins, based on the attenuation values of the light itself. At 100%, the light is attenuated according to the light parameters, not the volume parameters. Anything less than 100% moves the attenuation range closer to the light itself.

▲ **End %**. Works just like Start %, except that when the value is less than 100%, the light is attenuated beyond the light parameters.

With the last set of parameters you can add noise to the volumetric light. Much like noise in a material, or as a modifier, this parameter adds random variations of light and dark areas to the volumetric light to give a sense of non-uniformity and realism. In nature, a volumetric light is often the result of a foggy day or night. The constantly moving, shifting fog changes the way the light acts. With the noise set of controls, you can define how realistic or natural the fog looks or acts in a still frame, or over time. Following are brief descriptions of the options:

▲ **Noise On.** Turns the noise effects on or off.

▲ **Amount**. Enables you to define how much noise there is in the fog; 0 is no noise and 1 is all noise. A good range for realistic-looking fog is from about .4 to .6.

▲ **Uniformity**. Enables you to control the transparency of the fog. Valid values are from −1 to 1. As the number decreases, more of the fog becomes increasingly transparent.

▲ **Size**. Enables you to define the size of the tendrils of smoke or fog. Smaller values result in smaller tendrils.

▲ **Phase**. Enables you to control the animation rate of the fog, over time. In other words, the phase controls the rate at which the volumetric fog changes over time. Smaller values result in a slower moving fog whereas higher values result in a churning, more active fog.

▲ **Wind Strength**. Enables you to add wind from one of six directions for added emphasis in the animation of the fog.

▲ **Wind from the:**. Enables you to choose whether the wind comes from the front, back, left, right, top, or bottom of the scene.

The following exercise shows you how to create and use a volumetric light in a simple scene.

CREATING AND USING A VOLUMETRIC LIGHT

1. Load the scene CH16A.MAX from the CD.

2. Render the camera viewport to see the lighting at this point (see fig. 16.5).

3. Close the virtual frame buffer window.

4. Choose Rendering, Environment from the pull-down menus.

5. Choose the Add button in the Environment dialog box.

6. Choose Volume Light and then choose OK.

7. In the Volume Light Parameters section of the rollout, choose Pick Light.

8. Click on the spot light in any viewport. The name of the light, Spot01, appears in the drop-down list.

9. Set the density to 3.0.

10. Scroll down to the bottom of the parameters rollout.

11. Click on the check box next to Noise On to turn on noise.

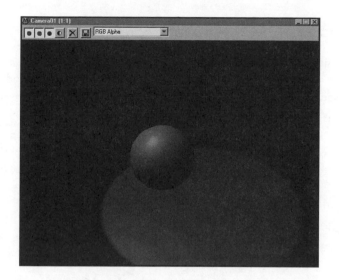

Figure 16.5

The CH16A.MAX scene at the start of the exercise.

12. Set the amount to 0.5.

13. Set the size to 10.

14. Set the uniformity to –0.5.

15. Set the phase to 1.0.

16. Close the Environment dialog box and render the scene, using Render Last. Figure 16.6 shows the rendered scene.

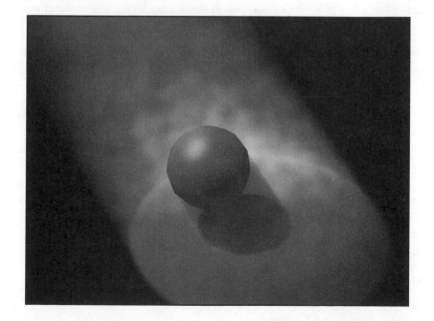

Figure 16.6

The Volumetric Light as used in the scene.

Volumetric Fog

Volumetric fog is similar to a volumetric light, but the fog permeates the whole scene. Volumetric fog is used instead of regular fog to give the fog some irregularity and make it look more realistic. When you choose this option from the list in the Add Atmospheric Effect dialog box, MAX displays the rollout shown in figure 16.7.

Figure 16.7

The Volume Fog Parameters rollout.

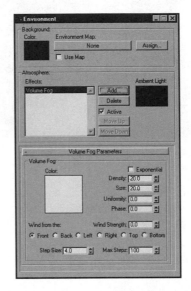

Volumetric fog has many of the same controls as volumetric lights. Only two of the controls are new. Descriptions of these two new controls follow:

▲ **Step Size**. Enables you to set the granularity of the fog. Use a large step size for a grainier fog; smaller step sizes make a finer fog. The default is 4.0, which is in the middle between fine and grainy.

▲ **Max Steps**. Enables you to control the rendering and sampling of the fog, so that MAX does not calculate fog for an infinite amount of time. 100 is the default setting for this option.

The following exercise shows you how to create and use volumetric fog.

CREATING AND USING VOLUMETRIC FOG

1. Load the file CH16B.MAX from the accompanying CD.

2. Render the scene to see what it looks like at the moment (see fig. 16.8).

3. Choose Rendering, Environment.

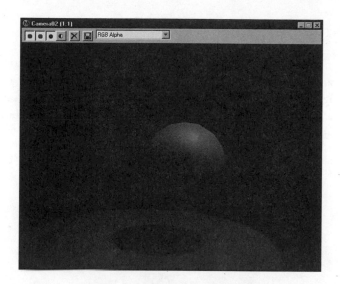

Figure 16.8

The Scene before adding volumetric fog.

4. Select the Add button.

5. Choose Volume Fog from the Add Atmospheric Effects dialog box..

6. Set the color to a light gray.

7. Set the Density and Size to 10.

8. Set the uniformity to 0.5.

9. Set the phase to 1.0.

10. Re-render the scene. Figure 16.9 shows the rendered scene.

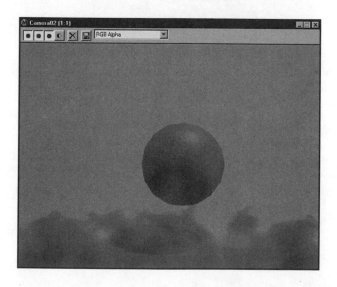

Figure 16.9

Volumetric fog has been added to the scene.

Fog

A fog atmospheric effect is a standard generic fog. When compared to a volumetric fog, a standard fog does not have very much in the way of noise controls to add non-uniformity and realism to the fog. Standard fog is based on the range settings for the current camera view. In other words, fog is *view dependent*. When you choose this option from the Add Atmospheric Effect dialog box, you see the rollout shown in figure 16.10.

Figure 16.10

The Fog Parameters rollout.

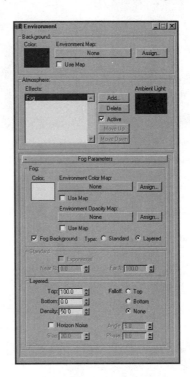

The Fog rollout is divided into three sections: Fog, Standard, and Layered. The Fog section enables you to control the way the fog appears in the scene. Descriptions of the parameters follow:

▲ **Color**. Enables you to control the color of the fog.

▲ **Environment Color Map**. Enables you to use a bitmap to vary the color of the fog. This type of bitmap uses environmental mapping to achieve the color control. (See the "Environment Mapping" section later in this chapter for more information.)

▲ **Environment Opacity Map**. Enables you to vary the density of the fog, using an opacity map.

▲ **Fog Background**. Enables you to apply fog to any backgrounds that might exist.

▲ **Type**. Enables you to choose the type of fog (Standard or Layered) you are creating. A layered fog varies the thickness of the fog between an upper and a lower limit, whereas a standard fog is based on distance from the camera.

Choosing the Standard fog type activates the Standard section of the dialog box, which has only three controls. Near % sets the percentage of fog at the near camera range, Far % sets the percentage of fog at the far camera range, and the Exponential control works the same as with volumetric fog.

At the bottom of this rollout is the Layered section. With a *layered fog*, you can vary the density of the fog from top to bottom. Brief descriptions of the layered fog parameters follow:

▲ **Top**. Enables you to define the upper limit of the fog, in world reference coordinate system units. This size is dependent upon where you want the fog to appear.

▲ **Bottom**. Enables you to define the lower limit of the fog, in world units.

▲ **Density**. Enables you to define how dense the fog is.

▲ **Falloff**. Enables you to force the fog density to drop off as it approaches the top or bottom of the fog. If you choose the None radio button, the density of the fog remains uniform.

▲ **Horizon Noise**. Enables you to add a little noise at the horizon line of the fog for a more realistic effect. When this option is enabled, you can use the following controls:

  ▲ **Size**. Enables you to control the size of the horizon noise.

  ▲ **Angle**. Enables you to set the angle away from the horizon line at which the noise will still have effect.

  ▲ **Phase**. Enables you to animate the horizon noise over time.

The following exercise shows you how to create a fog atmospheric effect.

CREATING AND USING FOG

1. Load the file CH16B.MAX from the CD. (Reload this file from scratch if you worked on the last exercise.)

2. Choose Select objects.

3. Click on the camera in the top viewport to select it.

4. Click on the Modify command panel tab.

5. Under Environment Ranges, choose Show.

6. Set the near range to 110 and the far range to 400. Figure 16.11 shows the correct camera ranges. The fog will start at the near range and grow progressively dense as it approaches the far range.

Figure 16.11

Figure 16.11

The correct camera range settings showing the range spheres.

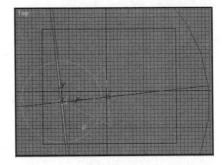

7. Choose Rendering, Environment.

8. Choose the Add button.

9. Choose Fog and OK in the Add Atmospheric Effects dialog box.

10. In the Standard section, set Near % to 20%.

11. Close the Environment dialog box.

12. Render the camera viewport. Figure 16.12 shows the rendered scene.

Figure 16.12

The scene, rendered with fog.

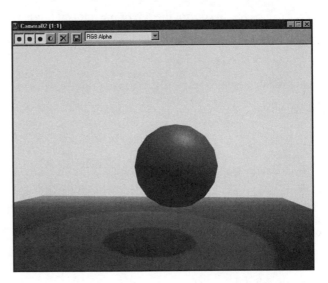

13. For further practice on your own, adjust the fog (making it a layered fog) and re-render the scene. Also, try using either an environment or an opacity map to see how it affects the fog.

Environment Mapping

Environment mapping enables you to map a bitmap to the environment, to give your scene realistic backdrops. For example, if you want to render your scene on top of a city background, you must use screen environment mapping. Also, if you want to create an animation of a scene with a sky background, you must use an environment background. To keep the sky from moving with the camera, you can use a spherical or cylindrical background type.

You can use four types of mapping for environmental mapping: screen, spherical, cylindrical, and shrink wrap. Spherical mapping, for example, creates an infinitely large sphere around your scene and maps the background to the inside of the sphere. The Environment Map controls are located in the Environment dialog box, above the atmospheric controls (see fig. 16.13).

Figure 16.13

The Environment Map controls.

These Environment Map controls are rather simple to use. By clicking on the color swatch, you can use the standard color picker to define a color (other than black) for the background. To the right of the color swatch is the Environment Map button. Before you can use this button, you must choose the type of map you are going to use as the environment. Choose the Assign button to display the standard material/map browser dialog box.

Because the environment map is a map, you can use any of the standard bitmap types such as gradient, bitmap, mask, and so on. When you choose a bitmap type, its name is displayed in the Environment Map button. To complete the assignment of the bitmap, you must assign it to a slot in the Materials Editor. You can do this by clicking on the Environment Map button after you have assigned the map. Figure 16.14 shows you the resulting dialog box.

Figure 16.14

The Put to Material Editor dialog box shows which slot the environment background will appear in.

In this dialog box, you select one of the six sample windows, or slots, from the Materials Editor. Then, whatever material you create in that window is used as the background. After you have assigned a slot, choose OK in the Put to Material Editor dialog box and close the Environment dialog box.

Warning

> After you create an environment map in a slot in the Materials Editor, you should not change that slot to another material. If you do, the other material will be used as the environment map instead of the material you want.

Now you must load the Materials Editor. When you do, the material in the assigned slot is now a black circle, as shown in figure 16.15.

The material in the slot is already set to use a bitmap as a diffuse map because that is the type of map necessary for use as a background. First, load the bitmap you want to use by choosing the blank button next to Bitmap in the Bitmap Parameters rollout. Now, having selected the bitmap you want to use, you must define how MAX is going to use it as an environment map. Figure 16.16 shows you the bitmap parameters rollout at this point.

If you look in the Coordinates section of the rollout, you will see that the environment coordinates have been chosen. To the right, the drop-down list is now active, and you can choose the type of environmental coordinates you are going to use. Descriptions of the four choices follow:

▲ **Spherical**. Enables you to map the environment map to the inside of an infinitely large sphere. Two things to watch out for here: First, be sure to use a high-resolution bitmap; otherwise, the background will look stretched and fuzzy. Second, there will always be a seam where the bitmap starts and ends on the sphere. You should always try to keep that seam behind the camera and out of view when rendering. (Both of these warnings apply also to cylindrical and shrink-wrap mapping.)

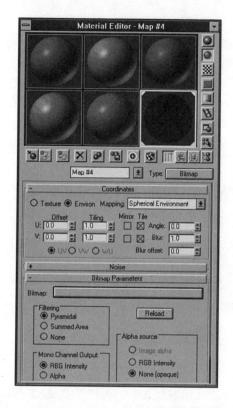

Figure 16.15

The Environment Map before creation.

▲ **Cylindrical**. Enables you to map the environment to the inside of an infinitely large cylinder, instead of a sphere.

▲ **Shrink Wrap**. Enables you to map the environment to the inside of a sphere, but only one copy of the bitmap is possible. Under spherical, you can control the tiling of the bitmap to make more copies appear on the cylinder. Shrink wrap bypasses this.

▲ **Screen**. Enables you to map the bitmap as a planar background. This is great for still images and must be used when you want to match your scene to a real background.

After you have chosen the environment mapping type, the environment is set; this is the way it will render until you disable the environment mapping in the Environment dialog box.

The exercise following figure 16.16 shows you how to create an environment map.

Figure 16.16

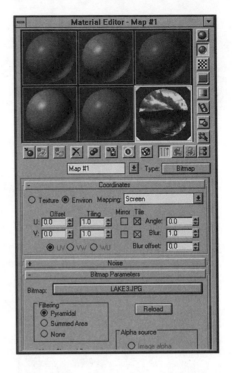

CREATING AND USING AN ENVIRONMENT MAP

1. Load the file CH16B.MAX from the CD. (Reload this file if you were just working on the last exercise.)

2. Choose Rendering, Environment from the pull-down menus.

3. Choose the Assign button in the Environment dialog box.

4. Double-click on bitmap in the Material/Map browser to assign it as the map type.

5. Click on the Environment Map button in the Environment dialog box.

6. Click on the Slot #6 button to assign the map to slot #6 in the Put to Material Editor dialog box.

7. Choose OK. To close the Put to Material Editor dialog box.

8. Close the Environment dialog box.

9. Start the Material Editor.

10. Click on sample window #6 to make it active.

11. Click on the blank button next to Bitmap in the Bitmap Parameters rollout to load a bitmap.

12. Load SUNSET90.JPG from your MAX Maps directory.

13. In the Bitmap Parameters rollout of the Materials Editor, under coordinates, set the environmental coordinates to a spherical environment.

14. Render the camera view. Figure 16.17 shows the rendered scene.

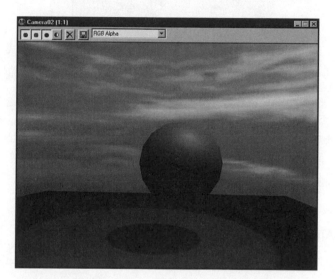

The scene with a spherical background.

Perspective Matching

Perspective matching makes use of a screen-environment mapped background and the camera's horizon line to match the perspective of your scene to the background. This is done when you want to render your scene into a photograph or other such background. Architects use this feature often, to render buildings into the site context. For best results, and to decrease rendering time, always try to use background bitmaps that are the same size and resolution as your final output.

After you have set up the environment map, use a shaded view of your camera viewport to perform the perspective match. In this shaded view, you can turn on the background and use the camera controls to change the camera view to match the perspective of the background. To turn on a background image, choose Views, Background image, which displays the dialog box shown in figure 16.18.

Figure 16.18

The Viewport Background dialog box where you can select a bitmap to appear in the background of a viewport for perspective matching.

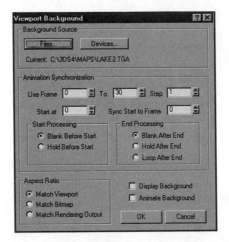

In the Background Source section, choose the Files button and load the same bitmap that you loaded into the Materials Editor for use as the screen environment map. When you choose OK, the image is displayed as the background of the current viewport.

The following exercise shows you how to create and use perspective matching.

CREATING AND USING PERSPECTIVE MATCHING

1. Load the file CH16B.MAX. (Again, reload this file if you are continuing from the last exercise.)

2. Choose Rendering, Environment.

3. Click on the Assign button.

4. Choose Bitmap as the type.

5. Click on the Environment button and assign the map to slot #6 again.

6. Close the Environment dialog box.

7. Open the Materials Editor and activate slot #6.

8. Load the file LAKE_MT.JPG as the bitmap from your MAX Maps directory.

9. Set the environmental coordinates to Screen coordinates.

10. Close the Materials Editor.

11. Click on the camera viewport name to activate it, if it is not already active.

12. Choose Views, Background Image.

13. Choose the Files button.

14. Load LAKE2.TGA again.

15. Choose Select objects from the main toolbar.

16. Click on the camera icon in any viewport.

17. Choose the Modify command panel tab.

18. Choose the Show Horizon option in the command rollout for the camera. A line will appear in the camera viewport, as shown in figure 16.19.

Figure 16.19

The horizon line is visible in the viewport.

19. Activate the camera viewport if it is not active.

20. Choose Orbit camera from the viewport control buttons.

21. Click and drag around in the viewport until the horizon line matches the horizon of the background image, then release the mouse button.

22. Render the camera viewport. Figure 16.20 shows the final rendering.

Figure 16.20

The final perspective-matched rendering.

Summary

Environmental effects are important to creating ambiance and mood in certain scenes. Backgrounds are necessary to provide an extra hint of realism to most renderings or animations. Making use of these tools will greatly enhance not only your skills, but your overall output quality.

This concludes the fundamentals on composition and rendering. While you have learned the basics here, there is much more to learn. This learning will come with experience. Practice these tools as they are the most important tools in producing a rich, powerful rendering.

Now that you have seen all the basic elements involved in creating still-image renderings, it is time to move on to animations.

PART V

ANIMATION FUNDAMENTALS

Basic Animation

Up to this point, you have explored numerous features of MAX: The user interface, modeling, editing, composition, materials, rendering, and environments. But these are only part of what MAX brings you. One of the most powerful features of MAX is its capability to animate just about any geometry, light, camera, or modifier.

This chapter examines the basics of computer animation in MAX. In this chapter, you will learn about the following topics and how they apply to animating with MAX:

▲ Time in computer animation

▲ Keyframing

▲ Creating an animation

▲ Working with the interactive renderer

Time in Computer Animation

When learning about computer animation, the most important element to understand is time. Computer animation is achieved by displaying a series of individual frames at a speed fast enough to create the illusion of motion. This is the same principle used in simple hand-drawn animation. Different figures are drawn on each sheet in a stack of paper, and when you flip through the stack of paper fast enough, the figures seem to move smoothly.

In general terms, animation playback is not considered smooth unless you can achieve a speed of at least 15 frames per second (FPS), but the actual speed for which you will design your animation depends on what medium you are going to record the animation. For example, the film industry has standardized on 24 frames per second for films such as

Jurassic Park or *Toy Story*. If you are recording to the PAL (European) video standard, 25 frames per second is used. For the NTSC (American) video standard, 30 frames per second is used. In general, if you are not sure what the final output will be, base your animations on 30 frames per second.

MAX enables you to set the overall playback speed of the animation to any of these standards, or any frame rate that you desire. (See the section "Time Configuration Controls" later in the chapter for details.) Once you have set this information, you can display and work with time in MAX as frames, minutes and seconds, or even fractions of seconds.

Animation Basics in MAX

The most common method used for creating animation is *keyframing*. Keyframing is a process whereby objects are positioned in critical frames and someone—or in the case of MAX, something—fills in the frames between the critical ones. A *keyframe* is any frame of an animation in which a specific event is supposed to occur. The frames between keyframes are called *in-betweens,* or sometimes just *tweens*.

Keyframing in MAX works by setting the current frame of the animation to a frame where you want a certain event to happen. Then you turn on the Animate button and create the event. MAX then interprets the motion between keyframes for the event.

For example, you could set a keyframe at frame 30 where you rotate an object 180 degrees. MAX will interpret the rotation to occur between frames 1 and 30. (All objects in MAX have an initial keyframe at frame 1 to indicate their start positions in the animation.)

You can tell an object has a key at a specific frame because a white bounding box will appear around the object. Figure 17.1 shows you a box with a keyframe assigned at frame 49 and a box without a keyframe at frame 49.

Note

A good technique to help you control animation over time in MAX is storyboarding. *Storyboarding* is the process whereby you hand-draw specific sections of animation for the scene and pre-plan as much of the animation as possible. This makes it very easy for you to translate the animation you want into MAX because you will know at what points in time you want to have a keyframe occur. Once you know this, you can easily create the animation using the tools in MAX. This technique is used by almost all animators.

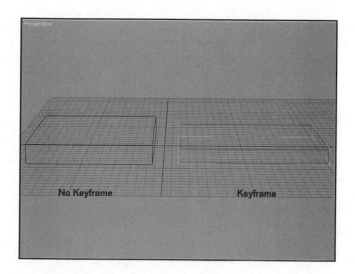

Figure 17.1

The box with a keyframe assigned has a white bounding box; the box without a keyframe assigned does not.

All animation in MAX is created when MAX is in animation mode. In this mode, any changes you make to geometry, materials, lights, modifiers, or any animatable parameters, are recorded as keyframes in the current animation frame. You can set MAX to animation mode by clicking on the Animate button at the bottom of the interface, to the left of the animation playback controls. When you do, the button turns red and the border around the current viewport turns red to indicate MAX is in animation mode.

Warning

It is very easy to forget that you are in animation mode in MAX. Remember, when you are in animation mode, any change you make to the scene is recorded as an animation keyframe. Always make sure you turn off the Animation button when you are done setting a key.

Motion Controllers

In MAX, animation is created because all changes are interpreted as some sort of motion. For example, if you move an object over time from one position to another, you are creating motion. Even if you created this motion using keyframes, a motion path is generated for the object to follow. MAX then assigns a motion controller to the path to determine how the path is interpreted.

For example, the path could be interpreted as a Bézier spline or as a TCB line. These two interpretations will produce different results in the overall motion of the object. Because you have a motion controller assigned to the object motion path, you can use the controller to control the pace, position, and orientation of the object along the motion path. (Chapter 18, "Track View," provides you with a full explanation of motion controllers.)

Animation Controls in MAX

There are many different ways for you to control animation and time in MAX. By using a variety of methods, you can achieve the animation timings for which you are looking. Some of the tools that MAX provides you to control animation and time are the following:

▲ Animation time slider

▲ Animation mode toggle

▲ Animation playback controls

▲ Time configuration controls

Animation Time Slider

The animation slider displays the current frame of the animation, as well as the overall number of frames or amount of time in the animation. By positioning this slider with the mouse, you can define the current frame or the length of the animation. When you play back an animation, the animation slider moves from left to right as it tracks the progress of frames and the passage of time; the time readouts on the slider change with the animation so you can always see what the current frame is or how much time has passed in the animation. Long animations can be broken down into active segments to make them easier to deal with. This way, you can work on a 10,000 frame animation, but only deal with a 1,000 frames at a time. The time slider can also show different time scales. For example, instead of showing you frame numbers, the time slider could show MINS:SECS if that is the current time format. These last two settings are dependent upon the settings in the time configuration dialog box.

Animation Mode Toggle

The animation mode toggle enables you to switch the system into and out of animation mode. When it is in animation mode, you can set keyframes for any animatable parameter in MAX. You know the system is in animation mode when the current viewport is outlined in red and the Animate button turns red. Figure 17.2 shows the interface in animation mode.

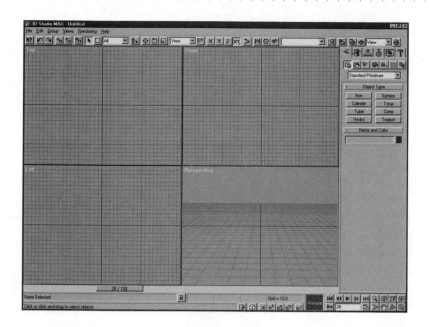

Figure 17.2

The interface in animation mode so you know when you are working with animation.

Animation Playback Controls

To the right of the animation mode button are a series of buttons that enable you to control the interactive playback of animations in MAX. Figure 17.3 shows these buttons.

Each of the animation slider and playback buttons is briefly described in the following list:

▲ **Go to start**. Sets the current frame to the beginning of the active animation segment.

▲ **Previous Frame**. Moves the current frame back one frame in the animation.

▲ **Play**. Plays the current animation in the current active viewport. Using shaded or wireframe mode, this is a great way to test your animation. This function makes the greatest use of a hardware accelerator to accelerate the HEIDI display.

▲ **Next Frame**. Moves the current frame forward one frame in the animation.

▲ **Go to End**. Sets the current frame to the last frame in the active animation segment.

▲ **Key Mode**. Toggles the system into key mode. Whenever this is active and you choose Next Frame or Previous Frame, you will be taken to the next frame that contains a key for the currently selected object. The next key that is selected will depend upon the current transform type selected. For example, if select and move is chosen, the next keyframe will be one that contains a position key.

▲ **Time Key In**. Enables you to enter a specific frame number or time. The animation is set to that frame when you press Enter.

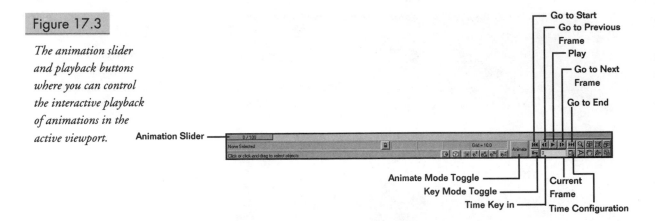

Figure 17.3

The animation slider and playback buttons where you can control the interactive playback of animations in the active viewport.

▲ **Time Configuration.** Enables you to configure how time is read and displayed in the animation, as well as how long the animation is and the intended playback rate. Alternatively, you can right click on any of the above buttons to access the time configuration dialog box as well. Figure 17.4 shows this dialog box.

Figure 17.4

The Time Configuration dialog box where you can define the length, playback rate, and time scale for the animation segment.

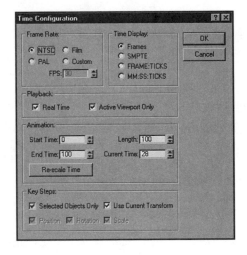

Time Configuration Controls

All animation time in MAX is configured and controlled through the Time Configuration dialog box. Here you can determine the overall amount of time in the animation, the animation playback speed, and the type of time readouts MAX will display. You can access the Time Configuration dialog box by either clicking on the Time Configuration button or right-clicking on any animation playback button. This dialog box is broken down into five different sections. Each section and their options are briefly described in the following list:

▲ **Frame Rate**. This section enables you to define the frame rate with which you are working.

▲ **NTSC**. NTSC stands for the National Television Standards Committee. The frame rate for NTSC is 30 frames per second. NTSC is the standard for the United States and for Japan.

▲ **PAL**. PAL stands for Phase Alternate Line. The frame rate for PAL is 25 frames per second. PAL is the standard for most European countries.

▲ **Film**. This is the frame rate for output to feature films. The frame rate is 24 frames per second.

▲ **Custom**. Enables you to set your own custom frame rates. The FPS spinner becomes available when you choose this option.

▲ **Time Display**. This section enables you to control how time is displayed on the animation slider and in any dialog box where you change the current time of the animation.

▲ **Frames**. Displays time as frames.

▲ **SMPTE**. This standard is developed by the Society of Motion Picture and Television Engineers. This option displays time as Minutes:Seconds.Frame.

▲ **Frames:Ticks**. MAX views time as ticks. There are 4800 ticks per second. Because there are 30 frames of animation per second in NTSC, each frame has 160 ticks per frame. This enables you to display time and control animation as 1/160 of a frame.

▲ **MM:SS:Ticks**. Enables you to view time as Minutes:Seconds.Ticks. Here the ticks can be as great as 4800, and you can display the time as 1/4800 of a second.

▲ **Playback.** Enables you to control the two options related to animation playback. These options are: Real Time and Active Viewport only.

▲ **Real Time**. Forces MAX to try to playback the animation in the viewport at the given frame rate. MAX will skip frames of animation to maintain the frame rate when this option is enabled. To see all frames in the interactive playback, turn off this option.

▲ **Active Viewport Only**. Enables interactive playback for the active viewport only.

▲ **Animation**. This set of controls enables you to define the overall length of the animation, as well as the current active segment.

▲ **Start Time**. Defines the start time, using the current time display, of the current animation segment.

▲ **End Time**. Defines the end time, using the current time display, of the current animation segment.

▲ **Length**. Defines the overall length of the current animation segment. This spinner is tied to the end time spinner. When you adjust one, the other is also adjusted.

▲ **Current Time**. Enables you to set the current time in the animation.

▲ **Re-Scale Time**. Enables you to re-scale the current active segment. All keys within this segment will be scaled equally. Choosing this button displays the dialog box shown in figure 17.5. You can re-scale the start, end, or length of the animation.

Figure 17.5

The Re-scale Time dialog box where you can rescale a segment of time in the animation.

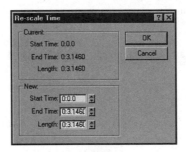

▲ **Key Steps**. This set of controls enables you to define how the key mode toggle works. The two controls here are Selected Objects Only and Use Current Transform.

▲ **Selected Objects Only**. When key mode is selected, this option causes the system to jump to the next frame containing a key assigned to the selected object. If no object is selected, using Go To Next Frame or Previous Frame will not work.

▲ **Use Current Transform**. Like selected objects, in key mode, the system will jump to the next frame with a key for the currently selected object in which the currently selected object is using the current transform. If you disable this option, you can select to jump to any of the three types of transforms.

When you are done setting your time configurations, choose OK to accept them. They will immediately appear in the time slider.

Creating an Animation

The following exercise shows you how to create a quick, simple animation in which you can animate a variety of objects.

CREATING A KEYFRAME ANIMATION

1. Load the file CH17A.MAX. Figure 17.6 shows what this file looks like before animation.

Figure 17.6

The scene before any animation has been applied to any objects.

2. Choose the Time configuration button.

3. Set the time display to SMPTE to display the time in a MINS:SEC.Frames, a readout that is much easier to understand that raw frame numbers.

4. Set the length of the animation to 0:4.0 or 4 seconds, and then choose OK.

5. Drag the time slider to 0:1.0 or 1 second.

6. Turn on the Animate button.

7. Select the tubular object in the middle using Select Objects.

8. Choose the Modify command panel tab.

9. Expand the deformations rollout and apply a Scale Deformation to the object.

10. Set the right endpoint of the deformation grid to 5, as shown in figure 17.7.

Figure 17.7

The scale deformation grid settings where you can control the deformation of the loft object.

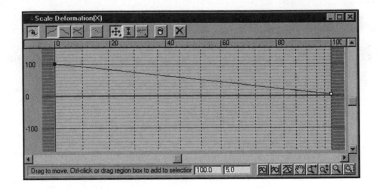

11. Set the time slider to 0:2.0 or 2 seconds.

12. Move the Scale endpoint back to its original position at 100.

13. Turn off the Animate Button.

14. Choose Go to Start in the animation playback controls.

15. Close the Scale Deformation Grid window.

16. Choose the Play button to see what the animation looks like at this point. If MAX skips too many frames, go back to the time configuration dialog box and turn off Real Time Playback.

17. Stop the playback when you are satisfied with it. You can stop it by clicking on the stop button in the animation playback controls.

18. Set the current frame to 0:2.0 by dragging the animation slider to the right.

19. Select the sphere on the right side of the scene using Select Objects.

20. Turn on the Animate button.

21. Choose Select and Non-Uniform Scale from the main toolbar so you can scale the object, but not equally in all axes.

22. Click in the front viewport and drag down and to the left until you get a shape close to the one shown in figure 17.8.

23. Set the time slider to 0:4.0 or 4 seconds.

24. Choose Select and Rotate from the main toolbar.

25. In the Top viewport, click on the sphere object and rotate it 720 degrees. You may want to turn on an angle snap to make this easier.

26. Turn off Animate.

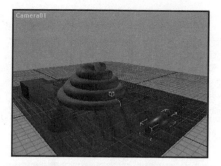

Figure 17.8

The sphere non-uniformly scaled to provide a slightly different animation effect.

27. Rewind the animation and play it back to see how it looks at this point.

28. Set the animation slider to 0:2.0 again by dragging the animation slider.

29. Choose Select Objects and choose the cone.

30. Open the Material Editor by clicking on the Material Editor button on the main toolbar.

31. Turn on Animate.

32. Activate the second material slot because it contains the material assigned to the cone. Notice the red outline indicating animation mode is on.

33. In the basic parameters rollout of the Material Editor, set the opacity to 100.

34. Drag the time slider to 0:4.0 and set the opacity to 0.

35. Turn off Animate.

36. Close the Material Editor.

37. Choose Rendering, Environment.

38. Add a volume light in the Environment Dialog box.

39. Assign the volume light to the spotlight in the scene by choosing Pick Light and clicking on the spotlight.

40. Set the following:

Density to 1.0
Noise On to On
Uniformity to 0.5
Size to 5.0
Phase to 1.0
Wind Strength to 0.5
Amount to 0.5

41. Close the Environment dialog box.

42. Turn on the Animate button.

43. Drag the time slider to 0:4.0 or 4 seconds.

44. Choose Select and Move.

45. Move the light itself to the right side of the scene in the Top viewport, as shown in figure 17.9.

Figure 17.9

The light in its new location providing a simple animation of the light.

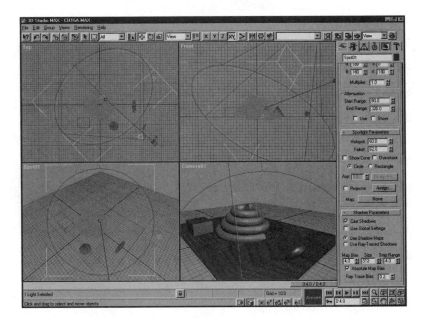

46. Set the time slider to 0:1.0 and then move the camera to the upper right corner of the Top viewport.

47. Set the time slider to 0:2.0 and then move the camera to the upper left corner of the Top viewport.

48. Set the time slider to 0:3.0 and then move the camera to the lower left corner of the Top viewport.

49. Set the time slider back to 0:4.0 and then move the camera back to its original place in the lower right corner.

50. Turn off animate.

51. Save the file as CH17B.MAX. This file is provided on the CD for reference purposes. This file will be used in later exercises to illustrate other points, so keep it handy.

52. Activate the camera viewport and play back the animation. At this point, you should see the camera view rotate around the model, the light and shadows constantly changing, the sphere spinning and shrinking, and the wound up tube getting smaller at the top.

This exercise illustrates some points about keyframe animation and how easy it is to use. For now, you will not render the file; that will come in a later chapter. However, if you want to see the final rendering, load the file CH17B.AVI from the accompanying CD (use File, View File and select it). This will launch the media player that can play the AVI file.

Working with the Interactive Renderer

As you have seen in the previous exercise, the interactive renderer in MAX can be very helpful for viewing animations as you work on them. Every time you need to check the animation, you can do this with the interactive renderer, much as you did in the last step in the last exercise. The renderer is capable of showing not only shaded views, but textures, opacity, and lighting as well. This makes creating animations extremely easy as you can interactively view the animated objects.

Of course, having an accelerator card such as a GLint card makes a huge difference in the performance of the system. A GLint card will give you between three and four times the performance of the fastest standard video cards today.

Unfortunately, even with the fastest accelerator card, most scenes will not be able to play back smoothly in the interactive rendering, but you can use the speed of the renderer to generate preview animations.

Previewing Animations

A preview animation uses the interactive renderer to create a simple version of the animation. Animators use these mostly to check the motion of objects in the scene. Because it is generated using the interactive renderer, lighting, opacity, and materials can be applied. None of these are very accurate, however, and should only be used to help test the motion. To test the lighting, opacity, or materials, you should render individual frames of the animation.

Generating a preview animation is a simple task. Under the Rendering menu (Figure 17.10), you have three options you can choose: Make Preview, View Preview, and Rename Preview. The Make Preview option displays a dialog box (see fig. 17.11) from which you can set the preview settings.

Figure 17.10

The Rendering menu where you can select to create a preview animation.

Figure 17.11

The Make Preview dialog box where you can select the options necessary to create a preview animation.

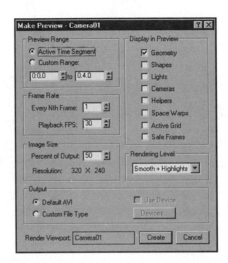

The Make Preview dialog box is broken down into six sections. Each is briefly described in the following list:

▲ **Preview Range**. Enables you to define the time segment you are going to include in the animation. You can choose the active time segment or a custom range.

▲ **Frame Rate**. Enables you to set the target frame rate for the animation file. Every Nth Frame allows you to create a preview of a regular sampling of the animation. Generating every other frame often is more than adequate and takes only half the usual time. Setting the Nth Frame spinner to 2 renders every other frame.

▲ **Image Size**. Enables you to set the size of the output file as a proportion of the image size set in the rendering dialog box. For example, if you set a rendering size of 640×480 in the render dialog box and the image size here is set to 50, the preview will be 50 percent of 640×480, which is 320×240.

▲ **Display In Preview**. Enables you to pick the types of objects to be shown in the preview animation.

▲ **Rendering Level**. Enables you to select the rendering level used by the interactive renderer to generate the preview animation.

▲ **Output**. Enables you to choose the output type or device. The default is an AVI or Video for Windows file.

When you have set all the options, you can generate the preview animation by choosing Create. Figure 17.12 shows a preview animation being generated.

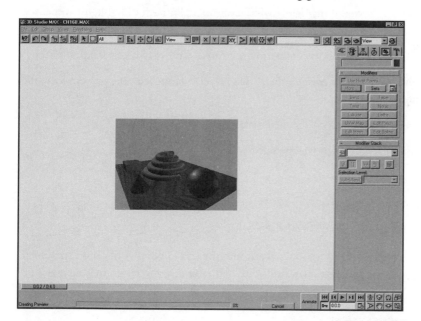

Figure 17.12

A preview animation as it is being generated showing you how the interface appears during this process.

The View Preview option from the Rendering menu loads the media player and the last preview animation that was generated. A preview animation has to be generated before you can use this option. You can rename the preview animation after it has been generated. MAX generates the preview animation under the filename SCENE.AVI in the PRE-VIEWS directory of your MAX installation. Rename enables you to change the name of the file so you do not overwrite it the next time you generate a preview animation.

The following exercise shows you how to generate and playback a preview animation. The preview animation is saved on the accompanying CD under the filename CH17B-P.AVI in case you don't want to wait for it to be generated by your system.

GENERATING A PREVIEW ANIMATION

1. Load the file CH17B.MAX that you created in the last exercise. It is also included on the accompanying CD-ROM if you did not complete the last exercise.

2. Activate the camera viewport.

3. Select Rendering, Make Preview.

4. Make sure the Preview Range is set to Active Segment, Smooth + Highlights are chosen as the rendering level, and the output is set to render a 320×240 file.

5. Choose Create. The preview animation is created. This may take several minutes.

6. When the animation is created, the media player is launched and you can view the animation.

7. Choose the Play button on the media player to see the animation.

8. Stop the animation when you are satisfied.

9. Exit the media player.

10. Choose Rendering, Rename Preview.

11. Rename the preview to CH17B-P.AVI.

At this point, you are encouraged to go back into the CH17B.MAX file and experiment with creating some more keyframes. Add your own geometry and try animating it as well.

Summary

As you can see, generating complex animation is very easy with keyframing. By creating a multitude of keyframes using any of a variety of animatable parameters, you can create almost any animation you want. In this chapter alone, you animated materials, positions, scales, loft deformations, cameras, and lights. Just about everything in MAX is animatable, so you are encouraged to explore more options and see what you can create.

However, you need to be able to control the keyframes with a greater level of detail than you have in this chapter. For example, you may not want the motion of an object to be constant between two keyframes. So, you need to be able to control and edit that motion. You can do this using the Track View dialog box, which is the focus of the next chapter.

18

Track View

In MAX, adding keyframes to an animation is a relatively simple task. But editing, modifying, and deleting one or more keys can be very difficult unless you use Track View. *Track View* is a powerful dialog box that enables you to edit all keyframes in your scene along a time line. Through this dialog box you can control the speed, motion, and spacing of keyframes, as well as create, delete, move, and copy keys.

This chapter explains how to use the Track View dialog box to edit an animation. In particular, this chapter focuses on the following items:

▲ Elements of the Track View dialog box

▲ Working in Edit Keys mode

▲ Working in Edit Time mode

▲ Working in Edit Ranges mode

▲ Working in Position Ranges mode

▲ Working in Function Curves mode

▲ Controlling animation with Track View

The Track View Dialog Box

You can access the Track View dialog box (see fig. 18.1) at any time by choosing the Track View button on the main toolbar.

Figure 18.1

The Track View dialog box.

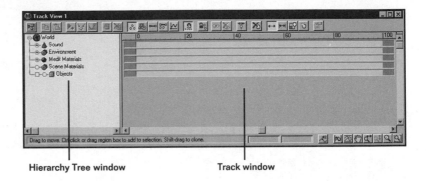

Hierarchy Tree window　　　　　　**Track window**

The Track View dialog box is divided into two windows and two rows of buttons: the Hierarchy Tree and Track windows, and the Control and View buttons. These elements of the Track View dialog box are explored in the following sections.

The Hierarchy Tree and Track Windows

The Hierarchy Tree window, on the left of the Track View dialog box, is an expandable tree list of all elements in the scene, including materials, sounds, objects, and environments. You can expand any of these tree's branches by clicking on the plus (+) button next to the branch name. Figure 18.2 shows you an expanded tree.

Figure 18.2

An expanded Track View tree showing you how detailed the hierarchy tree can get.

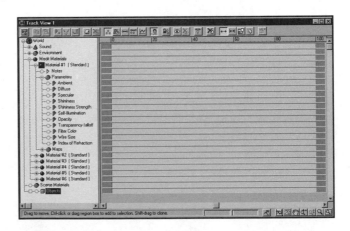

As you can see from figure 18.2, even something as simple as a material can have 12 or more tracks associated with it. When you create a key, you create it for a specific parameter of an object, such as its position or rotation. If an object has a key in a specific track, that key will appear in the Track window, the right side of the dialog box, at the frame where the key is located. Frames are numbered across the top of the Track window, in a time line. Figure 18.3 shows you a Track View with some keys assigned.

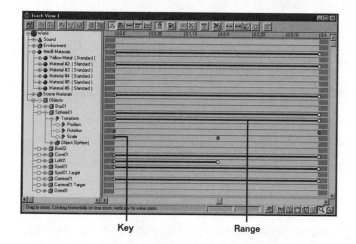

Key   **Range**

Figure 18.3

The Track View showing two position keys and two scale keys.

Take, for example, the Sphere01 object shown in the Hierarchy Tree window. If you expand its tree, as shown in the previous figure, you can access the transforms or the object parameters themselves. This Track View is the one from the file CH17B.MAX you created in the last chapter. As you may recall, you rotated the sphere 720 degrees at time index 0:4.0. The keys for the rotation of the sphere show up under the rotation transform track.

In the Track View window, to the right of the Transform entry, the start and end times of the transforms are represented by the white boxes at each end of the *range* (the heavy black line). The range represents the total length of time that this object is being animated by some sort of transform. The specific transforms are located below the Transform entry in the tree.

In the rotation track in figure 18.3, the gray spheres at time 0 and at time 0:4.0 represent (in the time line) the keys you created in the animation. From Track View, you can delete the individual keys, move them, copy them, and so on. If you take the cursor and click on one of the gray spheres, it turns white to indicate that it has been selected. Once it has been selected, you can easily transform the key at will. Figure 18.4 shows you the Track View dialog box with a selected key.

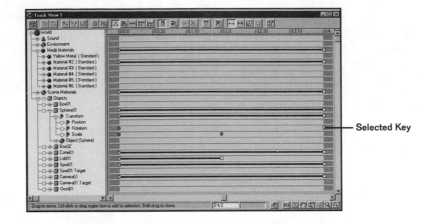

Selected Key

Control Buttons

Across the top of the Track View dialog box is a set of Control buttons that enable you to control aspects of the keys in Track View. Figure 18.5 shows you these buttons, and the following list describes each of the buttons.

Figure 18.5

The Track View Control buttons.

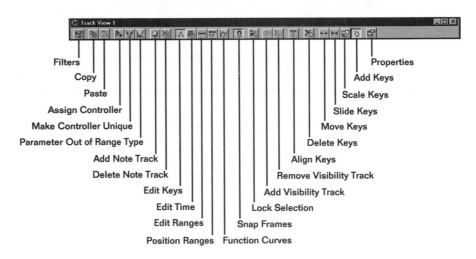

Filters — Properties
Copy — Add Keys
Paste — Scale Keys
Assign Controller — Slide Keys
Make Controller Unique — Move Keys
Parameter Out of Range Type — Delete Keys
Add Note Track — Align Keys
Delete Note Track — Remove Visibility Track
Edit Keys — Add Visibility Track
Edit Time — Lock Selection
Edit Ranges — Snap Frames
Position Ranges — Function Curves

Filters. Displays the Filters dialog box (see fig. 18.6) through which you can control what is displayed in the Track View dialog box.

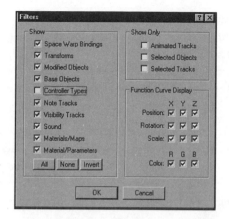

Use the Filters dialog box to control the display of tracks in the Track View dialog box.

On the left, you can choose what types of objects to show in Track View. On the right, you can define whether the display is animated or selected. In the lower-right section of the dialog box, you can determine which transforms show in the Function curves display (covered later in this section).

Copy. Enables you to make a copy of the selected keys so that you can paste them into another track.

Paste. Enables you to paste copied keys into the currently highlighted track.

Assign Controller. Each animated object in MAX is controlled by some sort of controller. Up to this point, you have used only transform controllers. You can use this button to assign a different controller to a track. (See Chapter 19, "Motion Controllers," for more information.)

Make Controller Unique. Converts an instanced clone of a controller to a copy. As you may remember, you can create a copy, instance, or reference of most objects in MAX—including animation controllers.

Parameter Curve Out-of-Range Types. Enables you to control how the animation of a selected track occurs outside the ranges you have defined. For example, you can use this option to make a defined animation pattern repeat over time. When you choose this type, you display the dialog box shown in figure 18.7.

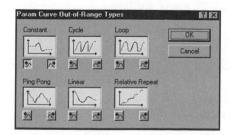

The Param Curve Out-of-Range Types dialog box where you can control animation outside of the keyframe ranges.

Below each out-of-range type are two buttons. The one on the left represents what happens to the selected track before the animation enters the range in which you defined the animation. The button on the right defines what happens when the animation leaves the range you defined. You can select the left or right button in any combination of out-of-range types. For example, you could have the animation constant entering the range and make it repeat after leaving the range.

Add Note Track. Enables you to add a note to a specific track, a feature that can be very helpful for future reference. Many of the things you can do in the Track View window get quite complicated. You can always leave yourself a note to remind you of why you did something. When you choose this option, a new track appears under the selected track. After you add the track, you simply add keys (discussed later in this section) to the track. Each key is a note that can be up to 16KB in size. By checking the properties of the key (discussed later in this section), you can enter information into the note through the Notes dialog box shown in figure 18.8. You can access this dialog box by double-clicking on the note in the track.

Figure 18.8

The Notes dialog box.

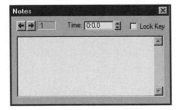

Delete Note Track. Deletes the currently selected note track. Note that choosing this button does not delete a single note only. It deletes all notes in the track, as well as the track itself. To delete a single note, delete the key it is attached to.

Edit Keys. Sets Track View to Edit Keys mode, in which you can edit individual or selection sets of keys in Track View. The buttons to the right of the Lock Selection button on the toolbar will change to match this mode. These buttons are shown in figure 18.1.

Edit Time. Sets Track View to Time mode, in which you can add, delete, stretch, or shrink time. The buttons to the right of the Lock Selection button on the toolbar change to match this mode. Figure 18.9 shows you these buttons.

Figure 18.9

The Edit Time Track View toolbar buttons.

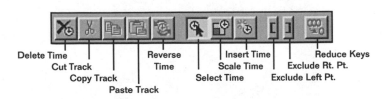

Edit Ranges. Sets Track View to Edit Ranges mode, in which you quickly can slide or move groups of keys. In this mode, individual keys are not shown. The button to the right of the Lock Selection button on the toolbar changes to match this mode (see fig. 18.10).

Figure 18.10

The Edit Ranges Modify Subtree button.

Position Ranges. Sets Track View to Position Ranges mode. This mode enables you to create some special effects by editing ranges independent of their associated keys. The buttons to the right of the Lock Selection button on the toolbar change to match this mode (see fig. 18.11).

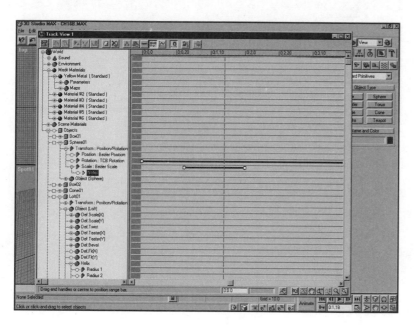

Figure 18.11

The Position Ranges button.

Function Curves. Enables you to edit animated keys as curves. Function curves may appear as curves, or as straight lines, depending upon the function and its current settings. These curves make it easier for you to see how an object is acting in the animation. For example, a position function curve may have sloped lines. The steeper the lines, the faster the object is moving. When this option is chosen, the buttons to the right of the Lock Selection button change, as does the right side of the Track View dialog box, as shown in figure 18.12. The function curve displayed will vary according to the type of animation curve you are looking at.

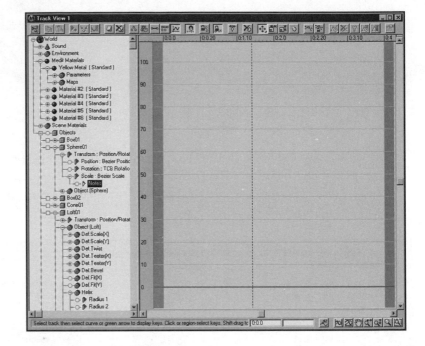

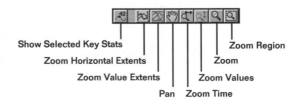 **Snap Frames**. Forces MAX to snap keys to individual frames when you are editing the keys in a particular track. Otherwise, the keys could end up assigned to a subframe tick.

Lock Selection. Locks the current selection of keys so that you cannot mistakenly select another key when you are trying to edit the selection set.

Any buttons displayed to the right of the Lock Selection button are covered in the appropriate sections later in this chapter.

View Buttons

At the bottom of the Track View dialog box are several buttons that enable you to control the view of Track View elements. These buttons, shown in figure 18.13, are described in the following list.

Show Selected Key Stats

Zoom Horizontal Extents

Zoom Value Extents

Pan

Zoom Time

Zoom Values

Zoom

Zoom Region

Show Selected Key Stats. In Function Curve mode, this button displays the stats for the selected key spot to the right of the key. For example, a display of `0,0,0:100.0` represents the X, Y, and Z transform scales at frame 0, all with a value of 100.

Zoom Horizontal Extents. Enlarges or reduces the right side of the Track View dialog box to show the active time segment.

Zoom Value Extents. In Function Curve mode, enlarges or reduces the right side of Track View vertically to show the entire active time segment.

Pan. Enables you to pan around either side of the Track View window, as you can in any standard viewport.

Zoom Time. Horizontally zooms the content of the right side of the window.

Zoom Values. Vertically zooms the content of the Function Curve window.

Zoom. Enables you to zoom in and out of track window. Track View of Track View (like using the Zoom command for a standard viewport).

Zoom Region. Enables you to zoom in to a specific region of the Track View window by defining a window around that region. (Works just like a Region Zoom in a standard viewport.)

Track View's Modes

As mentioned earlier, Track View works with different modes to achieve different levels of functionality. When Track View is set to a specific mode, you can only edit the tracks in certain ways, depending upon the mode. For example, in key mode, you can edit individual keys, but in ranges mode, you can only edit a range of keys, not an individual key. Each mode is activated by selecting the appropriate mode button from the Track View toolbar. Each mode is listed below:

▲ Edit Keys

▲ Edit Time

▲ Edit Ranges

▲ Position Ranges

Edit Keys Mode

With Edit Keys mode enabled, you can edit individual keys or selection sets of keys in Track View. The buttons to the right of the Lock Selection button on the toolbar will change to match this mode. Descriptions of these buttons follow:

Add Visibility Track. Adds a new track to the selected object. This track controls the visibility of the object over time. When you add keys to the visibility track, the keys set the visibility of the object to either 0 (off) or 1 (on). When the time passes a key, the visibility of the object is set until another key or the end of the animation is reached. You can control the value of a key through the Properties button (described later in this list).

Delete Visibility Track. Deletes the entire visibility track.

Align Keys. Enables you to set all currently selected keys to the current frame.

Delete Keys. Enables you to delete any selected keys.

Move Keys. Enables you to move any selected keys through time.

Slide Keys. Enables you to slide a track forward or backward in time, without having to adjust the spacing of the keys in the track.

Scale Keys. Scales the time between the selected keys and the current frame.

Add Keys. Enables you to add a key to any track.

Properties. Enables you to view the properties of any selected key. The dialog box that pops up when you choose this button differs between animation controllers. Figure 18.14 shows you the properties dialog box for a rotation key.

Figure 18.14

A Properties dialog box for a rotation key controlled by a TCB animation controller.

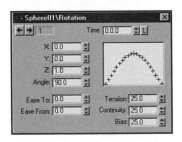

The most common use for Edit Keys mode is to add, delete, or move keys from one position to another in the Track View. The exercise in this chapter's "Controlling Animation with Track View" section shows you how to use Edit Keys mode.

Edit Time Mode

With Track View set to Edit Time mode, you can add, delete, stretch, or shrink time. When this mode is active, all keys and ranges are grayed out; you can select time by clicking and dragging across the window. The buttons to the right of the Lock Selection button on the toolbar change to match this mode. Brief descriptions of these buttons follow:

▲ **Delete Time**. Deletes the selected segment of time and any keys within that time.

▲ **Cut Track**. Cuts the selected section of time on the selected track so that you can paste it into the same track or another track. When you cut the track, the time and all keys are removed.

▲ **Copy Track**. Makes a copy of the selected section of time on the selected track so that you can paste it into the same track or another track. Unlike the Cut Track button, the Copy Track button does not remove the time and keys.

▲ **Paste Track**. Enables you to paste cut or copied sections of time into other tracks or in a different location in the same track.

▲ **Reverse Time**. Reverses the position of the keys in the selected area.

▲ **Select Time**. Enables you to select a segment of time in the current track by clicking and dragging. The time selection turns black and is surrounded by two vertical yellow lines (see fig. 18.15).

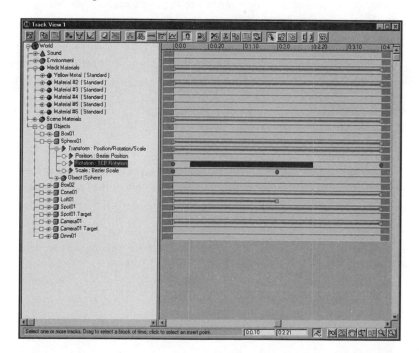

Figure 18.15

The Track View with selected time.

▲ **Scale Time**. Enables you to select a segment of time and scale that segment up or down. This change of scale will affect keys at various points in the animation.

▲ **Insert Time**. Enables you to add time to the current track.

▲ **Exclude Left End Point**. When you copy a segment of time to the clipboard, the first frame might contain a key that you do not want copied. In such a case you would use this button to exclude that key.

▲ **Exclude Right End Point**. Same as the Exclude Left End Point button, but this one works on the right (last) frame.

▲ **Reduce Keys**. Enables you to reduce the number of keys in a segment of animation and maintain nearly the same animation movements. This feature is very helpful when your animations have hundreds of keys.

Edit Time is a powerful method of controlling how much time you have in your tracks in Track View. See the exercise in this chapter's "Controlling Animation with Track View" section for an example of how to use this feature.

Edit Ranges Mode

With Track View set to Edit Ranges mode, you can slide or move groups of keys quickly (individual keys are not displayed). A single button to the right of the Lock Selection button on the toolbar is used in this mode. Following is a brief description of this button:

▲ **Modify Subtree**. Enables you to adjust the ranges of a group of keys. With this option enabled, you can adjust the ranges of the top-level object and all keys below that level in the hierarchy tree on the left side of the Track View dialog box.

Position Ranges Mode

With Track View set to Position Ranges mode, you can edit ranges (independent of their associated keys) to create some special effects. The button to the right of the Lock Selection button on the toolbar changes to match this mode. A brief description of this button follows:

▲ **ReCouple Ranges**. Enables you to move the ranges bar without moving the key. After you move the ranges bar, use this button to recouple it to the keys.

Function Curves Mode

Function Curves mode enables you to edit animated keys as curves instead of dots on a time line. These curves make it easier for you to see how the object is acting in the animation. For example, a position function curve may have sloped lines. The steeper the lines, the faster the object is moving. Figure 18.16 shows you a scale function curve.

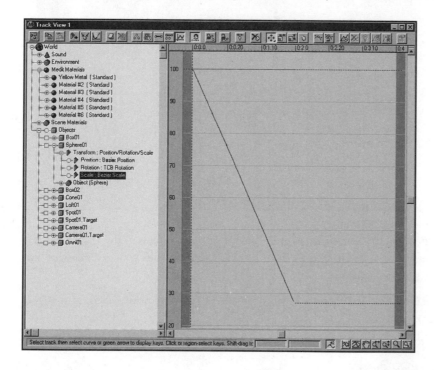

Figure 18.16

The Scale function curve for the Sphere01 object shows that the animated sphere is moving fast.

The function curves display each axis as a different color; X, Y, and Z are red, green, and blue, respectively. When you scale all three axes together, you see only one line, as in the example shown in figure 18.16. The curve in this example reads as follows: at frame 0, the object is equally scaled in all axes at 100 percent; from time index 0 to time index 0:2.0 the object is constantly scaled down in the Y and Z axes to a value of approximately 27 percent of its original size; the X axis stays constant at 100% for the duration of the animation. A selected key appears as a black box at a vertex on the curve line, as shown in figure 18.17.

Figure 18.17

A function curve with a selected key.

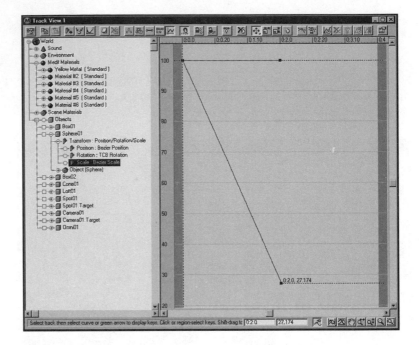

When Function Curves mode is enabled, the buttons to the right of the Lock Selection button change, as does the right side of the Track View dialog box. Following are descriptions of these buttons:

▲ **Freeze Non Selected Curves**. Freezes any curves you have not selected, so that you cannot change them.

▲ **Align Keys**. Aligns (to the current frame) all selected keys on all curves.

▲ **Delete Keys**. Deletes any selected keys.

▲ **Move Keys**. Enables you to move any selected keys to a new position in the curve. This button's flyout has two other Move options, used to restrict movement horizontally and vertically.

▲ **Scale Keys**. Scales the time between the selected keys and the current frame.

▲ **Scale Values**. Enables you to scale keys vertically by adjusting their values rather than their positions in time.

▲ **Add Keys**. Enables you to add keys to a function curve.

▲ **Show Tangents**. Enables you to adjust the tangent of the curves as they enter and leave certain keys. To adjust the tangents separately, press and hold down the Shift key.

▲ **Lock Tangents**. Enables you to lock a tangent so that you cannot adjust it.

The rest of the buttons in the Function Curves section get rather complicated rather quickly and easily exceed the scope of this book. Please consult the online documentation for more information on these controls.

The exercise in the next section demonstrates how to use function curves to control an animation.

Controlling Animation with Track View

As you will learn from the following exercise, the capability of controlling animation with Track View is a powerful feature of MAX. Through this feature, you will learn how to control animation and the keys on the Track View time lines.

This exercise takes the animation file you created in the last chapter and modifies the animation to create different effects, without actually having to create new animation.

USING TRACK VIEW TO CONTROL ANIMATION

1. Load the file CH17B.MAX that you created in the last chapter. It is also available on the CD-ROM if you did not complete the last exercise.

2. Click on the Track View icon to display the Track View for this file. Figure 18.18 shows the initial Track View window. You may need to resize the Track View window to see all of it.

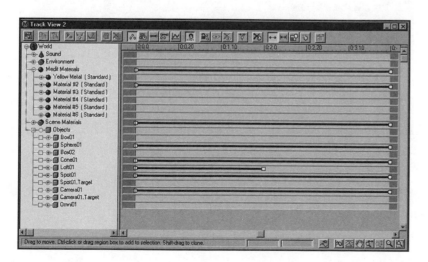

Figure 18.18

The Track View window for CH17B.MAX.

3. If you look closely at the way CH17B.MAX is created, there really isn't a good way to change the height of the lofted tube in the middle of the animation. Expand the Loft01 object tree on the left. Expand all options until the tree on your screen resembles the one shown in figure 18.19.

Figure 18.19

The hierarchy tree for the Loft01 object.

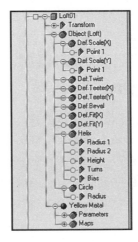

4. If you look under Loft01/Parameters/Helix, you will see all the parameters for the loft path, which was a helix. Choose Add Keys from the toolbar.

5. In the Helix Height track, click at time 0:2.0, and at 0:4.0 to add two keys, as shown in figure 18.20. These keys will be used to animate the height of the helix over time.

Figure 18.20

Three keys have been added to the Helix Height track.

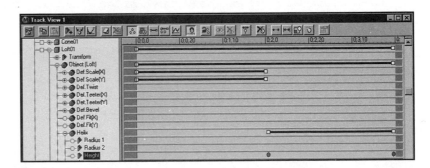

6. Right-click on the middle key, displaying a Properties dialog box.

7. In this dialog box, set the value to 100. This changes the height to 100 at this frame.

8. Close the Properties box.

9. Close Track View.

10. Play back the animation and watch the center loft object grow in height.

11. Stop the animation playback.

12. Save the file as CH18A.MAX. (This file is also provided on the CD.)

Now you'll see how to add time, using Edit Time mode.

13. Open Track View again.

14. Choose Edit Time mode on the toolbar.

15. Click on the Height track in the hierarchy tree to make it active.

16. Click and drag from approximately 0:1.0 to 0:1.15 on the right side of the dialog box, as shown in figure 18.21.

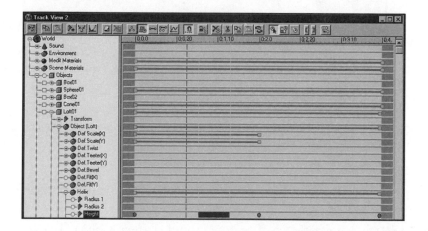

Figure 18.21

The Track View Time selection showing you the correct amount of time to select.

17. Choose the Delete Time button. Now, with the time segment deleted, the loft object will rise a little faster than it will fall.

18. Close the Track View window.

19. Play back the animation to see how it reacts.

The final segment of this exercise explains how to use a function curve to edit the animation keys.

20. Start Track View again.

21. Switch to Function Curves view. You may want to resize the Track View dialog box, making it larger so that it is easier to see and work with.

22. Click on the same Height track you have been working on. Figure 18.22 shows you the function curve for this track.

Figure 18.22

The Function Curves view of the Height track.

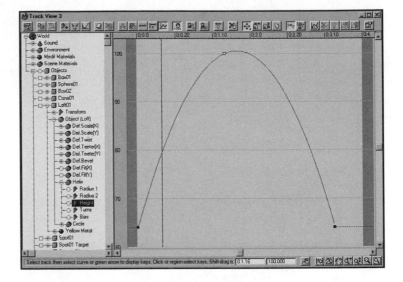

23. Choose the Move Keys button, and click once on the function curve. Two black boxes and a white box appear, representing the keys you just created. The white box is the currently selected key.(These boxes also are shown in fig. 18.22.)

24. When you right-click on the box near the top of the curve, you will see the dialog box in which you originally set the height for the key.

25. Close the dialog box.

26. Choose Zoom Values and expand the Track View window to show the function curve at a slightly smaller scale.

27. Click and drag the box near the top of the curve up vertically from a value of 100 to a value of 120.

28. Close the Track View window.

29. Play back the animation. As you can see, the loft object now rises to a height of 120 instead of 100.

There is a lot more to using the Track View dialog box, such as the capability to edit motion controllers (see next chapter). As you work through the remaining chapters in this book, you constantly return to this dialog box to adjust animations or learn more about how MAX handles animations (particularly as you learn about parameters and trajectories in Chapter 19).

Summary

The Track View dialog box is very helpful for controlling an animation, but it is not the only method you can use. As you will learn in the next chapter, you can also use the Motion command panel in MAX to control parameters and trajectories related to animation keys.

Motion Controllers

Whenever you create animation in MAX, some sort of controller is always assigned to the animated objects. These controllers, called *motion controllers*, affect the way the animation reacts when it enters or leaves a keyframe over time. Motion controllers are assigned any time you create animation. You can change motion controller through either the Track View dialog box or the Motion Command panel. As with any controller, there are always several options that you can control about the motion.

This chapter shows you how to use motion controllers to control animation keyframes. Many of the topics covered in this chapter are related to Chapter 18, "Track View," a MAX feature that also makes heavy use of controllers. This chapter focuses on the following topics:

▲ Trajectory motion controllers

▲ Trajectories

▲ Using a motion controller

You can access the motion controller functions from the Motion command panel. When you create an object and apply a keyframe to it, you can control the animation parameters. The animation parameters will vary depending on the motion controller that you are using. When you click on the Motion command panel tab with an animated object selected, you get the rollouts shown in figure 19.1.

Figure 19.1

*The Motion command
panel rollouts.*

Trajectory Motion Controllers

When you create animation in MAX, the keyframes are converted to a motion path that is usually a line such as a Bézier line. This conversion is automatic and necessary to create the animation. For example, when you animate a box moving from one position to another, MAX draws a line between the two keyframes and the box follows that line. The line is hidden so that you cannot see it and it does not render. A controller effects the curvature and spacing of this line. Different controllers affect the curvature and spacing differently.

The methods you use to control the motion of an object vary according to which animation controller is assigned to the object. You can adjust the parameters of the controller by using the Parameters option on the Motion command panel or the Track View Properties dialog box for any key.

MAX has eight basic animation controllers:

▲ TCB controller

▲ Bézier controller

▲ Linear controller

▲ Expression controller

▲ Path controller

▲ Noise controller

▲ List controller

▲ Look at controller

These basic controllers will change slightly to match the object type you are working with. The animated parameters for the controllers will change for each different type of object you assign the controller to.

Note

When you are working in Track View, you can select the Filters button and turn on the display of Controller Types. When you do, any tracks that have controllers assigned to them will show the controller name to the right of the track name in the hierarchy view.

To work with an animation controller, first create the object and assign some animation to it. Then select the object. At the top of the Motion command panel, you will see an Assign Controller rollout. Expand this rollout to see which controllers are assigned to the object (see fig. 19.2).

Figure 19.2

The Assign Controller rollout shows which controllers are assigned to the object.

In figure 19.2, you are looking at the controllers for a box that has been rotated in a keyframe. As a result of the rotation of the box, two types of controllers have been assigned to the three basic transforms. In this example, both the position transform and the scale transform have a Bézier controller, but the rotation transform has a TCB controller. You can change controllers by highlighting the transform type you want to change and clicking on the Assign Controller button at the top of the window to display the Replace Position Controller dialog box shown in figure 19.3.

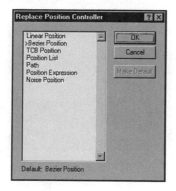

Figure 19.3

The Replace Position Controller dialog box with the list of controllers.

As you can see from the list of controllers shown in figure 19.3, seven of the eight basic animation controllers can be assigned to the position track of the rotated object. When you select a controller from this list, you have the option of making it the default controller. If you do, all objects that are animated by using a position transform will be assigned the default controller.

When you choose a controller from this list, the bottom of the command rollout changes, displaying any parameters for the controller. You may then change how the controller acts. The next sections discuss how you change the parameters for the different types of controllers.

Figure 19.4

The KeyInfo rollout for a Rotation TCB controller.

Figure 19.5

Controls in the Track View Box01/ Rotation KeyInfo dialog box are the same as those in the KeyInfo rollout.

TCB Controller

A TCB controller controls tension, continuity, and bias. Using this controller, you can control the spacing of keys around the keyframe by adjusting the tension, continuity, and bias of the motion curve around the keyframe. When you select a track with a TCB controller, MAX displays in the Motion command panel a KeyInfo rollout similar to the one shown in figure 19.4.

To access the same controls in Track View (see fig. 19.5), you right-click on the key spot in the rotation track.

At the top of the rollout is the time, or frame number, of the current key. By adjusting this number you can change the location, in time, of the key. Use the two black arrow buttons in the rollout's top left corner to move to the next or previous keyframe in which the selected object has a key. Alternatively, you can click on the L button next to the spinner to lock the key into this time slot so that you cannot move it by accident.

Below the frame number are X, Y, and Z spinner fields that show the current position of the object in the current frame, and an Angle (rotation) spinner that displays the current rotation value. Adjusting any of these parameters adjusts the key and the location and rotation of the object.

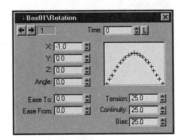

Below the Angle spinner are the TCB controls. Brief descriptions of these controls follow:

▲ **Key Curve Chart**. This chart shows you the spacing and position of keys around the keyframe. A red cross represents the keyframe. The black crosses are the frames before and after the key. By adjusting the TCB values, you adjust the curvature of these keys, and hence the motion of the object.

▲ **Ease To**. This spinner goes from 0 to 50 and places more keys closer to the key as the animation enters the keyframe. This has the effect of slowing down the animation as it gets closer to the key, or "easing" into the keyframe. In figure 19.6 you see the key curve with Ease To set to 50.

▲ **Ease From**. Ease From is similar to Ease To, but places more keys closer to the keyframe as the animation *leaves* the keyframe. The effect is that motion starts slowly and accelerates.

▲ **Tension**. This spinner controls the overall tension in the line. The higher the tension value, the less curvature there is in the line. This spinner can be set from 0 to 50. When tension is high, the curve is a straight line and causes a jerky animation. When tension is low, the curve has even more curvature and animation is much smoother. Figure 19.7 shows the key curve with tension set to 50.

▲ **Continuity**. This spinner affects the angle at which the frames in the key curve enter the keyframe. Higher values result in a dipped curve, which produces a hitch in the animation. Low values more closely approximate the tension set to 50. In figure 19.8, continuity is set to 50.

▲ **Bias**. This spinner affects overshoot and undershoot of frames around the keyframe. Higher values produce an overshoot animation where the motion of the object goes past the keyframe before returning to the original path. Lower values produce an undershoot animation where the motion of the object stops short of the keyframe. Figure 19.9 shows you the key curve with bias set to 50.

The TCB controller is an "older" method of working with and controlling animation around keys. (In the DOS version of 3D Studio, it was the primary way to control animation around keys.) In MAX, TCB is the default controller only in situations in which a Bézier controller does not work well.

Bézier Controller

The most commonly used controller—a Bézier controller—converts motion paths to Bézier splines. In the Assign Controller box shown in figure 19.2 you saw two transforms with Bézier controllers. When you select one of these transforms (with the Bézier controller), you see the Basic and Advanced KeyInfo rollout shown in figure 19.10.

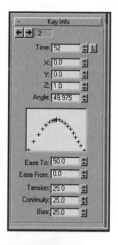

Figure 19.6

The Key Curve with Ease To set to 50.

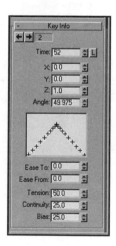

Figure 19.7

The Key Curve with Tension set to 50.

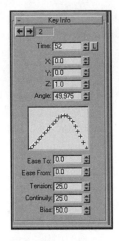

Figure 19.8

*The Key Curve with
Continuity set to 50.*

Figure 19.9

*The Key Curve with
Bias at 50.*

Figure 19.10

*The Bézier controller
KeyInfo rollouts.*

This basic KeyInfo rollout has the same keyframe number and lock controls, and the same X, Y, and Z spinners as the TCB controller rollout. Below these familiar features are two large buttons that control the motion of the object as it enters (In) and leaves (Out) the keyframe. These buttons enable you to define how the tangent of the Bézier line is defined on the in or out side of the key. When you click and hold on the large buttons, you can see the different tangent types, as shown in figure 19.11.

Figure 19.11

*The Bézier Keyframe
Tangent controls.*

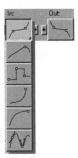

Each of the six Bézier tangent controls causes the tangent curve of frames before or after the keyframe to react slight differently, in much the same way the TCB controls affect the key curve.

The default is the first tangent curve type, which produces a nice smooth motion through the keyframe. The reaction of the others is similar to the graphic representation on the button. For example, the second button from the top of the list has sharp corners and causes very jerky animation, with rigid transitions.

The last Bézier tangent controller is a custom controller. When you choose this button, the KeyInfo Advanced rollout becomes available, as shown in figure 19.12.

Figure 19.12

The activated KeyInfo Advanced rollout.

The In and Out controls on the Advanced rollout enable you to control the rotation of the tangent handles of the curved line so that you have precise control over the tangent points. These new values essentially replace the preset curve values and create new tangent curves based on the In and Out values. Adjusting the tangent points is better done in Track View as the tangent points can be directly manipulated there, and the results of these changes on the curve can be seen directly The Normalize Time control takes an average of the keys over time. Constant Velocity keeps the velocity of an object the same between keys.

For the most part, you will use the default Bézier controller. If you need to, you can use other forms of the Bézier controller, or generate your own. The advanced Bézier controller types are beyond the scope of this book. If you need more information on these topics, consult the MAX documentation or Help.

Linear Controller

A linear controller is a very simple animation controller. It makes the curves between two keyframes straight lines, which is great for creating rigid, mechanical animations. Because it is a straight-line controller, there are no parameters to change within the controller.

Expression Controller

With the expression controller, you use mathematical expressions to control the motion of objects between keyframes. This controller has several parameters that must be accessed from within Track View. To use the expression controller, highlight the track you want to assign it to, then choose the Assign Controller button from the Track View toolbar. In the Replace Position Controller dialog box, choose Expression controller and choose OK to assign this controller to the track. To access the parameters, simply right-click on the track to display the dialog box shown in figure 19.13.

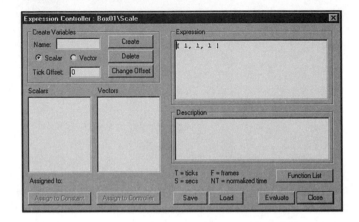

Expression controllers are well beyond the scope of a Fundamentals book. They are mentioned here just so that you know what they are. For their actual use, refer to your MAX documentation.

Path Controller

The path controller enables you to assign an object's motion to a spline path that you have already drawn. When you assign this type of controller to the object, the rollout displayed in the Motion command panel resembles the one shown in figure 19.14. Generally, you will assign path controllers to position tracks only. This is because a path controller assigns a Bézier line as the motion path, which only affects the position track of an object.

Figure 19.14

The Path Controller parameters.

The Pick Path button enables you to choose the path that you attach the object to. After you have attached the object, you have two other choices: Follow and Bank.

The Follow option forces the object to reorient itself as it travels along the path, always pointing in the same direction as the path. When you do not choose Follow, the object moves along the path without ever changing its orientation. The Bank option forces the object to bank as it travels along the curves of the spline. When Bank is active, you can set both the amount and the smoothness of the bank.

For example, you could draw a spline through your scene that is representative of where you want to have your camera. Create a free camera and attach it to this path. Then, you can turn on follow, and optionally, banking. This makes it very easy for you to control the motion of your camera. You can control the number of frames or amount of time the object follows the path by adjusting the track in Track View.

Noise Controller

The noise controller is used to add random dips and valleys to the motion curve. In much the same way you add noise to a volume light, you can add noise to a motion path. You must apply this type of controller (as you apply expression controllers) in the Track View dialog box. Like expression controllers, this controller has several parameters that must be accessed from within Track View. Then, right-click on the track to which you assigned the controller to display the Noise Controller dialog box shown in figure 19.15.

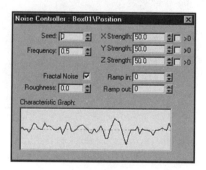

Figure 19.15

The Noise Controller dialog box where you can set the parameters of the noise motion controller.

You can control the following parameters in the Noise Controller dialog box:

▲ **Seed**. Gives the random number generator a starting point.

▲ **Frequency**. Enables you to control the randomness of the curve. The higher the values, the more ragged and discontinuous the curve.

▲ **X, Y, and Z Strengths**. Enable you to control the scale factors applied to each axis of the object's motion. Next to the X,Y, and Z strengths are ">0" checkboxes. If a box is checked the curve for that axis is offset by half the strength.

▲ **Fractal Noise**. Enables the use of fractal algorithms to generate the noise.

▲ **Roughness**. A fractal function, roughness controls the fractal dimension of the curve, which makes it look rougher.

▲ **Ramp In**. Enables you to control how quickly the noise curve takes over the motion path from the start frame.

▲ **Ramp Out**. Enables you to control how quickly the motion path returns to normal at the end of the noise curve.

▲ **Characteristic Graph**. A representative graph of the motion's appearance.

List Controller

You use a list controller to generate a list of controllers that you will combine to provide different effects for the animation. When you choose this option, you get the rollout shown in figure 19.16.

Figure 19.16

*The List Controller
Rollout.*

Each motion controller you add to the list controller track gets added to the list. You can cut, copy, delete, and paste controllers into and out of this list. In Track View, a new track appears below the selected track. This new track is a placeholder, used to add or paste new controllers to the List Controller.

Look at Controller

You use a look at controller to force one object to always look at another. A look at controller is applied at the Transform level, and when this is applied, the Position/

Rotation/Scale transforms are replaced with Position/Roll Angle/Scale. For example, a target camera uses a look at controller to force the camera to always look at the target icon. When you choose this option, you get the rollout shown in figure 19.17.

Figure 19.17

The Look at Controller rollout.

The only new option here is Pick Target, which you use to choose the target object.

Most of the motion controllers mentioned here are used for special purposes. Generally, you will use either a TCB or Bézier controller. For example, when you animate an object moving from one position to another, the default controller is a Bézier controller. You can also easily assign a TCB or Path controller to achieve similar results. A noise controller or a list controller, however, would not work as they would not yield the same or similar animation results.

Trajectories

Clearly, being able to control motion in a scene is terrific—but so is being able to see the motion path in the scene. To see the motion path, first select the object that is in motion, then choose the Trajectories button in the Motion command panel. MAX displays the motion path for the selected object, as shown in figure 19.18.

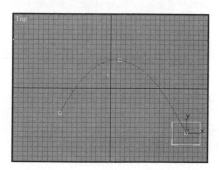

Figure 19.18

The Motion Path for an object.

The motion path is displayed as a blue line, with white boxes on the line representing the position keys for the object. Depending on which motion controller you use, this path can be a straight line, a Bézier line, or a TCB line. In this case, it is a Bézier line.

To interactively change the position of keys, choose the Sub Object button at the top of the Trajectories rollout, then use a transform (such as Select and Move) to reposition any key. As you do this, you can watch the changes that occur in the motion path.

You can use the motion path also to see how a motion controller affects the path. To do this, choose the Parameters button and set the motion controller. When you again display Trajectories, you can see the changes caused by the controller. Figure 19.19 shows the same motion path shown in figure 19.18, but with a noise controller applied.

Figure 19.19

The motion path shows the effects of the noise controller.

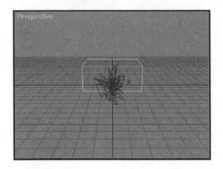

The Trajectories rollout also has the following controls:

▲ **Delete Key**. Use this button, which becomes available when the sub objects for keys are enabled, to delete keys from the path.

▲ **Add Key**. For this option, as for the Delete Key, sub objects must be enabled. Add key enables you to add as many keys as you like to the path.

▲ **Start Time**. Enables you to define the start time for the spline conversion.

▲ **End Time**. Enables you to define the end time for the spline conversion.

▲ **Samples**. Enables you to define the sampling rate for the spline conversion. Higher samples represent a more accurate conversion.

▲ **Convert To**. Enables you to convert the motion path to a regular spline, using the preceding settings.

▲ **Convert From**. Enables you to convert a spline to a motion path.

Using a Motion Controller

The following exercise shows you how to use a motion controller. In this exercise, you will apply different motion controllers to different objects to produce different results in the same animation.

USING MOTION CONTROLLERS

1. Load the file CH19A.MAX.

2. Click on the Motion command panel tab.

3. Play back the animation, to see what it looks like at this point. (It is a simple block, moving up and down, created using three keys.)

4. Select the light blue block.

5. Click on the Trajectory button. The motion path appears (see fig. 19.20).

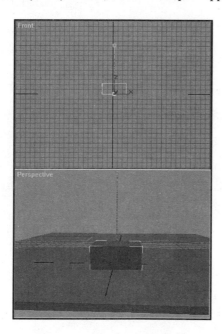

Figure 19.20

The motion path for the block.

Figure 19.21

The angular tangent method for the Bézier curve.

6. Choose the Sub-Object button.

7. Choose Select and Move from the main toolbar.

8. Select the key at the top of the motion path, and move it to the right in the front viewport.

9. Play back the animation to see the changes.

10. Choose Undo.

11. Turn off Sub-Object selection.

12. Click on the Parameters button in the rollout to return to the parameters section.

13. Set the animation to frame 50, which is a keyframe.

14. Set the In button to the angular tangent method, as shown in figure 19.21. You can accomplish this by clicking and holding on the In button until the flyout buttons appear. Then choose the angular tangent button.

15. Rewind the animation and play it back. Notice how the block jumps, instead of moving smoothly.

16. Choose Undo.

17. Expand the Assign Controller rollout.

18. Click on the Position controller to highlight it.

19. Choose the Assign Controller button.

20. Select the Linear position controller, and choose OK.

21. Play back the animation. Notice how much more rigid the animation is.

22. Choose Undo.

23. Expand the rollout again, and select Position.

24. Choose Assign Controller again.

25. Assign the noise controller.

26. Play back the animation. The noise controller makes a nice shaking box.

27. Choose Undo.

28. Go to the Display command panel and unhide the object named Line01.

29. Click on the Go to Start button in the animation controls.

30. Return to the Motion command panel, and expand the Assign Controller rollout.

31. Choose Position again.

32. Choose Assign Controller again.

33. Select Path, and choose OK.

34. Select the Pick Path button.

35. Click on the Line01 object. The box is repositioned at the beginning of the path.

36. Play back the animation.

37. Turn on Follow, and again play back the animation. Notice that the box now turns with the path.

38. Turn on Bank, and play back the animation again. Notice that the box now banks with each curve (but too much).

39. Set the Bank amount to 0.15, and play back the animation.

40. Open the Track View window.

41. Expand the Objects hierarchy.

42. Expand the Box02 hierarchy, as well as the Transform hierarchy under Box02. The Position track should show a range. This range is the length of time over which the box is traversing the line.

43. Click on the right endpoint of the range and move it to frame 50 (see fig. 19.22).

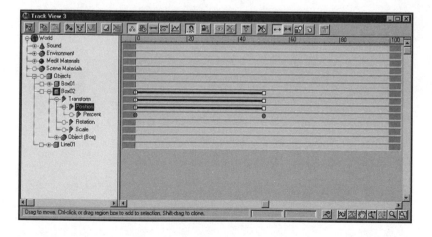

Figure 19.22

The new location for the range bar appears.

44. Close the Track View window.

45. Play back the animation. Notice that the box now moves along the path twice as fast.

Summary

Motion controllers are essential to creating realistic, lifelike animation. By controlling the motion between keyframes, you can make the motion of objects look much more realistic. You can take this a step further and use other methods to help generate your keyframes. The next chapter shows you how to animate characters by using hierarchical linking and Inverse Kinematics (IK).

Linking and IK

One of today's most popular uses for animation packages such as 3D Studio MAX is to animate characters. *Character animation*—animating a person or creature that has arms, legs, facial expressions, and so on—is one of the most difficult types of animation to create. Capturing human or animal movement in an animation requires tremendous patience, thought, and careful observation.

Creating character animation is much easier to do with MAX, using some of the program's built-in tools, than with some other animation packages. This chapter focuses on these tools, with particular emphasis on using them in the following ways:

▲ Controlling pivot points in animation

▲ Linking objects together

▲ Forward kinematics versus inverse kinematics

▲ Using IK to create character animation

By the end of the chapter, you will have a good idea of how to link objects together and how to control the joints between the objects using IK. At the end of the chapter, you will work through an exercise showing you how to link a robotic arm together. Then, use IK to animate that arm with real-world joint restraints.

Controlling Pivot Points in Animation

After you work with animation for a while in MAX, you will realize that you need to rotate certain objects around a specific point, such as the center of the object, or one end of the object. In many cases, regardless of the reference coordinate system you choose, you cannot create the rotation you need. At this point, you have two choices: You can either create a point helper object and use that as the reference coordinate system to rotate about, or you can simply move the pivot point.

The *pivot point* is defined as a point around which the rest of the object rotates. This point is generally the center of the object, unless the pivot point has been moved. You can access the pivot point controls for an object by selecting the object and clicking on the Hierarchy command panel tab to display the command panel shown in figure 20.1.

On the Hierarchy command panel are three buttons that enable you to work with three different aspects of hierarchical relationships between objects. The Pivot button, which displays the rollouts shown in figure 20.1, enables you to control where a pivot point for an object is located. The IK button enables you to create and assign IK values to linked objects (a topic discussed later in this chapter). The Link Info button enables you to define how one object is linked to another, when you actually link them together.

As you can see from the figure, the Pivot option on the Hierarchy command panel has two rollouts. The Adjust Pivot rollout enables you to control the location and orientation of an object's pivot point. The Adjust Transform rollout enables you to transform and align an object to a coordinate system.

Descriptions of the buttons on the Adjust Pivot rollout follow:

▲ **Affect Pivot Only**. When this option is enabled and you adjust the pivot point of an object, only the pivot point is adjusted. The object is not affected.

▲ **Affect Object Only**. When this option is enabled and you adjust the pivot point of an object, the object is adjusted around the pivot point, which is stationary.

▲ **Center to Object**. Centers the pivot point to the center of an object.

▲ **Align to Object**. Aligns the pivot point's coordinate system to that of the object.

Figure 20.1

The Hierarchy command panel where you can adjust the Pivot, IK, and Link Info of the selected object.

▲ **Align to World**. Aligns the pivot point's coordinate system to the world coordinate system.

The Adjust Transform rollout has the following buttons:

▲ **Affect Object Only**. When this option is enabled and you adjust the transform of an object, only the object is affected, not the pivot point.

▲ **Align to World**. Aligns the objects to the world coordinate system.

▲ **Align to Parent**. Aligns the object to its parent's coordinate system. (Parents are discussed later in this chapter.)

▲ **Transform**. Enables you to reset the transformation matrix of an object to the world coordinate system. When you create an object, a transformation matrix is created. When you transform the object, the matrix is changed. This option resets the matrix to match the world coordinate system.

▲ **Scale**. Same as transform, but it resets the scale of an object.

The following exercise shows you how to use the Pivot options on the Hierarchy command panel.

CREATING AND USING PIVOT POINTS

1. Load the file CH20A.MAX, which is used for all exercises in this chapter. Figure 20.2 shows this file loaded in MAX.

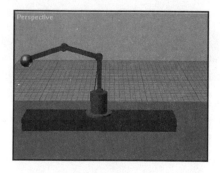

Figure 20.2

The exercise file in MAX before any pivot point adjustments.

2. Choose Select and Rotate.

3. Click on one of the arms of the object.

4. Rotate it a couple of degrees. Notice how it rotates around one end point.

5. Choose Undo.

6. Click on the Hierarchy command panel tab.

7. Choose Affect Pivot Only. The pivot icon appears as a tripod, as shown in figure 20.3.

Figure 20.3

The pivot icon where you can control the pivot point location and orientation.

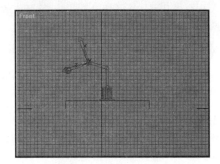

8. Choose Center to Object. The pivot point is centered on the object.

9. Turn off Affect Pivot Only.

10. Try to rotate the object again. It now rotates around the pivot point.

11. Turn on Affect Pivot Only.

12. Choose Select and Move.

13. Click and drag the pivot point to a new location on the screen.

14. Again, turn off Affect Pivot Only, and try to rotate the arm. It rotates around the pivot point.

15. Choose Affect Object Only.

16. Choose Select and Move, and move the arm to a new location. Notice how the arm moves and the pivot point does not. Again, if you try to rotate the object, it will still rotate around the pivot point.

17. Finally, under Adjust Transform, choose Align to World. This object is now aligned to the world coordinate system.

 Tip

> Whenever you are animating an object and need to change the center of rotation, adjusting the pivot point is usually much easier than creating a point helper to use as the rotation point.

Linking Objects Together

Clearly, adjusting the pivot point of an object is of great benefit when you are animating a single object. But there will be times, especially in character animation, when you will want to animate an object by transforming it, and have other objects repeat the same transform. For example, if you animate the upper arm of a character, you will want the lower arm, wrist, and hand to animate with the upper arm, as it would in real life. You could accomplish this in Track View by copying and pasting keys between tracks—but that process quickly becomes tedious.

The solution here is to link one object to another and form a hierarchical chain. The linked object becomes the child, and the object it is linked to becomes the parent, which is the basis for *forward kinematics*. When the parent object is transformed, the child object is transformed also, unless you change the Link Info settings. But if you transform the child, the parent is *not* transformed. This is the basis for something called *forward kinematics*.

To link two objects together, you must use a selection tool called Select and Link. You can see this tool and its sister tool (Select and Unlink) on the main toolbar in figure 20.4.

Figure 20.4

The Select and Link and Select and Unlink buttons.

To link an object as a child to another (parent) object, simply choose Select and Link. When you place the cursor over an object, it will change to the select link cursor. Then, click on the object you want to be the child and drag to the object you want to be the parent. A line will form between the two, and the cursor will change to the accept link cursor. When you release the mouse button while the accept link cursor is visible, both objects are highlighted for a moment and then return to normal. Although they look the same as they did before you linked them, they do not act the same. Now, when you move the parent, the child moves with it.

Using this manner of linking, you form a hierarchical tree which, as you can imagine, can be very powerful for character animation. For example, you can link a torso object to an upper arm, the upper arm to a forearm, and the forearm to a hand of the character. And, using the previously mentioned pivot-point adjustments, you can place the pivot points for each respective object at the joint locations. Then, when you rotate the upper arm, the forearm and hand rotate with it.

When the child object is selected, you can control which parameters are linked from the parent by clicking on the Link Info button on the Hierarchy command panel to display the rollouts shown in figure 20.5.

Figure 20.5

The Link Info rollouts where you can control which transformation axes of a parent object are passed on to the child.

The first of these Link Info rollouts is the Locks rollout. When you select any axis of the transform sections, you cannot transform the selected object along that axis. Inherit, the second rollout, determines which aspects a child object inherits from the parent. You can restrict the inheritance to specific axes under specific transforms, if necessary. For example, if you create a Ferris wheel, you would attach the cars of the wheel as child objects. When the Ferris wheel rotates, so do the cars. But, you would only want to inherit the rotation in one axis. Otherwise, the cars will rotate with the Ferris wheel and dump their passengers out!

The following exercise shows you how to quickly link objects together.

LINKING OBJECTS TOGETHER

1. Load the file CH20A.MAX again. (If you are continuing from the last exercise, please reload the file from the CD.)

2. Choose Select and Link, and click on the ball at the end of the last arm (see fig. 20.6).

3. Click and drag up to the first arm, and let go over the first arm. The ball and arm should highlight briefly to indicate that they are linked.

4. Link the first arm to the first circular joint.

5. Link the first circular joint to the second arm.

6. Link the second arm to the second circular joint.

7. Link the second circular joint to the third arm.

8. Link the third arm to the fourth circular joint.

9. Choose Select and Rotate.

10. In the front viewport, select the fourth circular joint, and rotate it 45 degrees. Notice the way the rest of the arm responds.

11. Rotate the third joint 30 degrees. Notice that the rest of the arm (which is lower in the hierarchy chain) moves, but that the objects higher in the hierarchy chain do not move. This type of animation is the basis of forward kinematics. By applying this type of animation with keyframes, and with some work, you can produce character animation.

12. Save the file as CH20B.MAX for use in a later exercise.

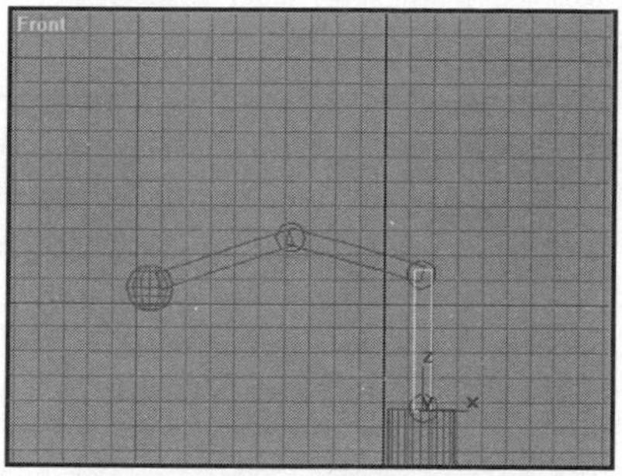

Figure 20.6

The arm to select.

Forward Kinematics versus Inverse Kinematics

There are two ways to create character animation efficiently and effectively. The first is forward kinematics, which you have just seen. In forward kinematics, you animate a hierarchical chain by transforming parent objects and affecting child objects with that transform.

Inverse kinematics (IK) does just the opposite. Instead of transforming the parent, you transform the child—and the parent objects are affected, all the way up through the chain. This is only part of IK's power. IK also enables you to define how the joints work. In IK, you can use two types of joints: rotating and sliding. You can limit these joints in any axis, to any number of degrees or any distance. And by setting information such as joint precedence, damping, and so on, you can easily make the character's animation more lifelike.

The downside of IK is that you give up some control of the animation to the IK system. You rely upon the IK system to calculate certain keyframes and motion—good in some cases, but troublesome in others. Despite its downside, IK is extremely powerful for the creation of character animation.

Using IK to Create Character Animation

To use IK in character animation, you must first perform the linking operation used in forward kinematics. Always start with the last object in the chain and work your way back to the parent object when linking. Because it is inverse kinematics, the child objects affect the parent, and hence, the last object on the link chain should be a child object. After you have linked the objects, you can apply the IK parameters to the joints between the objects.

After the IK parameters have been set, you turn on inverse kinematics by choosing the IK button on the main toolbar (see fig. 20.7). Then, whenever you manipulate an object that is part of an IK chain, the IK constraints are used. When the IK button is active, it turns blue. When the button is inactive, the chain acts like a normal hierarchical chain.

Figure 20.7

The Inverse Kinematics button.

When you set up the hierarchical chain between objects, it is nice to be able to see the links between the objects. You can do this with the Link Display rollout at the bottom of the Display command panel (see fig. 20.8).

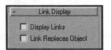

Figure 20.8

The Link Display rollout.

The first option in this rollout, Display Links, draws a bonelike structure that represents the link for all selected objects. When the second option, Link Replaces Object, is enabled, the object is replaced by the link, which makes it easier to understand how the IK works. In figure 20.9, you can see the arm scene with both types of displays.

Figure 20.9

The mechanical arm, showing links.

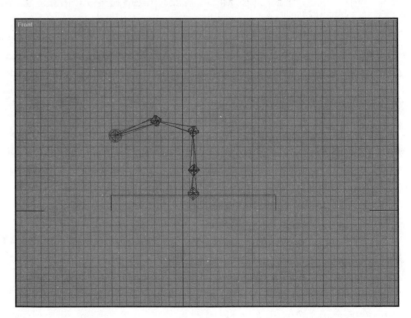

When the links are visible, you can select either the object you want to work with, or the link object. When you transform one, the other is transformed also.

Tip

> You can use dummy objects in your hierarchical chain to define joints or points of rotation. Dummy objects, found on the Create command panel under Helpers, do not render, but will add another link to the chain when necessary.

To apply the IK, you must first select the object to which you want to apply IK, and then select the IK button on the Hierarchy command panel to display the rollouts shown in figure 20.10.

The four rollouts—Inverse Kinematics, Object Parameters, Sliding Joints, and Rotational Joints—and their options are described next.

The Inverse Kinematics rollout enables you to solve the motion for an IK chain that is attached to a follow object. Whenever the last object in the kinematic chain is attached to a follow object, the motion of the follow object is translated into the kinematic chain. Solving the kinematic chain finds all the position and rotation keys for each joint, necessary to make the animation occur correctly. This rollout provides the following options:

▲ **Apply IK**. Solves the kinematic chain for follow objects.

▲ **Update Viewports**. Used for updating viewports as the chain is solved.

▲ **Clear Keys**. Removes all keys from the kinematic chain.

▲ **Start, End**. Enables you to define the range of time for which the solution is created.

The Object Parameters rollout enables you to define the objects in the chain and their precedence, bindings, and order in the chain. This rollout offers the following options:

▲ **Terminator**. Enables you to define the end of the IK chain by selecting one or more objects. After you have selected objects as terminators, objects above the terminator in the chain are not affected by IK calculations.

▲ **Bind Position**. Enables you to bind the selected object to its position. When this option is enabled, the selected object will not change position until the IK calculations force it to.

Figure 20.10

The IK rollouts.

▲ **Bind Orientation**. This option forces the selected object to maintain its orientation until the IK calculations force it to change.

▲ **Bind To Follow Object**. Binds the selected object to a follow object. Then, when you animate the follow object, the IK chain is animated. Any other object can be used as a follow object, but dummy objects generally are used because they do not render.

▲ **Precedence**. Enables you to set the precedence, or importance, of the object in the kinematic chain. Precedence defines an object's importance in the solution to the IK chain.

▲ **Child–Parent**. Sets the precedence for the entire chain as child, then parent. In this case, all child objects have a higher precedence than their parents.

▲ **Parent–Child**. The exact opposite of Child–Parent.

▲ **Copy, Paste**. Enables you to copy and paste rotating and sliding joint parameters between objects.

The Sliding Joints rollout enables you to define joints as sliding joints, and to define how those joints act when IK is enabled. A *sliding joint* is able to move in any defined axis. If rotating joints are applied, the joint will be able to rotate as well as slide. By default, sliding joints are disabled.

▲ **Active**. Defines whether the selected object can slide in this axis. The axis is defined by the local coordinate system for the object.

▲ **Limited**. Enables you to limit the motion of the sliding joint.

▲ **Ease**. Enables the joint to resist movement or rotation as it nears the limits of its motion.

▲ **From**. Enables you to define the upper limit of motion for the object in the selected axis.

▲ **To**. Enables you to define the lower limit of motion for the object in the selected axis.

▲ **Damping**. Enables you to dampen the motion of the object, making it more resistant to IK forces. Values range from 0 to 1 (with 1 the highest damping force). You dampen the motion of an object to simulate real-world situations, such as inertia.

The Rotational Joints rollout enables you to define joints as rotating joints, and to define how those joints act when IK is enabled. The options on this menu are the same as those on the Sliding Joints menu, except that the To and From fields are measured as angles. Rotational joints are similar to your knee, elbow, and shoulder joints. They all rotate around a defined point, and do not slide.

An IK Example

The following exercise shows you how to use IK to animate the arm scene in this chapter.

USING IK TO ANIMATE A SCENE

1. Load the file CH20B.MAX that you created earlier in this chapter. (If you did not complete the earlier exercise, the file is provided on the accompanying CD.)

2. Select the entire mechanical arm, except the ground object.

3. Click on the Display command panel tab.

4. Expand the Link Display rollout.

5. Turn on both Display Links and Links Replace Objects. Figure 20.11 shows the resulting object.

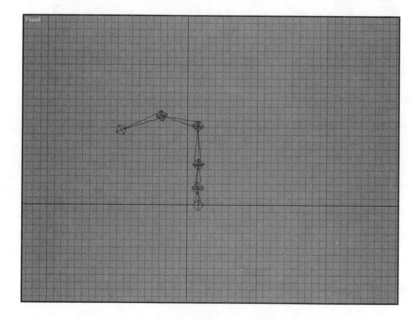

Figure 20.11

The links of the mechanical arm.

6. Select one of the middle arms and rotate it quickly to see how it affects the rest of the object. As you can see, objects above and to the left of the selected arm rotate also. (This is forward kinematics.)

7. Choose Undo.

8. Select the second arm on the left, as shown in figure 20.12.

Figure 20.12

The correct arm is selected.

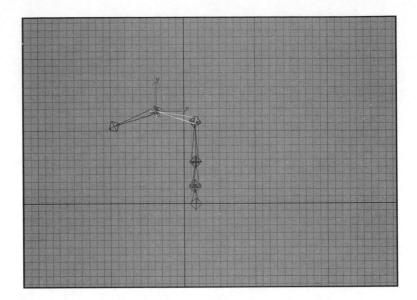

9. Click on the Hierarchy command panel tab.

10. Choose Child–Parent to set the joint precedence in this order. The selected joint should have a precedence of 70.

11. Move up the rollouts until you can see all the rotational joint parameters.

12. Deactivate the X and Z axes.

13. Turn on Limited for the Y axis. Set the From value to 110, and the To value to –10. (If you use the spinners, you can see the joint move interactively, which makes it easier to define the limits, if you decide to do so.)

14. Select the next arm to the right.

15. Deactivate the X and Z axes.

16. Turn on Limited for the Y axis. Set the From value to 75, and the To value to –60.

17. Select the next arm in the chain.

18. Turn off rotation in all axes.

19. Select the last arm in the chain.

20. Turn off all axes.

21. Expand the Sliding Joint rollout, activate the sliding joint in the X axis, and set Damping to 1.0.

22. Select all links using select objects.

23. Click on the Display command panel.

24. Turn off Display Links and Links Replace Objects.

You have set all the circular joint parameters. Now, you must go back and set the arm parameters themselves.

25. Choose Edit, Select None.

26. Select the large base box.

27. Turn off all rotating and sliding joints.

28. Select the vertical base cylinder. Turn off all rotating and sliding joints.

29. Select the first arm above the cylinder.

30. Turn off all rotating joints, except the Z axis.

31. Repeat for the other two arms. On the second arm, limit the motion to –50 and 50.

32. Choose Select and Move, and move the ball on the end of the arm. Notice that only the ball moves (because it is a child object, without IK on).

33. Choose Undo.

34. Turn on IK.

35. Move the ball at the end of the arm again. Now, because IK is on, all the other arms move correctly (as they would in real life). For correct animation, you would combine forward and inverse kinematic techniques.

The file at this point is saved on the CD as CH20C.MAX; you can check your work against it, if you want.

To animate the arm, simply turn on the Animate button and begin setting position keys. The rest of the arm will react appropriately and position itself correctly. Always create the animation by adjusting the position of the last object in the chain. Another way to animate a kinematic chain, shown in the next couple of steps, is to use a follow object.

36. Click on the Create command panel tab.

37. Choose the Helpers button.

38. Choose Dummy.

39. Click at –70,30 in the front viewport, and create a dummy object about the size of the ball. (Dummy objects are created in much the same way you create cube boxes.)

40. Set the animation slider to frame 100.

41. Turn on Animate.

42. Move the dummy object vertically 170 units.

43. Turn off Animate.

44. Select the ball on the end of the mechanical arm.

45. Click on the Hierarchy command panel tab.

46. Choose Bind, under Bind to Follow Object.

47. Click on the ball, drag over to the dummy object, and let go when you see the cursor change.

48. Choose Apply IK.

49. Now, having created the animation and position keys for all objects in the IK chain, you can create a camera and a light, and render the animation. The file CH20C.AVI shows you the animation.

50. On your own, play with the joint parameters. See whether you can set up the IK chain so that the arm rotates around its base. Also, set up the base cylinder so that it can slide along the base box. Then you might want to apply some materials, lights, and cameras to complete the scene.

Summary

Having learned about the basic suite of animation tools in MAX, including the powerful character-animation tools (inverse and forward kinematics), all you need is a lot of practice and a little intuition. Now, it is time to learn the ins and outs of rendering an animation, which is the focus of Chapter 21, "Rendering Animations."

CHAPTER 21

Rendering Animations

In MAX, rendering an animation is similar to rendering a still frame, except for the fact that you are actually rendering multiple still frames and compiling them into some animation format. You need to be aware of three new options in the Render Scene dialog box that must be addressed for rendering an animation versus a still frame. In addition, MAX enables you to render the animation from two different locations: the Render Scene dialog box and Video Post. Video Post is a special MAX dialog box in which you can perform image-editing and compositing special effects and is discussed in the next chapter.

This chapter focuses on the different aspects of rendering an animation both from the Render Scene dialog box and from Video Post. In particular, this chapter focuses on the following topics:

▲ Animation rendering options

▲ Object motion blur

▲ Field rendering

▲ Network rendering

▲ Output options

Animation Rendering Options

To render an animation, simply activate the view that you want to render. Then, choose the Render View button on the main toolbar, just like you would for a still frame. The Render Scene dialog box appears, as you would expect. In the Render Scene dialog box (see fig. 21.1), several settings are worth a further look. They include the time range, video color checking, object motion blur, field rendering, and net rendering.

Figure 21.1

*The Render Scene
dialog box.*

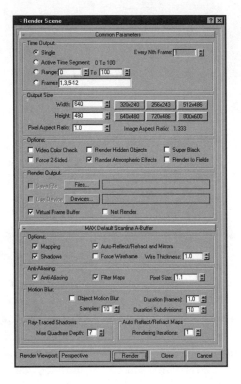

Animation is nothing more than the display of a sequence of images at a rate fast enough to give the illusion of motion. Hence, you have to render many still frames to achieve this effect. Under the Time Output section of the Render Scene dialog box, you can define the amount of time and the number of frames you are going to render. You can render the active time segment, a specific range, or specific sets of frames.

Animations typically are rendered with the intent of outputting the animation to videotape. Unfortunately, videotape is not a great medium, because both the NTSC and PAL video standards do not support as wide a color range as MAX does. Hence, if you are rendering the animation with the intention of taking it to videotape, you should turn on the Video Color Check checkbox in the Options section of this dialog box. Video color checking checks the colors of each output image versus acceptable color ranges for the videotape type (NTSC or PAL) that you are recording to. You can define how they work by choosing File, Preferences and choosing the Rendering tab in the Preferences Settings dialog box (see fig. 21.2).

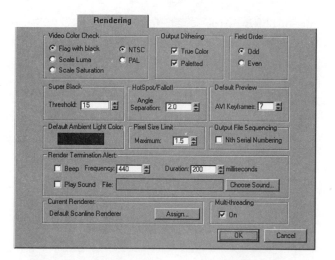

Figure 21.2

The Rendering tab of the Preference Settings dialog box.

Under the Video Color Check section in the upper-left corner of the Rendering tab, you can determine how MAX handles the checking. First, and most important, you should choose the video standard to which you are outputting. In the United States and Japan, it is NTSC. In other places, it may be NTSC or PAL; more than likely, it is PAL. Then you can determine what MAX does when it finds colors in your images that are not compatible with the standards.

Each option of the Video Color Check section is described in the following list:

▲ **Flag with Black**. When this option is enabled, each pixel that is out of the acceptable color range is colored black. You can go back and adjust the materials or lighting so that the material does not exceed acceptable color limits.

▲ **Scale Luma**. When this option is enabled, each pixel's luminance is scaled up or down until the color is within the acceptable range. If the pixel's color is already within the range, it is not scaled.

▲ **Scale Saturation**. When this option is enabled, each pixel's color saturation is scaled up or down until the color is within the acceptable range.

Object Motion Blur

Object motion blur is a special effect that you use to blur the motion of an object as it passes across the screen. Motion blur is used in many instances to give an object in an animation the illusion that it is moving much faster than it really is, or to create a special look for that object by blurring its motion.

You can set the object motion blur in two places. The first is in the Object Properties dialog box, and the second is in the Render Scene dialog box.

To set the motion blur for an object, simply right-click the object to access its pop-up menu. Then choose Properties. Figure 21.3 shows the resulting Object Properties dialog box.

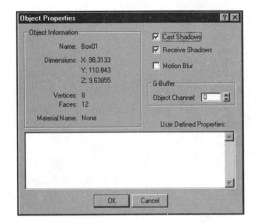

In this dialog box, you simply check the Motion Blur checkbox. When this option is enabled, MAX renders multiple copies of the object into the image to create the illusion of motion blur. How MAX renders the multiple copies is determined in the Motion Blur section of the Render Scene dialog box, as shown in figure 21.4.

In the Render Scene dialog box, you first must turn on Motion Blur. Then you can choose from the three settings that affect how the motion blur is created for the object. They are as follows:

▲ **Duration (Frames)**. Using this spinner, you can set how long the "virtual shutter" is open. The longer it is open, the more exaggerated the motion blur effect is.

▲ **Duration Subdivisions**. Using this spinner, you can set the number of copies of the object in a frame.

▲ **Samples**. Using this spinner, you can determine how many duration subdivision copies are sampled.

When you turn on and set all these options, the objects with their motion blur property enabled have this effect. You should note, however, that using motion blur can slow down the rendering process substantially. Use this option only when necessary.

Field Rendering

Probably the most important aspect of rendering an animation for video output is *field rendering*. Video output displays information in an interlaced manner. This means that the video output displays every other scanline of information. Then it repeats by displaying the scanlines it missed the first time. Most computer monitors are non-interlaced, so all scanlines are refreshed in order.

To get the smoothest motion in your animations when played back on a TV, you should always use field rendering. MAX then renders every other scanline of the frame. Then it comes back and renders the scanlines it missed. But, when MAX renders the second set of scanlines, it moves forward in time in the animation by one half of a frame. Field-rendered images don't look as good as still frames because of this effect, but the motion on a videotape is excellent. Rendering to fields, of course, increases the overall processing time for the animation.

When you render to fields, you must determine which field of the frame is rendered first. You can either render odd or even fields first. You set this value in the Preference Settings dialog box under the Rendering tab, as shown in figure 21.2. Before you decide which field order to use, you should match this to the output device you are using. A DPS Personal Animation Recorder, for example, can accept either order of field rendering. You just need to match the setting in MAX to the settings on the PAR. You should check the documentation on your output hardware or software to see which field order to use.

When you do field render, the playback of the animation changes slightly. Instead of referring to the playback speed as 30 frames per second, you now say that it plays back at 60 fields per second. Remember, each frame has two fields. So, if you see in the documentation of a specific output device 60 fields per second, it refers to the field-rendering playback speed.

Network Rendering

When rendering an animation, you can spend enormous amounts of time just waiting for the rendering of each frame to finish. Waiting 2, 3, 5, 10, 20, or more days for animations to finish is not uncommon, depending on the complexity of the scene, rendering options, and overall number of frames. MAX offers several ways to decrease this amount of time.

First, you can use multiple processors in a single system. Second, you can use different processor architectures such as DEC's Alpha chip running NT. (MAX has not been ported yet to other platforms but will be in the future.) Probably the most important method of increasing the overall rendering speed in an animation, however, is network rendering.

In network rendering, a TCP/IP (Transmission Control Protocol/Internet Protocol) network is used to link a series of NT workstations together. As the animation is processed, the next frame of the animation that needs to be rendered is sent to the next available machine on the network for processing. So, a two-machine network cuts the rendering time of an animation in half if both machines are configured the same. Three machines cuts the time by three and so on.

Large animation houses typically have rendering farms of 10 or more machines that are strictly dedicated to rendering animations. In this situation, you can work on an animation at your workstation, and when you want to test it, you can start a network render and send it out across the rendering farm. Depending on the size and complexity of the animation, you could get the finished result back much more quickly than by using a single machine.

Note

> You can use network rendering only when you are rendering to a sequence of bitmap files. You cannot use it to create an AVI or an FLC animation file. This is because of the way the animation is saved. Each frame must be saved in order to a temporary file. On a network rendering, depending on the configuration of the slave machines, you probably will not get the frames back in the proper order. To create these types of files, you must run the rendering on a single machine or compile the individual frames into an AVI or FLC using Video Post or a nonlinear editing suite such as Adobe Premiere.

The four basic components to network rendering in MAX are described in the following list:

▲ **TCP/IP Networking**. TCP/IP is a common networking protocol that is used by a large variety of operating systems. This network protocol was chosen for MAX because it is so widely used. Because TCP/IP is the protocol for the Internet, you could, theoretically, do network rendering across the Internet as well. You must have your NT workstation set up with TCP/IP installed, however, before you can do any network rendering. (Consult your NT documentation on how to set up TCP/IP.)

▲ **Manager**. This Windows NT service is installed during installation of MAX. The manager service controls what animations are in the network queue, when they are processed, and which machines on the network get what frames. This process occurs transparently to most end users because the manager service is installed on only one machine on the network.

▲ **Server**. This Windows NT service also is installed during installation of MAX. The server service queries the manager for the next frame of the animation. When it receives the information, the server launches MAX and renders the frame. When the frame is finished, the server notifies the manager that it is ready for another frame. Again, this process happens transparently.

▲ **Queue Manager**. This stand-alone program is used to manage the network queue. You can manage the queue from any NT or Windows 95 workstation that is connected to your network running TCP/IP. You can use Queue Manager to check the status, change the order, or delete animations that exist in the rendering queue.

Setting Up Network Rendering

When MAX is initially installed, you are given the option of installing the manager and server components. If you choose either or both, they are automatically installed as services under NT. In all cases, when you install the server service during the installation routine, you need to give the installation routine the IP address of the machine that will serve as the manager. You provide this address so that the server service knows which machine to query for new jobs.

Alternatively, if you do not elect to install these services at installation time, you can install them manually at a later date, or run the services in their own DOS shell windows. To install the server or manager service manually, do the following:

1. Start a DOS shell window.

2. Switch to the \3DSMAX directory, or wherever you have MAX installed.

3. To install the manager service, type **MANAGER -I**.

4. To install the server service, type **SERVER -I**.

5. To uninstall either service, type **MANAGER -R** or **SERVER -R**.

After you install the services, you need to set up how the services work under NT, regardless of whether you installed the services manually or during the installation of MAX itself. You basically have two choices for file storage: saving files locally on each machine or saving them to a network directory.

MAX handles network rendering differently depending on the method you choose. Most people want to save the rendered files to a network drive. In many network rendering farms, a drive array may be set up to handle the enormous amount of data that can be generated when network rendering. Typically, you will pick the machine with the largest hard drive and save all the files to that machine. This is especially true if you are using a PAR, or Perception Animation Recorder, because you will want to save files directly to the PAR.

When running the network render to save files locally on each drive, you simply specify a drive that is the same on each machine, such as the C: drive, in the Render Scene dialog box. Then you execute the net render. When you do, you see MAX load on each machine and begin processing the animation.

The problem occurs when you want to save files to a network drive. Under the default installation of the server service, MAX cannot write any information to the network drive due to a user rights error. To solve this problem, you must set up the server service to work with a specific account under NT. To this end, you should probably set up an account with network connection rights specifically devoted to network rendering. (See your NT documentation for more on how to set up new user accounts with specific rights.)

The following steps show you how to set up the server service to work with a specific account:

1. Open the Control Panel. Under NT 3.51, it is located in the Main program group. Under NT 4.0, go to Start and choose Settings, Control Panel.

2. In the Control Panel, double-click the Services icon. The Services dialog box then appears, as shown in figure 21.5.

Figure 21.5

The Services dialog box.

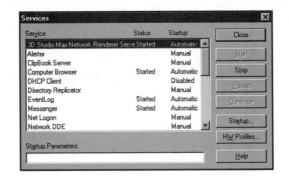

3. Click the 3D Studio MAX Network Renderer Server entry.

4. Choose the Startup button. Figure 21.6 shows the resulting dialog box. In this Service dialog box, you can define the parameters that the service uses every time it is started.

Figure 21.6

The Service dialog box where you can set up the service startup parameters.

5. In the Log On As section, choose the This Account radio button. To the right, the text field should now say LocalSystem.

6. Choose the button with three dots to the right of LocalSystem. The Add User dialog box then appears, as shown in figure 21.7.

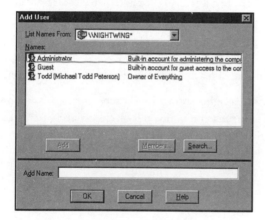

Figure 21.7

The Add User dialog box where you can restrict use of the service to a specific user.

7. In this dialog box, select the account that you want to use for network rendering from the list of existing accounts.

8. Choose the Add button and then choose OK to close the Add User dialog box. The account name and computer name should appear in place of LocalSystem in the Service dialog box, as shown in figure 21.8.

Figure 21.8

The Service dialog box
with correct user.

9. Delete both entries in the Password and Confirm Password fields. Under NT 3.51, they are already empty. Under NT 4.0, they have a series of asterisks. This service should not require a password to use it. Otherwise, you will have to enter a password every time the MAX renderer tries to start.

10. Choose OK to return to the Services dialog box and then close it by choosing the Close button.

11. Restart your system to make the changes take effect.

You must repeat these steps on all machines that are going to run as servers.

As a consequence of the new user rights settings for the server service, you cannot see MAX when it is running on the server machines. If you look closely at figure 21.6, you will see that with the permissions set to the System Account, the service is allowed to interact with the desktop. This means you can see the service when it is running. Under any other circumstance, you cannot tell that MAX is running.

 Warning

> You must authorize MAX before using it. You also must authorize MAX on all network server machines. Otherwise, after MAX loads, a message box appears asking you to authorize it (see fig. 21.9). When you set up the service to run under a specific account, it cannot interact with the desktop. This means that you cannot choose OK to the warning message box and allow MAX to continue to load. Authorizing MAX on every machine, of course, does not mean that you have to purchase a copy of MAX for each machine. You simply run the authorization program on each machine.

Figure 21.9

*The MAX warning
message.*

After you set up the server to run the way you want, you are ready to execute a network rendering. Before you start the network render, make sure that all machines you want to use in the network are set up and turned on. (This instruction might sound silly, but you don't want to come into work some morning only to find your previous night's rendering stalled by a downed computer.) If you are going to save the files to a network drive, make sure that all machines are connected into the same network drive using the same drive letter. N: (for Network), for example, makes a good network drive letter. Of course, you can use any free drive letter you want. (You can set up network connections in the File Manager. Refer to your NT documentation for more information on this process.)

Then you can load your scene by following these steps:

1. Choose Render View (or whatever it is you want to render) to access the Render Scene dialog box.

2. In the dialog box, set any options, the time range, output size, and output file names. For the output file name, make sure that you use a bitmap file type and save it to the network drive location, if you are using that method.

3. Select the Net Render checkbox under the Render Output section.

4. Choose the Render button. At this point, the Network Job Assignment dialog box appears, as shown in figure 21.10. You use this dialog box to submit the network rendering job to the queue.

5. Under Job name, give the animation a job name. All job names in the queue must be unique.

6. You can either elect to set a bitmap path to a network drive or choose the Include Maps checkbox. When Include Maps is turned on, the maps are copied into the temporary directory where all servers access the MAX file from the manager.

7. Under Network Manager, click the blank field of the drop-down list and type in the IP address of the manager machine.

8. Choose Connect to connect to the manager machine.

9. A list of servers appears in the list window of the dialog box. Select the machines you want to have render the animation. Machines with green dots are available. Gray dots indicate machines that are present but not available. When you select a machine, an arrow appears over the dot, as shown in figure 21.11.

Figure 21.10

The Network Job
Assignment dialog box.

Figure 21.11

The Network Job
Assignment dialog box
showing servers.

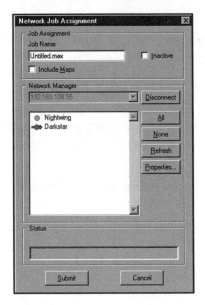

10. If you are not sure about the configuration of a server machine, select it and choose the Properties button. Figure 21.12 shows the resulting Server Properties dialog box.

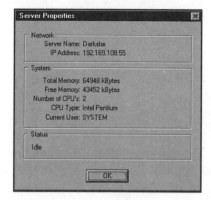

Figure 21.12

The Server Properties dialog box.

11. Choose OK to close the Server Properties dialog box and return to the Network Job Assignment dialog box.

12. Choose Submit to submit the job to the network. It is placed at the end of the queue and processed when it is at the top of the queue.

Note

After you start a network rendering on a server machine, you can no longer work in MAX on that machine. Only one copy of MAX can run on a single system at a time. If you are saving files to a network drive, you cannot see MAX running on the individual machines. Use Queue Manager to see which machines are working on an animation. Alternatively, you can use the performance monitor to monitor CPU activity on individual machines or PVIEW to monitor active threads. (PVIEW is a utility that ships with the Microsoft Developer's Network Subscriptions and is used to monitor all active threads (programs) in the system.)

After you start the animation on the network, you can use Queue Manager to monitor the activity of the network rendering. Queue Manager is a separate utility that you can run on any machine connected to the network with TCP/IP. Figure 21.13 shows the Queue Manager interface.

*The 3D Studio MAX
Queue Manager where
you can control the
rendering queue.*

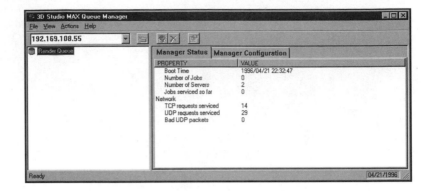

Again, you have to enter the IP address of the manager and choose the Connect button.
The connect button is located to the right of the Manager IP drop down list. After you
do, each network job is listed on the left of the Queue Manager under the Render Queue.
Any failed jobs appear with red icons next to them. Figure 21.14 shows the Queue
Manager with a job listed.

*The Queue Manager
with one job.*

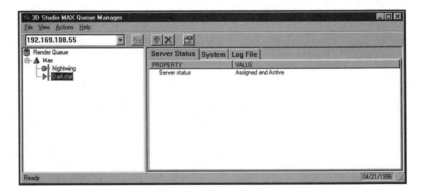

After you select a job and expand its view, you can see all the server machines that are
working on it. If you click and highlight one of these machines, three tabbed boxes appear
on the right side of the Queue Manager, as shown in figure 21.14. Here, you can access
the server status, system properties, and the log file. The log file tells you which frames have
been submitted to the server and when the server finished each frame.

You can activate and deactivate server machines at any time by selecting the server and
choosing Activate/Deactivate from the Queue Manager's Actions menu, or right-clicking
the server name. You can also delete any server or job from the queue at any time.

The last option you can use Queue Manager for is to assign times of the day when a server
will be available for network rendering. To do so, select the server under the job name on
which you want to set times. Then choose the Properties button from the toolbar. Figure
21.15 shows the resulting Server Properties dialog box.

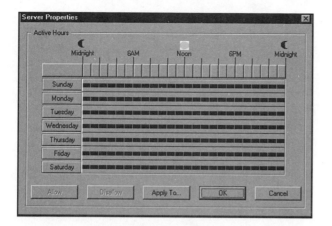

Figure 21.15

The Server Properties dialog box.

To set the times when a server is active or inactive, click and drag across a time slot. Time slots are broken down into hour increments. After you highlight a time slot, choose Allow or Disallow. When you choose the Allow button, the time slots turn green. If you choose the Disallow button, they turn red. When the time slots are blue, the server is always available. After you set the times, choose the Apply To button. A list of active servers then appears in the Apply Server Properties dialog box, as shown in figure 21.16.

Figure 21.16

The Apply Server Properties dialog box.

Figure 21.17 shows a server setting that disables network rendering during working hours.

Generally speaking, you do not have to set server properties because machines to which you will be network rendering are dedicated to that purpose. But having the ability to schedule network renderings in this manner is always nice.

Network rendering is a powerful capability of MAX, but it can get fouled up occasionally. If it does, restart all machines, including the manager machines. The network rendering will take up where it left off.

Figure 21.17

Server properties for working hours disallowance.

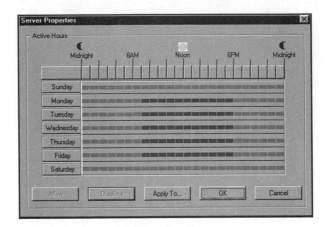

Output Options

The last thing to look at when it comes to rendering animations is your output options. Animations can be output to a variety of file formats and hardware devices. The most common formats and hardware devices are described in the following list:

▲ **Individual Bitmap Files**. Animations can be rendered to individual bitmap files such as TARGA, TIF, GIF, and so on. These files are numbered corresponding to their order in the animation. Use the Nth serial numbering option if you choose this method often. This method is the most common and works great with network rendering.

▲ **AVI Files**. Microsoft's Audio Video Interleaved format is a digital video format that you can play back using the Media Player. This format is popular for preview animations or distribution on CD-ROM. You cannot use it with network rendering.

▲ **FLC Files**. You cannot use Autodesk's proprietary online animation format with network rendering.

▲ **Accom WSD Device**. This specialized device records 30 or 60 seconds of uncompressed animation with the best quality possible. This device uses a special driver in MAX. You access it by choosing Devices instead of Files in the Render Scene dialog box.

▲ **PAR or Perception Card**. This device uses individual bitmaps and records them to a proprietary animation format on a dedicated hard drive that can be played back at 30 or 60 fields per second. Watch out when using network rendering because files may not come back from the network in the correct order to record to the PAR or Perception card.

▲ **Other**. You can use many other devices with MAX to compile and play back animations. You can use, for example, MPEG cards, other MJPEG cards, and software such as Adobe Premiere or Speed Razor.

Summary

Rendering an animation correctly with the correct options is essential to good animation productivity. MAX provides you with many tools, including powerful network rendering to increase your power and reduce the time necessary to render animations.

Now that you have learned the fundamentals in MAX, take a brief look at some intermediate skills in the next few chapters to give you an idea of where you can explore from here. The next chapter also deals with animation rendering skills by using the Video Post.

Video Post

When you create animations in MAX, you may occasionally want or need more power and flexibility than what is available in the renderer. For example, you might want to apply special image filters, or composite two images together. To compensate for this shortage, you can use the Video Post to render animations.

This chapter focuses on the Video Post and how to use it. In particular, you learn about the following:

▲ Understanding the Video Post

▲ Adding queue entries

▲ Rendering from Video Post

Understanding the Video Post

The Video Post is a special dialog box in which you can add special effects such as image processing, transitions, or loops to an animation. These special effects are generally added to each frame immediately after the frame is rendered. You can access the Video Post by choosing Rendering, Video Post. The Video Post dialog box then appears, as shown in figure 22.1.

Figure 22.1

*The Video Post
dialog box.*

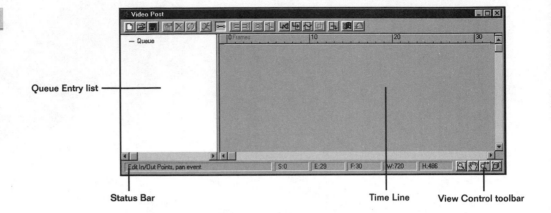

Figure 22.1

*The Video Post
dialog box.*

Queue Entry list

Status Bar   Time Line   View Control toolbar

The Video Post is broken down into five main areas: the toolbar, queue entry list, time line, status bar, and view control toolbar.

The toolbar at the top of the dialog box enables you to control the Video Post queue by executing, adding, and deleting queue events. Each button of the toolbar is described in the following list:

New Sequence. This button enables you to start a new Video Post sequence and queue. When you do, the existing sequence is removed.

Open Sequence. This button enables you to load a saved Video Post sequence of events.

Save Sequence. Using this button, you can save a Video Post sequence of events to disk. Video Post sequences have a file extension of .VPX.

Edit Current Event. This button enables you to edit the currently selected queue event. Choosing this button opens the dialog box with which you created the event.

Delete Current Event. Using this button, you can delete the currently selected event from the queue.

Swap Events. This button enables you to swap two or more selected events.

Execute Sequence. You can choose this button to render the animation sequence using the entries in the Video Post queue.

Edit Range Bar. Using this button, you can edit the range over which a Video Post queue event is active. This process is similar to editing ranges in TrackView. Figure 22.2 shows the Video Post with an event in the queue.

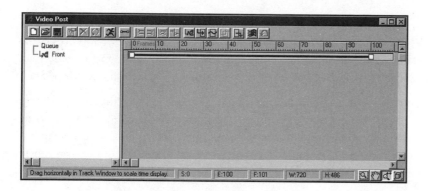

Figure 22.2

The Video Post with a queue entry.

Align Selected Left. This button aligns the left side of all selected events so that they start at the same frame.

Align Selected Right. You use this button to align the right side of all selected events so that they end at the same frame.

Make Selected Same Size. This button sets the length of all selected events to the same size.

Abut Selected. This button aligns the end of an event with the start of the next event.

Add Scene Event. Using this button, you can add a Video Post event from the current scene in MAX.

Add Image Input Event. Using this button, you can add still images as an event in Video Post.

Add Image Filter Event. This button enables you to add special image-processing filters as an event in Video Post.

Add Image Layer Event. This button enables you to combine two or more tracks into a layer where they can be processed together.

Add Image Output Event. Using this button, you can add an event for the output of images. You can add multiple output events to output the final images to multiple destinations.

Add External Event. This button enables you to add events that call external programs.

Add Loop Event. This button enables you to add an event that causes a loop back in time.

Whenever you add something to the Video Post queue, it is called an *event*, and it appears in the Video Post queue list. The order of this list is very important. MAX processes the queue from top to bottom. So, if you were to composite a basketball on top of a basketball court animation, the basketball would be first in the queue and the court would be second.

At the bottom of the Video Post dialog box is a status bar that tells you the current settings of the Video Post. S: represents the current start frame, E: represents the end frame number, F: represents the total number of frames in the Video Post, W: is the current output image width, and H: is the current output image height. You can control these settings in the Execute Sequence dialog box.

The parameters in this dialog box are set just like any other typical rendering in MAX.

To the right of the status bar in the Video Post dialog box are the view control buttons. Each is described in the following list:

▲ **Zoom Region**. This button enables you to zoom in or out of the time line window by creating a rectangle.

▲ **Pan**. This button enables you to pan around either the queue entry list or the time line window.

▲ **Zoom Time**. This button enables you to zoom horizontally in or out of the time line window.

▲ **Zoom Extents**. This button enables you to expand the view to the maximum extents of all queue events in the time line.

The G-Buffer

Some of the events that you can add to the Video Post, such as an image filter event that uses a glow filter, are intended to work on specific pieces of geometry. To this end, you must have a method of linking the geometry to the Video Post event. You accomplish this feat by using the *G-buffer*, or geometry buffer. The G-buffer is used to transfer geometry information to video post processes.

Each object you create in MAX has a G-buffer object channel. The object channel assigns an ID number to it, so the video post will know which objects to process using Image filters such as glow. You can access it by accessing the Object Properties dialog box, as shown in figure 22.3. The Object Properties dialog box is accessed by right-clicking on a selected object to make the transform pop-up menu appear. Then, simply choose properties at the bottom of the pop-up menu.

Figure 22.3

The Object Properties dialog box.

By default, all objects have an object channel value of 0, but you can set this channel number as high as you want. Then all you have to do is match the object channel value to that in the image filter event. Then the image filter is applied only to the appropriate objects.

You also can accomplish the same task at the material level instead of the object level. To do so, you simply set the materials effect channel in the Material Editor. Then you set the corresponding effect channel in the image filter event entry. Materials are limited to nine different effect channels, though.

Adding Queue Entries

To use the Video Post, you must add entries to the Video Post queue. As mentioned previously, these entries are called events. You can add seven types of events:

▲ Scene events

▲ Image input events

▲ Image filter events

▲ Image layer events

▲ Image output events

▲ External events

▲ Loop events

In the next several sections, you explore each of these event types.

Scene Events

A scene event is any scene in MAX; it is generally any viewport, such as a camera viewport, where you have defined geometry, lights, cameras, or animation. When you choose the Add Scene Event button on the Video Post toolbar, the Add Scene Event dialog box appears, as shown in figure 22.4. At the top of the dialog box, you can select the view for the scene from a drop-down list. Then you can set the rendering options for the scene by choosing the Render Options button. Figure 22.5 shows the corresponding Render Options dialog box.

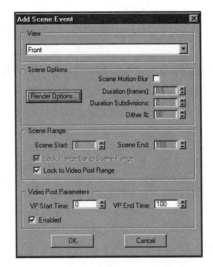

You can set the scene motion blur in the Add Scene Event dialog box by selecting the Scene Motion Blur checkbox. This option is different from the motion blur option in the Render Scene dialog box. Here, the motion blur is applied to the scene as a whole, not to an individual object within the scene. The three options for the scene motion blur work the same as the object motion blur options, though.

You also can define the range of time over which the scene occurs. Generally, this is taken from the active time segment for the assigned scene. At the bottom of the Add Scene Event dialog box, you can set the Video Post parameters. They include the range of time in the Video Post where the event is active and whether it is enabled. Your ability to turn on or off the event is nice when you are working with combinations of multiple events. By turning an event off or on, you can see what effect it has in the final image.

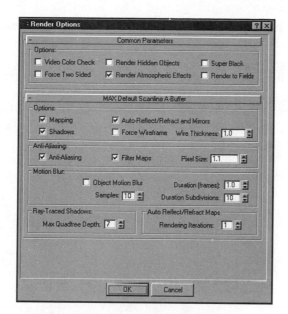

Figure 22.5

*The Render Options
dialog box.*

Image Input Events

The image input event enables you to add a series of still images or an animation file to
the Video Post queue. You generally add images to post process the images through an
image filter or compile them into an animation format such as AVI. Choosing the Add
Image Input Event button from the Video Post dialog box displays the Add Image Input
Event dialog box, as shown in figure 22.6.

Figure 22.6

*The Add Image Input
Event dialog box.*

At the top of the dialog box, you can choose to add files or images from a device such as the Accom WSD device. If you choose the Files button, a standard file browser dialog box appears. From here, you can select one or more files to add to the queue. To add a series of files, you can select files such as A*.TGA. By using the wild-card character, you can select all files that begin with the letter A and have a .TGA extension. When you choose OK to load the files, the Options button becomes available in the Add Image Input Event dialog box. If you choose this button, the Image Input Options dialog box then appears, as shown in figure 22.7.

Figure 22.7

The Image Input Options dialog box.

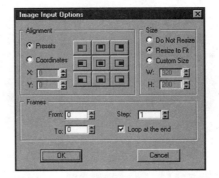

Here, you can define the alignment of the image in the scene by either choosing one of the presets or specifying X and Y coordinates in pixels. You also can determine what to do with the size of the image file. If the size of the image file does not match the size of the Video Post rendering, the image must either be resized to fit, resized to a specific size, or not resized at all. You can also determine the range of time over which these images occur. Choosing OK returns you to the Add Image Input Event dialog box.

The Image Drive section of the dialog box is used for plug-in image drivers that enable you to load file formats not supported by MAX at this time. If the driver has any options, the Setup button becomes available. In this dialog box, you also can set Video Post parameters to define how long the event lasts in the Video Post.

Image Filter Events

An image filter event is a special type of processing that modifies the look of a frame after it has been rendered. This processing is similar to applying a filter in Adobe Photoshop. Choosing the Add Image Filter Event button from the Video Post dialog box displays the Add Image Filter Event dialog box, shown in figure 22.8.

Figure 22.8

*The Add Image Filter
Event dialog box.*

Filters are applied to any scene event in the video post queue. You simply select the scene in the queue, then add the image filter event. The scene queue entry will appear as a sub-entry to the filter event. At the top of the Add Image Filter dialog box, you can choose the type of image filter to apply. MAX ships with six default filter types. Each is described in the following list:

▲ **Fade**. This filter enables you to fade an image in or out over time. Figure 22.9 shows the setup dialog box for this wipe.

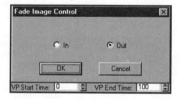

Figure 22.9

*The Fade Image
Control dialog box.*

▲ **Glow**. Using this filter, you can add glow to an object or a material, based on the object's material or object channel settings. Figure 22.10 shows the setup dialog box for this filter.

Figure 22.10

*The Glow Control
dialog box.*

▲ **Image Alpha**. Using this filter, you can replace certain sections of an image's alpha channel with the mask file chosen in the Mask section of the Add Image Filter Event dialog box. No setup is required.

▲ **Negative**. This filter enables you to invert the colors in an image, making a negative. No setup is required.

▲ **Pseudo Alpha**. Using this filter, you can create a pseudo alpha channel for images that do not have alpha channels. The alpha channel is based on the color of the pixel in the upper left-hand corner. No setup is required.

▲ **Simple Wipe**. This filter enables you to wipe an image from the screen over time. Figure 22.11 shows the setup dialog box for this filter.

Figure 22.11

The Simple Wipe Control dialog box.

After you decide on the filter type, you can determine whether you want to use a mask. A mask is a bitmap that is used to block all or part of the image or effect. For example, a mask bitmap might be black letters on a white background. When applied as a mask, the white areas of the bitmap will mask, or hide, the underlying image or effect. Like a material mask, a filter mask hides the effect of the filter on the image. If you use set the Mask option in the Add Image Filter Event dialog box, you should use a mask bitmap that has an alpha channel for the best results, just like you would with a material mask. (For more information on masks, refer to Chapter 12, "Basic Materials," Chapter 13, "Mapped Materials," and Chapter 14, "Advanced Materials.") You also can set the Video Post parameters in this dialog box.

Image Layer Events

You use the image layer event only when you have two events next to each other that you want to composite together in some way. To access this option, you must first select the two queue events. Then, by choosing the Add Image Layer Event button from the Video Post dialog box, MAX displays the Add Image Layer Event dialog box, shown in figure 22.12.

Figure 22.12

The Add Image Layer Event dialog box.

The image layer event is similar to the image filter event. It works by applying certain filters to the selected events. The difference here is that filters are applied to create a transition or composition between the two selected events.

At the top of the Add Image Layer Event dialog box, you can select the type of image layer event you want to use. Each is described in the following list:

▲ **Alpha Compositor**. This type enables you to compose the image in the top event over the top of the image in the second event, using the alpha channel of the first image for transparency.

▲ **Cross Fade Transition**. This type enables you to cross fade the images in event 1 with the images in event 2. As event 1 fades out, event 2 fades in. The length of the fade is determined by the length of the option in the Video Post.

▲ **Pseudo Alpha**. Using this event type, you can perform alpha compositing with images that do not have an alpha channel.

▲ **Simple Additive Compositor**. This type enables you to perform cross-fade transitions with images that do not have an alpha channel.

▲ **Simple Wipe**. This type enables you to perform a wipe that erases or pushes one image to reveal another.

Again, in the Add Image Layer Event dialog box, like in the Image Filter Event dialog box, you can mask the effect and set your Video Post parameters.

When you apply an image layer event, the queue entries change to reflect this fact. Figure 22.13 shows the queue entry list with two events compositing with a simple wipe.

Figure 22.13

The Video Post queue entry list with a layer event where two queue entries are now combined into one "layered" entry.

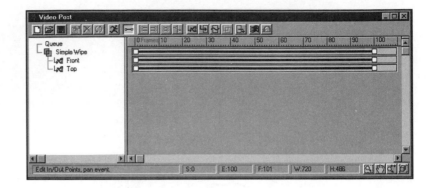

Image Output Events

The image output event enables you to render Video Post events and save them to disk in any of a variety of formats. As a matter of fact, by adding more than one output event, you can save the images to multiple files or devices at the same time. Without an output event, you can render Video Post events, but they are not saved to disk.

Choosing the Add Image Output Event button from the Video Post dialog box displays the Add Image Output Event dialog box, shown in figure 22.14. This dialog box is very much like the Add Image Input Event dialog box. You can save the processed events to either files or devices. You can also use plug-in drivers and set Video Post parameters.

Figure 22.14

The Add Image Output Event dialog box.

External Events

External events enable you to send each frame to be processed by a program separate from MAX. This program must, however, accept command-line parameters to work. For example, Image Alchemy is a DOS command-line program that frequently is used to convert images from one format to another, or from one size to another. This program has about 100 command-line options to it. You can plug in the program name and options you want into the external event and have MAX execute the program for each frame in the animation. Choosing the Add External Event button in the Video Post dialog box displays the Add External Event dialog box, shown in figure 22.15. All you have to do is browse around to find the external program. Then you can plug in any command-line parameters and off you go.

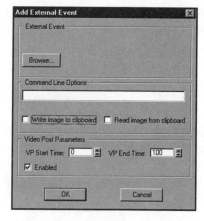

Figure 22.15

The Add External Event dialog box.

Loop Events

A loop event forces some sort of repeat in the currently selected event. Choosing the Add Loop Event button in the Video Post dialog box displays the Add Loop Event dialog box, shown in figure 22.16.

Figure 22.16

The Add Loop Event dialog box.

The loop event can either be a complete repeat of the event or a ping-pong effect where the event runs backward and then forward; simply choose the appropriate radio button. You also can set how many times the loop occurs by setting the spinner in the middle section of this dialog box. When you add this type of event, the selected event to which it is applied is moved down and to the right in the Video Post queue, as shown in figure 22.17.

Figure 22.17

The Video Post queue with an add loop event.

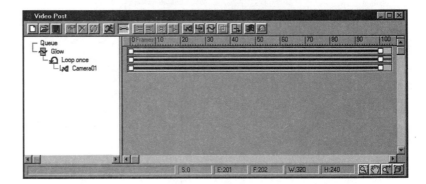

Rendering from Video Post

The following example shows you how to create a simple Video Post rendering.

A Simple Video Post Rendering

1. Load the file CH22A.MAX from the CD-ROM.

2. Choose Rendering, Video Post.

3. In the Video Post dialog box, choose the Add Scene Event button. The Add Scene Event dialog box then appears.

4. Select Camera01 as the view for the scene event and choose OK to close the dialog box.

5. Choose the Add Scene Event button again. The Add Scene Event dialog box reappears.

6. Select Top as the view for the scene event and choose OK to close the dialog box again.

7. In the Video Post dialog box, click on the camera entry in the queue.

8. Hold down the Ctrl key and click on the Top entry.

9. Choose the Add Image Layer Event button in the Video Post dialog box. The Add Image Layer Event dialog box then appears.

10. Select Cross Fade transition as the Layer Plug-In type and choose OK to close the dialog box.

11. Choose the Add Image Output Event button in the Video Post dialog box.

12. Enter CH22.AVI as the file name and choose OK.

13. Choose OK to close this dialog box and return to the Video Post dialog box. Figure 22.18 shows the video queue at this point.

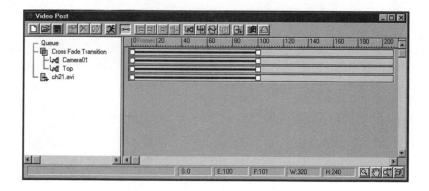

Figure 22.18

The Video Post at the end of the exercise.

14. Choose the Execute Sequence button.

15. In the Execute Sequence dialog box, select Range as the time output. Make sure that the start and end ranges are set from 0 to 100, respectively.

16. Set the output size to 320×240.

17. Choose Render. The sequence is then rendered and composited together. The resulting file is contained on the CD-ROM as CH22.AVI; you can view this file if you don't want to render the Video Post sequence at this time.

Experiment with this exercise by trying to add an image filter. See, for example, if you can make one of the balls glow. Also, you might try different image layer compositors as well.

Summary

Video Post is a powerful tool for creating transitions, compositing, and processing images of animations. This is particularly handy if you do a lot of image processing of your renderings. By using video post, you can process your images while they are rendered. You can also use video post to add special effects such as glowing objects or transitional effects between animation sequences. You should learn it well because it is handy for creating many special effects.

One of the fun aspects of computer animation is special effects. Special effects are events in an animation that add a sense of sensationalism to the scene. For example, smoke, fog, fire, wind, snow, or even exploding objects are all forms of special effects. The next chapter focuses on some of the special effects that are built into MAX.

PART VI

SPECIAL EFFECTS FUNDAMENTALS

Special Effects Fundamentals

Up to this point in the book, you have seen many tools and techniques for creating basic models, materials, renderings, and animations. All of these tools are powerful and can be used to create just about anything you need. Eventually, however, you will need the capability to create a special effect. A special effect is an effect that greatly enhances the realism or sensationalism of a scene, such as fire, smoke, explosions, rain, or even snow. In instances where you need these types of effects, MAX provides tools for you to handle them.

This chapter focuses on some of the basic tools that MAX provides. This chapter is intended as an introduction and is by no means a complete reference on special effects in MAX. This chapter explores two different types of special effects: space warps and particle systems. The "Space Warps" section of this chapter covers all the MAX space warps:

▲ Ripple

▲ Wave

▲ Wind

▲ Deflector

▲ Bomb

▲ Gravity

▲ Displace

The "Particle Systems" section demonstrates the two particle systems included with MAX:

▲ Snow

▲ Spray

Additionally, this chapter will cover one other special effect: morphing.

Space Warps

A *space warp* is a plug-in for MAX that affects an object as it moves through the space influenced by the warp. For example, a space warp can be an effect such as gravit, or an exploding object. The space warp affects the 3D space in and around the object, to affect how the object behaves. When you create a space warp, an icon for the warp will appear in the scene. To be affected by a space warp, you must bind an object to the space warp by using the Bind to Space Warp tool found on the main toolbar. To use this tool, click on the object you want to bind, drag it to the space warp, and let go. Both objects will be highlighted briefly to indicate the acceptance of the new relationship. The MAX space warps may be found by choosing the Space Warp button on the Create Command Panel. This displays the rollouts shown in figure 23.1.

Figure 23.1

The space warp rollouts where you can create and define the parameters for any space warp.

MAX provides you with seven different default space warps to work with. Other space warps will undoubtedly be developed by third party developers. The MAX space warps—Ripple, Wave, Wind, Deflector, Bomb, Gravity, and Displace—are discussed in the following sections.

Ripple

The ripple space warp is used to create concentric ripple effects in any deformable object. You can use ripple to create effects such as rippling water or a rippled rug. The object simply needs to have enough faces to show the ripple effect well. If an object does not have enough faces, the ripple effect will be limited or not appear at all. As a general rule of thumb, make your objects fairly complex for use with space warps. When you choose this option, you get the rollout shown in figure 23.2.

To create the ripple, click to place the center of the ripple and drag out to place the outer edge in any viewport, in much the same way you would create a circle. Once you have defined the location and size, by moving the mouse up and down the screen, you can define the height of the ripple. The ripple space warp icon will appear in the scene, as shown in figure 23.2. The first rollout that appears is the Supports Objects of Type. This rollout simply displays the types of objects this particular space warp can affect. Then you may adjust any of the parameters of the ripple space warp to achieve the affect you want. To animate the effect, adjust the parameters at various points in time with the Animate button ON. The following list briefly describes each parameter:

Figure 23.2

The ripple rollouts and the ripple icon where you can define how the ripple space warp works.

▲ **Amplitude 1**. Creates a ripple motion in one direction.

▲ **Amplitude 2**. Creates a second ripple motion that moves at 90 degrees to the first.

▲ **Wave Length**. Enables you to set the distances between the waves.

▲ **Phase**. Enables you to shift the position of the waves over the object. Lower numbers move the ripples closer to the center.

▲ **Decay**. Enables you to limit the effect of the ripple.

▲ **Circles**. Enables you to define the number of circles shown in the space warp icon. This does not affect the size of the ripple.

▲ **Segments**. Enables you to define the number of segments in the space warp icon.

▲ **Divisions**. Enables you to define the number of divisions in the space warp icon.

The following exercise shows you how to use a ripple space warp.

CREATING AND USING A RIPPLE SPACE WARP

1. Create a box that is 100 units by 100 units and 1 unit tall. Set the number of Length and Width segments to 50.

2. Choose the Space Warp button.

3. Select a Ripple warp.

4. Click on the center of the box in the Top viewport and drag out until the icon is roughly the same size as the box, and then let go.

5. Move the mouse up and down to set the amplitude. Choose an amplitude of somewhere around -4.

6. Choose Bind to space warp.

7. Click on the box object and drag it over the space warp. When the icon changes, let go to bind the warp. Figure 23.3 shows you the resulting object.

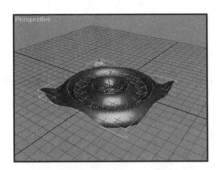

8. Now animate the properties of the space warp over time. This is accomplished by turning on the Animate button and adjusting any parameter in any frame you want.

Wave

The wave space warp is used to create a wave-like effect across any deformable object. The object simply needs to have enough faces to show the wave effect well. The wave space warp is very similar to a ripple space warp, except that it is a linear effect instead of a concentric effect. When you choose this option, you get the rollout shown in figure 23.4.

To create the wave, click and drag in any viewport, in much the same way you would create a box. The wave space warp icon will appear in the scene, as shown in figure 23.4. You may then adjust any of the parameters of the wave space warp to achieve the effect you want. To animate the effect, adjust the parameters at various points in time with the Animate button ON. The wave parameters are basically the same as the ripple parameters; refer to that section for more information on the parameters.

Wind

The wind space warp is used to create the appearance of blowing wind in a particle system. This space warp only affects particle systems. When you choose this option, you get the rollout shown in figure 23.5.

To create the wind, click the center of the wind space warp and drag out to the outer edge in any viewport, in much the same way you would create a rectangle. A rectangular icon with an arrow will appear, showing you the size and direction of the wind space warp. The wind space warp icon will appear in the scene, as shown in figure 23.5. Rotate the space warp to point in the direction you want the wind to blow and then bind it to the desired particle system. You may then adjust any of the parameters of the wind space warp to achieve the effect you want. The following list briefly describes each parameter:

▲ **Strength**. Enables you to define the overall strength of the wind.

▲ **Decay**. Enables you to control the rate at which the force of the wind decays as it gets farther away from the icon.

▲ **Planar**. Enables you to set the shape of the wind's force field to *planar*.

▲ **Spherical**. Enables you to set the shape of the wind's force field to *spherical*.

▲ **Turbulence**. Enables you to define the amount of turbulence in the wind.

▲ **Frequency**. Enables you to define the apparent speed of the turbulence in animated effects.

▲ **Scale**. Enables you to scale the particles before the turbulence is applied. With larger scales, the particles become more random and wild.

▲ **Icon Size**. Enables you to define the size of the icon.

The following exercise shows you how to use a wind space warp. (You may need to refer to the "Particle Systems" section later in this chapter for more information on the particle system used in this exercise.)

CREATING AND USING A WIND SPACE WARP

1. Load the file ch22a.max from the CD.

2. Set the current frame of the animation to around 60 so you can see the particle system.

3. Choose the Space Warp button on the Create command panel.

4. In the Front viewport, click at approximately the center of the spray and drag until you create a box as large as the spray.

5. In the Top viewport, move the wind icon toward the top of the screen until it is just outside the spray.

6. Choose Bind to Space Warp.

7. Click on the particle spray, drag it to the Wind icon, and then let go. Both icons will be highlighted briefly and then return to normal. The particle system will immediately show the effect of the wind, as shown in figure 23.6.

Figure 23.6

The wind space warp affecting the motion of a particle spray.

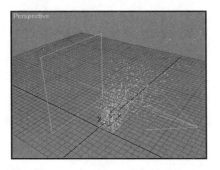

8. For further practice, try adjusting the parameters of the wind to create different effects on the spray.

Figure 23.7

The deflector rollouts showing you the deflector icon and the parameters you can set for this space warp.

Deflector

The deflector space warp is used to deflect particle systems in a different direction. This space warp only affects particle system objects. When you choose this option, you get the rollout shown in figure 23.7.

To create the deflector, click and drag in any viewport, in much the same way you would create a rectangle. The deflector space warp icon will appear in the scene, as shown in figure 23.7. Once you bind the deflector to any surface, the surface is then capable of deflecting particle systems. You may then adjust any of the parameters of the deflector space warp to achieve the effect you want. The following list briefly describes each parameter:

▲ **Bounce**. Enables you to define how much a particle will bounce off the deflector surface. A value of 1 produces a bounce equal to the incoming force of the particle. A value of 0 causes all particles to stick to the deflector.

▲ **Width/Height**. Enables you to define the size of the deflector space warp icon.

The following exercise shows you how to use a deflector space warp. (Again, you may need to refer to the "Particle Systems" section later in this chapter for more information on the particle system used here.)

CREATING AND USING A DEFLECTOR SPACE WARP

1. Load the file ch22b.max.

2. Choose the Space Warp button in the Create command panel.

3. Choose Deflector.

4. Click in the Top viewport at the lower-left corner of the ground box, drag to the upper-right corner, and then let go.

5. In the Front viewport, rotate the deflector icon 45 degrees.

6. Choose Bind to space warp.

7. Select the spray emitter, drag it to the deflector icon, and then let go when the icon changes.

8. Set the current frame to 60 to see the results, as shown in figure 23.8.

9. Choose select objects and select the deflector space warp.

10. Click on the Modify Command Panel tab.

11. Set the bounce to 4.0 and see the result in the Front viewport.

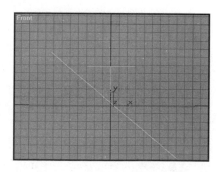

Figure 23.8

A particle system spray being deflected by a deflector space warp.

Figure 23.9

The bomb rollouts showing the bomb icon and the various parameters you can set for the space warp.

Figure 23.10

The gravity rollouts show you the gravity icon and the parameters that you can set for the space warp.

Bomb

The bomb space warp is used to explode one or more objects into many smaller objects. The object simply needs to have enough faces to show the explosion effect well. When you choose this option, you get the rollout shown in figure 23.9.

To create the bomb, click on any point in any viewport. The bomb icon appears at this location, as shown in figure 23.9. You may then adjust any of the parameters of the bomb space warp to achieve the effect you want. The following list briefly describes each parameter:

▲ **Strength**. Enables you to define the strength of the explosion.

▲ **Gravity**. Enables you to define how gravity affects the exploded particles.

▲ **Chaos**. Enables you to determine the randomness of the exploded particles. The higher the values, the more random and natural looking the explosion will be.

▲ **Detonation**. Enables you to set the frame number where the bomb explodes.

Gravity

The gravity space warp is used to create the effect of gravity in a particle system. When you choose this option, you get the rollout shown in figure 23.10.

To create the gravity effect, click and drag in any viewport, in much the same way you would create a circle. The gravity space warp icon will appear in the scene, as shown in figure 23.10. You may then adjust any of the parameters of the gravity space warp to achieve the effect you want. Each parameter of the gravity space warp is similar to the wind space warp; refer to that section for details, as well as a brief exercise. Repeat that exercise, but create the effect of gravity from above rather than the effect of wind from the side.

Displace

The displace space warp is used to modify the shape of an object or particle system by using a bitmap. This is similar to a bump map, but the displacement map actually deforms the geometry to create the ridges and valleys.

(A bump map achieves this effect by changing the lighting on the surface of the material.) The object simply needs to have enough faces to show the displacement effect well. When you choose this option, you get the rollout shown in figure 23.11.

To create the displacement map, click and drag in any viewport, in much the same way you would create a rectangle. Next, select the bitmap to apply to the geometry as a displacement map. Once you have selected the map, you can choose the type of mapping, much like you do for a texture-mapped material. Once you have these set up, the displace space warp icon will appear in the scene, as shown in figure 23.11. You may then adjust any of the parameters of the ripple space warp to achieve the effect you want. The following list briefly describes each parameter:

▲ **Strength**. Enables you to set the overall strength of the displacement map. Higher values result in greater exaggerations in the geometry.

▲ **Decay**. Enables you to decay the effect of the displacement map as the distance from the center increases.

▲ **Center Luminance**. Enables you to use the color grey as the lowest level of displacement instead of black.

▲ **Image**. Enables you to select an image to use as the displacement map.

▲ **Blur**. Enables you to apply a blur to the image.

▲ **Mapping**. Enables you to define the type of mapping with which to apply the bitmap. These mapping controls are the same as the mapping controls for texture mapped materials.

The following exercise shows you how to use a displace space warp.

CREATING AND USING A DISPLACE SPACE WARP

1. Create a box that is 100 units by 100 units. Set the length and width segments to 50.

2. Click on the Space Warp button in the Create command panel.

3. Choose Displace.

4. In the Top viewport, click at approximately the center of the box and drag out until the icon is approximately the same size as the box.

5. Select the None button under Image.

Figure 23.11

The displace rollouts showing you the icon and the parameters that you can set for the space warp.

6. Choose Cloud2.jpg from your 3DSMAX\MAP directory as the image.

7. Set the strength to 10.

8. Choose Bind to Space Warp.

9. Click on the box and drag it over the displace icon until the cursor changes and then let go. The displacement map appears in the geometry, as shown in figure 23.12.

Figure 23.12

The box showing how a displacement map changes the overall shape of the box.

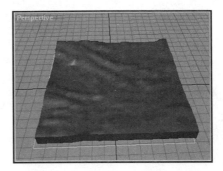

Space warps are a powerful way of influencing an object and creating special effects. With space warps, you can blow up, displace, or even distort an object. But, you may have noticed that some of the space warps only affect particle systems. Particle systems are complex systems of many small objects used to create effects such as rain, smoke, flames, or snow.

Particle Systems

Particle systems are used to create the effect of many small particles in motion, such as snow, fire, smoke, rain, or just about any type of spray. MAX provides you with two default particle systems that you can use: Snow and Spray. To access these, choose the Particle Systems option from the Geometry drop-down list on the Create command panel. Figure 23.13 shows you the resulting rollouts.

Figure 23.13

The particle systems rollouts showing you the particle systems you can create in MAX.

To create a particle system, you must create an *emitter*—an object from which the particles will appear over time. The emitter is a rectangular object with an arrow to indicate the side on which the particles will appear. The emitter does not render in the scene.

Snow

The snow particle system is used to create the effect of snow or other similar particles. When you choose this option, you get the rollout shown in figure 23.14.

To create the snow emitter, click and drag in any viewport, in much the same way you would create a rectangle. The snow icon will appear in the scene, as shown in figure 23.14. You may then adjust any of the parameters of the snow particle system to achieve the effect you want. The following list briefly describes each parameter:

▲ **Viewport Count**. Enables you to define the number of particles visible in the viewport.

▲ **Render Count**. Enables you to define the number of particles visible at any one time in the final rendering. Generally, this number will be somewhat high for the final animation.

▲ **Flake Size**. Enables you to define the size of the snowflake.

▲ **Speed**. Enables you to define the speed at which the snowflake moves.

▲ **Variation**. Enables you to define the amount of variation in the movement of the snowflake.

▲ **Tumble**. Enables you to define whether or not the snowflake tumbles as it falls.

▲ **Tumble Rate**. If tumble is selected, you can define the rate at which the flake tumbles.

▲ **Flakes, Dots, Ticks**. Enables you to choose the particle type as either a flake, dot, or tick.

▲ **Render**. Enables you to define what type of geometry is used in the final rendering of the particle system.

▲ **Start**. Enables you to define the start frame for the particle system.

Figure 23.14

The snow rollouts.

▲ **Life**. Enables you to define the overall length of time a particle will appear on the screen.

▲ **Birth Rate**. Enables you to define how quickly new particles appear in the rendering.

▲ **Constant**. Enables you to define whether or not the birth rate is constant.

▲ **Width/Length**. Enables you to define the overall size of the icon for the spray system.

▲ **Hide**. Enables you to define whether or not the icon shows in the viewports. It does not render under any circumstances.

The following exercise shows you how to use a snow particle system.

CREATING AND USING A SNOW PARTICLE SYSTEM

1. Choose the Particle Systems option from the drop-down list under the Create command panel, when Geometry is chosen.

2. Select the Snow button.

3. In the Top viewport, click at -50,-50, drag to 50,50, and then let go.

4. Choose Select and Move.

5. Click in the Front viewport and move the snow system vertically 50 units.

6. Set the current frame of the animation to 50 to see the snow.

7. Choose the Modify command panel tab.

8. Set the viewport count to 1,000.

9. Set the variation to 5.

10. Set tumble to 0.5.

11. Click in the Perspective viewport to activate it.

12. Turn off real time playback in the Time configuration dialog box.

13. Play back the animation to see how the particle system looks. Play with other parameters to see how they affect the overall animation.

Spray

The spray particle system is used to create the effect of rain, fire, or other spray-like effects. When you choose this option, you get the rollout shown in figure 23.15.

To create the spray emitter, click and drag in any viewport, in much the same way you would create a rectangle. The spray icon will appear in the scene, as shown in figure 23.15. You may then adjust any of the parameters of the spray particle system to achieve the effect you want. Each parameter is similar to those of a snow particle system; refer to the section on snow particle systems for descriptions of the parameters. Repeat the snow exercise, but use a spray instead.

Morphing Objects

Morphing objects is the process of transforming one object into another over time. Many morphing effects were used in the movie *Terminator 2* to create the T-2000 Terminator made of liquid metal. In MAX, you can easily create a morph between two objects. There is only one restriction: both objects must have the same number of vertices. This is because as the morph is generated, MAX simply moves the vertices in the first object to match the locations of the vertices in the second object.

To create a morph, first, draw the first and last morph objects. The last morph object is called the target morph because that is what you are going to morph into. Once you have created both objects, simply select the first morph object. Then, under the Create command panel, choose the Compound objects option from the Create geometry drop-down list, much as you would for a Boolean object. Then, select the Morph button. The Morph rollouts appear.

All you can do in these rollouts is select the morph targets and create a morph key.

The following exercise shows you how to use this rollout to create a morph.

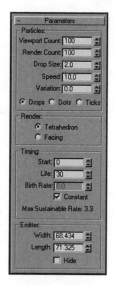

Figure 23.15

The spray rollouts.

CREATING A MORPH

1. In MAX, create a box that is 50 by 50 by 10. Name the box **Morph1**.

2. Create a second box that is 10 by 10 by 100 and name it **Morph2.**

3. Choose Select Objects.

4. Select Morph2.

5. Set the animation slider to frame 100.

6. Turn on the Animate Button.

7. In the command rollout, choose Pick Target.

8. Click on the Morph1 object.

9. Choose Create Morph Key in the Current Targets rollout.

10. Turn off Animate.

11. Activate the camera viewport and do a zoom all.

12. Play back the animation to see the morph in action.

When working with morph objects, you can use instances, references, moves, or copies to create the morph targets. That's all there is to creating a morph object.

Summary

MAX provides you with many tools to create a variety of special effects. Particle systems, space warps, morphs, and projector spotlights are just a few of the tools you can use. With a little imagination, you can create an enormous variety of special effects.

The next chapter is a long exercise to refresh your memory on many of the topics covered in this book, as well as to reinforce the interaction between the various parts of MAX that is necessary to create an effective scene or animation.

Bringing It All Together

Up to this point, you have seen many different aspects of MAX and what it is capable of doing. But it is easy to lose sight of how to make all of it work together. This chapter brings all the aspects of working with MAX together in a long exercise that illustrates the usage of MAX in a production environment. The skills and techniques shown here represent one way of modeling, rendering, and animating in MAX. There are always other ways of accomplishing the same tasks. Feel free to explore methods other than those presented here.

Creating a Dinner Table Scene

The following exercise shows you how to create a dinner scene. This scene will include some modeling, materials, lights, cameras, special effects, and animation to help bring everything together that you have learned from this book. Feel free to add more detail to the model presented in this chapter.

CREATING A DINNER TABLE SCENE

1. Load MAX.

2. Set up the scene by choosing Views, Units Setup.

3. Set the unit type to US Standard and select Feet w/ Fractional Inches, and then choose OK.

4. Choose Views, Grid and Snap Settings.

5. Set the snap spacing to 6" and then choose OK.

6. Turn on the 2D snap toggle.

Modeling Objects

With the units set and snap turned on, you are ready to begin modeling.

1. Choose Box from the Create command panel.

2. Make the box 16'×10' with a height of -1'. Start the lower left corner of the box at 0,0. Name the box **Floor**.

3. Choose Zoom Extents All.

4. Create four boxes that are 6" wide and 8' tall around the outer edge of the floor object. Name these boxes **Wall1** through **Wall4** respectively.

5. Choose Select and Move. Set the axis restriction to Y.

6. Hold down the shift key and click on the floor object in the Front viewport. Drag the object to the top of the Wall objects and let go.

7. Choose Copy as your clone option and name the new object **Ceiling**. Choose OK to create the copy.

Note

> At this point, you have created an enclosed room. Obviously, there are extra faces above the ceiling and below the floor that will never appear in the final rendered scene. Feel free to delete these extra faces. This is a good practice to get into, to help you save memory and increase rendering speeds. By reducing the number of faces and vertices in your scene, you reduce the amount of memory and the number of calculations necessary to render the scene or animation.

Figure 24.1 shows the scene at this point.

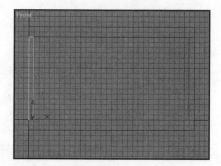

Figure 24.1

The scene showing you the completed wall, floor, and ceiling objects.

Creating a Camera

Before continuing to model the scene, you need to create the camera to simplify the modeling process.

1. Choose the Camera button in the Create command panel.

2. Choose Target.

3. Click at 14',1' and drag to 1',9' in the Top viewport.

4. Choose Select and Move. Turn on Y-axis restriction.

5. Click on the Camera in the Front viewport.

6. Move the camera vertically 6'.

7. Click on the target and move it vertically 5'.

8. Click on the title of the perspective viewport, activate it, and press the C key on your keyboard to change the view to a camera view.

9. Choose Select Objects from the main toolbar.

10. In the Front viewport, select the camera object.

11. Click on the Modify Command Panel tab.

12. Set the lens length of the camera to 35mm so you can see more of the room.

13. Right click on the Camera viewport title. Set the shading limit to Smooth + Highlights. Figure 24.2 shows the scene at this point.

14. Choose File, Save. Name the file **FUNFINAL.MAX** and choose OK.

Figure 24.2

*The Scene with a
Camera.*

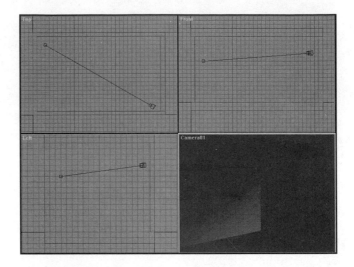

Modeling the Window

Now that you have a basic camera view to give you an idea of composition, it is time to continue modeling objects for the scene. First, cut out a Window in the back wall.

1. Click on the Create command panel. Choose the Geometry button, and then choose Box.

2. Click at -1',2' and create a box that is 4' long, 1'6" wide, and 4' tall.

3. Use Select and Move to move the box vertically in the scene so the top of the window is at 6'6". (Normally, the top of a window is at 6'8", but for this scene 6'6" will do.)

4. Click on the drop-down list in the Create command panel and choose Compound objects.

5. Select the Boolean button.

6. Set the operation type to Subtraction (B-A).

7. Turn off Optimize Result to avoid any problems with the final Boolean object. You can apply an optimize modifier on your own if you want.

8. Choose Pick Operand B.

9. Click on the back wall. The Boolean is created.

10. Rename the back wall object **Window Wall**. Figure 24.3 shows the scene with the window hole.

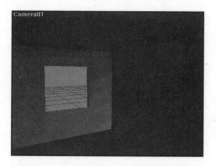

Figure 24.3

The wall showing the hole for the window.

With the hole in the wall, you can now begin to add details to the window to give it a realistic effect.

11. Create four boxes that are 1" square and 4' long. Position them around the edges of the window opening as a window frame. Create a fifth box that is positioned horizontally half way up the window. Figure 24.4 shows the window after this step.

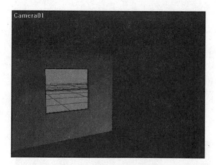

Figure 24.4

The scene showing the window opening with window trim.

12. On your own, create smaller boxes to represent the mullions, and add a sill to the window. Finally, add a 4'×4'×1" box as a piece of glass in the window. Name each object appropriately (such as Mullion1, Mullion2, and so on). Figure 24.5 shows a final window. Your window may have more detail or less detail.

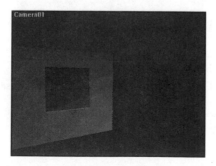

Figure 24.5

The completed window showing the opening, frame, mullions, and glass.

Adding Detail: Furniture

Now that you have created the basics of the room, it is time to model some furniture and place it around the room. For the purposes of this exercise, model one or two pieces of furniture. Later you can model as much furniture to add to the scene as you like. To help illustrate this, you will load the file CH15A.MAX you created earlier in the book, in Chapter 15, "Rendering a Scene." Then you will add a few details to finish off the modeling of the room.

Note

> Please note that many animators simply use library models to populate their scenes with furniture. This is a great time saver and should be used when necessary.

1. Choose File, Merge.

2. Select the file CH15A.MAX that you created earlier in this book. If you did not complete that exercise, load the file from the CD-ROM.

3. In the Merge dialog box, select the Box05 and Teapot01 objects, and then choose OK.

4. The table and teapot appear in the scene. Choose Select and Move to move the table to the center of the room. Then move the teapot so it rests somewhere on the table top. Figure 24.6 shows a possible configuration of the teapot and the table.

Figure 24.6

The scene with the table and teapot merged into the room.

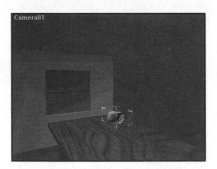

5. Save the file.

6. Choose Shapes under the Create command panel, and then choose Line.

7. Draw an outline similar to the one shown in figure 24.7. This is a profile of a plate.

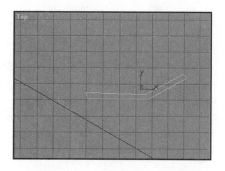

8. Create a second outline that is a profile of a wine glass.

9. Select the plate outline.

10. Click on the Modify command panel tab and choose Lathe.

11. Set the alignment to minimum.

12. Select the Glass profile.

13. Again, choose Lathe and set the alignment to minimum.

14. Use Select and Move to position the new objects on top of the table.

Note

Depending on how you created the profiles, you might need to rotate or scale the final objects to match the table scale.

15. In the Top viewport, make four copies of the plate and glass and position them around the table. Figure 24.8 shows you the scene at this point.

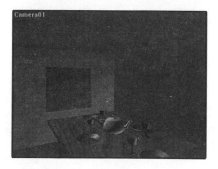

Figure 24.8

The scene showing you the plates and glasses correctly modeled and positioned on the table top.

16. Save the file.

17. Create a candle holder and a candle using the lathe command and place them at the center of the table. Figure 24.9 shows an example of a candle in the center of the table.

Figure 24.9

The scene showing you a possible candle and holder positioned on the table top.

18. Create four boxes that are 1'6"×2' with a height of 0. Place these boxes under each place setting.

19. Save the file again.

For the purposes of this exercise, this will be all the modeling. However, you can continue to add more and more detail to the scene. The more detail you add, the better the scene will look. For example, you can create chairs, silverware, serving dishes, food, flowers, other furniture in the room, people, chandeliers, molding, and trim. Explore the modeling tools of Max and see what you can do.

Creating the Lighting

For the rest of this exercise, you will create lighting, assign materials, render, and do a little animation. First, the lighting.

1. Click on the Create command panel tab.

2. Choose the Lights button.

3. Select Omni.

4. Place a light in the center of the room at a height of 5'. This light will provide general illumination for the scene. Set the multiplier of the light to 0.5 so it does not wash out the walls.

5. Choose Target from the command panel.

6. Click near the ceiling in the Front viewport and drag down to the floor.

7. Set the Hotspot to 150 degrees and the Falloff to 170.

8. Turn on Shadow Casting and set the Shadow Type to Ray-Traced.

9. Use Select and Move to position the light in the center of the room over the table.

10. Click on the camera viewport name to activate the viewport, and then choose Render View.

11. Turn off Auto Reflect mirrors and maps. (The teapot is a reflective surface and will take a long time to render.)

12. Set the resolution to 640×480 and choose Render. Figure 24.10 shows the scene at this point.

Figure 24.10

The scene showing you the correct lighting.

Assigning Materials

Now it is time to assign some materials and begin to add some life to this scene. The table and teapot that were imported already have materials, so you do not need to worry about them.

1. Choose the Materials editor button from the main toolbar.

2. Using Select Objects, select one of the glasses on the table.

3. The material in slot one should be active. Click on the Diffuse Color swatch.

4. Set the color to a light grey, such as RGB 183, 183, 183.

5. Turn on 2-Sided because this is going to be a glass material.

6. Click on the Background button to turn on the checkered background in the sample window.

7. Set the Opacity to 30.

8. Set Shininess to 40 and Shininess Strength to 100. Figure 24.11 shows the Material Editor with this material.

Figure 24.11

The glass material.

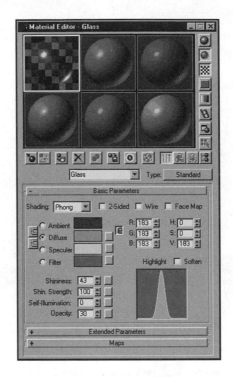

9. Name the material **Wine Glass**.

10. Choose Put To Library.

11. Choose OK to the message to verify the name of the material in the material library.

12. Choose Apply Material to selection.

13. Select each glass object in the scene, including the window, and apply the material to them.

14. Select one of the placemats in the scene.

15. Click on the material in slot 2 in the Material Editor.

16. Name the material **Placemat.**

17. Click on the Maps button to extend the maps rollout.

18. Click on the None button next to diffuse.

19. Double-click on Bitmap as the map type.

20. Click on the blank button next to bitmap to select a bitmap for use in the scene.

21. Select PAT00027.TGA from the 3DSMAX\MAPS directory and choose OK.

22. Turn off the tile options for both the U and V axes under Coordinates.

23. Turn on the Show Bitmap In Viewport button.

24. Choose Assign Material To Selection. The placemat in the scene should turn white to indicate this. You must now apply mapping.

25. Click on the Modify command panel tab.

26. Select UVW Mapping. The bitmap immediately appears in the shaded camera viewport.

27. Choose Bitmap Fit and select the file PAT00027.TGA from the 3DSMAX\MAPS directory again.

28. Turn on Sub-Object.

29. Choose Select and Rotate from the main toolbar.

30. In the camera viewport, click on the yellow box surrounding the placemat and rotate it 90 degrees.

31. Choose Select and Scale.

32. In the camera viewport, click on the yellow box and drag up or down until the box is approximately the same size as the placemat.

33. Turn off Sub-Object.

34. Select another placemat using Select Objects.

35. Choose UVW Mapping to apply the mapping.

36. Choose Acquire.

37. Click on the placemat that you just finished.

38. Set the Acquire Type to relative and choose OK.

39. In the Material Editor, choose Assign Material To Selection.

40. Repeat steps 35 through 39 for the other two remaining placemats. Figure 24.12 shows you the scene at this point.

41. Save the file.

Figure 24.12

The scene showing the placemats in their correct position on the table with correct materials.

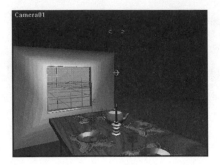

At this point, all you need to do is create materials for the rest of the objects in the scene. On your own, create materials for the floor, walls, window trim, ceiling, candle, candle holder, and plates. If you added other objects to the scene, create and apply materials to them. Figure 24.13 is a rendering of a possible scene at this point. The scene is starting to look like a mountain cabin, based on the materials that were chosen. Your scene might look completely different.

Figure 24.13

The scene showing you all the objects with the correct materials.

Adding a Background

To finish the look of a mountain cabin, a background for the window is needed.

1. Choose Rendering, Environment.

2. Choose Assign under Background.

3. Choose Bitmap as the background type. Choose OK to the return to the Environment dialog box.

4. Click on the Environment Map button.

5. Assign the map to Slot 6 and choose OK.

6. Close the Environment dialog box.

7. Click on the Material Editor button.

8. Click in Slot 6 to activate the slot.

9. Set the Mapping Type to Screen.

10. Click the blank button next to bitmap.

11. Choose LAKE_MT.JPG from the 3DSMAX\MAPS directory.

12. Close the Material Editor.

13. Save the file.

14. Render the scene again. Figure 24.14 shows the resulting image with the new background in the window.

Figure 24.14

The room with a scenic view in the window.

Adding a Flame for the Candle

The last item to add to the scene is a flame for the candle.

1. Click on the Create command panel tab.

2. Select the Geometry button.

3. In the drop-down list, choose Particle Systems.

4. In the top viewport, zoom in on the candle.

5. Select the Spray button.

6. Click to place the center of the emitter and drag out to about the size of the candle flame.

7. Choose Select and Move.

8. In the Front viewport, move the spray emitter to the top of the candle.

9. Choose Select and Rotate to rotate the emitter so it points up into the air.

10. Click on the Modify command panel tab.

11. Set the Render Count to 1000.

12. Set the Particle Size to 1/32".

13. Set the Speed to 0.5 and the Variation to 0.25.

14. Set the Current Frame to 65.

15. Set the Particle Type to Dots.

16. Choose Select and Scale to scale down the particle system until it is the right size for the flame. Figure 24.15 shows you the particle emitter at the correct scale.

Figure 24.15

The scaled down particle emitter shown at the top of the candle.

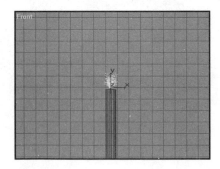

17. Right click on the particle system to access the pop-up menu, and then select Properties.

18. Set the G-Buffer Object Channel to 1 so the Video Post Glow filter will know which objects to glow.

19. Choose OK to return to MAX.

20. Save the file.

21. Open the Material Editor.

22. Create a bright yellow-red material and assign it to the particle system.

Adding the Events

Now that you have created the particle system on the candle, it is time to create a glow around the candle to make it look like a real flame. This is accomplished through the video post.

ADDING THE GLOW

Continue with the previous exercise.

1. Choose Rendering, Video Post.

2. Choose Add Scene Event.

3. Select the camera view as the view to add and choose OK.

4. Click on the Scene event in the queue to select it.

5. Choose Add Image Filter Event.

6. Select Glow as the filter type.

7. Choose Setup.

8. Select Object Channel as the source. Set the Object Channel spinner to 1.

9. Choose OK, and then OK again.

10. Choose Add Image Output Event.

11. Choose Files.

12. Enter **FUNFINAL.TGA** as the file name.

13. Choose OK.

14. Choose Execute.

15. Set the Time Output to single and set the Frame to 65.

16. Set the Output Size to 640×480.

17. Choose Render.

18. Save the file.

Creating a Little Animation

Now that you have an animated candle, it is time to add a little animation to the scene. Just for fun, pretend there is an earthquake that destroys all of the cabin, except the candle. The following steps show you how to do this through the use of some basic animation, space warps, and Track View.

ADDING ANIMATION

1. Choose Zoom Extents All.

2. Choose Select Objects and select the glass nearest the camera in the camera viewport.

3. Set the animation slider to frame 15.

4. Activate the Left viewport.

5. Choose Zoom Window and zoom in on the selected glass.

6. Turn Animate on.

7. Choose Select and Rotate.

8. Rotate the glass to the left 15 degrees in the front viewport.

9. Set the animation slider to 25.

10. Rotate the glass to the right until it is horizontal to the table. (This should be around 105 degrees).

11. Set the animation slider to 30.

12. Rotate the glass to the left 5 degrees.

13. Set the animation slider to 35.

14. Rotate the glass back to the right 5 degrees. This gives the illusion that the glass bounced a little when it fell over.

15. Turn Animate Off.

16. Save the file.

Working with Track View

Now that you have set up the animation for one glass, Track View will be used to copy the animation to the other glass objects.

USING TRACK VIEW

1. Choose Select Objects again.

2. Hold down Ctrl and click on the other glasses in the scene to select them.

3. Choose the Track View button.

4. Choose the Filter button to filter out the Track View display.

5. Choose Selected Objects under Show Only.

6. Choose OK.

7. Expand the Objects section of the hierarchy window to show all the parameters of all four glasses. Because the glass objects were originally created as lines, the object names might appear as Line1 through Line4.

8. Choose Edit Ranges.

9. Under the Transform/Rotation track, you should be able to see the range of keys for the animation you just created. Click once on this range to highlight it.

10. Choose the Copy button from the toolbar.

11. Select the Rotation track for any of the other glasses in the scene.

12. Choose the Paste button from the toolbar.

13. In the Paste dialog box that appears, choose Copy as the paste type and choose OK.

14. Repeat steps 11,12, and 13 for the other two glasses.

15. When you are done, close the Track View window.

16. Save the file.

Creating the Explosion

Now, just for fun, you are going to blow up everything in the scene, except the candle and the background. This will make it seem as though the earthquake was extremely violent, but somehow, forgot the candle.

CREATING THE EXPLOSION

1. Choose Edit, Select None.

2. Click on the Create Command Panel tab.

3. Choose the Space Warps button.

4. Select bomb as the space warp type.

5. In the Top viewport, click at roughly the center of the room to place the space warp.

6. Set the Detonation value to 40, so the bomb will go off in frame 40.

7. Set the Chaos value to 5 to make a more naturalistic looking explosion.

8. Choose Select by Name.

9. Select everything in the scene, except lights, cameras, the candle, candleholder, or the particle system.

10. Choose the Select button to create the selection set.

11. Choose Bind to Space Warp.

12. Click on any selected object in the Top viewport and drag over to the space warp.

13. When the cursor changes over the space warp, let go and all the objects will be bound to the space warp.

14. Save the file.

15. Choose Rendering, Video Post.

16. Double click on the output event to modify it.

17. Choose Files.

18. Enter a name of **FUNFINAL.AVI** in the filename section of the dialog box.

19. Choose OK to return to the Edit Image Output Event dialog box.

20. Choose OK to set the changes and return to the video post.

21. Close the video post and save the file.

The Final Rendering

Now, you have set up the animation and it is time to make the final animation. This animation file is saved on the CD as FUNFINAL.AVI if you choose not to finish this section.

RENDERING THE SCENE

1. Choose Rendering, Video Post.

2. Choose Execute Sequence.

3. Select the Range button under Time Output.

4. Make sure the range is set from 0 to 100.

5. Set the output size to 320×240 if it is not already set.

6. Choose Render. The file is rendered and saved to FUNFINAL.AVI. Use the Windows Media Player to view it when it is finished.

Summary

This exercise should have given you a brief review and overview of how to piece together the elements of MAX discussed earlier in this book. The exercise is not very detailed. You are highly encouraged to explore different methods and try to enhance the scene as much as possible.

Well, you have finally reached the end. Now you are ready to begin using one of the most powerful rendering and animation systems in the world. This book is just a starting point; there is much more for you to learn about MAX. Much of the learning will come through experience. Refer back to this book whenever you need a refresher on any of the subjects covered here. Otherwise, may you have the best of luck and let your imagination go!

PART VII

APPENDICES

Appendix A: File Extensions in MAX

Appendix B: Cursors in MAX

File Extensions in MAX

When working with MAX, you will undoubtedly notice a large number of different file types that you can use. This appendix lists and describes the file extensions you'll see with MAX.

3DS. 3D Studio 4.0 for DOS file formats.

AVI. Microsoft Audio/Video Interleave animation files.

BMF. Filter DLLs (dynamic link libraries).

BMI. Bitmap import DLL. System file necessary to be able to import any type of bitmap. Bitmap import plug-ins will have this extension.

BMP. Microsoft Windows bitmap file format.

BMS. Storage DLLs.

CEL. Old image file format from Animator Pro.

CFG. Configuration files for various aspects of MAX.

DLC. Standard controls DLL for MAX.

DLE. Object Export DLL. System file necessary to export objects to other formats.

DLI. Object Import DLL. System file necessary to import objects into MAX.

DLL. General DLL.

DLO. Object primitive library in DLL format.

DLR. Plug-in rendering DLLs.

DLT. Material DLLs.

DXF. Drawing exchange format file. Used for importing and exporting files to and from other CAD programs.

EPS. Encapsulated PostScript file format.

FLC. Kinetix high-resolution animation format.

FLI. Kinetix low-resolution animation format.

FLT. General filters used in MAX.

GIF. CompuServe image file format.

HDI. Graphics interface drivers for working with the HEIDI renderer.

HLP. Windows Help files.

INI. Initialization files to set startup parameters for use every time MAX is launched.

JPG. Highly compressed image file format.

LOG. Log files to track certain events such as network rendering.

MAX. 3D Studio MAX scene files.

PRJ. 3D Studio 4.0 project files.

PS. PostScript file format.

RLA. Wavefront image file format.

SHP. 3D Studio 4.0 shape files.

TGA. Targa image file format. Supports 16-, 24-, and 32-bit files with compression.

TIF. TIFF image file format. Supports grayscale, 8-, 16-, 24-, and 32-bit files with compression.

TTF. TrueType Fonts.

VP. Video Post sequences.

WAV. Sound files.

WRI. Microsoft Write files.

YUV. YUV image file format. This is the file format used for component video recording with devices such as the ACCOM WSD.

ZIP. Compressed archive file formats.

Cursors in MAX

Throughout this book, mention has been made of the various cursors that indicate the current state of MAX. This appendix shows each of these cursors and provides a brief explanation of when they appear.

Align. Appears when the align command is selected.

Bind to Space Warp. Appears when you choose the Bind to Space Warp button. This is used to bind the selected object to a space warp. This cursor appears only when the cursor is over a valid space warp.

Create. Appears whenever you are going to create any type of geometry.

Dolly Camera. Appears whenever the Dolly Camera button in the Viewport control panel is active in a camera viewport.

FOV. Appears whenever the FOV button in the Viewport control panel is active for any camera viewport.

Get Shape or Get Path. Appears whenever you are creating a loft object and you are using the Get Shape or Get Path option.

Help Mode. Appears whenever you select the Help Mode button on the main toolbar.

Linking. Appears whenever you choose the Select and Link button. This icon appears when the cursor is over the object to which you are linking.

Move. Appears anytime the Select and Move command is active when the cursor is over the selected object.

Normal Align. Appears when the Normal Align command is active.

Orbit Camera. Appears when the Orbit Camera command in the Viewport control panel is active for any camera viewport.

Pan. Appears anytime a Pan command, Rollout Scroll, or Hierarchy View Scroll option is available.

Perspective. Appears whenever the Perspective option in the Viewport control panel is active for any camera viewport.

Place Hilite. Appears when the Place Hilite command is active.

Region Zoom. Appears when the Region Zoom command is active in the Viewport control panel.

Roll Camera. Appears when the Roll Camera button in the Viewport control panel is active for any camera viewport.

Rotate. Appears anytime the Select and Rotate tool is active and the cursor is over the selected object.

Scale. Appears anytime the Select and Scale tool is active and the cursor is over the selected object. The cursor adjusts to match each of the three Select and Scale commands.

Select for Linking. Appears whenever you choose the Select and Link command and you are about to select the object you want to link.

Select for Space Warp. Appears whenever you select the Bind to Space Warp command and you are about to select the object you want to bind to a space warp.

Select. Appears anytime you are using the Select Objects command and the cursor is over a selectable object.

Spotlight Falloff. Appears when the Spotlight Falloff button in the Viewport control panel is active for any spotlight view.

Spotlight Hotspot. Appears when the Spotlight Hotspot button in the Viewport control panel is active for any spotlight view.

View Rotate. Appears anytime you are using the View Rotate command in the Viewport control panel.

Zoom All. Appears anytime you are using the Zoom All command in the Viewport control panel.

Zoom. Appears anytime you are using the Zoom command in the Viewport control panel.

INDEX

Symbols

3D primitives (objects)
editing, 177-182
extrude modifier, 178-179
lathe modifier, 180-183
3D Studio MAX
configuring, 12-13
GLint Based Card option, 12-13
Software Z Buffer option, 12-13
hardware requirements, 14-21
Accom WSX digital video recorder, 21-22
GLint chip video cards, 20-22
memory, 15-18
Perception board, 20-22
processors, 14-21
swap file space, 15-18
video cards, 18-19
installing, 10-13

A

Accom WSX digital video recorder,
requirements for, 21-22
adaptive degredation, 34, 42-44
Adjust Transform rollout buttons, 410
Affect Region option (Vertex-level
editing), 204-206
Align button, 33
Align cursor, 497
alignment controls (mapping), 294
Acquire button, 294
Bitmap Fit button, 294
Center button, 294
Fit button, 294

Normal Align button, 294
Reset button, 294
Alpha source (Bitmap Parameters
rollout), 283
ambient lighting, 246
Animate button, 33
animation, 360-366
color, copying, 75
controlling with Track View, 389-392
creation overview, 64-84
3D text creation, 67-71
camera creation, 71-73
light creation, 71-73
lofted object creation, 67-71
material assignment, 74-77
rendering the model, 74-77
stage creation, 64-67
dinner table exercise, 473-491
event additions, 487-488
explosion creation, 490
lighting creation, 480-481
material assignment, 481-487
object modeling, 474-480
Track View, 489
dinner table exercise, rendering, 491
free cameras, 243
interactive renderer, 371-374
Keyframe, creating, 367-371
kinematics, 415
Make Preview dialog box, 372
Display in Preview, 372
Frame Rate, 372
Image Size, 372
Output, 373
Preview Range, 372

M

. . . .

WANT MORE INFORMATION?

CHECK OUT THESE RELATED TOPICS OR SEE YOUR LOCAL BOOKSTORE

CAD

As the number one CAD publisher in the world, and as a Registered Publisher of Autodesk, New Riders Publishing provides unequaled content on this complex topic under the flagship *Inside AutoCAD*. Other titles include *AutoCAD for Beginners* and *New Riders' Reference Guide to AutoCAD Release 13*.

Networking

As the leading Novell NetWare publisher, New Riders Publishing delivers cutting-edge products for network professionals. We publish books for all levels of users, from those wanting to gain NetWare Certification, to those administering or installing a network. Leading books in this category include *Inside NetWare 3.12*, *Inside TCP/IP Second Edition*, *NetWare: The Professional Reference*, and *Managing the NetWare 3.x Server*.

Graphics and 3D Studio

New Riders provides readers with the most comprehensive product tutorials and references available for the graphics market. Best-sellers include *Inside Photoshop 3*, *3D Studio IPAS Plug In Reference*, *KPT's Filters and Effects*, and *Inside 3D Studio*.

Internet and Communications

As one of the fastest growing publishers in the communications market, New Riders provides unparalleled information and detail on this ever-changing topic area. We publish international best-sellers such as *New Riders' Official Internet Yellow Pages, 2nd Edition*, a directory of over 10,000 listings of Internet sites and resources from around the world, as well as *VRML: Browsing and Building Cyberspace*, *Actually Useful Internet Security Techniques*, *Internet Firewalls and Network Security*, and *New Riders' Official World Wide Web Yellow Pages*.

Operating Systems

Expanding off our expertise in technical markets, and driven by the needs of the computing and business professional, New Riders offers comprehensive references for experienced and advanced users of today's most popular operating systems, including *Inside Windows 95*, *Inside Unix*, *Inside OS/2 Warp Version 3*, and *Building a Unix Internet Server*.

Orders/Customer Service **1-800-653-6156**   Source Code **NRP95**

New Riders Publishing   201 West 103rd Street ◆ Indianapolis, Indiana 46290 USA